EMPIRE OF ELOQUENCE

The global reach of the Spanish and Portuguese empires prompted a remarkable flourishing of the classical rhetorical tradition in various parts of the early modern world. *Empire of Eloquence* is the first study to examine this tradition as part of a wider global renaissance in Europe, the Americas, Asia and Africa, with a particular focus on the Iberian world. Spanning the sixteenth to the early nineteenth centuries, the book argues that the classical rhetorical tradition contributed to the ideological coherence and equilibrium of this early modern Iberian world, providing important occasions for persuasion, legitimation and eventual (and perhaps inevitable) confrontation. Drawing on archival collections in thirteen countries, Stuart M. McManus places these developments in the context of civic, religious and institutional rituals attended by the multiethnic population of the Iberian world and beyond, and shows how they influenced public speaking in non-European languages, such as Konkani and Chinese.

STUART M. MCMANUS is Assistant Professor of World History at the Chinese University of Hong Kong and an Affiliated Scholar of the Faculty of Law's Center for Transnational and Comparative Law. His published work ranges widely across Hispanic and global history from antiquity to the present, and has been supported by prestigious fellowships from Princeton, Brown, Yale and SIFK at the University of Chicago.

T0384843

IDEAS IN CONTEXT

Edited by David Armitage, Richard Bourke and Jennifer Pitts

The books in this series will discuss the emergence of intellectual traditions and of related new disciplines. The procedures, aims and vocabularies that were generated will be set in the context of the alternatives available within the contemporary frameworks of ideas and institutions. Through detailed studies of the evolution of such traditions, and their modification by different audiences, it is hoped that a new picture will form of the development of ideas in their concrete contexts. By this means, artificial distinctions between the history of philosophy, of the various sciences, of society and politics, and of literature may be seen to dissolve.

The series is published with the support of the Exxon Foundation.

A full list of titles in the series can be found at:
www.cambridge.org/IdeasContext

EMPIRE OF ELOQUENCE

*The Classical Rhetorical Tradition in Colonial Latin
America and the Iberian World*

STUART M. MCMANUS

The Chinese University of Hong Kong

CAMBRIDGE
UNIVERSITY PRESS

Shaftesbury Road, Cambridge CB2 8EA, United Kingdom

One Liberty Plaza, 20th Floor, New York, NY 10006, USA

477 Williamstown Road, Port Melbourne, VIC 3207, Australia

314–321, 3rd Floor, Plot 3, Splendor Forum, Jasola District Centre, New Delhi – 110025, India

103 Penang Road, #05–06/07, Visioncrest Commercial, Singapore 238467

Cambridge University Press is part of Cambridge University Press & Assessment, a department of the University of Cambridge.

We share the University's mission to contribute to society through the pursuit of education, learning and research at the highest international levels of excellence.

www.cambridge.org
Information on this title: www.cambridge.org/9781108821735

DOI: 10.1017/9781108909181

First published 2021
First paperback edition 2024

A catalogue record for this publication is available from the British Library

Library of Congress Cataloging-in-Publication data
NAMES: McManus, Stuart M., 1986– author.
TITLE: Empire of eloquence : the classical rhetorical tradition in colonial Latin America and the Iberian world / Stuart M. McManus.
DESCRIPTION: Cambridge, UK ; New York : Cambridge University Press, 2021. | Series: Ideas in context | Based on the author's dissertation (doctoral)– Harvard University, 2016. | Includes bibliographical references and index.
IDENTIFIERS: LCCN 2020043221 (print) | LCCN 2020043222 (ebook) | ISBN 9781108830164 (hardback) | ISBN 9781108821735 (paperback) | ISBN 9781108909181 (epub)
SUBJECTS: LCSH: Rhetoric, Ancient–Study and teaching–Spain–History. | Rhetoric, Ancient–Study and teaching–Latin America–History. | Latin philology–Study and teaching–Spain–History. | Latin philology–Study and teaching–Latin America–History. | Latin language, Medieval and modern–Rhetoric. | Latin language–Church Latin–Rhetoric. | Rhetoric–Religious aspects–Catholic Church. | Spain–Colonies–History. | Spain–Intellectual life–History.
CLASSIFICATION: LCC PA2065.S7 M36 2021 (print) | LCC PA2065.S7 (ebook) | DDC 808/.046–dc23
LC record available at https://lccn.loc.gov/2020043221
LC ebook record available at https://lccn.loc.gov/2020043222

ISBN   978-1-108-83016-4   Hardback
ISBN   978-1-108-82173-5   Paperback

Matri optimae

Contents

Figures

Acknowledgments

This book would not have been possible without the help and support of numerous people scattered across multiple continents. There is not enough space here to include every person who deserves to be thanked, but I hope that in this act of *praeteritio* those whose names do not appear will find some small measure of the appreciation they deserve.

In the thirteen countries that I visited in the course of my research, I relied heavily on the expertise and assistance of numerous librarians and archivists. I also benefited from the company of many local guides and fellow travelers. In the sprawling cities of the Americas, I would have been lost (often literally) without Deidre Moore and Tatiana Seijas in Mexico City; Ximena Gómez in Lima; and Andrew Redden in Santiago de Chile. In Manila, Madrid and Seville, Jorge Mojarro showed me the way to the archives and the best local eateries. In Tokyo, Aki Watanabe and his colleagues in the Japanese Association of Renaissance Studies made me feel very welcome. I also owe a heartfelt *Deu borem korum* and a *muito obrigado* to Antonio Pereira and his family who hosted me in Goa. To all those I met on my travels, I only wish that I could have stayed longer to get to know you better.

Like many other books, this one began life as a dissertation. At Harvard, I benefited immensely from the advice and camaraderie of numerous advisors and friends. It was Bernard Bailyn who first encouraged me to turn my attention to Latin America, and for this I will be forever grateful. I also could not have wished for a more supportive dissertation committee who deserve much more than this short *gratiarum actio*: to Jim Hankins for giving me the most complete training an historian of the Western humanities could have asked for and for the faith he has shown in me over the years; to Tamar Herzog for her sage advice, perceptive criticisms and advice on archives and libraries in Latin America and beyond; to Ann Blair for her unfailing support from beginning to end; to David Armitage for his constant encouragement to ask bigger questions; and to Peter Mack for sharing with me his deep knowledge of rhetorical theory. In addition, I was fortunate to be part of two communities of enthusiastic young scholars in my two intellectual homes, the Departments of History and the Classics, including my *Doktorbrüder und -schwester*, the Drs. Tworek, and my good friend Tom Keeline. Beyond Harvard, I also benefited from the advice of Andrew Laird, *rerum Romanarum Mexicanarumque peritus*, and the cartographical expertise of Cheryl Cape.

During my time "abroad" (wherever exactly that is), I received financial support from many organizations. At Harvard, I received short-term grants from the David Rockefeller Center for Latin American Studies, the Harvard Asia Center, the Weatherhead Center for International Affairs, the Reischauer Institute of Japanese Studies and the Harvard Center for American Political Studies. An eighteen-month period of research was also funded by a Social Science Research Council International Dissertation Research Fellowship with funds provided by the Andrew W. Mellon Foundation and a Mellon Fellowship for Dissertation Research in Original Sources administered by the Council on Library and Information Resources. Lastly, the John Carter Brown Library in Providence also proved a wonderful place to spend a semester conducting preliminary research.

The completed dissertation subsequently began its metamorphosis into a book at the Stevanovich Institute on the Formation of Knowledge (SIFK) at the University of Chicago, where I spent two glorious years, first as the inaugural postdoctoral fellow, then in the company of my fellow fellows: Margaret Carlyle, Jennifer P. Daly, Damien Droney and Eduardo A. Escobar. SIFK's Steering Committee, Shadi Bartsch-Zimmer, Bob Richards, Haun Saussy and Clifford Ando (we never did go on that bike ride along the lakefront!), were also always there for me with advice and wine, not forgetting the wonderful staff: Macol Cerda, Jessica Velazquez and Vicky Lim. Thanks to their support and that of the members of the Committee on Southern Asian Studies (COSAS), especially Philip Engblom, I was also able to complete Chapter 4, which I hope gives some sense of the richness of the surviving missionary sources in Konkani (*amchi Goenchi bhas*).

The final touches to the book were added at the Chinese University of Hong Kong during a turbulent period in Hong Kong's post-handover history. Come rain or shine in this great city where the mountains rise straight out of the ocean and the skyscrapers out of the mountains, my wonderful colleagues have always been generous with their time and knowledge of premodern Chinese history and other topics: Professors

Lai Ming-chiu, Poo Mu-chou, Ho Pui-yin, Puk Wing-kin, Ian Morley, Noah Shusterman, Rowena He and my fellow Scotsman, James Morton. I received a Direct Grant from the Faculty of Arts, which allowed me to enlist the help of Terence Tze-wai Chan who provided much linguistic and other assistance, and at different stages I had the assistance of a number of student helpers, including Chung Ling Fung, Lee Marcus Sherray and Tang Edward. Finally, I wish to thank the two anonymous reviewers and the staff at Cambridge University Press, especially Liz Friend-Smith and Atifa Jiwa, as well as Michael Henry who compiled the index and the Faculty of Arts of the Chinese University of Hong Kong, which provided a publication subvention.

Over the decade it took to research and write, this book stole many hours, days and months. Throughout the process, Janine May was a source of constant support and encouragement. However, it is to my family, Fiona Crosbie, James McManus, Ruth McManus, Shona, Clare and the newest arrival Caleb, that I owe the greatest debt.

Abbreviations

AGI	Archivo General de Indias, Seville, Spain
AGN	Archivo General de la Nación, Mexico City, Mexico
AGS	Archivo General de Simancas, Valladolid, Spain
AHSI	*Archivum Historicum Societatis Iesu* (Journal)
ARSI	Archivum Romanum Societatis Iesu, Rome, Italy
BNM	Biblioteca Nacional de México, Mexico City, Mexico
BNP	Biblioteca Nacional del Perú, Lima, Peru
BPB	Biblioteca Pública, Braga, Portugal

Introduction
An Empire of Eloquence in a Global Renaissance

On June 23, 1721 Cayetano de Cabrera y Quintero (1698–1775) gave a "job talk" (*lección de oposición*) for the chair of rhetoric at the Royal and Pontifical University in Mexico City.[1] For Cabrera and the other candidates, this was no small undertaking. Indeed, the aspiring rhetoricians were each given only twenty-four hours to compose and deliver from memory an elegant Latin lecture on a passage from one of Cicero's orations. To prevent collusion, this passage was selected at random from a fine Renaissance edition of Cicero's speeches by a local boy who was by design too young to have studied Latin. Thankfully for Cabrera, on this occasion luck was on his side. He was given the opening lines of Cicero's well-known speech *In Vatinium*, in which the Roman orator celebrated his own triumphant return to the Eternal City following a period in exile. The gobbet also ended with a typically self-aggrandizing rhetorical question that provided plenty of grist to Cabrera's mill: "what then more honorable could have happened to me, what more desirable for the immortality of my glory and everlasting perpetuation of my name, than that all my fellow-citizens should think that the good of the state was bound up with my own welfare?"[2]

In the course of his lecture on this passage delivered in the great hall (*aula mayor*) that stood above the submerged ruins not of republican Rome, but of the Aztec metropolis of Tenochtitlan, Cabrera did not simply offer an analysis of the text, its historical context, structure and form in the most elegant Latin he could muster, as the rules of the competition required. Instead, he delivered a long meditation on the relationship between civic life and rhetoric. Cicero, he argued, had been right to equate himself with the republic, as eloquence (which the ancient orator personified) was the foundation of any

---

[1] BNM, ms. 27, fols 78r–85r.

[2] Cicero, *In Vatinium*, 8: "Quid ergo ... praestantius mihi potuit accidere, quid optabilius ad immortalitatem gloriae atque ad memoriam mei nominis sempiternam, quam omnes hoc cives meos iudicare, civitatis salutem cum unius mea salute esse coniunctam?" All translations are my own.

well-functioning society.[3] Like Athens, New Spain (*res publica Mexicana*) depended on persuasive speech, which served to unite its citizens under the banner of the Hispanic Monarchy, resist the rise of tyrants, defend it from external enemies and maintain the true religion. Mexico City, the "Rome of the New World," as the early Franciscan missionary Pedro de Gante had called it, could not do without a qualified scholar-orator to lecture on Cicero's orations, teach rhetorical theory and oversee student declamations; and Cabrera was the only man up to the task – or at least so he argued!

To underline the utility of classicizing eloquence, Cabrera also told a revealing story about a dying man who could not decide which of his sons deserved to inherit his wealth: the physician or the orator. This was no competition, Cabrera informed the jury in Latin verses that he had dashed off the night before:

> You ask, my sons, who will inherit my wealth,
> But I ask: who could be of more use to his homeland?
> Believe me, eloquence is the life blood of cities.
> Medicine has not sometimes, but always spelled death.[4]

Although these verses were probably meant somewhat tongue in cheek – a jab perhaps at the members of the medical faculty who were also vying for the chair of rhetoric – Cabrera's larger celebratory account of the classical rhetorical tradition deserves our attention, as we find it in every corner of the early modern Iberian world where its value was understood in almost identical terms.

Indeed, across the Hispanic Monarchy (the patchwork global polity often erroneously referred to as the "Spanish Empire") rhetoric was taught in colleges and universities. This, in turn, influenced the secular and sacred public speaking that resounded in churches, cathedrals, gubernatorial palaces, plazas and university halls, through which orators sought to unite listeners in the pursuit of shared societal goals.[5] For instance, sacred orators in Oran in Spanish North Africa celebrated the triumphs of monarchs in Madrid as part of multisensory civic rituals that reminded the inhabitants

---

[3] Osorio Romero, *Tópicos sobre Cicerón en México* (Mexico City: Universidad Nacional Autónoma de Mexico, 1976), 83–84.

[4] BNP, ms. 27, folio 83v:

> "Quaeritis, heraedes, istum cui competat aurum
> Et quisnam patriis aptior esse potis?
> Urbibus est igitur facundia, credite, vita
> Non modo, sed semper mors medicina fuit."

[5] Although sermons and orations are usually treated as separate genres of public speaking (one "religious" and the other "secular," whatever that really means in the premodern context), here I treat them together as expressions of the same classical rhetorical tradition.

of the Spanish *presidio* of the king whose interests they defended. In Spanish Manila, we find the same reliance on classicizing public speaking on occasions as divers as royal funeral commemorations and the inauguration of the academic year at the city's numerous colleges, where the combined praises of humanist learning, Christian piety and loyalty to the Crown were sung to generations of students. This was no less the case in the disparate parts of the world under the Crown of Portugal, before, during and after the Iberian Union (1580–1640). Along the sinuous trade route that linked Brazil to Lisbon, Goa and Macau, Jesuit missionaries from Iberia and elsewhere taught the *studia humanitatis* (the Renaissance curriculum centered on the classical rhetorical tradition) and delivered classicizing orations and sermons in a variety of languages that made similar calls for unity around Iberian Catholicism. At the same time, classicizing rhetoric and oratory did more than just follow the flag. It also spilled out into areas that were not under the direct control of any Iberian monarch, but were touched by the outward migration of Iberian merchants and missionaries. Black-robed Jesuit humanists carried the classical rhetorical tradition with them to Japan and China as tools to evangelize and instruct native populations, while native Christians also quickly embraced the tradition to bolster their newfound faith. All this had the effect that the classical rhetorical tradition, as part of what we might call a "Global Renaissance," became one of the first intellectual currents to traverse the Americas, Europe, Asia and Africa, where it contributed in tangible ways to the stability and longevity of the patchwork of societies that made up the Iberian World.[6]

Thus, the classical rhetorical tradition, Cabrera believed and *Empire of Eloquence* argues, contributed to the ideological coherence and equilibrium of the early modern Iberian World, providing important occasions for persuasion, legitimation and eventual (and perhaps inevitable) confrontation. While bureaucratic "chains of paper," commercial networks and the threat of violence (real or perceived) played an important role in holding together the composite monarchies of Spain and Portugal, the oratorical "chains of words" that resonated both within and beyond the areas we normally associate with Iberian empire were also very much in the mix. This said, it would be wrong to characterize them as merely means for the imperial center to exert power. Like the ability to petition the Crown or leverage business interests, these orations gave agency to thousands of

---

[6] Peter Burke, Luke Clossey and Felipe Fernández-Armesto, "The Global Renaissance," *Journal of World History* 28 (2017), 1–30.

individual orators, both Iberian and Iberianized non-European, who sought to harmonize and shape the organic societies in which they lived. At the same time, speaking on particular occasions in front of particular audiences meant that orators had to craft their arguments to the needs and expectations of those in attendance, thus handing over some of their own (already decentralized) agency in the interests of building consensus. Consequently, the many hundreds of surviving orations and classicizing sermons offer a window onto the myriad unique, but (orators hoped) ultimately converging perspectives on politics, religion and society that characterized and shaped the Iberian World. This geographical diffusion is, in turn, a boon for global historians, as it is well suited to the sort of historical analysis that transcends national, national-imperial, regional and civilizational history. The aims of *Empire of Eloquence* are therefore three-fold: one cultural, one intellectual, and one meta-geographical.

Cultural History: Building Empires

Over the years, historians have given numerous cultural explanations for the longevity of Iberian political hegemony and Catholic religious unity. In particular, writing, the law and bureaucratic tools are often seen as foundational, supplemented by the power of imagery and architecture.[7] In contrast, *Empire of Eloquence* makes the case that it was also through the early modern incarnation of the classical rhetorical tradition that the rubber of ideology met the road of society. Indeed, during the Iberian World's Global Renaissance, neo-Roman public speaking was the

---

[7] José Antonio Maravall, *La Cultura del Barroco: Análisis de una Estructura Histórica* (Barcelona: Esplugues de Llobregat, 1975); Walter D. Mignolo, *The Darker Side of the Renaissance: Literacy, Territoriality, and Colonization* (Ann Arbor: University of Michigan Press, 1995). The legal apparatuses of the Spanish and Portuguese crowns are often seen as the prime movers of empire, contributing to an "empire of law" in which Iberians, indigenous peoples and others were integrated into a political and cultural system through self-interested interactions with the law, much as had happened in the Roman Empire, their law's ultimate source: Susan Kellogg, *Law and the Transformation of Aztec Culture, 1500–1700* (Norman: University of Oklahoma Press, 1995); Sylvia Sellers-García, *Distance and Documents at the Spanish Empire's Periphery* (Stanford, CA: Stanford University Press, 2014); Brian Philip Owensby, *Empire of Law and Indian Justice in Colonial Mexico* (Stanford, CA: Stanford University Press, 2008); cf. Clifford Ando, *Imperial Ideology and Provincial Loyalty in the Roman Empire* (Berkeley: University of California Press, 2000). On visual culture and empire, see Daniela Bleichmar, *Visible Empire: Botanical Expeditions and Visual Culture in the Hispanic Enlightenment* (Chicago: University of Chicago Press, 2012); Carolyn Dean, *Inka Bodies and the Body of Christ: Corpus Christi in Colonial Cuzco, Peru* (Durham, NC: Duke University Press, 1999). On civic rituals, see Alejandro Cañeque, *The King's Living Image: The Culture and Politics of Viceregal Power in Colonial Mexico* (New York: Routledge, 2004); Alejandra B. Osorio, *Inventing Lima: Baroque Modernity in Peru's South Sea Metropolis* (Basingstoke: Palgrave Macmillan, 2008).

archetypal ordering mode in Iberian urban settings, and a powerful tool for spreading ideas, building political consensus, bolstering religion and articulating standards of public behavior that could take place in Latin, European vernaculars and indigenous languages.

Of course, the importance of ancient Mediterranean culture to Europe and other parts of the early modern world affected by European expansion is well known. As Sabine MacCormack taught us, Greco-Roman antiquity as revived in the Renaissance provided nothing less than "a framework for the construal of historical experience" in the early modern Andes and elsewhere.[8] Similarly, Ángel Rama famously argued that educated urban elites (*letrados*) living in "lettered cities" (*ciudades letradas*) dominated all aspects of intellectual life, applying their scholarly tools, many inherited from Greece and Rome, to build the ideological foundations of a new "Latin" America out of the ruins of pre-Columbian polities.[9] Yet, there was also an oral, and specifically an oratorical dimension to the Renaissance world of Iberian and Iberianized *letrados* that contributed in important ways to its stability and longevity. In this sense, there are both identifiable links and striking parallels between Rome's "world state" and the Iberian World, which were both knitted together by law, culture, religion and, of most significance for our purposes, oratory.[10] This is because premodern state formation (be it "national" or "colonial") was fundamentally unlike its modern (i.e. industrial and post-industrial) counterpart, such that the neo-Roman social technologies of the Iberian World mirrored Roman precedents both by technological necessity and overt imitation.[11]

---

[8] Sabine MacCormack, *On the Wings of Time: Rome, the Incas, Spain, and Peru* (Princeton, NJ: Princeton University Press, 2007), xv.

[9] Ángel Rama, *La Ciudad Letrada* (Hanover, NH: Ediciones del Norte, 1984). The term *letrado* has both a general meaning of "learned individual" and "degree-holding jurist." Rama employs the term in the former more general sense, and I follow his usage here.

[10] Josiah Osgood, *Rome and the Making of a World State, 150 BCE–20 CE* (Cambridge: Cambridge University Press, 2018), 2; Emma Dench, *Empire and Political Cultures in the Roman World* (Cambridge: Cambridge University Press, 2018), 29–33. Indeed, anyone who dips into the last fifty years of scholarship on the empires of both ancient Rome and early modern Iberia will be struck by the fact that almost all the debates and insights of early modernists are prefigured in the historiography on Rome. Given that we now know how little was exceptional about premodern Western Eurasia, it is tempting to conclude that these various parallels were a reflection of a larger premodern pattern, rather than something uniquely "Western": Walter Scheidel (ed.), *Rome and China: Comparative Perspectives on Ancient World Empires* (Oxford: Oxford University Press, 2009).

[11] On state-building in the Iberian World, see: Tamar Herzog, *Upholding Justice: Society, State, and the Penal System in Quito (1650–1750)* (Ann Arbor: University of Michigan Press, 2004), 1–8. In using "neo-Roman," I am purposefully repurposing Quentin Skinner's epithet for the early modern republican tradition: Quentin Skinner, *Liberty Before Liberalism* (Cambridge: Cambridge University Press, 1998).

This is, however, not to say that this neo-Roman system was entirely free from coercive elements. Creating consensus by coaxing the unwilling with honeyed words was for sure not the same as demanding loyalty or conversion at the point of a sword, but it was the product of the same intention and led to the same result. It was a means for imperial, missionary and local actors to exert power, just as much as any civic, scholarly or artistic practice. Yet, it also bears underlining that like alphabetical writing or painting the classical rhetorical tradition was not wedded to one particular worldview, but was a conduit for the orator to contribute to public discourse, while advancing his own agenda. Described by Cicero and all those who followed in his footsteps as means to teach, delight and move listeners to action (*docere, delectare, movere*), classicizing public speaking was a versatile instrument of consensus building, which could be put to differing, even contradictory, ends depending on the circumstances. Codified at the level of theory at the elite level, such processes took place across the social spectrum in the Iberian World, as public speaking was characteristic of a whole host of occasions and linguistic sub-contexts.

Intellectual History: A Treasure-Trove of Ideas

It is highly unusual to center an intellectual history on public speaking.[12] After all, ornate displays of spoken eloquence belong to that no-man's-land between history and literature that few care to enter, a space too literary for historians and too historical for literary scholars. Selected sermons may have attracted the interest of historians of religion, but for the most part the *orationes, oraciones, orações, sermones* and *sermões* remain unread.[13] In the Iberian World, however, rhetoric mattered. It was a high prestige activity that could result in significant financial and social rewards. It stood at the heart of elite education. It crowned important civic and religious rituals in all urban contexts. The fact that historians have paid so little

---

[12] The notable exceptions all come from Renaissance historiography: Anthony F. D'Elia, *The Renaissance of Marriage in Fifteenth-Century Italy* (Cambridge, MA: Harvard University Press, 2004); James Hankins, "Renaissance Crusaders: Humanist Crusade Literature in the Age of Mehmed II," *Dumbarton Oaks Papers*, 49 (1995), 111–207; John M. McManamon, *Funeral Oratory and the Cultural Ideals of Italian Humanism* (Chapel Hill: The University of North Carolina Press, 1989).

[13] Félix Herrero Salgado, *La Oratoria Sagrada Española de los Siglos XVI y XVII*, 2 vols., (Madrid: Fundación Universitaria Española, 1996–1998); Perla Chinchilla Pawling, *De la Compositio Loci a La República de las Letras: Predicación Jesuita en el Siglo XVII Novohispano* (Mexico City: UIA, 2004). The most important Anglophone study of preaching in the Hispanic World remains Hilary Dansey Smith, *Preaching in the Spanish Golden Age: A Study of Some Preachers of the Reign of Philip III* (New York: Oxford University Press, 1978).

attention to this widespread and influential civic practice is therefore more the product of our modern disciplinary boundaries and a post-Romantic mistrust of skillful displays of eloquence than a reflection of its historical importance, although the challenges of dealing with these written accounts of oral performances as sources are real.

Furthermore, the particular corpus of sermons and orations treated in *Empire of Eloquence* has been overlooked by intellectual historians for linguistic reasons, namely that a large proportion of it is in postclassical Latin, or requires an understanding of Latin to comprehend its intellectual context fully. This is because in an age of national languages it is tacitly presumed that all Latin and Latinate public speaking was devoid of real content, and in any case probably incomprehensible to its audience.[14] However, we must not forget that these classicizing orations and sermons – be they in Latin, European or non-European vernaculars – were designed to be understood, with the choice of language and conventions being carefully calibrated for the particular circumstances and audience. Although there must have been instances when the audience did not fully grasp the orator's meaning, this was likely the exception rather than the rule. Indeed, the whole culture of classicizing public speaking and the institutional infrastructure that underpinned it was premised on the idea that listeners would be moved by what they heard. This only worked if the words being spoken were actually comprehensible to the listeners. As distant as it may be from our modern experience, this was equally the case for orations in Latin, the sacred language of the large Brahmanical class of *letrados* in the Iberian World, although, of course, unlike Sanskrit, it was not expressly forbidden to other castes.

If classicizing public speaking was an important and legible cultural practice, we should therefore take seriously the ideas put forward in it. Indeed, centering such a history on rhetoric and oratory offers a treasure trove of new insights. First, it bypasses a certain Eurocentric bias in Iberian intellectual history. These were specific *local* expressions of *local* ideas. In other words, these orations and sermons composed and delivered in Mexico City, Lima and Goa, to name but a few examples, offer a window onto a variegated world that the more commonly studied set-piece histories and works of political theory – frequently written and printed in Spain,

---

[14] The type of scenario envisioned is akin to the satirical portrait of late colonial culture painted by the Filipino novelist José Rizal in a passage of his novel *Noli Me Tangere* (1887), in which he describes a sermon delivered by a Spanish friar that was incomprehensible to his indigenous congregation: Vicente L. Rafael, *Contracting Colonialism: Translation and Christian Conversion in Tagalog Society under Early Spanish Rule* (Durham, NC: Duke University Press, 1988), 19.

Portugal and Italy – do not.[15] Second, they offer a less rarefied perspective than the aforementioned genres. Normally articulated within the context of epideictic rhetoric that aimed to rally a wide range of office holders, clerics and commoners around widely held beliefs, the orations of the Iberian World had to reflect mainstream views by necessity. We should not be afraid that the ideas expressed in them were the idiosyncratic creation of a single wild-eyed scholar. Third, by following the ideas espoused in orations and sermons from Latin into European vernaculars and indigenous languages, it is possible to begin to move across ethnic and class lines in a way that is otherwise difficult. They are therefore of potential interest to ethnohistorians and others interested in "history from below," as well as intellectual historians in the traditional mold. In short, studying the classical rhetorical tradition offers many advantages, both historical and historiographical.

Historical Meta-Geography: Defining the Iberian World

The final purpose of *Empire of Eloquence* is meta-geographical. That is to say, it offers a sketch map of the early modern Iberian World as a whole, with an emphasis on the place of the Americas within it (Figure I.1).[16] This approach is far from typical. When this sprawling series of polities, diasporic enclaves and cultural zones has been studied, it has been traditionally viewed from the perspective of the part not the whole. Protonational and regional traditions of scholarship dominate. The Iberian Atlantic has a distinctly imperial and cis-Atlantic flavor.[17] Iberian Asia is normally divided into its constituent Hispanophone and Lusophone parts with Brazil nowhere to be seen.[18] Self-declared historians of Iberian global

[15] David A. Brading, *The First America: The Spanish Monarchy, Creole Patriots, and the Liberal State, 1492–1867* (Cambridge: Cambridge University Press, 1991); Thomas James Dandelet, *The Renaissance of Empire in Early Modern Europe* (Cambridge: Cambridge University Press, 2014); Anthony Pagden, *Lords of All the World: Ideologies of Empire in Spain, Britain and France c. 1500–c. 1800* (New Haven, CT: Yale University Press, 1995).

[16] On the concept of meta-geography, see: Martin W. Lewis and Kären Wigen, *The Myth of Continents: A Critique of Metageography* (Berkeley: University of California Press, 1997).

[17] Jorge Cañizares-Esguerra and Benjamin Breen, "Hybrid Atlantics: Future Directions for the History of the Atlantic World," *History Compass*, 11 (2013), 597–609.

[18] Sanjay Subrahmanyam, *The Portuguese Empire in Asia, 1500–1700: A Political and Economic History* (London: John Wiley & Sons, 1993). Even the wide-ranging work of Charles Ralph Boxer focused largely on just one of the Iberian Peninsula's two kingdoms, for the most part in Africa and Asia: Charles Ralph Boxer, *The Portuguese Seaborne Empire, 1415–1825* (London: Hutchinson, 1969). On the life and scholarship of Boxer whose influence can be found throughout this study, see Dauril Alden, James S. Cummins and Michael Cooper, *Charles R. Boxer: An Uncommon Life: Soldier, Historian, Teacher, Collector, Traveller* (Lisbon: Fundação Oriente, 2001).

Figure I.1   Diachronic map of the early modern Iberian World (anthropological terms).
Made with the assistance of Cheryl Cape

empire have taken a similarly bifurcated approach. In almost all instances, territorial rather than anthropological definitions of the empires of "Spain" and "Portugal" dominate, with "borderlands" being considered the exception rather than the rule.[19] Of course, this does not mean that the Iberian World was homogenous and without conflicts, even during the Iberian Union (1580–1640). What political or cultural space is? Rather, as will become apparent there is a value to widening the panorama, to placing Goa, Mexico or Macau in a larger context, which few to date have done.

In *Empire of Eloquence*, in other words, the Iberian World is understood not as a nation *in ovo*, nor even as the sum total of the areas under Iberian political control. While large parts of the supposedly "conquered" Americas remained minimally Iberianized, Iberian influence extended beyond claimed political borders, including to allied states and de facto protectorates like Genoa and Tuscany, as well as to the Portuguese commercial zones and missionary fields that stretched from the Kongo to Kyūshū. Here, the hallmarks of "empire" in the sense of both the political and the sociocultural space created by Iberian expansion from the late fifteenth century onward were Iberian political influence (although

---

[19] Henry Kamen, *Empire: How Spain Became a World Power, 1492–1763* (New York: Harper Perennial, 2004).

not necessarily sovereignty), Iberian trade networks and Iberian cultural forms, including food, dress, language and above all Iberianized Catholicism. These "Iberian" traits could come from either the Iberian Peninsula itself or some other part of the Iberian World.[20]

This is the spatial scaffold I have used to build the "Empire of Eloquence." While there is extensive evidence of the important role played by classicizing public speaking in public life in France, Britain, German-speaking lands, Venice, imperial Russia and elsewhere, it nonetheless had a particular set of manifestations and applications in the Iberian World that mean that it can be usefully studied within this context without prejudicing any future attempt to place it within an even wider geographical frame. All these settings featured virtue-driven funeral orations and inaugural orations at universities. However, in the Iberian World these were delivered by orators living under (or in the shadow of) particular crowns, or teaching in institutions modeled on particular universities and colleges in the Iberian Peninsula where a particular brand of Catholicism was practiced that differed subtly from those of Italy and France.[21] That is to say, geography, history and religion conspired to create a particular set of circumstances in the Iberian Peninsula that would cast a long shadow, such that while not "exceptional," the Iberian World had a set of identifiable features that makes it a useful heuristic for historical study.[22] At the same time, the Iberian World is a particularly convenient starting point for

[20] Here, I am purposefully taking an anthropological approach to the question of Iberian "empire," drawing on: Gary W. McDonogh, *Iberian Worlds* (New York: Routledge, 2009).

[21] Marc Fumaroli, *L'Age de l'Eloquence: Rhétorique et "Res Literaria," de la Renaissance au Seuil de l'Epoque Classique* (Geneva: Librairie Droz, 1980); Peter Bayley, *French Pulpit Oratory, 1598–1650: A Study in Themes and Styles, with a Catalogue of Printed French Pulpit Oratory* (New York: Cambridge University Press, 1980); Max J. Okenfuss, *The Rise and Fall of Latin Humanism in Early-Modern Russia: Pagan Authors, Ukrainians, and the Resiliency of Muscovy* (New York: Brill, 1995); Johan Anselm Steiger, "*Oratio Panegyrica versus Homilia Consolatoria*. Ein Exemplarischer Vergleich Zwischen einer Römisch-katholischen Trauerrede (Wolfgang Fuchs) und einer Lutherischen Leichenpredigt (Johann Gerhard)," in Birgit Boge and Ralf Georg Bogner (eds.), *Oratio Funebris. Die katholische Leichenpredigt der frühen Neuzeit. Zwölf Studien. Mit einem Katalog Deutschsprachiger Katholischer Leichenpredigten in Einzeldrucken 1576–1799 aus den Beständen der Stiftsbibliothek Klosterneuburg und der Universitätsbibliothek Eichstätt* (Amsterdam: Rodopi, 1999), 103–130; Lucy Wooding Kostyanovsky, "From Tudor Humanism to Reformation Preaching," in Peter McCullough, Hugh Adlington and Emma Rhatigan (eds.), *The Oxford Handbook of the Early Modern Sermon* (Oxford: Oxford University Press, 2011), 329–347; Stuart M. McManus, "*Classica Americana*: An Addendum to the Censuses of Pre-1800 Latin Texts from British North America," *Humanistica Lovaniensia: Journal of Neo-Latin Studies*, 67.2 (2018), 421–461; George V. Bohman, "Rhetorical Practice in Colonial America," in Karl R. Wallace (ed.), *History of Speech Education in America; Background Studies* (New York: Forgotten Books, 1959), 60–79.

[22] This case is made particularly well by: Bartolomé Yun Casalilla, *Iberian World Empires and the Globalization of Europe, 1415–1668* (Singapore: Palgrave Macmillan, 2019).

exploring not only the relationship between classicizing public speaking and certain Iberian political projects, but also the interactions between the classical rhetorical tradition and similar traditions from Asia and the Americas, since it was the birthplace of syncretic cultures of Indo-Humanism (Chapter 4). These might otherwise slip through the cracks if either a wider or a narrower lens is employed.

Of course, the novelty of taking the Iberian World as a starting point raises the question of how exactly we should conceptualize it. Here, the traditions of historical scholarship on colonial Latin America are instructive. For the last half-century or so, the parts of the Americas subject to Iberian expansion have often been characterized as "colonial." This model suggests an Iberian World divided into a European "center" and American, Asian and African "peripheries" or "semi-peripheries," categories inherited from World Systems Theory and Dependency Theory. This has recently been challenged by a new school of Iberian imperial history that has proposed a "polycentric" model that questions the primacy of "many bilateral relations arranged in a radial pattern" and instead underscores "many different interlinked centers that interacted not only with the king but also among themselves, thus actively participating in forging the polity."[23] While recognizing the European origins of the classical rhetorical tradition, this study takes inspiration from the polycentric approach to foreground individual lived experiences of orators and audiences often living under slowly centralizing Iberian monarchies, and the self-reproducing and independently expanding cultures of classicizing learning that grew up in the centuries following 1500.[24]

To build such a polycentric vision of the Iberian World, this book consists of six case studies that cover its length and breadth, while overlapping geographically. These use, as far as is possible, nontraditional meta-geographical subunits based on a coherent series of orations or the lived experience of individual orators. By breaking out of traditional

---

[23] In this sense, this book builds on the insights of: Pedro Cardim, Tamar Herzog, José Javier Ruiz Ibáñez and Gaetano Sabatini (eds.), *Polycentric Monarchies. How Did Early Modern Spain and Portugal Achieve and Maintain a Global Hegemony?* (Brighton: Sussex Academic Press, 2012); Óscar Mazín and José Javier Ruiz Ibáñez (eds.), *Las Indias Occidentales: Procesos de Incorporación Territorial a las Monarquías Ibéricas (siglos XVI a XVIII)* (Mexico City: El Colegio de México, 2012); and José Javier Ruiz Ibáñez, "Les Acteurs de l'Hégémonie Hispanique, du Monde à la Péninsule Ibérique," *Annales. Histoire, Sciences Sociales*, 69 (2014), 927–954.

[24] Here, I am following in the footsteps of Byron Hamann who in his study of the global reception of Nebrija's Castilian dictionary wrote of "constellations of print shops": Byron Ellsworth Hamann, *The Translations of Nebrija: Language, Culture, and Circulation in the Early Modern World* (Amherst: University of Massachusetts Press, 2015).

national and regional paradigms, this book offers multiple frameworks for understanding the Iberian World that highlight the potential for connected and comparative histories of this polycentric global space, which consisted of multiple "skewed mirrors ... in a unified space that existed contemporaneously," to use the words of Tamar Herzog.[25] These at times underline the importance of maintaining the traditional distinction between "colonial" and "metropolitan" contexts, and at others belie it.

This said, all histories, even global (i.e. self-consciously transregional) histories, must have a fulcrum.[26] In this case, that fulcrum is located not in Europe, where the classical rhetorical tradition originated, but in the Americas. As such, it takes seriously the observation of Mexico City's first major Spanish-language poet, Bernardo de Balbuena (1561–1627), who wrote in his *Grandeza Mexicana* (1604) that Mexico City was the place where "Spain is joined to China, Italy to Japan and finally a whole world in trade and order."[27] In other words, this is a polycentric global history written with reference to a map of the early modern world centered not on the Greenwich Meridian, but somewhere around 80° West.[28] Such an approach has value both as an alternative to most global histories, which are distinctly Eurasian in focus, and as the beneficiary of developed and unique traditions of historical scholarship from this part of the world that can enrich the practice of global history.

Building a larger global framework around the Americas has numerous additional advantages. Due to the sheer extent of early modern Iberian expansion, unparalleled in premodern history, the Americas as part of the Iberian World is the ideal laboratory to explore the diffusion and development of ideas across multiple continents in both hemispheres in the

---

[25] Tamar Herzog, *Frontiers of Possession: Spain and Portugal in Europe and the Americas* (Cambridge, MA.: Harvard University Press, 2015), 11.

[26] Sebastian Conrad, *What Is Global History?* (Princeton, NJ: Princeton University Press, 2016), 162–184.

[27] Bernardo de Balbuena, *Grandeza Mexicana*, 2 vols., (Mexico City, 1604), I, fol. 89r:

> "En ti se junta España con la China
> Italia con Japón, y finalmente
> Un mundo entero en trato y disciplina."

[28] This approach is also to be found in: Serge Gruzinski, *Les Quatre Parties Du Monde: Histoire D'une Mondialisation* (Paris: Points, 2004); Tamar Herzog, *Frontiers of Possession: Spain and Portugal in Europe and the Americas*, and Kris E. Lane, *The Colour of Paradise: Emeralds in the Age of the Gunpowder Empires* (New Haven, CT: Yale University Press, 2010). When the term "Latin" America is used in this study, it is merely a term of convenience chosen more for its currency in the Anglophone historical profession as a catchall for the Iberianized parts of the Western Hemisphere, than for its implied relationship to any other imagined "America," Anglophone or otherwise: Mauricio Tenorio-Trillo, *Latin America: The Allure and Power of an Idea* (Chicago: University of Chicago Press, 2017).

sixteenth, seventeenth and early eighteenth centuries, which Anglo-centric global historians have tended to overlook because large-scale British imperial expansion was a largely modern affair.[29] Treating the history of an intellectual current that has its roots in the ancient Mediterranean world primarily from the perspective of the Americas also produces a certain "alienation effect" (*Verfremdungseffekt*) for historians of the classical tradition more accustomed to looking out at the world from Europe. Finally, expanding outward from the Americas historiographically also has the advantage of allowing a detailed treatment of the relationship between learned culture, identity and empire that can benefit from a rich tradition of scholarship on these themes.[30]

As the conventional chronologies and surviving documentation from the different parts of the Iberian World do not always line up neatly, this meta-geographical approach necessitates a similarly expansive periodization. To permit this, *Empire of Eloquence* draws inspiration from David Armitage's "serial contextualism," and offers a series of "transtemporal" moments, which overlap as far as possible, while bridging the gap between Columbus and Napoleon.[31] In Latin American historiography, this is a period normally marked by a division of labor between historians of conquest and colonization (*c.* 1500–1700) on the one hand, and historians of enlightenment and revolution (*c.* 1700–1850) on the other.[32] However, this line in the sand severs important continuities in rhetorical education and practice. To underline the continuities between the worlds of late humanist orators on the one hand, and of enlightenment and early national orators on the other, I have used the term "post-humanism." This draws attention to the fact that in the early eighteenth-century Latin

---

[29] For this critique, see Sanjay Subrahmanyam, "Global Intellectual History Beyond Hegel and Marx," *History and Theory*, 54 (2015), 126–137 (129).

[30] This point is made in Jeremy Adelman, "Latin American and World Histories: Old and New Approaches to the Pluribus and the Unum," *Hispanic American Historical Review*, 83 (2004), 399–409. An example of the usefulness of specifically Latin America categories for global history is Arnulf Becker Lorca, *Mestizo International Law: A Global Intellectual History 1842–1933* (Cambridge: Cambridge University Press, 2014). We await with interest Jeremy Adelman's forthcoming global history of Latin America.

[31] David Armitage, "What's the Big Idea? Intellectual History and the *Longue Durée*," *History of European Ideas*, 38 (2012), 493–507.

[32] Eric Van Young "Brading's Century: Some Reflections on David A. Brading's Work and the Historiography of Mexico, 1750–1850," in Susan Deans-Smith and Eric Van Young (eds.), *Mexican Soundings: Essays in Honour of David A. Brading* (London: Institute of Latin American Studies, 2007), 42–64 (49). On the colonial-national divide in Latin American history, see Jeremy Adelman, "The Problem of Persistence in Latin American History," in Jeremy Adelman (ed.), *Colonial Legacies: The Problem of Persistence in Latin American History* (New York: Routledge, 1999), 1–13.

declamation and late humanist handbooks or their translations remained the gymnasium in which speakers were trained for a predominately vernacular world increasingly characterized by new ideas. This tradition, of course, came to be replaced by a wholly vernacular neoclassical culture of rhetoric and oratory by the end of the eighteenth century following the rise of *belles lettres* out of the ashes of late Renaissance culture.[33] This, as the final chapters of *Empire of Eloquence* will show, took place across the Iberian World.

The Classical Rhetorical Tradition

Before proceeding, it is important to clarify exactly what we mean by the "classical rhetorical tradition," as "rhetoric" has both a general and a specific meaning, with the latter being the topic of *Empire of Eloquence*. In its early modern form, the classical rhetorical tradition (vs. "classical rhetoric") was a cultural conglomerate of ancient, late antique, medieval and early modern European currents centered on the Greco-Roman codification of best practices in public speaking.[34] At its core, it depended on the revival of one of the two pre-Socratic educational models that arose in the Greek-speaking world of the fifth and fourth centuries BCE. The first of these, which we might call "philosophy," sought to know all things, so as to provide a critique of received social norms, while the other, which we might call "rhetoric" or "sophistry," wished to shape and direct public behavior through persuasive speech. These contrasting intellectual and educational visions grew up simultaneously and soon came into conflict. As Plato described in his dialogue *Gorgias*, philosophers attacked sophists for teaching (at an exorbitant price) a mere "knack" (ἐμπειρία) that did not lead to any true knowledge, while sophists accused philosophers of peddling schoolroom tricks that did not advance the interests of the speaker in the law courts or the public assembly.[35] While the conflict was never fully resolved, these traditions came to coexist in Greek education (παιδεία), which prepared future citizens for philosophically informed, active

---

[33] My use of the term post-humanism has no connection to the philosophical system that rejects anthropocentrism: Cary Wolfe, *What Is Posthumanism?* (Minneapolis: University of Minnesota Press, 2010), ix–xxvi.

[34] The best general introduction to this topic is: George A. Kennedy, *Classical Rhetoric and Its Christian and Secular Tradition from Ancient to Modern Times* (Chapel Hill: University of North Carolina Press, 1999).

[35] Plato, *Gorgias*, 462c.

participation in civic life, including public speaking in political, judicial and ceremonial contexts.[36]

Sharpened to a point in the Greek-speaking Mediterranean, the rhetorical tradition of the sophists was soon taken up by the elites of an expanding Rome. Fed by the needs of Roman civic life with its deliberative assemblies and jury trials, the rhetorical training offered as part of the Romanized version of Greek education became a prerequisite for any ambitious young man in the *caput mundi* and its expanding sphere of influence.[37] For aspiring Roman statesmen, like Cicero, who studied under Greek teachers, rhetoric was the defining feature of a civilized, urban society, no less essential than paved streets and public baths. Indeed, societies, Cicero tells us in his youthful treatise on rhetoric, *De inventione*, only existed in the first place thanks to the efforts of eloquent orators:

> For there was a time when men wandered aimlessly over the fields, in the manner of beasts, and sustained themselves on nature's bounty; nor did they do anything by means of the reasoning powers of the mind; but almost everything by bodily strength . . . At this time then a man, a truly great and wise man perceived what materials there were, and what great fitness there was in the minds of men for the most important affairs, if anyone could only draw it out, and improve it by education. He, laying down a regular system, collected men, who were previously dispersed over the fields and hidden away in the woods, into one place, and united them, and leading them on to every useful and honorable pursuit – though, at first, from not being used to it they rebelled against it – he gradually, as they became more eager to listen to him on account of his wisdom and eloquence, made them gentle and civilized from having been savage and brutal . . . Once cities had been established, how could men possibly have been tempted to learn to cultivate integrity and to maintain justice, and to be convinced to obey others willingly, and to think it right not only to labor for the common good, but even to risk losing their lives, if men had not been able to persuade them by eloquence of the truth of those principles which they had discovered by reason?[38]

---

[36] Hans von Arnim, *Leben und Werke des Dio von Prusa: mit einer Einleitung, Sophistik, Rhetorik, Philosophie in ihrem Kampf um die Jugendbildung* (Berlin: Wentworth Press, 1898), 4–114.

[37] Elaine Fantham, *The Roman World of Cicero's De Oratore* (New York: Oxford University Press, 2004), 78–101; Thomas Habinek, *Ancient Rhetoric and Oratory* (Hoboken, NJ: Wiley-Blackwell, 2008), 1–15; Robert Morstein-Marx, *Mass Oratory and Political Power in the Late Roman Republic* (New York: Cambridge University Press, 2004), 34–57; Thomas J. Keeline, *The Reception of Cicero in the Early Roman Empire: The Rhetorical Schoolroom and the Creation of a Cultural Legend* (Cambridge: Cambridge University Press, 2018).

[38] Cicero, *De Inventione*, 1.2–3: "Fuit quoddam tempus, cum in agris homines passim bestiarum modo vagabantur et sibi victu fero vitam propagabant nec ratione animi quicquam, sed pleraque

This chimed with the judgment of the Greek historian Polybius who attributed at least some of Rome's success to the civilizing force of funeral oratory, which strengthened the resolve of the Roman youth by placing good models for imitation before them.[39]

With the advent of Christianity, this educational and civic program increasingly found new applications. In the hands of a sacred orator, classicizing eloquence and pious erudition were harnessed to exhort the faithful to higher standards of Christian behavior. As a result, the term "oration" (*oratio*) also came to mean a "prayer," with both meanings continuing into modern Spanish and Portuguese (*oración, oração*). In the age of the Church Fathers, new occasions appeared for Christianized public speaking. With these, new theories of ecclesiastical rhetoric arose that reworked existing models and practices for new Christian ends. As the political power of Rome declined, these traditions, equally classical and Christian, were codified and passed on to the new, but not unlearned world of Latin Christendom, while the traditions in the Greek-speaking part of the Roman Empire took their own path in Byzantium. There was also a parallel tradition in the Islamic World that drew occasionally from ancient Mediterranean models.[40] From the twelfth century, the universities of the High Middle Ages produced their own culture of religious rhetoric (*ars praedicandi*), and a new genre of public speaking, known as the "thematic sermon" that channeled the style of logical argumentation taught in the universities, while preserving the basic framework set out in classical rhetoric.

Towards the end of the fourteenth century, with a growing interest in the ancient urban culture that lay crumbling but not forgotten across Italy, scholars and statesmen in the burgeoning communes sought models for speaking in their own deliberative assemblies and law courts in antiquity. This, combined with a dissatisfaction with the dominant political and learned cultures of the day, led to a movement to revive the standards of behavior that the humanists of the Renaissance associated with their

---

viribus corporis administrabant ... Quo tempore quidam magnus videlicet vir et sapiens cognovit, quae materia esset et quanta ad maximas res opportunitas in animis inesset hominum, si quis eam posset elicere et praecipiendo meliorem reddere; qui dispersos homines in agros et in tectis silvestribus abditos ratione quadam conpulit unum in locum et congregavit et eos in unam quamque rem inducens utilem atque honestam primo propter insolentiam reclamantes, deinde propter rationem atque orationem studiosius audientes ex feris et inmanibus mites reddidit et mansuetos ... Age vero urbibus constitutis, ut fidem colere et iustitiam retinere discerent et aliis parere sua voluntate consuescerent ac non modo labores excipiendos communis commodi causa, sed etiam vitam amittendam existimarent, qui tandem fieri potuit, nisi homines ea, quae ratione invenissent, eloquentia persuadere potuissent?"

[39] Polybius, *Histories*, 6.53–54.
[40] George Makdisi, *The Rise of Humanism in Classical Islam and the Christian West with Special Reference to Scholasticism* (Edinburgh: Edinburgh University Press, 1990), 150.

idealized version of the ancient Mediterranean past.[41] Rhetoric and its application in oratory was to be the trumpet of ancient virtue.[42] This reforming (but not revolutionary) movement was spearheaded in turn by the new embodiments of Quintilian's ideal of the "good man skilled in speaking" (*vir bonus dicendi peritus*), Latinate statesman-scholars educated according to the principles of a revived *paideia*, supremely eloquent according to the standards set by the best authors of antiquity and with a mastery of classical history, literature and philosophy.[43] Combining the knowledge and most importantly the virtues imparted by the reading of ancient texts with the ability to make the lessons of both pagan and Christian antiquity sing, the Renaissance heirs of Cicero hoped to revive the glory that was Rome, an ancient polity onto which a vast array of visions could be projected.

As much of the elite of Renaissance Italy and then Europe came under the influence of this classicizing craze, any and all occasions were exploited to exhort listeners to virtuous behavior on the basis of classical models. Civic events, triumphal entries, the appointment of officials and military leaders, the opening of universities, ecumenical councils, funerals, weddings and even birthday celebrations throughout what many intellectual historians called the "Republic of Letters," featured displays of classicizing public speaking in Latin and the vernacular.[44] This also influenced preaching in Europe's Jewish communities.[45] In response to this elite obsession

---

[41] Ronald G. Witt, *In the Footsteps of the Ancients: The Origins of Humanism from Lovato to Bruni* (Leiden: Brill, 2000), 338–391, 443–494; Hanna H. Gray, "Renaissance Humanism: The Pursuit of Eloquence," *Journal of the History of Ideas*, 24 (1963), 497–514; Patrick Baker, *Italian Renaissance Humanism in the Mirror* (Cambridge: Cambridge University Press, 2015), 36–89; Stephen J. Milner, "'Le Sottili Cose non si Possono Bene Aprire in Volgare': Vernacular Oratory and the Transmission of Classical Rhetorical Theory in the Late Medieval Italian Communes," *Italian Studies* 64 (2009), 221–244.

[42] Paul Oskar Kristeller, *The Classics and Renaissance Thought* (Cambridge, MA: Harvard University Press, 1955), 11–12, 22.

[43] On humanist education, see Paul F. Grendler, *Schooling in Renaissance Italy: Literacy and Learning, 1300–1600* (Baltimore, MD: The Johns Hopkins University Press, 1989); Robert Black, *Humanism and Education in Medieval and Renaissance Italy: Tradition and Innovation in Latin Schools from the Twelfth to the Fifteenth Century* (Cambridge: Cambridge University Press, 2001); *ibid.*, *Education and Society in Florentine Tuscany* (Boston: Brill, 2007).

[44] Whereas the rhetorical theory of the Renaissance has been the subject of sustained study, its application in classicizing public speaking is still poorly mapped: Johannes Helmrath, "Der Europäische Humanismus und die Funktionen der Rhetorik," in Thomas Maissen und Gerrit Walther (eds.), *Funktionen des Humanismus. Studien zum Nutzen des Neuen in der Humanistischen Kultur* (Göttingen: Wallstein Verlag, 2006), 18–48 (29–34).

[45] Elliott Horowitz, "Speaking of the Dead: The Emergence of the Eulogy among Italian Jewry of the Sixteenth Century," in David B. Ruderman (ed.), *Preachers of the Italian Ghetto* (Berkeley: University of California Press, 1992), 129–162.

with ancient eloquence, new treatises were written on increasingly specific applications of classical theory.[46] This was no less the case in the Iberian Peninsula, and it is from here that we take up the story.[47]

Chapter Outlines

Each chapter of *Empire of Eloquence* addresses the role of the classical rhetorical tradition in forging the Iberian World from a single meta-geographical perspective that throws the Americas into relief either in a connected or in a comparative way. Chapter 1 argues that the foundations of the Iberian "Empire of Eloquence" were laid in the sixteenth century in a process of intellectual and educational expansion that mirrored the territorial and cultural growth of the Iberian World. This takes the form of a case study of the Valley of Mexico placed within the context of this larger space. As well as offering a thumbnail sketch of the "Empire of Eloquence" as a whole, this chapter makes the case for significant continuity or at least parallels across the pre-/post-Columbian divide. For instance, the colleges where classical rhetoric was taught were often built on the site of earlier indigenous institutions, while Renaissance rhetoric and oratory replaced similar indigenous forms of consensus building, most notably Aztec *huehuetlatolli* ("sayings of old men"). In other words, the classical rhetorical tradition may have been new, but it was not necessarily entirely alien.

Chapter 2 argues for the pivotal role of classicizing funeral oratory for Spanish monarchs in shaping and disseminating the political thought of the global Hispanic Monarchy. Rather than taking a protonation state like Mexico or Peru as the unit of analysis, it considers all the surviving orations delivered at the funeral commemorations for Philip IV (1605–1665) in Spanish America, Iberian Asia, the Iberian Peninsula, Spanish North Africa, Spanish Italy and the Spanish Netherlands. Grounded in epideictic rhetoric, these orations presented listeners with absolute standards for imitation embodied in the person of the king ("virtue politics"). At the same

---

[46] Marc Fumaroli, *L'Age de l'Eloquence: Rhétorique et "Res Literaria," de la Renaissance au Seuil de l'Époque Classique*; Peter Mack, *A History of Renaissance Rhetoric (1380–1620)* (Oxford: Oxford University Press, 2011).

[47] Johannes Helmrath, "Diffusion des Humanismus. Zur Einführung," in Johannes Helmrath, Ulrich Muhlack and Gerrit Walther (eds.), *Diffusion des Humanismus: Studien zur Nationalen Geschichtsschreibung Europäischer Humanisten* (Göttingen: Wallstein Verlag, 2002), 9–29; Paul Oskar Kristeller, "The European Diffusion of Italian Humanism," *Italica*, 39 (1962), 1–20. On Spain in particular, see Ottavio di Camillo, "Humanism in Spain," in A. Rabil, Jr. (ed.), *Renaissance Humanism. Foundations, Forms, and Legacy*, 3 vols. (Philadelphia: University of Pennsylvania Press, 1988), II, 55–108.

time, they also left space for institutionalized resistance or "negotiation" in the face of unjust local officials who could be measured according to these standards and held accountable by petitions to the monarch, the ultimate source of justice. In addition, the orations open up rich possibilities for connected and comparative histories of the Iberian World, which included areas that were not strictly speaking territories of the Spanish Habsburgs, but were tied to it by bonds of alliance and cultural kinship, such as the Grand Duchy of Tuscany, Papal Rome and the Republic of Genoa.

Chapter 3 argues that the classical rhetorical tradition in its Renaissance humanist garb was a valuable tool for celebrating and thereby bolstering Jesuit efforts to expand the boundaries of Catholicism, a project that was at times imagined in highly militaristic terms. While Jesuit "spiritual conquest" is normally discussed in the context of the Americas, this chapter follows the career of a Japanese humanist, Hara Martinho (*c.* 1568–1629), from his early education in the Jesuit College at Arima in Japan, to his participation in the Tenshō Embassy to Rome, and finally to the crowning achievement of his humanist career, the delivery of a militaristic Latin panegyric oration to his fellow Jesuits at Goa. The case of this Japanese Cicero also reminds us that Jesuit missionary projects were instrumental in forging parts of the Iberian World that did not fall under the direct jurisdiction of Iberian monarchs, such as Southern Japan, which was partially Christianized and Iberianized in this period, but never conquered per se. Although largely unknown to *american-istas*, the case of Catholicism in Japan in general, and Hara Martinho in particular, has important implications for our understanding of the Western Hemisphere, where territorial conquest and conversion were symbiotic, but not necessarily identical processes.

Chapter 4 similarly explores the role of the classical rhetorical tradition in bolstering Iberianized Catholicism among native converts in Paraguay and Portuguese India. In particular, it addresses the culture of what is dubbed here "Indo-humanism," the hybrid but naturalized classicizing culture produced by interactions between Jesuit missionaries and native peoples. By taking a connected and comparative approach to the application of the classical rhetorical tradition by Jesuit missionaries and its reception by native audiences in the Konkani-speaking areas of coastal western India, this chapter demonstrates that local social and caste structures, not only factors internal to the classical rhetorical tradition, shaped sacred oratory in indigenous languages. In so doing, this chapter places Latin American ethnohistory in a new meta-geographical context, and argues for the important constitutive role played by non-European languages, peoples and cultural practices in the Iberian World.

Chapter 5 makes the case that the classical rhetorical tradition was not only a means to disseminate Iberianized Catholicism or the "negotiated" political ideology of the Hispanic Monarchy. It was also a conduit for expressing the local identities, usually called in Latin American historiography "creole patriotism" (*patriotismo criollo*). This can be seen most clearly in a little-known late humanist Latin oration delivered in 1745 at the Royal and Pontifical University in Mexico City, which represents the first "Mexican" reaction to the *Bibliotheca Mexicana* controversy, a transatlantic debate started by a prominent Spanish antiquarian, Manuel Martí (1663–1737), who claimed that the New World was an intellectual desert. This reveals that the identity of the so-called creoles (American-born ethnic Spaniards) centered on their particular kingdom of the Hispanic Monarchy, in this case New Spain, which as a possession of the House of Bourbon looked constantly to Castile where the monarchs resided. Furthermore, we learn that membership in the political community of this kingdom did not depend exclusively on birth, but could also be based on long-term residence, which mirrored concepts of citizenship inherited from Roman Law. This Novohispanic identity, in turn, existed within a larger Pan-Hispanic context and membership of the "Republic of Letters."[48]

Chapter 6 turns to the disintegration of the polities of the early modern Iberian World, and addresses the role of the classical rhetorical tradition in articulating and spreading new ideas in both the Atlantic and the Pacific (*c.* 1750–1850). To this end, it begins by showing that Enlightenment wine was frequently put in post-humanist bottles, focusing on the orations delivered at meetings of the Royal Patriotic Society of Manila (*Real sociedad patriótica de Manila*) in the Philippines. By taking a transpacific rather than transatlantic perspective, this chapter aims to challenge the Atlanticist myopia of much of the scholarship on the Iberian Enlightenment. It then shows that a similar pattern can be seen in the oratory of the Age of Revolutions in Mexico. While the public ceremonial oratory of the early Mexican Republic is often portrayed as having arisen spontaneously to fulfill the needs of the new nation, this chapter argues that this was merely the last in a long line of applications in the Iberian World of a civic and scholarly practice inherited from Mediterranean Antiquity.

Finally, it bears underscoring that all global historical projects present certain logistical challenges. In this case, since the many hundreds of

---

[48] Tamar Herzog, "Los Americanos Frente a la Monarquía: el Criollismo y la Naturaleza Española," in Antonio Álvarez-Ossorio Alvariño and Bernardo J. García García (eds.), *La Monarquía de las Naciones. Patria, Nación y Naturaleza en la Monarquía de España* (Madrid: Fundación Carlos de Amberes, 2004), 77–92; *eadem, Defining Nations: Immigrants and Citizens in Early Modern Spain and Spanish America* (New Haven, CT: Yale University Press, 2003).

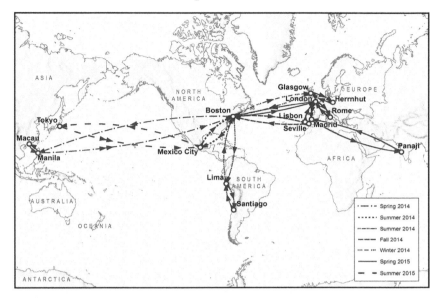

Figure I.2 McManus Research Itinerary, 2014–2015. Made with the assistance of Cheryl Cape

orations and sermons, editions of relevant classical texts and student notes that form the basis of *Empire of Eloquence* frequently survive only in their original manuscript or early modern printed form and in disparate collections, the researching and writing of this book required the author to visit archives and libraries on four continents over a period of several years (Figure I.2). This book is therefore very much the product of the globalizing, if not quite fully globalized, world of the early twenty-first century. This said, *Empire of Eloquence* is not a panegyric of globalization, past or present.[49] Rather, it is an archaeological project to uncover the vestiges of a lost world order that lies buried beneath our modern conceptions of nations, continents and civilizations, and to which we are heirs only indirectly, if at all.

---

[49] We must remember that the increasing connectedness of humanity in the early modern period – what Christopher Bayly called "archaic globalization" – was fundamentally different from our own, characterized as it was by militant universalizing monarchies (both European and non-European), expansionist religions and biomoral understandings of human health: Christopher A. Bayly, *Birth of the Modern World, 1780–1914* (Malden, MA: Wiley-Blackwell, 2004), 41–48.

CHAPTER I

The Foundations of the Empire of Eloquence

Thirty-two years after Hernán Cortés and his army of indigenous, African and Iberian conquistadors captured Mexico-Tenochtitlan, Francisco Cervantes de Salazar (*c.* 1514–1575) took his students for a walk through the new city that was rising out of the rubble of the former capital of the Aztec Triple Alliance. This was, however, not a perambulation in the physical sense. Rather, it was an imaginary tour that was to be repeated by generations of students who studied the Ciceronian Latin dialogues that Cervantes de Salazar composed in his capacity as the inaugural professor of rhetoric at the city's newly founded university. If we follow in the footsteps of his interlocutors, it becomes clear that by 1554 many Iberian buildings and institutions, frequently modeled on Roman archetypes, already stood alongside – or more often atop – pre-Columbian structures. Where there had once been a vast Mesoamerican temple complex that represented the center of the Nahua cosmos, there was now a Hispanic *plaza de armas* that acted as the ceremonial and commercial center of the nascent Viceroyalty of New Spain.[1] To the north of the *plaza*, the twin temples to Tlaloc and Huitzilopochtli had been torn down and a humble church erected that would act as a placeholder until the construction of a grand cathedral began in 1573.[2] On the northwest side, Cortés had built himself a fine medieval castle on the site of the earlier palace of the Mexica emperor Axayacatl (*c.* 1449–1481), while the viceroy and the *audiencia* occupied another palace originally built by Cortés atop the more recent palace of Montezuma II (*c.* 1466–1520) (Figure 1.1).[3] There, the viceroy and his

---

[1] Francisco Cervantes de Salazar, *México en 1554*, Joaquín García Icazbalceta (ed.) (Mexico City: Universidad Nacional Autónoma de México, 2001), fol. 260v.

[2] *Ibid.*, fols. 265v–266r.

[3] On the palace of Axaycatl, see Susan Toby Evans, "Aztec Palaces and Other Elite Residential Architecture," in Susan Toby Evans and Joanne Pillsbury, *Palaces of the Ancient New World* (Washington, DC: Dumbarton Oaks Research Library and Collection, 2004), 7–58 (20–21).

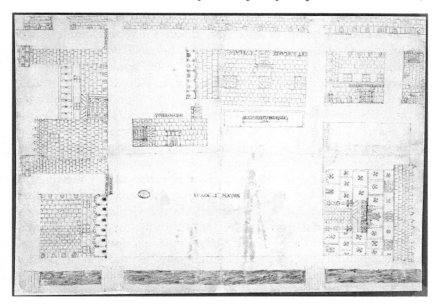

Figure 1.1   Map of the main square in Mexico City (c. 1562), *Plano de la Plaza Mayor de México, de los edificios y calles adyacentes y la acequia real* (Spain, Seville, Ministerio de Cultura y Deporte, Archivo General de Indias, MP-MEXICO, 3)

judges (*oidores*) issued decrees and passed judgment on legal cases brought to them by litigants from all corners of the viceroyalty.[4]

This said, the former Aztec city had not disappeared. After touring the central *traza* (an urban space on the Iberian model that was home to the majority of the city's 3,000 Spaniards), Cervantes de Salazar's interlocutors crossed one of the city's causeways, noting that it saw more traffic than the Via Appia that Cicero had eulogized in his speech *Pro Milone*. They then climbed Chapultepec Hill just outside the city. There, they were struck by the fact that the population and built environment remained largely unchanged, punctuated only by the occasional stone church. Viewing this patchwork Aztec city populated by ethnic *españoles* and *indios* – as well as Africans and eventually Asians, none of whom made it into Cervantes de Salazar's account – they described Mexico City as a "microcosm" that

---

[4] *México en 1554*, fols. 262r–263v. On the process of viceroyalty-building and the formation of a "parasitic civic nobility," see Jose-Juan Lopez-Portillo, *"Another Jerusalem" Political Legitimacy and Courtly Government in the Kingdom of New Spain (1535–1568)* (Leiden: Brill, 2017).

united the "Old" World and the "New."[5] This, then, was the navel of an Iberian World, the origins of whose shared norms may be traceable back to an isolated outcrop at the edge of Eurasia, but that was constituted by peoples and cultural forms from across the globe, resulting in a richness that was at least partly visible from Chapultepec Hill.

Of course, the process by which this New World metropolis was incorporated into the Hispanic Monarchy and the larger Iberian World took place in a number of steps, none of which was preordained. It began with Cortés' wild-eyed adventurism on the American mainland, which quickly led to an unsanctioned military intervention in a regional dispute between the Aztec Triple Alliance and its tributary states. Following this Mesoamerican civil war, in which a small group of Iberians and Iberianized non-Europeans were the senior partners on the victorious side, a neo-European political system slowly developed with the cooperation of indigenous elites who saw their interests tied to those of a distant monarch and the growing number of transatlantic immigrants. To this nascent political hierarchy was added a legal apparatus that allowed the resolution of disputes under the watchful eye of delegates of the Crown, both Iberian and indigenous. This process of integration into the Hispanic Monarchy and the wider Iberian World was aided by the rapid expansion of the Catholic religion, which gave the growing political consensus a spiritual underpinning, and was to prove as important as asymmetrical military might to the slow expansion of this system outward from increasingly Iberianized urban centers. All this is well known. What is less well known, however, is that this political, legal and spiritual expansion was accompanied by the spread of a set of intellectual, and specifically rhetorical, ideas and practices at the hands of orators and educators. These masters of the classical rhetorical tradition played an important role in smoothing out the wrinkles in the new social order.

Although public speaking is by nature ephemeral, the infrastructure that supported this rhetorical culture left an indelible mark on Mexico City. In the decades following the siege, the city saw the construction of colleges, seminaries and universities where humanist rhetoric was taught and practiced, sometimes even on the site of pre-Hispanic centers of learning. Simultaneously, occasions for eloquent speech were instituted, which filled new or existing spaces with the booming voices of learned Christian orators. In 1551 Cervantes de Salazar himself delivered the first inaugural oration in Latin at the new university. He has also left us a description of

[5] *México en 1554*, fol. 284r–v.

the grand funeral commemorations performed for the death of Charles V, when the archbishop of Mexico, Alonso de Montúfar y Bravo de Lagunas (1489–1572), delivered a funeral oration in praise of the "emperor" (*césar imperador*) of New Spain.[6] In a city characterized by multiple linguistic traditions, it is important to remember that this new rhetorical culture was not limited to politicized speech in European languages. Rather, the classical rhetorical tradition spilled out into indigenous languages, a fact that the Spanish humanist highlighted when he directed the attention of his inter-locutors to the city's Franciscan church, where the university's grammar master Blas de Bustamante (dates unknown) delivered sermons in Nahuatl.[7]

In preparation for the rest of the book, this chapter therefore argues that the foundations of the Iberian World's Empire of Eloquence were laid in the sixteenth century by the expansion of neo-Roman intellectual and educational traditions. This cultural conquest, however, did not mark a complete break with the past. While representing a new rhetorical order, there were also significant parallels, if not outright continuities across the pre-/post-conquest divide. These are visible not only in the well-known permanence of indigenous languages reimagined by missionaries on the model of Greek and Latin but also in the use of eloquent speech for social ends, most apparent in the correspondences between the educational pro-grams of the pre-Hispanic *calmécacs* and the Franciscan colegio de la Santa Cruz de Tlatelolco. Furthermore, by looking outward from Mexico City as a "microcosm" of the Iberian World, we will see that the expansion of the classical rhetorical tradition was not limited to the leading city in the premodern Americas but was part of a much larger phenomenon that linked the Americas to large parts of Asia, Europe and Africa. While Mexico City and other urban contexts in the Americas certainly saw some of the most dramatic applications of the classical rhetorical tradition, they were far from unique within the larger Iberian World.

Humanism in Renaissance Iberia

The humanist world of Cervantes de Salazar and his contemporaries in Mexico City did not arise *ex nihilo*. Rather, it was rooted in the particular

---

[6] Agustín Millares Carlo, *Apuntes para un Estudio Bibliográfico del Humanista Francisco Cervantes de Salazar* (Mexico City: Universidad Nacional Autónoma de México, 1958), 35.

[7] *México en 1554*, fols. 270r–271r; Francisco de Cervantes de Salazar, *Túmulo Imperial de la Gran Ciudad de México* (Mexico City, 1560), fol. 25v; Aysha Pollnitz, "Old Words and the New World: Liberal Education and the Franciscans in New Spain, 1536–1601," *Transactions of the Royal Historical Society*, 27 (2017), 123–152.

world of Renaissance Iberia, which was itself the product of a larger *translatio studii* from Italy to the rest of Europe. Indeed, due to close economic, social and political ties between the western Mediterranean's two main peninsulas, Spanish scholars corresponded regularly with Florentine, Milanese and Roman humanists from the late fourteenth century onward.[8] This continuing dialogue was enhanced not only by the ecumenical councils that brought together clerics from every corner of Christendom in the first half of the fifteenth century but also by the ongoing vitality of a shared late medieval culture of classicizing learning that meant that the same texts popular in medieval Italy also circulated in Iberia, including key rhetorical handbooks such as Cicero's *De inventione* and the anonymous *Rhetorica ad Herennium*, which were read alongside guides to preaching (*ars praedicandi*) and letter-writing (*ars dictaminis*).[9] Following the proliferation of Spanish colleges at Italian universities in this period, Spanish universities began to introduce chairs of rhetoric, beginning with Salamanca in 1403 where law students were eager to learn more about the new models for speaking and writing that were increasingly popular in Italy.[10] Under Portuguese royal patronage and thanks to close connections to scholars from both Italy and Northern Europe, the University of Coimbra too would become a center for humanist rhetoric in the sixteenth century as the explosion of academic oratory in Latin among students and faculty attests.[11] At the same time, many Iberian students also went to study in Paris where they were exposed to the newly institutionalized form of the humanist curriculum (*modus Parisiensis*), which would later become the model for the Jesuit curriculum (*Ratio studiorum*).[12]

In addition to Iberians bringing humanist culture home, there were also Italian and other foreign humanists who sought the patronage of Iberian

[8] Paul Oskar Kristeller, "The European Diffusion of Italian Humanism," *Italica*, 39 (1962), 1–20 (4–6); Ángel Gómez Moreno, *España y la Italia de los Humanistas: Primeros Ecos* (Madrid: Gredos, 1994).

[9] Charles B. Faulhaber, *Latin Rhetorical Theory in Thirteenth and Fourteenth Century Castile* (Berkeley: University of California Press, 1972).

[10] Pero Díaz de Toledo, *Libro Llamado Fedrón: Plato's Phaedo*, Nicholas Grenville Round (ed.) (Rochester, NY: Tamesis Books, 1993), 62–76.

[11] Belmiro Fernandes Pereira, *Retórica e Eloquência em Portugal na Época do Renascimento* (Lisbon: Imprensa Nacional-Casa da Moeda, 2012); Arnaldo Fabrício, Sebastião de Pinho, Maria José Pacheco (eds.), *Orações de Sapiência, 1548–1555* (Coimbra: Imprensa da Universidade de Coimbra, 2011).

[12] Américo da Costa Ramalho, *Para a História do Humanismo em Portugal* (Coimbra: Imprensa da Universidade de Coimbra, 1988). See also the essays in Maria Louro Berbara and K. A. E. Enenkel (eds.), *Portuguese Humanism and the Republic of Letters* (Leiden: Brill, 2012).

royal houses in both Iberia and Italy as the wealth and prestige of these kingdoms rose in the course of the fifteenth and sixteenth centuries. For instance, the famous Milanese translator of Plato, Pier Candido Decembrio (1399–1477), cultivated connections with the Spanish nobility and briefly served Alfonso the Magnanimous (1396–1458) following the latter's conquest of Naples in 1442. As a result, many of Decembrio's works were translated into Spanish, alongside those of the Florentine Chancellor Leonardo Bruni (*c.* 1370–1444) who also enjoyed a considerable reputation in Spain. Similarly, Peter Martyr d'Anghiera (1457–1526) became court chaplain to Ferdinand and Isabella, while the Sicilian Lucio Marineo Sículo (*c.* 1444–1533) gave lectures in poetry and rhetoric at the University of Salamanca and later served as royal historian to the Catholic Monarchs.[13] Around the same time, the Kingdom of Portugal hosted the Flemish grammarian Nicolas Cleynaerts (1495–1542) and the Scottish historian and poet George Buchanan (1506–1582). Such scholars were invited not because humanist learning was connected to a particular locale or political ideology but because it was seen as an essential ornament to any court or noble house, since, it was believed, it had the power to make "men" (*viri*) out of mere "human beings" (*homines*).[14]

With the increasing prominence of Renaissance humanism in schools, in universities and at court, the humanist strain of the classical rhetorical tradition naturally came to influence public speaking by Iberians and in Iberia. Already in the mid-fifteenth century, Íñigo López de Mendoza y de la Vega (1398–1458) owned a collection of classical and Renaissance orations, including speeches by Cicero, Greek orations in Latin translation by Italian humanists such as Bruni and Spanish translations of the works of the Renaissance republican Stefano Porcari (d. 1453).[15] By the third quarter of the fifteenth century, Iberians themselves were delivering humanist orations in Latin. In 1481, the bishop of Évora, Garcia de Meneses (d. 1484), addressed Pope Sixtus IV celebrating the decision of

---

[13] Erika Rummel, "Marineo Sículo: A Protagonist of Humanism in Spain," *Renaissance Quarterly*, 50 (1997), 701–722.

[14] Luis Gil Fernández, *Panorama Social del Humanismo Español (1500–1800)*, 2nd ed. (Madrid: Tecnos, 1997); Ottavio di Camillo, "Interpretations of Humanism in Recent Spanish Renaissance Studies," *Renaissance Quarterly*, 50 (1997), 1190–201; *ibid.*, "Humanism in Spain" in Albert Rabil, Jr. (ed.), *Renaissance Humanism: Foundations, Forms and Legacy*, 3 vols. (Philadelphia: University of Pennsylvania Press, 1988), II, 55–108; Jeremy N. H. Lawrance, "Humanism in the Iberian Peninsula," in Anthony Goodman and Angus MacKay (eds.), *The Impact of Humanism on Western Europe* (London: Routledge, 1990), 220–258; Francisco Rico, *El Sueño de Humanismo* (Madrid: Editorial Crítica, 1993).

[15] Angel Gómez Moreno, *España y la Italia de los Humanistas*.

the Portuguese to assist in the recovery of Otranto, which had been captured by the Turks. This was a typical crusading oration of the sort delivered throughout Italy following the fall of Constantinople (1453) that bespeaks Meneses' complete command of the sub-Ciceronian Latin style typical of the early Renaissance. As the printed marginal notes to a later 1561 edition point out, it also had a distinctly classicizing structure ([*exordium*], *narratio, propositio, confirmatio, confutatio* and *conclusio*).[16]

Within a decade, classicizing public speaking would become a regular feature of court life in Spain. In 1492, Alfonso Ortiz (1455–1503) addressed Ferdinand and Isabella on the occasion of their visit to Barcelona in a typical Renaissance panegyric that lauded the Catholic Monarchs as liberators of Granada and defenders of Catholicism who had reunited *Hispania* for the first time since antiquity.[17] Of course, this sort of elite Latin oratory was not the only outlet for the classical rhetorical tradition. Other sorts of secular and sacred public speaking in the vernacular also began to be modeled to a greater or lesser extent on humanist oratory, with the panegyric sermon rising to particular prominence in the seventeenth century often modeled on Pliny's *Panegyricus* for Trajan or the sacred oratory of the Church Fathers.[18] In turn, the practical usefulness of this new incarnation of the classical rhetorical tradition spurred the production of Iberian rhetorical handbooks in both Latin and the vernacular. This began with a rhetoric by Renaissance Spain's leading grammarian, Antonio de Nebrija (1444–1522). The sixteenth century would then see the publication of many Ciceronian, anti-Ciceronian, Ramist and neo-Byzantine rhetorical handbooks first in Spain and then in Portugal, culminating in Cipriano Soáres' *De arte rhetorica* (Coimbra, 1562) that would become a staple of Jesuit classrooms throughout the world for the next 200 years.[19]

[16] *Garsias Menesius Eborensis Praesul quum Lusitaniae Regis Inclyti Legatus & Regiae Classis Aduersus Turcas Hydruntem in Apulia Preaesidio Tenentes Praefectus ad Vrbem Accederet, in Templo diui Pauli Publice Exceptus apud Xistum iiii Pontificem Maximum & apud Sacrum Cardinalium Senatum, Huiuscemodi Orationem Habuit* (Coimbra, 1561). On the genre of the crusading oration, see James Hankins, "Renaissance Crusaders: Humanist Crusade Literature in the Age of Mehmed II," *Dumbarton Oaks Papers* 49 (1995), 111–207.

[17] Tomás Fanego Pérez, "'Ad Illustrissimos Fernandum et Helisabeth Hispaniarum Regem et Reginam Potentissimos Alfonsi Ortiz Doctoris Oratio' de Alfonso Ortiz: Edición Crítica de las Versiones Latina y Castellana," *Humanistica Lovaniensia*, 50 (2001), 91–117.

[18] See Chapter 2.

[19] Don Paul Abbot, "*La Retórica y el Renacimiento*: An Overview of Spanish Theory," in James Jerome Murphy (ed.), *Renaissance Eloquence: Studies in the Theory and Practice of Renaissance Rhetoric* (Berkeley: University of California Press, 1983), 95–104; Jorge Fernández López, "Rhetorical

It was into this world that Cervantes de Salazar was born. Like that of his contemporaries, Cervantes de Salazar's education from the 1530s onward was of the typical humanist sort starting with grammar, rhetoric and canonical classical authors. This began at a local grammar school attached to the University of Toledo that was presided over by the great Renaissance pedagogue Alonso Cedillo (d. 1565), and where he was also taught by Alejo Venegas de Busto (1497–1562), the famous lexicographer and admirer of Erasmus. He then studied canon law at Salamanca where it seems that Hernán Núñez de Toledo y Guzmán (1475–1553) and the precocious Diego de Covarrubias y Leyva (1512–1577) held the chairs of rhetoric and canon law respectively, although both were equally steeped in humanist learning. Indeed, the former wrote commentaries on Seneca and Pliny the Elder, while the latter, although better known as a jurist, has left us a collection of Latin orations composed for examinations and other occasions, some of which Cervantes de Salazar may have even heard himself. These mix the scholastic Latin terminology of canon law with the structural and stylistic conventions of the revived classical rhetorical tradition to make the Ciceronian argument that the honor bestowed on the learned (*doctores*) should be the same as that given to military men (*milites*), as the societal value of arms and letters (*arma et litterae*) was the same.[20]

While Covarrubias went on to become a leading member of the School of Salamanca, Cervantes de Salazar went to Flanders in 1539 as part of a diplomatic mission on behalf of Charles V. There, his humanist training opened many doors, including allowing him to converse with one of the leading Spanish-born humanists of the age, Juan Luis Vives (1493–1540), whose works Cervantes de Salazar would translate and republish in both Spain and New Spain. With some experience as a humanist diplomat (*orator*) under his belt, Cervantes de Salazar then entered the service of Cardinal Juan García de Loaysa y Mendoza (1478–1546) through whom he met Hernán Cortés. Between 1548 and 1550 he would hold the chair of rhetoric at the University of Osuna before departing for New Spain. There, he would contribute to the transatlantic *translatio studii* of the humanist tradition in general and the humanist incarnation of the classical

Theory in Sixteenth-Century Spain: A Critical Survey," *Rhetorica: A Journal of the History of Rhetoric*, 20 (2002), 133–148.

20 Katherine Elliot Van Liere, "Humanism and Scholasticism in Sixteenth-Century Academe: Five Student Orations from the University of Salamanca," *Renaissance Quarterly*, 53 (2000), 57–107.

rhetorical tradition in particular, which would soon become a feature of education and civic life in all parts of the growing Iberian World.[21]

Rhetoric across the Pre-/Post-conquest Divide

In the century before Cervantes de Salazar's interlocutors took their imagined walk around Mexico City, the most northerly district (*calpulli*) of the city's main island Tlateloco had seen many changes. Brought under the political control of its neighbor Tenochtitlan in 1473, the former independent city-state was the site of the last stand of the forces loyal to Cuauhtémoc, the cousin of Montezuma II, who would briefly retire to a house near Tlateloco's market square before being executed in 1525 for allegedly plotting an uprising.[22] Throughout the period of dominance by Tenochtitlan, Tlateloco's market remained a significant hub for the sale of goods coming from the surrounding conurbation and beyond, as well as a center of learning and rhetorical culture. Indeed, attached to the temple that towered over the market square was a small *calmécac* of the sort that was attached to all the temples in Mexico-Tenochtitlan.[23] Here, noble Nahua males (*pipiltin*) and some commoners received moral, ceremonial and intellectual training in preparation for the Aztec priesthood. Daily life in these Aztec hothouses was tough. Military drills, fasting, prayers and domestic chores were the order of the day, and harsh punishments for infringement of the rules were common. In these schools, ethics and morals were considered a sign of – if not the path to – true nobility, and these had to be beaten into young men. It was within this Spartan environment that the flower of the Nahua youth studied cosmology, philosophy and the interpretation of dreams and committed to memory the correct interpretations of logographic texts.[24]

---

[21] José Luis Madrigal, "Cervantes de Salazar, Francisco," *Real Academia de la Historia*, http://dbe.rah .es/biografias/11971/francisco-cervantes-de-salazar; María del Carmen Vaquero Serrano, "El Maestro Alonso Cedillo (1484–1565): Escritos, Testamento e Inventario: Su Biblioteca," *Lemir: Revista de Literatura Española Medieval y del Renacimiento*, 21 (2017), 33–106.

[22] Francisco González Rul, *Urbanismo y Arquitectura en Tlatelolco* (Mexico City: Instituto Nacional de Antropología e Historia, 1998), 53–55.

[23] The space allotted to the *calmécac* seems to have been somewhat smaller than in the *templo mayor* complex: *ibid.*, 100.

[24] Edward Calneck, "The Calmecac and Telpochcalli in Pre-conquest Tenochtitlan," in J. Jorge Klor de Alva et al. (eds.), *The Work of Bernardino de Sahagún: Pioneer Ethnographer of Sixteenth-Century Aztec Mexico* (Albany, NY: Institute for Mesoamerican Studies at SUNY-Albany, 1988), 169–178; Miguel León Portilla, *Aztec Thought and Culture: A Study of the Ancient Nahuatl Mind* (Norman: University of Oklahoma Press, 1963), 137–143.

Students at the *calmécac* also received training in rhetoric and oratory. By memorizing poetic songs and *huehuetlatolli* ("sayings of old men"), students learned ancestral lore clothed in the "lordly language" (*tecpillatolli*). As the famous Mexican antiquarian Francisco Javier Clavijero (1731–1787) described:

> Those who were destined to be orators were instructed from childhood to speak well, and they made them learn by memory the most famous speeches of their forebears, which had been passed down from father to son. In particular, they used their powers of eloquence in diplomacy, in political deliberations and congratulatory orations for new kings.[25]

With the help of his indigenous collaborators, the Franciscan friar and ethnographer Bernardino de Sahagún (c. 1499–1590) recorded many of these *huethuetlatolli* in a chapter of book six of the Florentine Codex, entitled "On the Rhetoric and Moral Philosophy of the Mexicans," which represents the single largest collection of such texts.[26] While it is probably impossible to disentangle the pre-Columbian reality fully from the Renaissance world of the friar and his indigenous collaborators who were primed to find an equivalent of the classical rhetorical tradition in every society they encountered, there was clearly a long-standing tradition of Nahua public speaking, although it embraced a much wider range of occasions than its European counterpart.[27] In Sahagún's collection alone, there are speeches to be delivered for a host of ceremonial and social occasions. Religious ceremonies that required ornate invocations of the gods are particularly prominent, but there are also political orations for the election of a new king, in which the speaker urges the monarch to rule justly and piously. Further down the social ladder, merchants departing on trading missions also received exhortations to fair conduct, while an oration often accompanied the sacrifice of a slave to placate the gods. Finally, although women could not attend a *calmécac*, there are speeches for the occasion of a woman visiting a friend, as well as for pregnancy, birth and marriage. Therefore, although we lack normative statements about its ultimate purpose, it is clear that Aztec ceremonial public speaking served an important role in conserving societal knowledge, norms and hierarchies, while also being rich in metaphors and parallel phrases (known as

---

[25] Francisco Javier Clavigero, *Historia antigua de México*, Mariano Cuevas (ed.) (Mexico City: Editorial Porrua, 1964), 241.
[26] Thelma D. Sullivan, "The Rhetorical Orations, or *Huehuetlatolli*, Collected by Sahagun," in Munro S. Edmundson (ed.), *Sixteenth-Century Mexico: The Work of Sahagún* (Albuquerque: University of New Mexico Press, 1974), 83–89.
[27] Pollnitz, "Old Words and the New World."

diphrasis), thereby providing models for creative imitation not just verbatim recitation.[28]

By the time Cervantes de Salazar's interlocutors visited Tlateloco, the temple and *calmécac* were gone. Yet, not everything had changed.[29] The vast marketplace remained where merchants continued to sell all manner of foodstuffs and medicinal plants. Overlooking this was the palace of the *cacique* (indigenous lord of the area), a prison and a silent stone gallows, new incarnations of long-standing institutions. There was even an echo of the *calmécac*. To the north side of this vast market square, which saw the daily toing and froing of 20,000 buyers and sellers, stood a Franciscan convent. This housed a college for the native nobility, known to posterity as the colegio de la Santa Cruz de Tlateloco. This had been founded in 1536 by the first bishop of Mexico, Juan de Zumárraga (1468–1548), and it was here that Sahagún taught grammar to the sons of indigenous nobles immediately following his arrival in New Spain. At the time of the composition of the dialogue, however, the students were being taught by an indigenous teacher, named Antonio Valeriano, who was, in the words of Cervantes de Salazar, "in no way inferior to our grammarians, very well versed in Christian doctrine and a lover of eloquence."[30]

Like their parents in the *calmécac*, the students at the Franciscan college were subject to a rigorous program in preparation for future careers not as Aztec priests, but as governors in New Spain's burgeoning *cacique* bureaucracy. Students lived, ate and studied together in monastic seclusion. The curriculum was Christian and humanist, covering grammar, rhetoric, philosophy and some theology, and took place in a classroom where Latin and Nahuatl were the only languages of instruction. This was aided by a library that contained the full gamut of Christian and classical texts.[31] After passing through the college, we are told, the best students could deliver polished humanist orations and write Latin verse, reports that are easy to believe if we peruse the surviving Latin texts written by former

---

[28] Don Paul Abbott, *Rhetoric in the New World: Rhetorical Theory and Practice in Colonial Spanish America* (Columbia: University of South Carolina Press, 1996), 24–40.

[29] Barbara E. Mundy, *The Death of Aztec Tenochtitlan, the Life of Mexico City* (Austin: University of Texas Press, 2015), 77–84.

[30] *México en 1554*, fol. 276r: "Ad septentrionem, quod quartum latus claudit Franciscanorum positum est monasterium et in ipso Indorum collegium, qui latine loqui et scribere docentur. Magistrum habent eiusdem nationis Antonium Valerianum nostris grammaticis nequaquam inferiorem, in legis Christianae observatione satis doctum et ad eloquentiam avidissimum."

[31] Edward V. George, "Humanist Traces in Early Colonial Mexico: Texts from the Colegio de Santa Cruz de Tlatelolco," in Ferran Grau Codina, José María Maestre Maestre, and Jordi Pérez Durà (eds.), *Litterae Humaniores: Del Renacimiento a la Ilustración* (Valencia: Universidad de València, 2009), 279–291.

students that include a number of letters addressed to Charles V.[32] Of course, not all contemporaries believed in the usefulness of educating the native population, and the college slowly declined toward the end of the sixteenth century and was eventually abandoned. Yet, as long as the college remained open the students were more than capable of defending themselves from these detractors. For instance, during a visit of the commissioner general of the Franciscans in 1584, the students put on an allegorical drama (a common schoolroom exercise that was sometimes also influenced by the classical rhetorical tradition) in a mixture of Spanish and Latin, in which they attacked those who wrongly believed that the *indios* were "like magpies and parrots who are hard to teach and quickly forget."[33] Certainly no one who knew the college's native teacher, Antonio Valeriano, would have come to this conclusion, since, as one missionary noted, he was "a great Latinist who could speak extemporaneously (even in the last years of his life) with such mastery and elegance that he brought to mind Cicero or Quintilian."[34]

Indeed, a Nahua Cicero was worth celebrating, since the rhetorical skills gained in the colegio de la Santa Cruz de Tlatelolco were considered essential for building the new Christian society that was springing up among the ruins of the Aztec Triple Alliance. As the *mestizo* rhetorician, Diego Valadés (1533–1582), put it in his famous handbook on preaching to the native inhabitants of New Spain, entitled *Rhetorica Christiana* (1579), a knowledge of the norms of eloquent speech was essential for a stable society:

> There is nothing more praiseworthy or outstanding than eloquence, which is ornamented by goodness, which has founded many cities, which has put an end to many wars, and which has given birth to the strongest societies, the firmest friendships, great goodwill and often the highest pursuits, as well

---

[32] Andrew Laird, "Nahuas and Caesars: Classical Learning and Bilingualism in Post-Conquest Mexico: An Inventory of Latin Writings by Authors of the Native Nobility," *Classical Philology*, 109 (2014), 150–169.

[33] Ignacio Osorio Romero, *La Enseñanza del Latín a los Indios* (Mexico City: Universidad Nacional Autónoma de México, 1990), XII-XLV: "tanquam picae et psittaci qui laboriose docentur et cito obliviscuntur."

[34] Juan Bautista, *A Iesu Christo S.N. Ofrece Este Sermonario en Lengua Mexicana* (Mexico City, 1606), "prólogo" p. 3: "fue también hijo del dicho colegio de Sancta Cruz, y uno de los mejores latinos, y rethoricos que del salieron (aunque fueron muchos en los primeros años de su fundación) y fue tan gran latino, que hablava extempore (aun en los ultimos años de su vejez) con tanta propriedad y elegancia, que parecia un Ciceron, o Quintiliano." Frances Karttunen, "From Court Yard to the Seat of Government: The Career of Antonio Valeriano, Nahua Colleague of Bernardino De Sahagún," *Amérindia*, 19 (1995), 113–120.

as having preserved peace, if we are to omit some of its lesser fruits, which it would take too long to enumerate.[35]

Echoing Cicero's view on the relationship between public speaking and urban life, this son of a Spaniard and a Tlaxcalan woman also stressed that the spread of Christian sacred oratory was part of a larger process that brought the native peoples of New Spain together into Christian towns and cities, where they could more easily hear the word of God from the mouths of eloquent preachers.[36] Urban life, social stability and public speaking were thus inexorably linked, but could not flourish without institutions such as the Franciscan college at Tlateloco.

Indeed, such was the prestige attached to oratory in the Iberian World that failure to achieve the expected standards could lead to ridicule and professional ruin. To take a single example, the Archdean of Mexico City Cathedral, Diego Suazo de Coscojales (dates unknown), once lost the thread of a sermon he was delivering in the cathedral, and was subsequently given a public dressing down in a pamphlet by Pedro de Avendaño y Suárez de Souza (*c.* 1654– 1705), the "Mexican Vieira," who had himself delivered a funeral oration for Carlos II in 1701. According to Avendaño, Suazo de Coscojales, a former professor of philosophy at the University of Alcalá de Henares, had strutted around Mexico City boasting of his abilities as a sacred orator and paying an excessive number of dubious social visits to noble women.[37] Avendaño then noted that when asked to show his skills by delivering a sermon at Candlemas, Suazo de Coscojales spent months scouring the local libraries for suitable sources. However, when he came to deliver it, he faltered during the opening (*salutación*) and was unable to continue, drawing the scorn of Avendaño and (seemingly)

---

[35] Diego Valadés, *Retórica Cristiana*, Tarsicio Herrera Zapién (ed.) (Mexico City, 1989), 2: "Nihil eloquentia laudabilius vel praestantius, quae bonitate ornatur, quae multas urbes constituit, plurima bella restinxit, firmissimas societates, sanctissimas amicitias, plurimas gratias, et maxima saepe studia perperit, pacisque ornamenta retinet, ut minores interea fructus (quos infinitum esset percensere) omittamus."

[36] *Ibid.*, 190: "Quondam in conversionis initio in montibus errabant atque ita non facile erat illos doctrina Christiana perfecte imbuere, quapropter non est mirandum tunc temporis inventos esse aliquos qui idololatriam commiserint. At postquam in vicos et civitates ad vitae societatem ineundam redacti sunt, politice admodum et Christiane victitant usque adeo, ut vel capitis gravedinem leviter sentient non modo ad confitendum, sed et ad consecrationem a religiosis impetrandam sese deferri currant. Tantam fidem illis habent, ut vel manu religiosi se contrectari sentient, existimant inde suam valetudinem confirmare."

[37] The events are described in Arnulfo Herrera, "Los traspiés de un sermón famoso: 'Fe de erratas al licenciado Suazo de Coscojales,' de Pedro de Avendaño," in Ignacio Arellano Ayuso, and Antonio Lorente Medina (eds.), *Poesía Satírica y Burlesca en la Hispanoamérica Colonial* (Madrid: Iberoamericana Editorial, 2009), 191–206.

other contemporaries. Regardless of whether Avendaño's telling is true in all its particulars, reputations were clearly made or lost in the pulpit.

To prevent the ruin of society at the hands of shoddy orators like Suazo de Coscojales, it was essential to create an educational apparatus to train competent orators. While the classical rhetorical tradition originated in the ancient Mediterranean, the reality was that across the Iberian World there grew up self-reproducing cultures of classicizing eloquence that were to a large extent independent of the European origins of the tradition. Indeed, it could have been no other way, as the possible occasions for public speaking far outstripped the number and capacities of the educated Iberians who left Europe for the Americas and Asia. In other words, the local manifestations of the classical rhetorical tradition in Mexico City or Goa could only be reinforced, and not replaced by those trained in Europe who were frequently held back in these contexts by their ignorance of local languages.

As Cervantes de Salazar described in one of his dialogues, in 1554 grammar and rhetoric were already taught at the city's newly founded university, where they were the prerequisites for the study of theology and Roman and canon law.[38] Much of this grammatical and rhetorical education would later be outsourced to the growing number of Jesuit colleges, which would come to dominate humanistic education in the city, the viceroyalty and the Iberian World as a whole. These not only trained those destined to join the Society of Jesus or even just those considering embarking on an ecclesiastical career. Rather, their numerous alumni filled all manner of civil and professional roles, which created a culture of connoisseurship among the elite that further reinforced the desire and appreciation for and the effectiveness of classicizing public speaking. This burgeoning educational eco-system also ensured that the classical rhetorical tradition crossed caste lines, as while the most famous Jesuit colleges, such as the colegio máximo de San Pedro y San Pablo, only admitted those who could prove their Spanish "blood purity" (*limpieza de sangre*), aspiring indigenous priests who began to reappear in increasing numbers in the late seventeenth century could receive a humanistic and rhetorical education in the city's diocesan seminaries.[39] In this way, what had once been a Mediterranean and European phenomenon percolated through the layers of Novohispanic and global Iberian society, creating a

---

[38] *México en 1554*, fol. 252r.
[39] Margarita Menegus Bornemann and Rodolfo Aguirre Salvador, *Los Indios, el Sacerdocio y la Universidad en Nueva España, Siglos XVI–XVIII* (Mexico City: Plaza y Valdes, 2006).

space unified by the application of the social technology at the core of the humanist movement.

Rhetorical Theory and Practice in the Iberian World

While the variation within the classical rhetorical tradition of Mexico City and the other urban contexts of the Iberian World is apparent from the textbooks and student notes studied in the following chapters, each of these diverse contexts may nonetheless be considered part of a unified tradition insofar as they relied on a set of core precepts and scholarly practices that remained extraordinarily stable across time and space. These were grounded in the rhetorical handbooks of the early first century BCE, such as the anonymous *Rhetorica ad Herennium* and Cicero's *De inventione*, as filtered through medieval and early modern rhetorics.[40] While rather light on philosophical discussions of rhetoric, these handbooks provided detailed practical advice about how to compose speeches. At the same time, contemporary rhetorical education contained elements taken from Cicero's later rhetorical works, such as *De oratore*, as well as Aristotle's *Rhetoric*, which influenced Cipriano Soáres' *De arte rhetorica*, a mainstay of the Jesuit classroom.[41] This said, rhetorical theory could only take a student so far. Indeed, the evidence suggests that among the triad of prerequisites for an orator, namely *ingenium* ("talent"), *ars* ("theory") and *exercitatio* ("practice"), students were encouraged to cultivate the third and final element as soon as possible in the interests of creating orators rather than rhetoricians. This involved the close reading of exemplary speeches and the composition and delivery of practice orations, known as declamations (*declamationes*), a smattering of which survive from the early modern Iberian World. In other words, while students and teachers were familiar with handbooks, such as the *De eloquentia sacra et humana* of Nicolas Caussin (1583–1651), and their precepts directly influenced public speaking, the imitation of ancient, patristic and contemporary humanist models was often equally if not more important.

This is, however, not to say that the classical rhetorical tradition was a cookie-cutter structuring system that added little of intellectual value to the orations and sermons delivered across the Iberian World. Rather, it

---

[40] During most of this period, the *Rhetorica ad Herennium* was attributed to Cicero: James J. Murphy and Michael Winterbottom, "Raffaele Regio's 1492 Quaestio Doubting Cicero's Authorship of the Rhetorica Ad Herennium: Introduction and Text." *Rhetorica: A Journal of the History of Rhetoric*, 17 (1999), 77–87.

[41] Peter Mack, *A History of Renaissance Rhetoric, 1380–1620*, 179–180.

existed as an integral part of an educational and cultural environment that belies a Manichean distinction between form and content. This conception of rhetorical culture as culture *tout court* was ingrained in classical rhetorical theory. Following Cicero's view that an orator had to command all domains of knowledge, the aforementioned Diego Valadés stressed that an aspiring orator needed to study not only rhetorical theory, but every art and science that pertained to the subject of his oration. In practice, this meant that a sacred orator should have an intimate knowledge of theology, to which must be added all seven liberal arts (grammar, rhetoric, dialectic, music, geometry, arithmetic and astronomy). It was this complete Christian humanist program of study that provided the orator with a vast array of ideas and models that could be channeled through rhetoric, which was the "ornament of the other domains of knowledge" (*aliarum scientiarum ornamentum*).[42]

While reliant on precepts that predated Christianity, the classical rhetorical tradition in the Iberian World was not divorced from religion. Far from it. Cicero and other pre-Christian authors were subject to highly pious readings, and as Valadés described, the training of the ideal orator also embraced many texts and scholarly practices that we usually associate with scholasticism and even theology. Indeed, it is no accident that when Cervantes de Salazar and his interlocutors toured the Royal and Pontifical University of Mexico City, they caught a glimpse of the great scholastic philosopher, Alonso de la Veracruz (1507–1584), whose work ranged from commentaries on Aristotle to original works on dialectic, "just war" and Indian marriage.[43] Following in his footsteps, many of the orators discussed in the following pages also held positions teaching philosophy, medicine and theology in universities and colleges in the Americas, Europe and Asia.[44] There were, as a result, orators who exhibited more or less "humanist" or "scholastic" tendencies. Some were wont to lay "secular" classical examples on thick while speaking in a neo-Ciceronian style. Others preferred to cite Thomas Aquinas and Peter Lombard. All, however, were familiar with both styles and modes of thought, and applied these when relevant and according to contemporary intellectual fashions, which, we shall see, were far from static.

---

[42] Valadés, *Retórica Cristiana*, 11–18.
[43] *México en 1554*, fol. 252r. On Alonso de la Veracruz, see Mauricio Beuchot, "Perfil del Pensamiento Filosófico de Fray Alonso de la Vera Cruz," *Nova Tellus*, 29 (2011), 201–214.
[44] On scholasticism, see John Patrick Doyle, "Hispanic Scholastic Philosophy," in James Hankins (ed.), *The Cambridge Companion to Renaissance Philosophy* (Cambridge: Cambridge University Press, 2007), 250–269.

At the same time, the classical rhetorical tradition in the Iberian World existed within a religious and philosophical framework that went well beyond an adherence to the basic tenets of Catholicism, but looked very much like a pious version of the "virtue politics" studied by James Hankins within the context of the Italian Renaissance.[45] For instance, when Cervantes de Salazar's interlocutors passed by the colegio de San Juan de Letrán, where the *mestizo* sons of Spanish men and indigenous women could study liberal arts or handcrafts depending on their abilities, one of them noted that the main benefit for society (*res publica*) of such colleges was the training of the youth in virtue as defined by the Christian and ancient examples taught there, since "never are the interests of a republic better served than when boys are trained in such a way that when they have imbibed virtue and have been strengthened in it, they are never able to abandon it."[46] One way to understand this link between humanist culture and virtue is offered by Cervantes de Salazar's extended edition of Hernán Pérez de Oliva's *Dialogue on the Dignity of Man* (1546), which he dedicated to Hernán Cortés.[47] Virtue, when combined with worthy accomplishments (in particular feats of learning, which Cervantes de Salazar thought, were a true reflection of internal character) was the root of the dignity of man. Such a worldview, which appears from time to time in the orations delivered in the Iberian World, could in some instances even lead to the espousal of an ideology of moral and intellectual meritocracy. This, of course, did not negate the inherited aristocratic and *casta* hierarchies that existed in the Iberian World, although its existence perhaps goes some way to explaining the patterns of thinking that allowed non-Europeans like Hara Martinho and Bartolomé Saguinsín to rise to positions of considerable authority by dint of their intellectual abilities.[48]

The "Nuts and Bolts" of the Classical Rhetorical Tradition

Regardless of the context or aim of the oration, the chief "duties of the orator" (*officia oratoris*), as Valadés (echoing Cicero) reminded his readers, were always to "teach" (*docere*), "move" (*movere*) and "delight" (*delectare*)

---

[45] For a full discussion, see Chapter 2.

[46] *México en 1554*, fol. 271v: "Nunquam est reipublicae tam bene consultum, quam cum sic formantur pueri, ut virtutem quam semel imbiberunt, confirmati postea, nunquam possint relinquere."

[47] Diane M. Bono, *Cultural Diffusion of Spanish Humanism in New Spain: Francisco Cervantes de Salazar's Diálogo De La Dignidad Del Hombre* (New York: Peter Lang, 1991), 68–69.

[48] See Chapter 3.

an audience. In order to achieve these ends, the orator should follow a fixed set of intellectual procedures. The orator first had to formulate logical arguments that were likely to persuade his audience (*inventio*). These ideas then had to be arranged to give a certain narrative arc to the oration (*dispositio*). For this, classical rhetorical theory dictated a basic five-part structure formed of an introduction (*exordium*), summary of the context (*narratio*), a statement of how the argument would be structured (*partitio*), the argument itself and/or a refutation of an opponent's argument (*confirmatio/confutatio*) and a conclusion (*peroratio/conclusio*).[49] It was, however, not required to follow this rigid structure blindly. Rather, like Cicero, whose orations rarely followed this conventional plan, orators in the Iberian World were expected to use it as a starting point in the creative process.

With the ideas and structure in place, the orator then had to embellish the speech (*elocutio*) according to whether it was to follow the "grand," "middling" or "plain" style. In practice, this meant the liberal application of tropes and figures, as well as potentially prose rhythm and other more advanced forms of ornamentation, as we shall see in Chapters 3 and 4. The final step before delivery (a moment when the orator had to pay particular attention to *pronuntiatio*) was committing the oration to memory (*memoria*). Of all the steps, these are by far the most difficult for the modern historian to reconstruct. In most cases, all we have to understand delivery is the occasional complimentary or critical comment regarding the orator's voice, and the normative statements found in rhetorical handbooks, which addressed the influence of different vocal registers on the emotions.[50] In the case of memorization, the sources are almost silent on actual practice, although we know that there were two main options available to the orator. He could either rely on repetition and the strength of his own powers of recollection, or apply the techniques of artificial memory (*memoria artificialis*), which prescribed the transubstantiation of the words of the oration into memorable icons (*imagines*) set against various backgrounds (*loci*), for instance a series of relevant household objects arranged in a room.[51] This latter technique was most famously advocated by the Jesuit missionary in Ming China, Matteo Ricci (1552–1610), who attempted to attract new adherents to Catholicism with the promise of

---

[49] Valadés was also heavily influenced by Raymond Lull: Linda Báez Rubí, *Mnemosine Novohispánica: Retórica e Imágenes en el Siglo XVI* (Mexico City: Universidad Nacional Autónoma de México, 2005).

[50] Valadés, *Retórica Cristiana*, 238–240.   [51] This is set out schematically in: *Ibid.*, 49.

improved memory for those taking the civil service examination. In the
end, Ricci was unsuccessful in his endeavor as the aspiring mandarins
complained that the techniques of artificial memory were more time
consuming to master than learning the Confucian texts in the first place![52]
Many in the Iberian World would have probably agreed.

If we take the authors of rhetorical handbooks like Valadés at their
word, we might also conclude that the occasions for public speaking in the
Iberian world also mirrored those common in the ancient Mediterranean:
judicial oratory (*genus iudicale*) for the courtroom; deliberative oratory
(*genus deliberativum*) for the assembly hall; and epideictic oratory (*genus
demonstrativum*) for ceremonial occasions. Indeed, these categories are
repeated throughout the rhetorical handbooks printed and studied across
the Iberian World and certainly shaped how contemporaries imagined
their rhetorical culture. They are, however, of somewhat less use for
understanding public speaking in practice. This is because classicizing
oratory in the Iberian World was for the most part restricted to
epideictic, that is to say ceremonial oratory focused on praise and blame.[53]
This does not mean that oratory was a rare occurrence. Rather, the early
modern Iberian World saw an unprecedented flowering of epideictic
oratory, which accompanied all manner of occasions and led to the
development of a number of highly specific subgenres of epideictic.

In this variegated world of early modern epideictic, both sacred and
secular, funerals were by far the most common occasion. As we shall see in
Chapter 2, the funeral commemorations (*exequias*) of Iberian monarchs
were the most prestigious occasions for such oratory, although similar
orations either in Latin or the vernacular frequently also graced the funerals
or funeral commemorations of queens, nobles, ecclesiastics and even
wealthy merchants. As we shall see in Chapters 3 and 5, colleges and
universities also regularly hosted classicizing epideictic orations (usually in
Latin), which punctuated the lives of elite males, both Spanish and
indigenous, during their formative years. Events of civic importance, such
as the arrival or investiture of office holders also featured epideictic
orations.[54] In other words, although largely focused on one of the three
classical "types of oration" (*genera causarum*), the culture of classicizing

[52] Jonathan D. Spence, *The Memory Palace of Matteo Ricci* (New York: Penguin Books, 1984).
[53] This reflects the norms of Italian Renaissance oratory: Paul Oskar Kristeller, *Studies in Renaissance Thought and Letter*, 4 vols. (Rome: Edizioni di storia e letteratura, 1996), IV, 236.
[54] The most striking examples of these were delivered by the historian and orator Diogo de Couto (1542–1616) in Goa for the arrival of the new viceroy, and for the unveiling of a state of Vasco de Gama on the city's main gate: Diogo do Couto, *Diogo do Couto Orador: Discursos Oficiais Proferidos*

public speaking in the Iberian World was in no way impoverished in comparison to its ancient counterpart.

It also bears mentioning that within the early modern culture of classicizing public speaking there was also considerable linguistic diversity. Following the universalizing drive inherited from antiquity, orators across the Iberian World applied the precepts of classical rhetoric when speaking both in learned languages like Latin, and in European vernaculars, such as Spanish, Portuguese, Italian or French. This said, Latin, remained the gymnasium in which orators were trained, regardless of the target language. Indeed, declamation continued in Latin well into the eighteenth century meaning that late humanist Latin eloquence retained its archetypal position even as public speaking in Latin became increasingly rare, creating a culture of post-humanist eloquence (Chapter 6). At the same time, indigenous languages did not necessarily exist outside this framework, although missionary orators in different parts of the Iberian World took vastly differing approaches, suggesting that rhetorical pragmatism rather than dogmatism was the rule (Chapter 4).

Looking Out at the Iberian World from Mexico City

When Cervantes de Salazar and his interlocutors reached the top of Chapultepec Hill, they saw all of Mexico City spread out before them. This view so struck one interlocutor, who was seeing the city for the first time, that he cried out:

> O immortal God! What a spectacle is displayed from here! How beautiful, how pleasing to the eyes and mind, how delightful in variety! I should dare to assert on excellent reasoning that both worlds have been joined and encompassed in this place and the term *microcosmos* that the Greeks employ for man, that is, a small universe, can likewise be said of the City of Mexico.[55]

Characterized by elements with origins in the two "worlds" (i.e. the Iberian Peninsula and Mesoamerica) known to this imagined visitor, Mexico City appeared like a globe in miniature, an assessment that is

---

na Câmara de Goa, Maria Augusta Lima Cruz, Rui Manuel Loureiro and Nuno Vila-Santa (eds.) (Lisbon: Arandis, 2016).

[55] *México en 1554*, fol. 284r–v: "AL: O Deum immortalem quam bellum quam gratum et oculis et animo, quanta quam varietate iucundum, se hinc spectaculum exhibet, ut summa cum ratione affirmare ausim, orbem utrumque hoc loco circumscriptum et circumductum esse et quod de homine Graeci tradunt, Microcosmon id est parvum mundum ipsum appellants idem de Mexico dici posse."

increasingly finding support (although expressed in decidedly different terms) in modern scholarship.[56] Indeed, this passing Hellenizing reference seems particularly farsighted from the vantage point of the city's later development, since, as the Iberian World expanded, the largest city in the Americas increasingly began to represent a true microcosm of the early modern Iberian *cosmos* that went far beyond Iberia and Mesoamerica. It is therefore the perfect starting point for understanding the Iberian World, the broad outline of which is worth briefly tracing in as far it was both a lived reality and meta-geographical category for Cervantes de Salazar and his contemporaries.

In terms of Cervantes de Salazar's "Old World," this period saw the parallel expansion of Iberian influence and the Empire of Eloquence. While the urban centers of the Americas were being gradually brought into the orbit of Iberian monarchs and Iberianized Catholicism, large parts of western Eurasia were similarly being Iberianized through a combination of military might, economic muscle and dynastic politics. Indeed, once the smoke had cleared following the reign of Charles V, the map of the Italian Peninsula resembled that of the Americas. Numerous formerly independent kingdoms and city-states now recognized the authority of the Spanish Habsburgs, including the Duchy of Milan and the parts of southern and insular Italy that had long been territories of the Crown of Aragon. This meant that educational institutions and ceremonial occasions in Naples, Milan and Palermo became integral parts of a nascent Iberian World at the same time as Renaissance education and its concomitant culture of public speaking reached its zenith.[57]

In addition, the Italian Peninsula reminds us that the Iberian World was not merely the sum total of the composite monarchies of the Habsburgs, Bourbons and Braganzas. As we shall see in Chapter 2, the Genoese Republic and the Grand Duchy of Tuscany were bound by economic, social and political ties to the Hispanic Monarchy. This was a mutually beneficial, although not always perfectly stable, arrangement in which the banking families of Genoa, on whom the Hispanic Monarchy came to rely for financing, raked in considerable profits.[58] Even in Tuscany, Iberian

---

[56] Meha Priyadarshini, *Chinese Porcelain in Colonial Mexico: The Material Worlds of an Early Modern Trade* (Cham: Springer International Publishing, 2018).

[57] On the origins of humanist rhetoric and oratory in Italy, see Ronald G. Witt, *The Two Latin Cultures and the Foundation of Renaissance Humanism in Medieval Italy* (New York: Cambridge University Press, 2012).

[58] Thomas Allison Kirk, *Genoa and the Sea: Policy and Power in an Early Modern Maritime Republic, 1559–1684* (Baltimore: Johns Hopkins University Press, 2005), 90–91.

influence was strong, since the Medici Grand Dukes owed their position to Charles V who subsequently supported their conquest of the last independent city-state in the region, the Republic of Siena. As a result, the Habsburgs retained the support of the Duchy's increasingly feeble ruling family, as well as control of the State of the Presidi, a series of fortresses on the Tuscan coast.[59] Alongside similar naval bases in North Africa, most notably Oran and Malzaquivir, this allowed the Hispanic Monarchy to maintain control of the western Mediterranean and from there to lead offensives against the Ottomans. As the twin defenders of Catholicism, the interests of the Habsburgs and the Papal States were thus also closely intertwined, a relationship that was made even closer by the presence of tens of thousands of Spanish immigrants in the Eternal City.[60] This, in turn, resulted in the *collegio romano* (as well as other Jesuit colleges in Italy) producing orators who would go on to eulogize Iberian monarchs in different settings for their own self-interested reasons (Chapter 2). Some even traveled to the Americas and Asia under the protection of Iberian monarchs where they sang the praises of Iberianized Catholicism in sermons in both European and non-European languages (Chapter 4).

Parts of Northern Europe too became caught in the Iberian web. While areas of the German-speaking territories of the Habsburgs became politically separated from the Iberian Peninsula, the formerly Burgundian Netherlands remained tied to the Spanish Habsburgs as part of Charles V's inheritance. Here again, local colleges and universities in Antwerp, Brussels and other towns and cities in the Low Countries produced clerics and laymen destined to become either classicizing orators or discerning listeners as public speaking was increasingly directed toward building consensus and advancing agendas within the context of Habsburg hegemony.[61] However, the urban contexts of the Spanish Netherlands were also quite different from other parts of the Iberian World. Thanks to the military and financial strength of the Dutch Republic following the Union of Utrecht (1579), they were also destined to be the most precarious and costly areas of the Hispanic Monarchy.

Parts of maritime Asia also partook in the larger process of uneven integration with New Spain and the wider Iberian World, both theoretically and in reality. This was due not only to the fact that Asian goods very

[59] See Chapter 2 for a more detailed discussion of Tuscany's relationship to the Hispanic Monarchy.
[60] Thomas James Dandelet, *Spanish Rome, 1500–1700* (New Haven, CT: Yale University Press, 2001), 9.
[61] On humanism in sixteenth-century Antwerp, see Marcel A. Nauwelaerts, "Humanisme en Onderwijs," in *Antwerpen in de XVIde eeuw* (Antwerp: Mercurius, 1975), 257–300.

quickly made their way to the Americas, but also because the Americas were conceptually closely tied to Asia. Indeed, for much of the early modern period Asia and the Americas were united under the banner of the "Indies," a catchall term for the tropical regions of the world that were the source of the rare and valuable commodities that Columbus had sought out in the late fifteenth century. It should come as no surprise then that the rich variety of goods sold by *indios* and *indias* in one of the city's markets brought to mind for Cervantes y Salazar's interlocutors the Virgilian line, "India sends ivory, and the soft Sabeans their incense" (*India mittit ebur, molles sua tura Sabaei* [Virgil, *Georgics*, I.57]).[62] Although it might clash with our modern continental and area-studies frameworks, this is no more a meta-geographical oddity than the current Anglophone division between "Latin" America and "North" America, and even chimes with a term currently in vogue, the "Global South."[63]

Of course, this loose commercial and conceptual relationship between the grandest city in the Americas and the source of many of its most desirable goods and manufactures would take on a political form not long after Cervantes de Salazar wrote his dialogues when Mexico City was brought into the same composite monarchy as the Iberianized pockets of South and East Asia. This was the result of one of Charles V's least celebrated achievements: his marriage to Isabella of Portugal (1503–1539). This meant that his son Philip II could lay claim to the Crown of Portugal, which he duly acquired following the Battle of Alcântara in 1580. During the resulting period of political union that lasted well into the seventeenth century, Mexico City and the cities that had been formerly loyal to the House of Aviz (including Goa, Cochin, Malacca and Macau) came under the same monarchy. This, in turn, led to a newfound interdependence between what had already been connected commercial and political systems, despite the agreement reached in the Cortes of Tomar (1581) to keep the interests of the two crowns separate.[64] Not only did Portuguese merchants increasingly trade commodities and slaves in Manila and Mexico City, but many residents of Portuguese cities

[62] *México en 1554*, fol. 273r.

[63] Ricardo Padron, "A Sea of Denial: The Early Modern Spanish Invention of the Pacific Rim," *Hispanic Review*, 77 (2009), 1–28. For a good discussion of the social origins of this meta-geography, see Mauricio Tenorio-Trillo, *Latin America: The Allure and Power of an Idea*.

[64] Pedro Cardim, *Portugal Unido y Separado: Felipe II, la Unión de Territorios y el Debate Sobre la Condición Política del Reino de Portugal* (Valladolid: Ediciones Universidad de Valladolid, 2014), 94–109; Jean-Frédéric Schaub, *Portugal na Monarquia Hispânica* (Lisbon: Livros Horizonte, 2001), 45–48.

made transatlantic crossings to and from Spanish America alongside the eastbound bullion and the westbound cottons and silks.[65]

Mexico City was thereby linked to other Iberian cities in Asia that were undergoing similar processes of intellectual and educational change as they were brought into the "Empire of Eloquence." Just like Mexico City, sixteenth-century Goa saw the foundation of colleges that nurtured local cultures of classicizing public speaking. These were largely the product of the worldwide expansion of the Iberian World's most active non-state actor, the Society of Jesus, which encouraged the study of Greco-Roman and South Asian grammatical and rhetorical traditions (Chapters 3 and 4) that were in turn combined and harnessed "for the greater glory of God" (*ad maiorem Dei gloriam*). Simultaneously, occasions for the delivery of public oratory were founded. Civic ceremonies in Goa featured classicizing speeches that exhorted the listeners to defend and expand Portuguese *imperium*. With the expansion of Catholicism, classicizing sermons in both European and indigenous languages came to resound through Jesuit churches in Asia. These formed part of a larger Jesuit zone that may have overlapped with the territories of Iberian monarchs, under whose protection the missionaries usually traveled, but it also transcended them. Indeed, while Jesuit missionaries clustered in Goa and Macau, they also plied their spiritual trade in areas to which Iberian monarchs had little territorial claim, such as Japan, Nepal and the Mogul court.[66]

Southeast Asia and the Pacific Rim were also part of this emerging Iberian World. After several abortive attempts to realize Columbus' ambition to reach Asia via a westward route, regular transpacific crossings began in the years following 1565. Maintaining this route and the missionary projects that grew up around it required the creation of permanent settlements in the region, and in particular in the area of the Malay Archipelago that was christened "The Philippine Islands" (*las islas Filipinas*), in honor of the future Philip II. To this end, the Islamic polities around the river Pasig on the archipelago's main island suffered the same fate as the Aztec Triple Alliance and were reoriented around a new Iberian city. In this new capital of a Captaincy General dependent on

---

[65] Tatiana Seijas, *Asian Slaves in Colonial Mexico: From Chinos to Indians* (New York: Cambridge University Press, 2014), 60; James C. Boyajian, *Portuguese Trade in Asia under the Habsburgs, 1580–1640* (Baltimore: The Johns Hopkins University Pres, 1993), 52, 141–142.

[66] Gauvin A. Bailey, *Art on the Jesuit Missions in Asia and Latin America, 1542–1773* (Toronto: University of Toronto Press, 1999), 112–118; Trent Pomplun, *Jesuit on the Roof of the World: Ippolito Desideri's Mission to Eighteenth-Century Tibet* (New York: Oxford University Press, 2010).

the viceregal court in Mexico City, schools, seminaries and colleges sprang up where once local elites had been taught to write in the Baybayin syllabary.[67] There, the Jesuits and Dominicans vied for supremacy in the teaching of grammar, rhetoric and philosophy, although anything beyond basic literacy in Spanish and Latin was reserved for the new ruling caste of *españoles* who had an almost complete monopoly on the highest echelons of learning until the enactment of a *cédula real* that mandated the inclusion of indigenous elites in the late seventeenth century.[68]

With the advent of Iberian civic and religious rituals, occasions for public speaking also proliferated rapidly in Manila. Sermons and orations of the sort found throughout the Iberian World were delivered for Catholic feast days, the deaths of Iberian monarchs, and other civic occasions.[69] As in New Spain, this newfound culture of eloquence was imagined and frequently practiced according to the conventions of the classical rhetorical tradition. It was therefore considered by many an essential means for creating unity and stability. For instance, in an "expert opinion" (*parecer*) appended to a Tagalog grammar, an indigenous priest and notable late humanist poet, Bartolomé Saguinsín (c. 1694–1772) underlined the importance of eloquence to the evangelization of the Philippine archipelago in terms highly reminiscent of Cicero's account of the origins of political communities:

> For with his style he [a particular missionary] knows how to convert the coarse and hardened wills of these my sorry countrymen in very sensitive and persuasive ways; he knows how to transform with his eloquence their wild and beastly habits into human and Christian virtues.[70]

Manila was not, therefore, only an entrepôt between East Asia and the Americas, but was also an integral part of the Empire of Eloquence that united Mexico City with other parts of the burgeoning Iberian World.

---

[67] William Henry Scott, *Barangay: Sixteenth-Century Philippine Culture and Society* (Quezon City: Ateneo de Manila University Press, 1994), 210–216.

[68] Horacio de la Costa, *The Jesuits in the Philippines, 1581–1768* (Cambridge, MA: Harvard University Press, 1961), 192–203.

[69] D. R. M. Irving, *Colonial Counterpoint. Music in Early Modern Manila* (New York: Oxford University Press, 2010), 215–229.

[70] Sebastián de Totanés, *Arte de la Lengua Tagala, y Manual Tagalog, para la Administración de los Santos Sacramentos* (Sampaloc, 1745), §§§§r: "Pues sabe convertir con su estylo a las piedras, o empedernidas voluntades de estos miseros mis paysanos en muy sensibles y compugnidas: sabe transformar con su eloquencia a las fieras, o ferinas costumbres de ellos en humanas, y christianas virtudes." On Saguinsín, see Dana Leibsohn and Stuart M. McManus, "Eloquence and Ethnohistory: Indigenous Loyalty, Chinese Treachery and the Making of a Tagalog *Letrado*," *Colonial Latin American Review*, 27 (2018), 522–574.

Returning to Cervantes de Salazar's dialogue, we also find that another part of the nascent Iberian World was never far from his mind: Africa and its diaspora. As his interlocutors surveyed the goods on sale in one of the city's marketplaces, one particular product caught their eye, *ogitl*. This was a tar-like substance that the *indios* smeared on their heads and legs for warmth and to kill parasites. When applied, it made a person, in the words of one interlocutor, "blacker than an Ethiopian."[71] Although a common ancient trope that echoed the ancient Mediterranean curiosity about Black people, this offhand remark also reflected the increasing visibility of Africans and those of African descent, both enslaved and free, in Mexico City.[72] As is well known, free Black Africans were among the forces that besieged and eventually captured Mexico-Tenochtitlan.[73] As the demand for labor in the Americas grew, the Portuguese forts along the West African coast later became the points of departure in a rapid transatlantic trade in African gold, ivory and slaves, which were exchanged for cloth, iron, copper and cowry shells from Europe and Asia.[74] This Transatlantic Slave Trade, which was particularly active in New Spain during the Iberian Union, brought tens of thousands of Africans to the viceroyalty, and in particular to Mexico City.[75]

Unfortunately, the role of the classical rhetorical tradition in integrating Africans and those of African descent into the Iberian World is so poorly documented that it is difficult to reconstruct in any detail. It is, however, possible to draw some tentative conclusions. The first stage in this process obviously involved the creation of a common language. To this end, missionaries in Cartagena and elsewhere studied African languages in order to minister to newly arrived Africans, while knowledge of Iberian languages seems to have been common in both the enslaved and free Black populations.[76] We also have evidence of occasions when Africans and *afrodescendientes* were present at the delivery of sermons and orations. For instance, African domestic slaves in Mexico City often accompanied

---

[71] *México en 1554*, fol. 273v.
[72] The classic study of sub-Saharan Africans in antiquity remains: Frank M. Snowden, *Before Color Prejudice: The Ancient View of Blacks* (Cambridge, MA: Harvard University Press, 1983).
[73] Matthew Restall, *Seven Myths of the Spanish Conquest* (New York: Oxford University Press, 2003), 44–63.
[74] John Thornton, *Africa and Africans in the Making of the Atlantic World, 1400–1800* (New York: Cambridge University Press, 1998).
[75] Herman L. Bennett, *Colonial Blackness: A History of Afro-Mexico* (Bloomington: Indiana University Press, 2009), 4–5; Jeanette Pinto, *Slavery in Portuguese India, 1510–1842* (Bombay, NY: South Asia Books, 1992).
[76] Pedro Días, *Arte da Lingua de Angola* (Lisbon, 1697).

their masters to church, where they too might have heard the sermons discussed in the following chapters.[77] Furthermore, Black confraternities played an important role in popular religious festivals, and their members may have heard the classicizing sacred panegyrics delivered on such occasions. In addition, these confraternities also organized religious festivals to commemorate their patron saints (e.g. Nicholas Tolentino, Benedict of Palermo, etc.), and we know these events included masses and sermons.[78]

Although these religious festivals are poorly documented in comparison to other occasions for sacred oratory, there survive several panegyric sermons delivered to Black confraternities in Brazil that give us some sense of the ways Africans and *afrodescendientes* may have experienced and participated in the Empire of Eloquence. These were all delivered in Salvador da Bahia by none other than António Vieira (1608–1697), probably the most famous sacred orator in the early modern Iberian World.[79] In this port city surrounded by sugar plantations, the large enslaved Black population was encouraged to form confraternities dedicated to our Lady of the Rosary as part of a wider effort to bolster Catholicism in the face of incursions from the Protestant Dutch to the north, and it was in this context that Vieira delivered his sacred panegyrics.

In these sermons structured and styled according the conventions of baroque sacred oratory, Vieira railed against the horrors of plantation agriculture and the excesses of ruthless slaveholders, while stopping short of condemning the institution of slavery itself. In so doing, Vieira integrated the experiences of his enslaved listeners into a larger providential vision. The fatal labor regimes, to which they were subject, he argued, brought them closer to Christ's suffering, while their transport to the Americas, where they were converted to Catholicism, was in fact a family reunion between Black Africans and Christ who was related to the Solomonic emperors of Ethiopia as a descendent of the House of David.[80] Vieira embellished these arguments with references to the

---

[77] Joan Cameron Bristol, *Christians, Blasphemers, and Witches: Afro-Mexican Ritual Practice in the Seventeenth Century* (Albuquerque: University of New Mexico Press, 2007), 86–87.

[78] Nicole von Germeten, *Black Blood Brothers: Confraternities and Social Mobility for Afro-Mexicans* (Gainesville: University Press of Florida, 2006), 14–21; Cristina Verónica Masferrer León, "Por las Ánimas de Negros Bozales: Las Cofradías de Personas de Origen Africano en la Ciudad de México (Siglo XVII)," *Cuicuilco*, 18 (2011), 83–104 (94–95).

[79] António Vieira, *Obra Completa*, João Francisco Marques (ed.), 30 vols. (Lisbon: Círculo de Leitores, 2014), VIII, 396–423; IX, 158–184, 340–367. This argument was echoed to some degree in the sermons delivered by contemporary Jesuits to slave masters: Jorge Benci de Arimino, *Economia Christãa dos Senhores no Governo dos Escravos* (Rome, 1705).

[80] Joan Meznar, "Our Lady of the Rosary, African Slaves, and the Struggle against Heretics in Brazil, 1550–1660," *Journal of Early Modern History*, 9 (2005), 371–397.

Bible, the Church Fathers and ancient Mediterranean history, literature and philosophy, all of which were chosen for their relevance to Africa or the institution of slavery. The "Empire of Eloquence," then, was not only intertwined with Iberia's global monarchies and Iberianized Catholicism (Chapters 2–4), but also with the labor systems on which large parts of the Iberian World were built.

We also know that the classical rhetorical tradition had an impact, albeit a limited one, in Africa itself. While early modern Iberian colonialism on the continent was largely restricted to coastal areas, Iberian Jesuits were responsible for the brief expansion of the "Empire of Eloquence" into the Ethiopian highlands. During the period between 1556 and 1632, Jesuit missionaries attempted to convert the Orthodox Christians of Solomonic Ethiopia to Catholicism, and with the assistance of Portuguese merchants and native collaborators, they produced manuscripts of Catholic works in local languages, constructed churches and delivered sermons.[81] While the evidence remains sparse, the Jesuit missionary Pedro Páez (1564–1622) describes one particularly illuminating incident during his time at the Ethiopian imperial court.[82] The Emperor of Ethiopia, he tells us, wished to experience the Catholic mass and a sermon, and so had a vast tent put up in front of his palace, under which Páez set up an altar and a preacher's chair. After reading the Gospel, which he had a Portuguese captain translate into Amharic as the Jesuits usually only learned Ge'ez, the sacred language of the region, Páez preached on a theme taken from the Parable of the Great Feast: "A certain man was preparing a great banquet and invited many guests" (*Homo quidam fecit coenam magnam et vocavit multos* [Luke 14:16]). This he delivered in Portuguese with the captain again providing a translation.

Although we do not have the text of the sermon, we are told that Páez structured it around the biblical parable from which the theme was drawn, taking care to explain each part carefully. When he had covered all the points he wished to make, Páez then put on a typically classicizing show of rhetorical modesty (*captatio benevolentiae*), excusing himself so as not to bore his audience, although they were apparently still in rapture. This then was a typical early modern sermon, which (as we shall see in Chapter 2) borrowed elements from the humanist oration and the medieval thematic

---

[81] Kristen Windmuller-Luna, "Guerra Com a Lingoa: Book Culture and Biblioclasm in the Ethiopian Jesuit Mission," *Journal of Jesuit Studies*, 2 (2015), 223–247.

[82] *Rerum Aethiopicarum Scriptores Occidentales Inediti a Saeculo XVI ad XIX*, Camillo Beccari (ed.), 15 vols. (Rome, 1903–1917), XI, 230–231.

sermon. What probably made this sermon particularly striking was the fact that despite Ethiopia being Christian, there was little in the way of vernacular preaching before the arrival of the Jesuits. Egyptian holy men (*abunäs*) did sometimes preach in Arabic perched on their donkeys, relying like Páez on interpreters to translate their words into Amharic. However, these sermons were likely not as spectacular as Jesuit sacred oratory, which overtly played on emotions and was the product of careful training in the art and practice of public speaking, including delivery.[83] The "Empire of Eloquence," then, was not only an American or Asian phenomenon, but also had an impact, albeit it a limited one, in Africa and its diaspora.

Conclusion

If we follow in the footsteps of Cervantes de Salazar's interlocutors as they tour Mexico City, we find that the expansion of Iberian political influence and cultural forms across significant stretches of the Americas, Europe, Asia and Africa in the years following 1500 was accompanied by a parallel expansion of the Renaissance incarnation of the classical rhetorical tradition. From Mexico City to Manila, and from Flanders to Florence, rhetorical theory was committed to memory; Ciceronian orations read and commented upon; declamations composed; and orations delivered in Latin, Romance and non-European languages. This new rhetorical culture provided opportunities for orators to shape society and politics in a nascent Iberian World that might rightly be described as an "Empire of Eloquence." At the same time, Cervantes de Salazar's humanist dialogues remind us that the Iberian World can be usefully viewed not only from a European vantage point, but also from the perspective of the Americas, and in particular of the Novohispanic metropolis of Mexico City.

---

[83] The best study of sermons in Ethiopia: Leonardo Cohen, *The Missionary Strategies of the Jesuits in Ethiopia (1555–1632)* (Wiesbaden: Harrassowitz, 2009), 77–94.

Philip IV's Global Empire of Eloquence

On July 21, 1666, the Galleon San José finally arrived in Manila from Acapulco after a four-month Pacific crossing (Figure 2.1). Three and a half weeks later the Concepción laid anchor at Palapag some 400 miles away on the island of Samar in the Eastern Visayas Islands. Both carried the same news to this distant outpost of Philip IV's global "composite monarchy" that stretched from the Philippines to Flanders and from Mexico to Milan. The king was dead. *¡Viva el rey!*

Following Philip's death in the *alcázar* in Madrid on September 17, 1665, the fateful news made its way across the length and breadth of the Hispanic Monarchy. From Cádiz, *cédulas reales* addressed to viceroys, *audiencias*, cities, bishops and heads of religious orders crossed the Atlantic, stopping in the Lesser Antilles, before parting company and traveling by land and sea to Mexico City, Tlaxcala and Manila in the Viceroyalty of New Spain, and to Quito, Trujillo, Lima, Cuzco, Asunción and Buenos Aires in the Viceroyalty of Peru, making use of a network of sea routes and "royal roads" (*caminos reales*) that formed the economic and administrative backbone of Spanish America.[1] The same news also made its way through the patchwork of kingdoms in the Iberian Peninsula itself, and was carried north to the Spanish Netherlands and across the Mediterranean to Mallorca, Sicily, Naples, Milan and Oran in North Africa.[2] Even this was not all. The news also traveled beyond the kingdoms

---

[1] The letters sent to the viceroyalty of Peru are recorded in AGI, Indiferente, 430, l.41, fols. 88r–94r. On communication in Spanish America, see Ernst Schäfer-Sevilla, "Der Verkehr Spaniens mit und in seinen amerikanischen Kolonien," *Ibero-amerikanisches Archiv*, 11 (1937/38), 435–455; Sylvia Sellers-García, *Distance and Documents at the Spanish Empire's Periphery*, 80–82; Carla Rahn Phillips, *Six Galleons for the King of Spain: Imperial Defense in the Early Seventeenth Century* (Baltimore: The Johns Hopkins University Press, 1986). For a chronology of the "communication revolution" in the premodern world, see Wolfgang Behringer, "Communications Revolutions: A Historiographical Concept," *German History*, 24 (2006), 333–374.

[2] "Forma de la celebración de las obsequias que en esta ciudad se hicieron a la muerte del rey nuestro señor Don Phelipe Quarto. En once de noviembre de 1665," in AGS, Guerra y Marina, Legajos,

Figure 2.1 Arrival of the Galleon *San José* bearing the news of the death of Philip IV in an illuminated initial (lower) (Manila, Archdiocesan Archives, Anales I, fol. 197v).
Image courtesy of the Archdiocese of Manila

of Philip's composite monarchy. Doges, kings and dukes in client and allied polities in Italy also received the sad tidings, while rumors of the death of the "most Catholic monarch" did not escape the attention of Philip IV's rivals in scheming France and heretical England.[3]

Philip IV had not met a dignified end. Renal failure had slowly sapped his strength, and bedridden and often delirious, he had spent his final days surrounded by relics and devotional images, which he kissed as he lay in the most exquisite agonies.[4] However, his funeral commemorations (*exequias*) belied this sorry demise. As the Queen Regent had instructed in her *cédulas reales*, each city, diocese and religious order paid its respects in the time-honored fashion. In Manila, as elsewhere in the Hispanic Monarchy, commissioners were named to oversee the nine days of mourning (*novenario*), quickly ordering the King's death be made public (*pregón*) and church bells rung throughout the city. In this Hispanic city in Southeast Asia where ethnic *españoles* were in the minority and the festival book documenting the event was printed by a Christian Tagalog, Simón Pinpin (dates unknown), the news had significance for the whole community. "Not only the Spanish residents and soldiers, but also the Indians, Japanese, Chinese, sangleyes, natives, Africans and many other nations put on mourning dress" the Philippine festival book tells us.[5]

Following a ceremony in the gubernatorial palace, which centered on a panegyric delivered by the eldest member of the *audiencia* that drew heavily on St Ambrose's funeral oration for the Roman Emperor Theodosius, on each day of the *novenario* a different religious order or institution held a procession, mass, prayers and sermon. This cycle was only broken for the acclamation (*aclamación*) of the new king, Charles II, before culminating in the "funeral" itself (*honras fúnebres*). Processing from the governor's palace, the great and the good of Manila entered the cathedral, which had been transformed by black drapery that cast the whole space in shadow, and drew the eye to the towering funeral pyre (known as a *túmulo*, from the Late Latin *tumulus* for "funeral mound")

03010. Beatriz Alonso Acero, *Orán-Mazalquivir, 1589–1639: Una Sociedad Española en la Frontera de Berbería* (Madrid: Consejo Superior de Investigaciones Científicas, 2000), XXV.

[3] AGS, Estado K-1390.

[4] Steven N. Orso, *Art and Death at the Spanish Habsburg Court: The Royal Exequies for Philip IV* (Columbia: University of Missouri Press, 1989), 1–5.

[5] Francisco Deza, *Cenotaphio Real de la Catholica Magestad de Philippo Quarto el Grande Rey de las Españas, y Emperador de las Indias* (Manila, 1668), fol. 7r: "Tan comunes fueron, y también recebidos de todos, que non solo los españoles, vecinos, y soldados, sino los indios naturales, japonés, chinos, sangleyes, terrenales, negros y otras muchas naciones que concurren en Manila, y hasta los niños, se pusieron luto, y hicieron demonstraciones de particular, y propio sentimiento."

that shone with the light of innumerable candles. Taking the place of the King's body lying in state, the octagonal *túmulo* stood under the cathedral's cupola and behind a new, temporary high altar. Bedecked with statues of the cardinal virtues of prudence, temperance, justice and fortitude, the multilayered ephemeral structure enclosed a rich canopy overhanging a red pillow, on which sat a replica of the Habsburg crown and scepter guarded by statues of ancient Iberian kings carrying swords. The pillars and parapets of the multilayered *túmulo* also featured a central Latin epitaph, which was flanked by emblems and learned verses in Latin, Greek, Castilian and Hebrew.[6] These celebrated the King's "heroic virtues" and expressed the shared grief of Philip's vassals in Asia, America, Europe and Africa. To crown the funeral commemorations, two learned clerics then took turns to address the assembled dignitaries, first in Latin and then in Castilian, singing the praises of the departed king with neo-Roman eloquence and pious erudition. In this way, Manila joined with cities across the global Hispanic Monarchy in celebrating Philip's virtues and underlining its place in a larger community based on shared cultural practices, values and interests.

According to the famous accounts of "baroque" culture in Europe and the Americas by José Antonio Maravall and Ángel Rama, the *exequias*, and, by inference, the accompanying classicizing public speaking, served as powerful technologies of class and colonial domination, which smothered the revolutionary impulses of the seething masses through baroque "shock and awe" tactics.[7] Recently, however, cultural historians and art historians have chosen to foreground their purely ritualistic and aesthetic aspects, and highlighted their role in "performing" and "imagining," rather than inculcating a hierarchical and harmonious model of society.[8] Although more

---

[6] On Hispanic panegyric verse, see Jesús Ponce Cárdenas, "El *Panegírico al Duque de Lerma*. Trascendencia de un Modelo Gongorino (1617–1705)," *Mélanges de la Casa de Velázquez*, 42.1 (2012), 71–93.

[7] José Antonio Maravall, *La Cultura del Barroco: Análisis de una Estructura Histórica*, 489: "son, como todos los productos de la cultura barroca, un instrumento, un arma incluso, de carácter político." Ángel Rama, *La Ciudad Letrada*, 27–28, which relies directly on Maravall. Reinhardt Wendt, "Philippine Fiesta and Colonial Culture," *Philippine Studies*, 46 (1996), 3–23. D. R. M. Irving, *Colonial Counterpoint. Music in Early Modern Manila* (New York: Oxford University Press, 2010), 215–229. These trends have been reinforced by Foucauldian conceptions of premodern public rituals as attempts by weak and ineffective states to present themselves as powerful, thereby achieving hegemony: Michel Foucault, *Surveiller et Punir* (Paris: Gallimard, 1975), 59–60. This view is echoed in Walter Mignolo's account of the role of learned culture in the colonization of the Americas: Walter D. Mignolo, *The Darker Side of the Renaissance: Literacy, Territoriality, and Colonization*, 125–170.

[8] Alejandro Cañeque, *The King's Living Image: The Culture and Politics of Viceregal Power in Colonial Mexico*. Alejandra B. Osorio, *Inventing Lima: Baroque Modernity in Peru's South Sea Metropolis*, 101–102. Francisco Javier Campos and Fernández de Sevilla, *Fiestas Barrocas en el Mundo Hispánico:*

recent studies have added much-needed nuance to these accounts, their careful readings of individual *exequias* have also led to a narrowing of focus in geographical terms. While Rama and Maravall, painting with broad brushstrokes, took a Pan-American and Iberian perspective respectively, revisionists have usually focused exclusively on the leading city of the proto-national unit (e.g. Lima in Peru or Mexico City in New Spain). Yet, the phenomenon was not isolated to these proto-national or regional spaces, either in conception or in reality. Very similar rituals took place simultaneously throughout the kingdoms of the Hispanic Monarchy in the Americas, Iberian Asia, Spanish Italy, the Spanish Netherlands, Spanish North Africa and the Iberian Peninsula itself, which modern categories such as "Latin America," "Europe" and "Mexico" have concealed. It even crossed ethnic lines, as the richly documented *exequias* performed in the indigenous Republic of Tlaxcala in Central Mexico attest.

Nor was all this a secret to people at the time. Like their contemporaries in the Americas, Europe, Iberian Asia and Spanish North Africa, the *guatemaltecos* and *milanesi* who commemorated Philip IV saw themselves performing rituals that expressed a sentiment common to every part of the Habsburgs' global composite monarchy. In Antigua in the Captaincy General of Guatemala, the Ionic columns of the *túmulo* were adorned with images and verses representing the Americas, Asia, Europe and Africa, while a visitor to the *duomo* in Milan would have been immediately greeted by a model of the globe and an arcade of statues, each representing a kingdom of the Hispanic Monarchy from Florida to Flanders, Chile to Castile.[9] If we are to understand the early modern Hispanic Monarchy, we should take these contemporary conceptions of space seriously. In other words, to understand fully the role of these archetypal royal rituals in a global Hispanic Monarchy that did not respect modern national and regional boundaries, we must thus take a holistic or "global" approach, for this is the only way to avoid the exceptionalist narratives that inevitably arise when one focuses on just one part of a larger whole.

Furthermore, we should not overlook one of the most important and well-documented features of these civic rituals. Long, brimming with

---

Toledo y Lima (Madrid: Ediciones Escurialenses, 2012), 28, 177. This final study is one of the few that treats *exequias* from more than one region.

[9] *Urna Sacra y Fúnebre Pompa con que los Señores President y Oidores de la Real Audiencia Desta Ciudad de Guatemala Celebraron las Reales Exequias, a las Augustas Memoriales de la Catholica Magestad de D. Felipe Quarto el Grande Rey de las Españas y de las Indias que esté en el Cielo* (Guatemala, 1666), 12r–13v. *Esequie Reali alla Catt. Maestà del Rè D. Filippo IV. Celebrate in Milano alli 17. Decembre 1665* (Milan, 1665), 33–34, 51–67.

classical references and usually written in a Latin or Castilian impenetrable or unpalatable to many modern readers, the sermons and orations delivered on these occasions are often sidelined in favor of the visual and ritual elements of the *exequias*. This has meant that historians have ignored an invaluable textual resource for understanding both the cultural landscape and the political thought of this vast and multiethnic territory.[10] Indeed, since these orations were delivered to large audiences of local elites – many if not most of whom were familiar with both Latin and the conventions of classicizing oratory thanks to their early education in Jesuit colleges – and were later printed and widely disseminated, they offer a window onto contemporary political ideas, which provides more explicit answers to the questions that intellectual and cultural historians ask than the visual and ritual aspects of the *exequias* that usually receive the bulk of scholarly attention. Furthermore, we can be assured that these sermons and orations were equally, if not more representative of contemporary political thought than the normative works studied by Anthony Pagden and others, since the genre of epideictic oratory itself, as we shall see, was not meant to be controversial but to reinforce views that were already widely held.[11] To neglect these sources, then, is to miss an opportunity to mine a rich vein of insights into how early modern ideas of global monarchy were constructed and disseminated.

This chapter, therefore, addresses the role of the classical rhetorical tradition in the Hispanic Monarchy, taking the totality of Philip IV's global composite monarchy as its unit of analysis. To this end, it interrogates forty-two *exequias* performed between 1665 and 1667 in every corner of Philip's composite monarchy (Figure 2.2).[12] As will become clear, these vast displays were not technologies of empire in the bare, instrumental

---

[10] Félix Herrero Salgado, *La Oratoria Sagrada Española de los Siglos XVI y XVII*, I, 328–355; Perla Chinchilla Pawling, *De la Compositio Loci a La República de las Letras: Predicación Jesuita en el Siglo XVII Novohispano*. The most important Anglophone study of preaching in the Hispanic world remains Hilary Dansey Smith, *Preaching in the Spanish Golden Age: A Study of Some Preachers of the Reign of Philip III*.

[11] Anthony Pagden, *Lords of All the World: Ideologies of Empire in Spain, Britain and France, c. 1500–c. 1800* and Colin M. MacLachlan, *Spain's Empire in the New World: The Role of Ideas in Institutional and Social Change* (Berkeley: University of California Press, 1988), 1–17.

[12] I have identified festival books that document the *exequias* performed in the following cities of the Hispanic Monarchy: Manila, Mexico City (3), Durango, Puebla, Morelia, Oaxaca, Tlaxcala, Antigua Guatemala, Lima (2), Cuzco, Arequipa, Antwerp, Brussels, Mechelen, Louvain, Milan (3), Naples, Lecce, Madrid (7), Toledo, Barbastro, Zaragoza, Pamploma, Valladolid, Salamanca (2), Oviedo, Figueres, Barcelona, Poblet, Lerida, Balga, Granada (3), Alcalá, Soria, Montilla, Villanueva de los Infantes, Valencia, Santiago de Compostela (2), Murcia, Villa de Fuentenovilla, Villa de Mula, Carmona, Mallorca, Oran. Looking beyond the Hispanic Monarchy, there were also *exequias* performed in Florence and Rome (3). This list is probably not exhaustive.

Figure 2.2   Map of surviving orations in Europe and the Americas for the death
of Philip IV. Made with the assistance of Cheryl Cape.

sense, nor were they only a means to imagine empire or make the king
present in parts of his realm he would never visit. Of course, as celebrations
of the deceased monarch and his successor, these orations and sermons,
alongside the *exequias*, emblems, poems and ephemeral architecture,
formed a multisensory ritual collage that served to display (and thereby
reinforce) allegiance to the Hispanic Monarchy and celebrate membership
in a larger political community centered on the king.[13] They were technologies of empire to be sure. Yet, this did not mean that kingship or the

[13] The unity of art and erudition in European civic ritual was ably shown by: Frances A. Yates, *Astraea:
The Imperial Theme in the Sixteenth Century* (London: Pimlico, 1975), 127–148.

rule of a particular king were taken for granted. Although kingship was based on hereditary claims, the funeral oratory for Philip IV demonstrated that contemporaries did not model kingship as purely hereditary or even absolute. Instead, drawing on the precepts of epideictic rhetoric (i.e. virtue-driven rhetoric of praise common in both Antiquity and Christian Late Antiquity) and the associated Renaissance intellectual tradition of "virtue politics," the funeral orations espoused an ideal of monarchical rule justified and legitimated by virtue, wisdom and piety, a monarchy that was simultaneously Greco-Roman and biblical, a monarchy that was exemplified by the life of the deceased monarch.[14]

Philip IV may have ascended to the throne due to his primogeniture in the Habsburg line and ruled kingdoms on five continents through either personal union (*aeque principaliter*) or earlier conquest and annexation.[15] However, in the context of the *exequias* such constitutional concerns were usually marginal. What really mattered was the King's position as a virtuous arbitrator of local disputes (like Augustus) and the primary defender of global Catholicism (like Constantine).[16] Success on the world stage was not even a good measure of a monarch in the Machiavellian world of the seventeenth century, as fortune (*fortuna*) frequently trumped virtue (*virtus*). If royal lineage had any role, it was only as a catalyst for virtue, since virtues, contemporary medicine taught them, were at least partly inheritable and needed only training and continual practice for their full expression. Only then could a monarch be worthy of his ancestors. Conversely, significant divergence from the path of virtue trod by the monarch's ancestors could lead to accusations of tyranny. Tyranny was the result of a monarch ruling not for the good of the commonwealth as a whole, but purely in his own interests, and represented the polar opposite of virtuous kingship. As the orator in Lecce in the viceroyalty of Naples put it: "the virtues are the characteristics of a monarchy and the elements that

---

[14] Throughout this discussion, I am indebted to the work of my teacher, James Hankins, *Virtue Politics: Soulcraft and Statecraft in Renaissance Italy* (Cambridge, MA: Harvard University Press, 2019); and the insights of Thomas James Dandelet, *The Renaissance of Empire in Early Modern Europe* and Marie Tanner, *The Last Descendant of Aeneas: The Hapsburgs and the Mythic Image of the Emperor* (New Haven, CT: Yale University Press, 1993), 183: "The Hapsburgs' revival of the dream of universal sovereignty under the Roman emperor's rule was similar to the ancients both in conception and premise. Seen as a mission, to which they had been elected by God, the claim to world dominion was based not on geopolitical strength, but on virtue, and above all on piety."

[15] J. H. Elliot, "A Europe of Composite Monarchies," *Past and Present*, 137 (1992), 48–71 (52–53).

[16] Tamar Herzog, *Frontiers of Possession: Spain and Portugal in Europe and the Americas*, 262–264; Kaius Tuori, *The Emperor of Law: The Emergence of Roman Imperial Adjudication* (Oxford: Oxford University Press, 2016).

form a prince, just as the vices do with a tyrant."[17] While virtuous kings could expect loyalty from their subjects, tyrants could expect violent resistance.[18]

At the same time, such displays of eloquence and artistic skill also served a parenetic function. Since epideictic oratory conventionally focused on praise and blame and featured exhortations to follow or eschew certain behaviors, they served to move listeners across Philip's global empire to higher standards of personal and professional conduct. In this way, classicizing public speaking was deployed in the service of the wider Christian humanist project of remaking their communities[19] This message was directed both at the listeners directly to encourage them to cultivate virtue and to remind them of the universal standards of conduct to which all of humanity was held. Significantly, this concentration on royal and personal virtue also opened the way for institutionalized resistance to unjust rule at the local level – what recent generations of historians have called "negotiation" – by offering an absolute standard of behavior for local officials whose divergence from this ideal could then be the source of complaints from aggrieved vassals to the highest authority, the king.[20] In this way, the *exequias* spoke to a desire on the part of local elites, intellectuals and the multiethnic population of the Hispanic Monarchy at large for consistent and evenhanded treatment from royal officials within the context of traditional Iberian constitutionalism (or Iberian social contract theory) that stressed local privileges over central direction. It served as a reminder to all vassals that their interests could and would be protected. This was a message around which all the inhabitants of Hispanic Monarchy could rally, even if it was not always reflected in reality.

This model was embraced throughout the Hispanic Monarchy, from Mexico City and the indigenous Republic of Tlaxcala in New Spain, to Madrid and Granada. Even in allied territories, such as Genoa, Papal

---

[17] *Pompe Funebri Celebrate all'Augusto Monarca Filippo Quarto il Grande* (Lecce, 1666), 5: "le Virtù sono i caratteri del Principato, e gli elementi, che formano il Principe, come i vitii il Tiranno."

[18] For an introduction to counter-reformation ideas of tyranny, see Quentin Skinner, *The Foundations of Modern Political Thought*, 2 vols. (New York: Cambridge University Press, 1978), II, 174–178.

[19] This is recognized to an extent in: Francis Cerdan, "La Oración Fúnebre del Siglo de Oro, entre Sermón Evangélico y Panegírico Poético Sobre Fondo de Teatro," *Criticón*, 30 (1985), 79–102.

[20] This recent emphasis on the role of community in creating societal norms and structures was identified and assessed by Silvia Marina Arrom, "New Directions in Mexican Legal History," *The Americas*, 50 (1994), 461–465. For the long-standing tradition of resistance theory in early modern political thought, see Martin van Gelderen, "So Meerly Humane: Theories of Resistance in Early Modern Europe," in Annabel Brett and James Tully (eds.), *Rethinking the Foundations of Modern Political Thought* (Cambridge: Cambridge University Press, 2006), 149–170.

Rome and Tuscany, we find, *mutatis mutandis*, the same patterns of thought that support the current scholarly consensus that the reach of the Hispanic Monarchy (and so the cultural and political dimensions of the Iberian World, of which it was a part) extended beyond the borders of territories that were technically under the Spanish Habsburgs. Only in two regions, do the *exequias* show variation. These were not in the "colonial" Americas, which we are used to seeing as fundamentally different from "metropolitan" Europe. The first was Spanish Italy, where the real and perceived decline of Spanish hegemony in Europe led learned orators to break the link between traditional virtue and political success and to champion instead a Stoic ideal of virtue. The second was in the Spanish Netherlands where the legitimacy of the Spanish Habsburgs had to be overtly defended in legal and constitutional terms, and a sharp distinction made between the king on the one hand and his frequently tyrannical officials on the other. However, before examining the *exequias* themselves, we must understand the culture of late humanist rhetoric in the age of Philip IV, and its relationship to moral and political thought.

Late Humanism in the Hispanic Monarchy

The funeral orations and sermons delivered for Philip IV were imagined as an offshoot of ancient public speaking.[21] In his widely read compendium of rhetorical theory, *De eloquentia sacra et humana* (1634), the Jesuit Nicolas Caussin (1583–1651) traced the origins of funeral oratory to Roman "funeral panegyrics" (*laudationes funebres*) and the Athenian custom of commemorating those who had fallen in battle for their country. However, as Caussin recognized, classicizing funeral oratory was not a timeless tradition, born complete in the ancient Mediterranean and received by later generations. Rather, it was a conglomerate of antique, late antique, medieval and early modern traditions that had formed in the course of the Renaissance revival of letters. Indeed, the most important model for most orators on these occasions was Pliny's *Panegyricus* for

---

[21] On humanist funeral oratory and its Christian uses, see John W. O'Malley, *Praise and Blame in Renaissance Rome: Rhetoric, Doctrine, and Reform in the Sacred Orators of the Papal Court, c. 1450–1521* (Durham, NC: Duke University Press, 1979), 36–76; John M. McManamon, *Funeral Oratory and the Cultural Ideals of Italian Humanism*; Frederick J. McGuinnes, *Right Thinking and Sacred Oratory in Counter-Reformation Rome* (Princeton, NJ: Princeton University Press, 1997); Paul Oskar Kristeller, "An Unknown Humanist Sermon on St. Stephen by Guillaume Fichet," in *Mélanges Eugène Tisserant*, 7 vols. (Vatican City: Biblioteca Apostolica Vaticana, 1964), VI, 459–497.

Trajan, which, although a fine example of epideictic oratory, was not a funeral oration at all. Furthermore, the funeral oratory of the Latin and Greek Church Fathers, such as St. Ambrose's oration for the death of the emperor Theodosius and Gregory of Nazianzus' oration for Basil the Great, cast a long shadow in funeral oratory thanks to their combination of classicizing eloquence and Christian themes. These provided the perfect prototypes for praising a pious Caesar.[22] This Roman imperial tradition was in turn supplemented by the medieval thematic sermon and Renaissance (especially Jesuit) humanist oratory, which offered highly Ciceronian examples of funeral oratory, although most orators preferred the Tacitean and neoscholastic prose style typical of the seventeenth century.

In classical and humanist rhetorical theory, funeral oratory belonged to the branch of oratory called epideictic. Whereas judicial oratory was suited to the rough and tumble of the courtroom and deliberative oratory to the political fisticuffs of the forum, epideictic grew out of less charged ceremonial contexts, such as funerals, weddings and thanksgivings where the audience did not have to be moved to believe something new, but entertained with elegant speech and presented with uncontroversial views around which they could rally. In epideictic oratory, the main subject was praise and blame, which was couched in terms of conventional morality.[23] Nonetheless, as Aristotle observed, praise and blame brought with them subtle exhortations. Just as the courtroom orator might include elements of epideictic to move his audience to condemn a defendant, or a statesman might praise a particular leader or course of action to induce senators to vote a particular way, a funeral orator praising the virtues of a king or potentate could not help but encourage his listeners to follow in the footsteps of the deceased.[24]

In praising individuals, the most important rhetorical topic was their "internal" state of body and mind (*natura*), which in practice meant their virtues. Education and upbringing (*institutio*) formed the soil in which these virtues could grow and eventually flower as deeds (*actiones*). To these "internal" features could also be added their "external" state (*fortuna*), including lineage, wealth, friends, and honors. However, external features played a much more limited role as they relied on factors independent of personal choices, and so did not directly reflect a person's *natura*. For

---

[22] Nicolas Caussin, *Eloquentiae Sacrae et Humanae Parallela Libri XVI* (Cologne, 1634), 478–479. On Caussin, see Peter Mack, *A History of Renaissance Rhetoric (1380–1620)*, 198–206. On late antique panegyrics, see Sabine MacCormack, "Latin Prose Panegyrics: Tradition and Discontinuity in the Later Roman Empire," *Revue d'Etudes Augustiniennes et Patristiques*, 22 (1976), 29–77.

[23] Caussin, *Eloquentiae Sacrae et Humanae Parallela*, 451–454, 460.

[24] Aristotle, *Rhetoric*, 1367b–1368a (I.9).

Caussin, the most important virtues included the cardinal virtues of prudence, justice, fortitude and temperance, to which he added clemency, liberality and Christian piety, all of which found their way into the funeral oratory for Philip IV. A popular alternative to Caussin's vision was the paradigm of the seven "heroic virtues." Growing out of an Aristotelian tradition of "divine virtue" (ἀρετή θεία), translated into Latin as "heroic virtue" (*virtus heroica*) and used by St. Augustine to describe the virtue of martyrs, the heroic virtues normally combined the cardinal virtues and the theological virtues (faith, hope and charity) and in the eighteenth century would become part of the official criteria for beatification.[25]

Knowledge of this epideictic tradition was widespread throughout the Hispanic Monarchy. By the seventeenth century, it was also no longer only a European current imported by Spanish or Italian clerics and administrators. Of course, some learned orators were educated in Spain, such as Francisco Santovo de Palma, born in Jaén in Spain and educated in Granada, who delivered the funeral oration for Philip IV in the cathedral in Lima. However, by 1665 the majority were born and trained within the extra-European *reinos* themselves, products of the self-reproducing culture of late humanism that had taken root following the foundation of colleges, seminaries and universities across the Americas and Iberian Asia. This was largely although not exclusively the work of the Society of Jesus. Indeed, by the time of the expulsion of the Jesuits in 1767, its colleges numbered over 200 in continental New Spain alone, and at the death of Philip IV in 1665 already ran to over 100.[26] This vast network of educational institutions teaching grammar, rhetoric and classical authors not only produced orators capable of delivering a classicizing oration or sermon, but also ensured the perpetuation of a local culture of Christian humanism. As a result, not only the speakers themselves, but also the clerics, officials and other dignitaries in the audience during the *honras fúnebres* were connoisseurs of the classical rhetorical tradition.[27]

---

[25] Nicolas Caussin, *Eloquentiae Sacrae et Humanae Parallela Libri XVI*, 461–462, 468–471; Risto Saarinen, "Virtus Heroica. 'Held' und 'Genie' als Begriffe des Christlichen Aristotelismus," *Archiv für Begriffsgeschichte*, 33 (1990), 96–114.

[26] Ignacio Osorio Romero, *Colegios y Profesores Jesuitas que Enseñaron Latín en Nueva España (1572–1767)* (Mexico City: Universidad Nacional Autónoma de México, 1979); Carmelo Sáenz de Santa María, *Historia de la Educación Jesuítica en Guatemala* (Madrid: Instituto Gonzalo Fernández de Oviedo, 1978); José del Rey Fajardo, *La República de las Letras en la Venezuela Colonial* (Caracas: Fuentes para la Historia Colonial de Venezuela, 2007).

[27] In the case of Spain, the only region for which we have figures, it is estimated that in 1600 the number of students studying Latin peaked at some 70,000: Richard Kagan, *Students and Society in Early Modern Spain* (Baltimore: Johns Hopkins University Press, 1974), 43–44.

In the Jesuit colegio de San Pablo in Lima as elsewhere, acculturation into late humanism began with grammar, "the origin and foundation of the liberal arts."[28] Rhetoric followed hard on its heels with particular attention to the works of Cicero who, as the rhetoric master Bartolomé Larrea reminded his *limeño* students in 1676, was:

> The equal in innate wisdom and fortune to mighty Rome itself, and the honied and Ambrosia-laden culmination of the virtues of all ages and talents in one man. A figure about whom you might wonder whether he was the personification of eloquence or eloquence itself. Certainly, there is nothing more fecund: there are as many virtues in him as there are types of eloquences, as many worthy features as there are pithy sayings.[29]

Even distant Manila could boast a Jesuit college, which vied for preeminence with the local Dominican *colegio*. Both institutions required the study of grammar and humanities, which included rhetoric, as prerequisites for the study of philosophy and theology, and ensured that on New Spain's Pacific frontier, the late humanist culture of classicizing eloquence and erudition was not absent.[30]

To support this bookish culture, relevant volumes were imported from Europe by the tens of thousands, and local presses in Mexico City, Lima and elsewhere churned out introductory works on grammar, rhetoric and poetics to meet the needs of local students.[31] Individual colleges amassed large libraries of such humanist books. In Lima, for instance, the library of the colegio de San Pablo kept several copies of the rhetorical treatises by Nicholas Caussin and his Protestant contemporary Gerardus Vossius (1577–1649) alongside an edition of the orations of the greatest of the early Jesuit Ciceronians, Pedro Juan Perpiñán (1530–1566), as well as numerous copies of classicizing sermons of the Latin and Greek Church

---

[28] BNP, ms. F116, fol. 1v.

[29] Archivo General de la Nación, Lima, Compañía de Jesús, 61.10, fol. 3v: "Par imperio Romano ingenium, sapiens, beatum, nectare et Ambrosia difluens ex omnium saeculorum, ingeniorumque virtutibus collecta in unum perfectio. Vir, de quo dubites, an ipse totus ex eloquentia ac ex ipso tota eloquentia sit confecta? Certe nihil est facundius; tot sunt in eo virtutes, quot genera eloquentiae, quot dicta, tot purpurae." On the Jesuit college in Lima, see Luís Martín, *La Conquista Intelectual del Perú. El Colegio Jesuita de San Pablo 1568–1767* (Barcelona: Editorial Casiopea, 2001).

[30] Horacio de la Costa, *The Jesuits in the Philippines, 1581–1768*, 503–508; Fidel Villarroel, *A History of the University of Santo Tomas: Four Centuries of Higher Education in the Philippines (1611–2011)*, 2 vols. (Manila: University of Santo Tomas Publishing House, 2012), I, 65–76.

[31] The case of New Spain has been best studied in this regard: Ignacio Osorio Romero, *Floresta de Gramática, Poética y Retórica en Nueva España (1521–1767)* (Mexico City: Universidad Nacional Autónoma de México, 1980). Magdalena Chocano Mena, "Colonial Printing and Metropolitan Books: Printed Texts and the Shaping of Scholarly Culture in New Spain, 1539–1700," *Colonial Latin American Historical Review*, 6 (1997), 69–90.

Fathers.[32] Libraries of this sort were not even restricted to the viceregal capitals of the Americas. The Jesuit college in Arequipa possessed Caussin's compendium in addition to a copy of the famous Italian Renaissance handbook of style, Lorenzo Valla's *Elegantiae linguae latinae*, and numerous editions of the works of Cicero.[33] Even in Manila, the Jesuit Colegio de San Ignacio could not do without a rich library of seventeenth-century Jesuit rhetorical works that provided students and masters with ample models for honing their rhetorical skills.[34]

This educational program, which spread throughout the Americas, Europe and Iberian Asia resulted in a surprisingly uniform culture of Christian humanism among the secular and ecclesiastical elite. These trained Ciceronians were, if not always fully bilingual, then highly proficient in Latin and steeped in classicizing erudition such that they could either deliver orations in Latin themselves, or at least appreciate the achievements of those who had mastered the art and been chosen to speak on important occasions. The resultant culture was equally important for public speaking in the vernacular and was reflected in the terminology used to describe sermons and orations in Spanish.[35] For instance, the classicizing sermon delivered by Juan de Poblete in the cathedral in Mexico City was published under the title "panegyric funeral oration," (*oración fúnebre panegyrica*), mirroring the common Latin term for an epideictic "funeral oration" (*oratio funebris*), to which was added the Greek term for an epideictic oration in praise of a person or place, "panegyric" (πανηγυρικός).[36] We find this pattern in all the funeral commemorations for Philip IV, which are variously titled "funeral oration" (*oración fúnebre*), "panegyric oration" (*oración panegírica*) and even "panegyric sermon" (*sermón panegírico*).

---

[32] BNP, ms. B 1943. Perpiñán's life ranged across the Iberian world and beyond, and so there are various spellings of his name used in contemporary sources and modern scholarship (e.g. Pedro Juan Perpiñán, Pedro João Perpinyá, Pierre-Jean Perpignan, Petrus Iohannis Perpinianus).

[33] BNP, ms. C 956.

[34] Although it has not been possible to identify the post-expulsion inventory of the Jesuit college library in Manila, an addition to it gives a sense of what it must have contained: "Adición a el índice de la librería particular del colegio que se tituló Máximo de San Ygnacio de Manila, por no haver sido en él comprehendidos los libros que acquí se expressan," in National Archive of the Philippines, Manila, Temporalidades, SDS 1826, S1–29.

[35] John W. O'Malley, *Praise and Blame in Renaissance Rome: Rhetoric, Doctrine, and Reform in the Sacred Orators of the Papal Court, C. 1450–1521*, 42–44. Bernarda Urrejola, "El Panegírico y el Problema de los Géneros en la Retórica Sacra del Mundo Hispánico. Acercamiento Metodólogico," *Revista Chilena de Literatura*, 82 (2012), 220–247.

[36] Juan de Poblete, *Oración Fúnebre Panegyrica a las Honras del Rey Nuestro Señor don Felipe Qvarto el Grande* (Mexico City, 1666). Nicolas Caussin, *Eloquentiae Sacrae et Humanae Parallela Libri XVI*, 471–472.

In other words, vernacular funeral orations and sermons were conceived of in highly classicizing terms, a fact that did not escape contemporary observers. For example, in his extravagant preface to the funeral sermon for Philip IV delivered in Arequipa, Francisco de Loyola Vergara (1609–1677), the archdeacon of Lima Cathedral, invoked St. Jerome's praise of Paulinus' funeral oration for the emperor Theodosius with its "Ciceronian purity" (*Tulliana puritas*), which he glossed with a reference to the classical scholarship of the famous Dutch humanist, Justus Lipsius (1547–1606):

> The style of the sermon, since it is replete with charm, beautiful without artifice, sententious without obscurity, discreet without pretense, clean with propriety, and "while it shines with Ciceronian purity, it is packed with maxims." It is very similar to the style that Seneca saw in the great orator Fabianus when he suggested Lucilius imitate him: "Fabianus does not so much seem to burst out (*effundere*), as pour forth (*fundere*) his words. The words are carefully chosen and are not of our times, which have only produced unnatural and perverted discourses. Instead, they have an honest and magnificent meaning. They are not forced into maxims, but float above the clouds." And glossing his commentary, Lipsius noted the same thing that I have identified in this sermon in that letter of Seneca: "not of course bursting out (*effundere*) with force and wildly, but pouring out (*fundere*) gently and in an orderly fashion."[37]

While imagined in largely classical terms, in practice vernacular funeral sermons combined humanist virtue-driven epideictic with elements of the medieval thematic sermon. This long-standing model for pulpit oratory required that the sermon be divided according to the parts of a scriptural passage chosen for the occasion, known as a "theme."[38] Whereas a typical panegyric was structured around the virtues of the individual (using a biographical narrative or focusing on each of the virtues in turn) the

---

[37] Juan de Almoguera, *Oración Panegyrica Funebre en las Exequias del Rey n. Senor d. Felipe Quarto el Grande, que Dios aya. Celebrolas la Ciudad de Arequipa en la Santa Iglesia Catedral della el Año de 1666* (Lima, 1667), A3r: "El estilo, porque es grave con suavidad, hermoso sin artificio, sentencioso sin obscuridad, discreto sin afectación, y aseado con propiedad, *et cum Tulliana luceat puritate crebrum est in sententiis*. Muy parecido al que celebró Séneca del grande Orador Fabiano, aconsejando a Lucilo su imitación: *Fabianus mihi non effundere videtur, sed fundere. Electa verba sunt, non huius saeculi more contra naturam posita et inversa, sensus honestos et magnificos habent, non coactos in sententiam, sed altius ductos.* Y glossando su comentador Lipsio la palabra *effundere* advirtió en essa epistola lo que yo he notado en este sermón: *non effundere cum impetu videlicet et turbide, sed fundere leniter et cum ordine.*" Cf. Seneca, *Epistulae morales*, 100.1–102.

[38] For an overview of the thematic sermon, see Thomas Worcester, "The Catholic Sermon," in Larissa Taylor (ed.), *Preachers and People in the Reformations and Early Modern Period* (Boston: Brill, 2001), 3–33 (3–9).

thematic sermon usually concentrated on the meaning and significance of specific words in the scriptural passage chosen for the occasion, and only then applied these insights to the circumstances of the oration. While these two traditions were far from identical, the selection of a suitable "theme" made it eminently possible to combine seamlessly a biblical theme and references to kingly virtue. In Cuzco, for example, the theme "He was a great man among all those from the East" (Job 1:3) introduced a discussion of the greatness of Philip, the great monarch in the "East" (i.e. Europe), that focused on his prudence, justice and fortitude. We find this same pattern across multiple vernaculars. In the French funeral sermon delivered in Brussels, for instance, the sacred orator made an even more astute choice of theme in "Praise ye him for his mighty acts: praise ye him according to the multitude of his greatness" (Psalms 150:2), which introduced a discussion of Philip IV's "greatness" with reference to the virtues of historical figures who had earned the epithet of "the Great," such as Alexander, Constantine and Charlemagne. This was all clothed in a Senecan Latin typical of the period.[39] Combining these ancient, medieval and humanist elements, orators thereby sang the praises of their monarch using the most effective tools available to them.

"Virtue Politics" and Good Government in Royal *Exequias*

The virtue-driven conventions of classical epideictic that found expression in the funeral oratory for Philip IV formed an integral part of a larger classical philosophical inheritance that has recently been dubbed "virtue politics." Since the time of Plato and Aristotle, there had been an important strand of political thought that put great store by defining the ideal constitution. The relative merits of monarchies, aristocracies and popular regimes were hotly debated, along with the optimal terms for magistrates and the necessity of certain laws. However, there was also a current, common in Antiquity, present in the Middle Ages and particularly prominent following the Renaissance revival of letters that played down concerns about constitutional models and issues of strict legality in favor of concentrating on the virtue of rulers. This "virtue politics" is commonly associated with the "mirror for princes" (*speculum principis*) genre that grew out of Seneca's treatise *On Clemency* addressed to the Roman Emperor Nero. Just like the Hispanic Stoic philosopher who argued that

---

[39] Charle-François Amounet de Hailly, *Harangue Funebre Prononcée aux Exeques de Philippe le Grand Roy Catholique des Espagnes et des Indes* (Brussels, 1665).

the only true power consisted in the exercise of virtue guided by universal reason, later authors defined a good polity as one ruled by a virtuous prince with all other institutional and legal factors receding into the background.[40] Reading the funeral orations for Philip IV, we see that virtue politics was the default ideological setting in the Hispanic Monarchy. The pros and cons of monarchy in general and the legitimacy of the Habsburg dynasty in particular may have been of interest to a select group of lawyers and political philosophers, but the majority of their vassals seem to have been more concerned with the standard of conduct of the monarch, royal officials and society at large, rather than the constitutional foundations of the political order.

Such a conception of monarchy found fertile soil in late humanist epideictic oratory, including in the Latin funeral oration and the Castilian sermon delivered by Nicholás del Puerto y Salgado (Figure 2.3) and Juan de Poblete respectively during the *exequias* organized by the *real audiencia* in Mexico City.[41] For instance, Del Puerto, a former holder of the chair of rhetoric at the city's Royal and Pontifical University followed the well-worn biographical route underlining Philip's virtues at each stage of his life beginning with his well-omened birth, his education under a learned Jesuit, his piety and relentless efforts on behalf of his vassals and the larger Catholic cause.[42] Similarly, after a brief exegesis of the theme "Give to the king thy judgment, O God: and to the king's son thy justice" (Psalms 72:1) Poblete gave a careful "judgment" of Philip's life, in which he stressed the King's virtues, this time within a thematic rather than biographical framework. In this way, he molded Philip IV into a modern day David and his son Charles II into a new Solomon famed for his "justice." Philip, he told his listeners, had also possessed "judgment," which was always tempered by his justice, temperance, benevolence,

---

[40] James Hankins, "Machiavelli, Civic Humanism, and the Humanist Politics of Virtue," *Italian Culture*, 32 (2014), 98–109 (102–103). On the tradition of princely virtue, the *speculum principis* genre and the Senecan tradition of political thought, see Peter Stacey, *Roman Monarchy and the Renaissance Prince* (Cambridge: Cambridge University Press, 2007).

[41] *Llanto del Occidente en El ocaso del más Claro Sol de las Españas: Fúnebres Demonstraciones que Hizo Pyra Real, que Erigió en las Exequias del Rey N. Señor D. Felipe IIII el Grande* (Mexico City, 1666), 11r: "Y que procurando el más autorizado desempeño de la iglesia, avía eligido para el sermón a su venerable Deán Doctor D. Juan de Poblete; y para la oración fúnebre latina, al doctor D. Nicolás del Puerto Canónigo, cathedrático jubilado de Prima de Cánones, comisario subdelegado general del triundal de la S. Cruzada desta Nueva España, consultor del S Officio de la Inquisición, provisor, y vicario general del Arzobispado; personas cuya autoridad y letras darían a tan graves actos todo el lleno, que pedían."

[42] It was later claimed that Del Puerto was indigenous *cacique* descent. On the question of Del Puerto's ethnicity, see Peter B. Villella, *Indigenous Elites and Creole Identity in Colonial Mexico, 1500–1800* (New York: Cambridge University Press, 2016), 235–241.

EL Ill.mo y R.mo S.r D.r D.n Nicolas del Puerto Salgado Colegial mayor de este Insigne Colegio, Cathedra.co de Rectorica, y Jubilado en Prima de Canones, Rector dos vezes, y Cancelario de esta R.l Univer.d Canonigo, y Thesorero de la S.ta Iglesia de Mexico, Prouisor y Vicario General de este Arzobispado, Consultor del S.to Offi.o Comissario G.l de la S.ta Cruzada, Presidente electo de la R.l Aud.a de Guadalaxara, el Consejo de S.M. dign.mo Obispo de Antequera, y fundador del Colegio de la S.ta Cruz de Oaxaca.

Figure 2.3   Portrait of Nicholás del Puerto y Salgado (Museo Nacional del Virreinato, Mexico). INAH.-FOTOTECA NACIONAL.-MEX. Reproducción Autorizada por el Instituto Nacional de Antropología e Historia

mildness, equity and clemency.⁴³ In both cases, piety is the leading virtue, from which all others flowed.

In some of the funeral orations for Philip IV, more extravagant methods were used to model virtuous kingship. In Milan, for example, the orator, senator Andrea Gambarana (dates unknown), recounted the famous story of the ancient Greek painter Zeuxis who, when asked to paint a picture of Helen of Troy for a temple in the City of Croton, could not find a single model who reached the requisite degree of perfection and so combined the best features of five different women. In contrast, the Milanese orator needed only one king to create an ideal image of royal virtue for imitation. Following in the footsteps of Zeuxis, Gambarana painted a portrait, in which Philip's prudence figuratively became the eyes, his fortitude the chest and his piety the heart.⁴⁴

It is also worth underlining that the tradition of virtue politics was reinforced by other parts of *exequias*, which like the 1680 triumphal arch described by the famous Novohispanic female mystic, Sor Juana Inés de la Cruz (1651–1695), spoke while remaining silent:

> This tongueless Cicero,
> This mute Demosthenes,
> Who with honied words,
> Tells us about your triumphs.⁴⁵

Such a view of the fundamental unity of the different parts of the larger civic ritual allowed Poblete to state, only somewhat hyperbolically that the *túmulo* could "tell us more with its silence than the orator with his eloquence."⁴⁶

Such an observation was possible because they delivered a parallel message in parallel terms. For instance, Mexico City's *túmulo* (designed by the artist and architect Pedro Ramírez) followed the same virtue-driven

---

⁴³ *Llanto del Occidente en El ocaso del más Claro Sol de las Españas,* fols. 140v–141r.

⁴⁴ *Eseqvie Reali alla Catt. Maestà del Rè D. Filippo IV. Celebrate in Milano alli 17. Decembre 1665* (Milan, 1665), 72: "Placet Zeuxis consilium, qui Helenam expressurus, ex quinque tantum lectissimae formae virginibus varias pulchritudinis species legit: ita plurimis ex virtutibus, quae maximum regem Philippum omnes supra Reges efformarunt, quinque illas deligam, qua prae ceteris impensius coluit Philippus, ne dicam quae ipsum excoluere Philippum."

⁴⁵ Sor Juana Inés de la Cruz, *Obras Completas,* Alfonso Méndez Plancarte and Alberto G. Salceda (eds.), 4 vols. (Mexico City: Fondo de Cultura Económica, 1951–1957), IV, 403:

> "este Cicerón sin lengua,
> este Demóstenes mudo,
> que con voces de colores
> nos publica vuestros triunfos."

⁴⁶ *Llanto del Occidente en El ocaso del más Claro Sol de las Españas,* fol. 135r: "Háblenos oy este túmulo, que dirá más con su silencio, que del orador la mayor eloquencia."

line of argument as Del Puerto's and Poblete's panegyrics. It featured a statue of Philip accompanied by exemplary ancient and biblical kings, including Alexander the Great and King Solomon who each represented particular virtues. The *túmulo* was then crowned with a statue of the theological virtue of faith (*fides*) dressed in white and carrying a cross in one hand and the Eucharist in the other.[47] These closely paralleled the orations delivered in front of the *túmulo* and reflected a common Christian humanist conditioning among architects and orators. Just as the orations were seen as modern reflections of Greek and Roman funeral oratory, so the *túmulos*, also sometimes called "catafalques" (*catafalcos*) and "funeral pyres" (*piras fúnebres*), were seen as the contemporary incarnations of the classical funeral pyre, as reconstructed from ancient accounts and material culture, but with a Christian twist (Figure 2.4).[48]

Neo-stoicism and Anti-Machiavellian "Virtue Politics"

In addition to a politics of virtue in the broad sense, the royal *exequias* also channeled anti-Machiavellian neo-Stoicism. This is despite the commonly held view that in the seventeenth-century Hispanic world there arose a Machiavellian conception of "political" virtue that challenged the long-standing dominance of "general" or humanist virtue.[49] It is, of course, true that Niccolò Machiavelli (1469–1527) attacked humanist virtue politics, and equated "virtue" (*virtù*) with a pragmatic notion of political prudence. This was because, he argued:

> There is such a difference between how men live and how they should live that those who choose what they should do over what is actually done end up seeking their own destruction rather than their preservation, because any man who under all conditions insists on being good will surely be destroyed among so many who are not good.[50]

---

[47] *Ibid.*, fols. 36v, 48r–v.

[48] Andrés Úbeda de los Cobos, *El Palacio del Rey Planeta. Felipe IV y el Buen Retiro* (Madrid: Museo Nacional del Prado, 2005), 206–209.

[49] José Antonio Maravall, *Teoría del Estado en España en el Siglo XVII* (Madrid: Centro de Estudios Constitucionales, 1997), 227–272; Ronald W. Truman, *Spanish Treatises on Government, Society and Religion in the Time of Philip II: The "De Regimine Principum" and Associated Traditions* (Boston: Brill, 1999), 361–383.

[50] Niccolò Machiavelli, *Opere Politiche*, 2 vols. (Rome: Salerno Editrice, 2006), I, 216 (XV.5): "perché elli è tanto discosto da come si vive e come si dovrerebbe vivere, che colui che lascia quello che si fa per quello che si dovrrebbe fare, impara più presto la ruina che la preservazione sua, perché uno omo che voglia fare in tutte le parte professione di buono conviene che ruini fra tanti che non sono buoni." Peter Stacey, *Roman Monarchy and the Renaissance Prince*, 205–206.

Figure 2.4   Sestertius of Faustina the Elder (141–142 CE) with a funeral pyre on the reverse Boston, Museum of Fine Arts, Theodora Wilbour Fund in Memory of Zoë Wilbour, 1978.41.
Photograph © 2021 Museum of Fine Arts, Boston

This was a distinction that certainly drew a number of adherents in the early modern Republic of Letters. However, the type of reasoning typical of the Machiavellians was not universal, or perhaps even common in the Hispanic Monarchy, and entirely absent from the funeral orations for Philip IV. Rather, they reflect a deep-seated attachment to the "fanciful notion," as Machiavelli put it, of traditional virtue-driven politics that was reinforced by the standard patterns of epideictic oratory.[51]

---

[51] Robert Bireley, *The Counter-Reformation Prince: Anti-Machiavellianism or Catholic Statecraft in Early Modern Europe* (Chapel Hill: University of North Carolina Press, 1990), 24–44. On anti-Machiavellianism in New Spain, see Mauricio Beuchot, "Algunos Opositores de Maquiavelo en

Whereas Machiavelli had argued against the Ciceronian and Stoic view that virtuous (*honestum*) governance was also the most expedient (*utile*), funeral orators continued to equate the two. As Del Puerto put it in his oration in Mexico City:

> Nor will my oration tell us about earthly or contemplative kingship in a pandering voice, but will sing the praises of Philip's reign according to his virtues, for it is a heavenly maxim, that power depends on virtue, is nurtured by virtue, is preserved by virtue, such that we all agree that the defining feature of this respectful terminology [for a king] and this glorious praise of his name will not be his greatness, but his piety.[52]

Some orators even challenged Machiavelli's vision of the ideal prince head-on. In Palermo, for instance, Machiavelli's argument that a prince must perfect the art of dissimulation earned a direct rebuke. Philip, the Jesuit orator told his listeners, never even considered diverging from the norms of honest speech, not even to curse, which he only did once or twice in his whole life. Furthermore, it was the works of anti-Machiavellians like Robert Bellarmine (1542–1621) and Jesuit ascetics like Juan Eusebio Nieremberg y Otin (1595–1658), rather than those of Machiavelli that he had kept by his bedside.[53] This distain for the "pseudo-prophet of political atheism" also found expression in the funeral oration delivered in Naples, where the idea that Philip had anything in common with those politicians "whose mouths did not express the feelings of their honest hearts" was simply anathema.[54]

Similarly, like the anti-Machiavellian thinkers who dominated Counter-Reformation political thought, most orators remained largely, if not completely wedded to a providential model of history, according to which

España y la Nueva España," *Signos Filosóficos*, 6 (2004), www.redalyc.org/articulo.oa?id=34301103 (consulted October 24, 2017).

[52] *Llanto del Occidente en El ocaso del más Claro Sol de las Españas*, fol. 114v: "Nec de terreno vel umbratili Dominio oratio nostra dicendi lenocinio referet testimonia, sed a virtutibus immarcescens PHILIPPI expromet imperium, cum sit apothema caeleste, a virtutibus imperia pendere, virtutibus enutriri, virtutibus perennari, ut innotescat universis, quod non a magnitudine, sed a pietate census nominis gloriosum erit elogium et vectigalis nomenclaturae character."

[53] Giacomo Lubrani, *L'Anfiteatro della Constanza Vittoriosa Oratione Funerale del P. Giacomo Lubrani della Compagnia di Giesù. Detta nel Duomo di Palermo per le Solenni Essequie Celebrate alla Cattolica Maestà di Filippo IV il Grande re delle Spagne e di Sicilia* (Palermo, 1666), 23: "Astutia nel fingere? È vero, che sincerissimo di genio non seppe articolare parola indorata di Equivoci, e con uniformità di labro, e di cuore, in tutta la vita due giuramenti gli usciron di bocca non più, testimonii di viva fede. Notitia de Macchiavelli Pseudoprofeti dell'ateismo politico? È verissimo, che nel suo studiuolo non rileggeva altri libri salvo, che le meditationi di Bellarmino, le differenze del temporale, ed Eterno di Nierembeg, pagine scritte da soliloquii religiosi."

[54] Tomaso Acquaviva D'Aragona, *L'Aquila Grande: Orazione per la Morte di Filippo Quarto il Grande Monarca delle Spagne* (Naples, 1666), 34.

any king who lived and ruled according to the precepts of standard Catholic morality would meet with success. In almost all circumstances, virtuous kingship stiffened with a strong dose of piety provided a "rampart" (*muralla*) against all possible foes.[55] However, in the wake of the Hispanic Monarchy's seventeenth-century crisis, this worldview began to show cracks, without ever collapsing entirely. For instance, the orator at the *exequias* organized by the Inquisition in Mexico City argued that Philip had put religion above political expediency when he refused an alliance with Cromwellian England. Adherence to Catholic piety had a geopolitical cost, but heavenly rewards.[56] In general, however, in the Americas and Spain itself the link between virtue and worldly success remained strong.

Predictably, it was in Philip's non-Hispanic domains, much reduced from their heyday under his grandfather, that the link between Philip's virtuous action and his success on the world stage was hardest to maintain. In Palermo, the diagnosis was particularly bleak:

> An accursed century, not without reason believed to be a harbinger of the Anti-Christ, a ravenous butcher of the peoples of the earth with plagues; it has, like a pyromaniac, set Vesuvius alight; it has violently shattered provinces with earthquakes; in immature India it has disembarked from its Dutch carracks heretical idols without regard for religion; like a murderer it has stripped France of Henry IV; like a tyrant acting through the Cromwells it has chopped down the tree of the illustrious Stuarts with an executioner's axe.[57]

---

[55] *Llanto del Occidente en El ocaso del más Claro Sol de las Españas*, fol. 139v: "Si le falta a la religión, culto, y veneración de las cosas sagradas, se pierden los Imperios; pero si se atiende al debido respecto a la Catholica religión, y a la observancia de las divinas leyes, y preceptos, es la más segura muralla, que los defiende, y principal apoyo, que los conserva, este solo fue el único, y principal cuydado de nuestro Catholico Rey viviendo, y este le continuó hasta la muerte, y en ella le encarga con tantas instancias a nuestra Reyna."

[56] *Honorario Túmulo Pompa Exequial y Imperial Mausoleo que más Fina Artemisa la Fe Romana por su Sacrosanto Tribunal de Nueva España Erigió y Celebró llorosa Egeria a su Catholico Numa y Amante Rey Philippo Quarto* (Mexico City, 1666), fol. B2r. In the anti-Machiavellian tradition there had always been those who argued that success in worldly affairs did not always flow from virtuous action, but that virtuous action was preferable because of its ultimate rewards beyond this life and its long-run consequences (intrinsic pragmatism): Robert Bireley, *The Counter-Reformation Prince: Anti-Machiavellianism or Catholic Statecraft in Early Modern Europe*, 26, 30–31.

[57] *Ibid.*, 6–7: "Secolo mal'auguroso, non senza ragione creduto foriero dell'Anticristo; mentre famelico macellò nationi con pestilentiose influenze, incendiario pose a fuoco Vesuvii: violento sconquassò co' tremoti Provinciae, sagrilego sbarcò dalle caracche Olandesi nell'India ancor Neofita Idoli di Eresia; assassino ne' ravigliacchi suentrò in Enrico Quarto la Francia; Tirannico ne' Cromvelli sottopose alle accette de Patiboli l'arbore de' diademi Stuardi."

Luckily, however, all was not lost. Fortune (*fortuna*) may not have always rewarded virtuous action, but the answer was not to "treat her roughly," as Machiavelli had suggested. Instead, for orators in Spanish Italy the solution was to fall back on Stoic traditions that were enjoying a particular resurgence in this period of bloody religious warfare. Although at the level of individual human experience virtue may not seem to be rewarded, when viewed from the perspective of eternity, justice was always served. Individuals must, therefore, cultivate temperance and constancy and seek to understand the workings of universal reason (λóγos).[58]

Such was the importance of this Stoic interpretation of kingly virtue that in Palermo the Jesuit humanist orator and poet Giacomo Lubrano (1619–1693) took the Stoic ideal of constancy as the theme, echoing Justus Lipsius' *On Constancy in Times of Public Calamity* (1584), the foundational text of neo-Stoicism. In the oration, printed under the title *The Amphitheater of Victorious Constancy*, he argued that misfortune was not a sign of divine displeasure at Habsburg rule. Rather, it provided an opportunity to show the Stoic virtues that befitted a monarch. Philip may have lost all but one of his sons and heirs, just like the Roman general Paullus Aemilius who, as Plutarch tells us, lost one son before his triumph over Macedon and another after. However, neither allowed grief to overcome him. Aemilius famously put aside his heartache to comfort the Roman people in their misfortunes and Philip showed similar resolve.[59]

Grafting Stoic virtues like "heroic temperance" onto an epideictic stem, Lubrano borrowed heavily from canonical figures in the tradition, such as Seneca whose works on clemency (*De clementia*) and on controlling anger (*De ira*) he invoked repeatedly to make Philip the ideal prince that Seneca's Nero was not. Indeed, he redefined Philip's "greatness," the ubiquitous theme in the funeral oratory for *Felipe el grande* in terms of the ability to

[58] Jill Kraye, "Marcus Aurelius and Neostoicism in Early Modern Philosophy," in Marcel van Ackeren (ed.), *Blackwell Companion to Marcus Aurelius* (Oxford: Wiley-Blackwell, 2012), 515–531. Peer Schmidt, "Neoestoicismo y Disciplinamiento Social en Iberoamérica Colonial," in K. Kohut and S. V. Rose (eds.), *Pensamiento Europeo y Cultura Colonial* (Madrid: Vervuert-Iberoamerica, 1997), 181–204; Pilar Ponce Leiva, "Séneca en los Andes. Neoestoicismo y Crítica Social en Quito a Fines del Siglo XVII," *Histórica (Lima)*, 31 (2007), 43–68; Giacomo Lubrani, *L'Anfiteatro della Constanza Vittoriosa Oratione Funerale del P. Giacomo Lubrani della Compagnia di Gesù. Detta nel Duomo di Palermo per le Solenni Essequie Celebrate alla Cattolica Maestà di Filippo IV il Grande re delle Spagne e di Sicilia* (Palermo, 1666), 6–7: "ove la constanza invincibile di FILIPPO rinovasse in se solo le atletiche bravure de' Cocliti, de Democrati, di Catoni."

[59] *Ibid.*, 39: "Che mi stanno a dir le storie de Roma la stoica faccia di Paolo Emilio, il qual nel trionfo amareggiato dalla morte di due figliuoli consolari, non diede a due funeral una lagrima?" Cf. Plutarch, *Aemilius Paullus*, 36.

face life's difficulties steadfastly.[60] Similarly, in Naples this idea of Habsburg virtue remaining constant in the face of hostile circumstances was placed within a larger historical context. Philip was no less virtuous than his more successful predecessors, Charles I and Philip II. He was merely less favored by fortune.[61]

Again, this message was reinforced by the visual aspects of the *exequias* in Palermo. As the assembled officials, clerics and military officers listened to this hour-long meditation on Stoic virtue, their eyes must have been drawn to the similar themes that surrounded them. Fortune's cruel treatment of Philip and his kingdoms stared out at them from between the columns in the form of statues of heresy, superstition and discord. From atop the *túmulo*, however, constancy, clemency and temperance and the other "political, moral and Christian virtues" looked down on Sicily's leading lights.[62] These were not Machiavellian "political" virtues, but the standard virtues celebrated by Seneca and his medieval and humanist followers.

Taking a single strand out of the larger "virtue politics" tradition and spinning it into a Stoic shroud to place over Philip's body, Lubrano constructed an image of virtuous kingship that could resist the slings and arrows of fickle fortune. This culminated in an appeal to his listeners to approach the *túmulo* and venerate a king turned Stoic sage:

> Go to the tomb to weep disheveled masses – what woe! The statues of the virtues encircle the tomb of Philip. May Fortune on bended knee stop turning her wheel and set his ashes alight, and may Fame with her golden trumpet sing to you eternal paeans of his victorious constancy.[63]

Now, some might be tempted to see in Lubrano's paean to Philip's Stoicism the cold hand of the nascent absolutist state.[64] However, another

---

[60] *Ibid.*: "Eh, bisogna riconoscer con Seneca il nome di Grande in FILIPPO, non per vocabolo di adulatione, ma per legittima della virtù, sempre indomita, sempre costantissima negli accidenti fortuiti. *Nullum est argumentum magnitudinis certius, quam nihil posse, quo instigeris, accidere* [Seneca, *De ira*, III.6]."

[61] *Ibid.*, 18: "L'invittissimo Carlo Quinto oprò maraviglie, *virtute duce, comite fortuna*; il famosissimo Filippo Secondo, *virtute firma, nec infirma fortuna*; il lodatissimo Filippo Terzo, *invariabili virtute varia fortuna*; ma il gloriosissimo Filippo Quarto *constante virtute, sed contraria fortuna*."

[62] Girolamo Matranga, *Le Solennità Lugubri e Liete in Nome della Fedelissima Sicilia nella Felice e Primaia Città di Palermo Capo del Regno Celebrate in Due Tempi*, 3 vols. (Palermo, 1666), II, 24.

[63] *Ibid*, 48: "Vanne dunque alle tombe plebe scapigliato a piangere, o lutto, a quella di Filippo faccian corona le statue delle Virtù; genuflessa la fortuna v'inchiodi le sue sfere volubili; la religione v'incensi le ceneri; e la Fama con trombe d'oro vi canti eternamente i peani della Costanza vittoriosa."

[64] On the political uses of neo-Stoicism, see Gerhard Oestreich, *Neostoicism and the Early Modern State* (Cambridge: Cambridge University Press, 1982), 28–38.

way to look at it is that Stoicism was the only means for Philip's vassals to remain wedded to Christian humanist ideas in the face of the Habsburgs' dynastic troubles and the slowly declining territories of the Hispanic Monarchy. This need was particularly acute in the context of a resurgent France and the ongoing challenges from the Protestant English and Dutch. It was not a call to meekness, but an exhortation to endure and to defend their shared values in the face of real threats in an age before the development of a realistic liberal alternative to Renaissance monarchy. It is no wonder that this call was heard most loudly in the non-Hispanic European kingdoms of the Hispanic Monarchy, where the decline of Habsburg fortunes was felt most acutely.

Lineage, Education and Virtue Politics

In Palermo, Lubrano had stressed that Philip's noble lineage was of secondary concern when praising him, since "a dwarf on the top of a mountain is still of diminutive stature."[65] In so relegating lineage to a minor role, he was following the precepts of humanist epideictic and the tradition of "virtue politics" as discussed, which defined nobility in terms of personal virtues and accomplishments, rather than titles and descent. In some exceptional cases, orators might even openly deny the role of inherited titles in forming nobility. In Naples, for instance, Tomaso Acquaviva D'Aragona maintained that "whoever praises noble birth, praises something alien to the person."[66] However, since lineage remained an undeniable feature of contemporary kingship, most orators in the Hispanic Monarchy were careful to strike a balance between paying lip service to conventional, inherited nobility and emphasizing that the only true nobility was a function of virtue alone.[67] As the Jesuit rhetorician Caussin explained:

---

[65] Giacomo Lubrani, *L'Anfiteatro della Constanza Vittoriosa Oratione Funerale del P. Giacomo Lubrani della Compagnia di Giesù. Detta nel Duomo di Palermo per le Solenni Essequie Celebrate alla Cattolica Maestà di Filippo IV il Grande re delle Spagne e di Sicilia* (Palermo, 1666), 8: "e un nano anche nella cima di un alpe, resta nell'accorciatura di un huomicciuolo."

[66] Tomaso Acquaviva D'Aragona, *L'Aquila Grande: Orazione per la Morte di Filippo Quarto il Grande Monarca delle Spagne* (Naples, 1666), 14: "qui genus laudat, aliena laudat."

[67] The view that all nobility was a function of virtue had originally grown up in fifteenth-century Italy, where many rulers had dubious claims to their positions. As a result, the idea of "true nobility" being based on virtue alone gained considerable traction, serving as it did to sidestep questions of legitimacy in states ruled by parvenus and strongmen as well as to elevate the social position of lowly born humanist scholars: James Hankins, *Virtue Politics*, 158–159; Albert Rabil, Jr., *Knowledge, Goodness and Power: The Debate over Nobility among Quattrocento Italian Humanists* (Binghamton, NY: Medieval & Renaissance Texts & Studies, 1991), 17–23.

Nobility, which is nothing else than luck of birth, occupies a special position in panegyrics of people. And this is not a gift from God to be sneered at, for if we show respect to the remains and likenesses of great men, how much more should we look up to living men who are the flesh and blood images of their fathers? ... In the theory and practice of this figure, first of all his ancestors should be praised. Then he should be praised as one who has inherited their virtues as well as their titles of nobility.[68]

Following this strategy, orators frequently used Philip IV's lineage as a yardstick for his virtue, rather than celebrating it in and of itself. For instance, in the *exequias* organized by the Inquisition in Mexico City, Philip was praised for having outdone his forefathers. Echoing Cicero's praise of the military virtues of Pompey the Great (who had ironically been of humble birth), he called Spain as a witness (*testis*) to Philip's resistance against the forces of heresy, an act that deserved even more praise given that he lived in much more troubled times than his predecessors.[69] Similarly, in Valladolid (modern Morelia) in New Spain, the orator spurned the hereditary *caput* of epideictic oratory except to say that Philip's lineage provided the standards by which to measure him:

> Therefore, I will rightly pass over the outstanding merits of his lineage and the age-old origins of his nobility that an intertwined and uninterrupted series of ancestors have propagated in our prince ... I may not tarry long here but, overcome with profound doubt, I will ask whether his distinguished predecessors brought Philip more honor and distinction, or

---

[68] Nicolas Caussin, *Eloquentiae Sacrae et Humanae Parallela Libri XVI* (Cologne, 1634), 463: "Praeclarum omnino locum in personae laudatione nobilitas occupant, quae nihil est aliud quam nascendi felicitas. Et hoc Dei quidem donum est non contemnendum, nam si illustrium virorum reliquias, et simulachra colimus, quanto magis liberos vivos, et spirantes patrum imagines suspicere debemus? ... In modo autem et tractatione eius loci primum laudandi parentes, deinde gratulandum illi, qui in se transfusam habeat cum maiorum fortuna virtutem."

[69] *Honorario Túmulo Pompa Exequial y Imperial Mausoleo que más Fina Artemisa la Fe Romana por su Sacrosanto Tribunal de Nueva España Erigió y Celebró llorosa Egeria a su Catholico Numa y Amante Rey Philippo Quarto* (Mexico City, 1666), fol. B1v: "Huius rei fidelis testis est Hispania, in qua cum tot haberes (o magne Philippe) praeclarissimorum praecedentium regum exempla, revocans in memoriam Pelayos, Ildephosos, Fernandos specialiterque atavum imperatorem maximum, infractae virtutis Sansonem Carolum V. Eximiae pietatis Davidem; avum prudentissimum Philippum II pacificum Salomonem, parentem tuum Philippum II, qui integerrimi religionis defensores ac firmissimi fidei propugnatores extiterunt memorque veteris catholicae observantiae ac veritus, ne aliqua tua culpa aut levi negligentia Hispania de honestata et maiorum Gloria obscurata videretur tam solicatam curam adhibuisti, ut inter saucias et furentes vicinas provincias Hispaniam incolumen ac nulla servitute infidelitatis oppressam habeamus. Tanto igitur ceteris regibus ac principibus antiquis superiorem gloriam adeptus fuisti, quanto praeclarius est, navim in aliquot formidoloso magno naufragio quam in placido securo portu referre quanto est famosius et magnificentius, Hispaniam ex tam pernicioso vicino incendio quasi iamiam fumantem ab ipsis saepe haereticorum crudelissimis unguibus eripuisse." Cf. Cicero, *De Imperio Cn. Pompei*, 30: "Testis est Hispania, quae saepissime plurimos hostis ab hoc superatos prostratosque conspexit."

whether he brought these to them, and thereby has secured eternal glory for himself?[70]

In the funeral oratory of Philip IV, it was generally acknowledged that Philip's right to rule was a function of his virtue, but that his lineage contributed directly to this virtue. By stressing the symbiotic relationship between the two, orators were able to avoid creating a hierarchy that would reduce the importance of either element, while still foregrounding personal virtue as the ultimate measure of a monarch.

Just as titles were hereditary, so were virtues. Sometimes the two could be one and the same, as in the case of the epithet, "the Catholic," which, as Del Puerto stressed in his oration delivered in the cathedral in Mexico City, had been passed on to each successive generation beginning with Alfonso the Catholic in the eighth century.[71] In Louvain in the Spanish Netherlands, the twin flames of "virtue" (*virtus*) and "lineage" (*stirps*) became a single beacon that burned even brighter.[72] In other words, listeners were observing, as the orator in Lecce in the viceroyalty of Naples put it, a Pythagorean reincarnation of virtues, a choice of analogy suited to the southern Italian origins of this particular philosophical school.[73]

Coming from good stock, or as the orator in Valencia put it, being a "branch" of the right "tree," offered some assurance (although not a guarantee) that virtue would be passed on along with other traits that we today would call biologically heritable.[74] This mirrored the view taken in

---

[70] *Solemníssimas Exequias, que la S. Iglesia Cathedral de Valladolid, Provincia de Mechoacan, Celebró a la Inclita y Grata Memoria del Catholicíssimo y Magnánimo Monarcha D. Felipe Quarto El Grande N. Rey, y Señor* (Mexico City, 1666), fols. 18r–v: "Quapropter consulto missum faciam eximium sanguinis splendorem, et /18v/ inveteratum nobilitatis primordia longa, consertaque et numquam interruptam maiorum gloriosa series in nostrum usque principem propagatum ... non ... possem multum immorar et vehementi dubio interceptus quaerere: an Philippo praesigniores ascendentes decus et ornamentum attulissent, an ipsis egregia cetera superfluant et dedisse Philippum ad gloriam sufficiat immortalem?"

[71] *Llanto del Occidente en El ocaso del más Claro Sol de las Españas,* fol. 116v: "IACET ALPHONSUS CATHOLICUS. A quo eius tituli velut haereditaria et iure sanguinis translatio traducebatur in posteros, et defluxit in ceteros, huius familiae proceres cognomentum."

[72] Henricus Loyens, *Oratio Fvnebris, in Exequijs Serenissimi ac Catholici Hispaniarum ac Jndiarum Regis Philippi Qvarti dum illi Academia Lovaniensis in Æde Divo Petro Sacra Lugibri & Solemni Pompa Parentaret...* (Louvain, 1665), fol. A4r: "non minus ingenio Philippus quam nomine, non minus virtute Austriacus quam stirpe, cuius in purpura nomen et ingenium, stirps et virtus radiorum quodam lumine et quasi luctamine coruscabant."

[73] *Pompe Funebri Celebrate all'Augusto Monarca Filippo Quarto il Grande* (Lecce, 1666), 22: "Se non fusse delirio filosofar' con Pittagora, io direi con più ragione, che l'Anima di Ridolfo trasfusa ne' Filippi, ne' Ferdinandi, e ne' Carli, passò in Filippo il Quarto à far pompa in lui solo, quasi in una basilica di tutte le attioni più riverite di quelli Eroi."

[74] Antonio Lazaro de Velasco, *Funesto Geroglífico, Enigma del Mayor Dolor, que en Representaciones Mudas Manifestó la muy Noble, Antigua, Leal, Insigne, y Coronada Ciudad de Valencia, en las Honras*

early modern learned medicine that blue blood was passed on by both the mother and the father in the course of conception, nursing and upbringing, with diet also playing a role. Just as the milk of a Jewish *conversa* wet nurse could cause a person to Judaize in later life, the milk of a virtuous, well-bred mother assured that a child would possess the right characteristics, both physical and emotional. These were then honed during the child's early years. Indeed, this is a view that the orator in the Pauline chapel of the palazzo Quirinale made explicit when he argued that Philip IV's virtue was the product of having been "reared among the fine pious examples of Philip III and between the devout breasts of Margaret of Austria, from which what could emerge except a milk that was worthy of this incarnation of majesty?" In this way, contemporaries believed, virtue could pass from one generation of Habsburgs to the next, just like physical characteristics and language, the so-called mother tongue.[75]

In addition to lineage and upbringing, it was also believed that education had an impact on personal virtue. This had its origins in the humanist tradition, according to which a classical education with its store of examples of virtuous behavior clothed in the most persuasive language was also essential to acquiring true nobility.[76] However, orators faced the problem that monarchs were rarely the best students and so praising their attainments was a delicate task. Admittedly, Philip IV was better than most. He

---

de su Rey Felipe el Grande IV en Castilla y III en Aragon (Valencia, 1666), 37–39: "dones que no solo por naturaleza resplandecieron en Filipo, sino que también adquiridos los tuvo por herencia de sus progenitores, los más excelentes príncipes del mundo, así Reyes, como Emperadores de la Casa de Austria, y de Castilla, digna memoria en Filipo que tener la supo de los mejores Reyes, para exceder a todos en grandeza. Heredó las más ilustres virtudes del tronco imperial de su Cesárea Casa Rodolfo primero, de quien tuvo siempre su mejor dechado."

[75] Antonio Pérez de Rúa, *Funeral Hecho en Roma en la Yglesia de Santiago de los Españoles à 18 de Diciembre de 1665: a la Gloriosa Memoria del Rei Catolico de las Españas Nuestro Señor D. Felipe Quarto el Grande en Nombre de la Nación Española* (Rome, 1666), 107: "educatus inter religiosissima Philippi tertii exempla, et inter piissima Margaritae Austriacae ubera, quid potuit surgere, nisi lac dignum nata maiestate." María Elena Martínez, *Genealogical Fictions: Limpieza de Sangre, Religion, and Gender in Colonial Mexico* (Stanford, CA: Stanford University Press, 2008), 55–56; Joanne Rappaport, *The Disappearing Mestizo: Configuring Difference in the Colonial New Kingdom of Granada* (Durham, NC: Duke University Press, 2014), 18–20; Emilie L. Bergmann, "Language and 'Mothers' Milk': Material Roles and the Nurturing Body in Early Modern Spanish Texts," in Naomi J. Miller and Naomi Yavneh, *Maternal Measures: Figuring Caregiving in the Early Modern Period* (Aldershot: Routledge, 2000), 105–120. On early modern ideas on the role of food in shaping a broad range of characteristics, see: Rebecca Earle, "If You Eat Their Food . . .": Diets and Bodies in Early Colonial Spanish America," *The American Historical Review*, 115 (2010), 688–713.

[76] James Hankins, *Virtue Politics*, xvii; Anthony Grafton and Lisa Jardine, *From Humanism to the Humanities: Education and the Liberal Arts in Fifteenth- and Sixteenth-Century Europe* (Cambridge, MA: Harvard University Press, 1986), xiv; David García Hernán, *La Nobleza en la España Moderna* (Madrid: Marcial Pons Historia, 1992), 205–206.

had retained at least some of his early classical education, and thanks to a special tutor in geography and painting he had acquired a love of maps and art. Like Elizabeth I of England, he also applied his limited literary skills to translation projects. Philip IV would never produce scholarly Latin tomes of the sort churned out by contemporary intellectuals, but he did take a personal interest in the language and history of Italy, and even personally labored in turning parts of Guicciardini's *History of Italy* from Italian into Castilian.[77]

Of course, for the erudite scholars and clerics who delivered the funeral orations for Philip IV in the Americas and elsewhere, not to mention their learned audiences, Philip's achievements did not pass muster. So rather than mentioning his feeble attempts at translating between two closely related vernacular languages, they chose to paint Philip as a new Augustus, under whose patronage every sort of knowledge had flourished. In Mexico City, Del Puerto lauded his support for scholars, academies and libraries: "How numerous are the marks of recognition he has given to the Republic of Letters: these splendid monuments to his name that will never die!"[78] For a prince, it was not necessary to command Latin eloquence and vast erudition. However, it did behoove him to recognize their value and cultivate them as much as was necessary for someone of his station. At Louvain, the foremost seat of learning in the Spanish Netherlands, the orator and four-time rector of the university, Hendrik Loyens (1607–1686) put it this way:

> He possessed all the ornaments of the arts and studies, but only as much as befits a monarch, which, if they exceed a certain measure, make a private citizen out of a prince. The measure is that when he had learned enough, he had a greater affection for learning than possession; he knew more than he practiced; he enjoyed it more than he cultivated it. He will be greater if he acts like a prince among the learned, rather than plays the *érudit* among princes.[79]

---

[77] Martha K. Hoffman, *Raised to Rule: Educating Royalty at the Court of the Spanish Habsburgs, 1601–1634* (Baton Rouge: LSU Press, 2011), 54–79.

[78] *Llanto del Occidente en El ocaso del más Claro Sol de las Españas*, fol. 122r: "Quanta reipublicae literariae attulit monumenta, speciosa sui nominis in sempiternum non emoritura suffragia!"

[79] Henricus Loyens, *Oratio Fvnebris, in Exequijs Serenissimi ac Catholici Hispaniarum ac Jndiarum Regis Philippi Qvarti dum illi Academia Lovaniensis in Æde Divo Petro Sacra Lugibri & Solemni Pompa Parentaret* (Louvain, 1665), fol. B1r: "illius igitur bonae artes ac studia fuere, sed quantum in principe laudari possunt, quae cum modum excedunt, ex principe privatum faciunt, modus vero ille est, ut ubi didicerit quantum satis, quantum didicerit amet magis, quam tractet, sciat quam excolat, usurpet quam ostentet; maior futurus, si inter doctos potius principem agat, quam si inter principes doctum."

Education and learning were prerequisites for true nobility. Yet, the standard to which princes were held was considerably lower than other members of the elite, for it was in the end the ability to resolve disputes justly, rather than to define or eulogize "justice" that really mattered to Habsburg subjects.

Virtue Politics As a Technology of "Negotiation"

Among the magnificent surroundings of Puebla Cathedral, Gregorio López de Mendizábal, a former professor of rhetoric at the Royal and Pontifical University in Mexico City, instructed his listeners: "Let us place [the image of Philip IV] before our eyes for careful inspection, for eager imitation and imprint it on our memories."[80] By displaying the rewards of virtue, the funeral oratory and the multifaceted *exequias* in Puebla and across the Hispanic Monarchy served to incentivize high standards of personal and professional conduct. This reflected the Christian humanist project of remaking society on the model of an idealized neo-Roman Christian commonwealth, which had received renewed impetus after the Council of Trent when humanist culture was championed as a tool for reforming Catholic society.[81] It was in this spirit that the *exequias* in their totality were addressed to the viceroy and the numerous other secular and ecclesiastical officials who stood in place of the king in the administration of justice in his various kingdoms. Office holders were required to represent not only the King's power, but also his virtues, foremost among which were his justice and religious zeal.[82] In Mechelen in the Spanish Netherlands, the orator made this exemplary role explicit:

[80] Gregorio López de Mendizábal, *Oratoria Parentatio, qua Caesareae Angelorum Urbis Americanae Magnum, Meritumque Dolorem Testatus est in Acerbo Philippi IV Magni Hispaniarum & Indiarum Regis Funere* (Mexico City, 1666), fols. 2v–3r: "Et augustissimis manibus parentatum convenimus, sacros magni regis cineres alte contemplemur, et quam propriis ipsemet virtutibus pro coloribus, quatuor, et quadraginta annorum spatio, utpote ad veram immortalitatem expressam, imaginem sui Philippus pie vivendo pinxit, et religiose moriendo absolvit, et quam praeclaros inter cineres mors impia contexit, ac tumulavit; excusso mortuali pulvere retegamus, nobisque ante mentis oculos avide intuendam, studiose imitandam et memori imprimendam. Ergo agite, quicumque mecum pii regis, chari patris, gratique, dum vita manebat, Philippi generosam animi effigiem de vultu nosse, et aestimare cupitis; ad sacram pyram hoc intra augustum mausoleum non tam extremis ardentem flammis, quam supremis nostri omnium studiis ac votis flagrantem, intrepide subeamus."

[81] Frederick J. McGuinnes, *Right Thinking and Sacred Oratory in Counter-Reformation Rome*, 13–14.

[82] Alejandro Cañeque, "Imaging the Spanish Empire: The Visual Construction of Imperial Authority in Habsburg New Spain," *Colonial Latin American Review*, 19 (2010), 29–68 (48–50); *ibid.*, "El Arco Triunfal en el México del Siglo XVII como Manual Efímero del Buen Gobernante," in José Pascual Buxó (ed.), *Reflexión y Espectáculo en la América Virreinal* (Mexico City: Universidad Nacional Autónoma de México, 2007), 199–218.

Certainly here, these royal ministers have an abundant supply of virtues in our king, which they might imitate. And you, noble men, senators of the highest royal senate, to whom our king gave the reins of administration in Belgium, being mindful of the royal will and the defense of the Church, have ordered on numerous occasions and on the basis of your just opinions such restorations of churches in similar cases, to which, although I may omit to mention them, this church, these columns, these very stones will testify. I pray that God will enhance the virtues you already possess, and I beseech you to continue to be defenders of the Church and justice according to the example set by this king whom you represent.[83]

This use of the person of the king as the paradigm of virtue was strengthened by the invocation of exemplary historical and biblical figures to whom Philip IV was linked and compared. As Caussin explained: "if it is done right, it is sublime, and an effective method of persuasion, since we are all more easily led by examples in particular than by words, and these are also a particularly good means to encourage people in virtue."[84]

These oratorical *exempla* for imitation were then reinforced by the representations of the same biblical, classical and mythological figures on the *túmulo* that remained in full view of the audience as they listened to the orator (Figure 2.5). In Mexico City, Philip was linked to the great chain of exemplary virtue through his royal insignia, which sat beneath a *labarum*, the military banner emblazoned with the Greek letters Chi-Rho, under which the first Christian emperor Constantine had marched into battle.[85] Together, as Del Puerto put it in the opening of his oration, Philip and Constantine spoke in one voice:

I am not embarrassed to say that from Constantine's *labarum* before us these words seem to emanate: "Philip IV, King of the Spains and the Indies, ever majestic emperor." Perhaps King Philip or his spirit that I perceive here

---

[83] Franciscus van den Venne, *Oratio Fvnebris, in Exequiis Magni & Catholici Hispaniarum Indiarumque Regis, Belgarum Principis Philippi IV* (Brussels, 1665), 20: "Habent sane hic ministri regii abundantissimas in rege nostro, quas imitentur virtutes: et vos habetis, amplissimi viri, supremi senatus regii conscripti patres, quibus primam in suo Belgio iustitiae administrationem rex noster commisit, qui regiae eius intentionis et ecclesiae defensionis non immemores, in similibus casibus iustissimis vestris sententiis, non semel ecclesiae tales fieri restitutiones jussistis, quas licet ego tacerem, templum hoc, hae columnae, hi lapides loquerentur. Hoc oro, ut confirmet hoc Deus, quod operatus est in vobis et vos obtestor, ut ad exemplum tanti regis, cuius personam geritis, ecclesiae et iustitiae, uti facitis, sitis perpetuo defensores."

[84] Nicolas Caussin, *Eloquentiae Sacrae et Humanae Parallela Libri XVI* (Cologne, 1634), 196–197: "si recte fiat, grandis est, et ad persuadendum efficax, cum praesertim omnes facilius ducamur exemplis, quam verbis, quibus ad incitamenta virtutis adduntur stimuli non mediocres."

[85] On the *labarum* and its significance as a Roman imperial symbol, see: Sebastián de Cobarrubias Orozco, *Tesoro de la Lengua Castellana o Española* (Madrid, 1611), 510–511 (*labaro*).

Figure 2.5   Túmulo constructed in Mexico City Cathedral, *Llanto del occidente en el ocaso del más claro sol de las Españas: Fúnebres demonstraciones que hizo pyra real, que erigió en las exequias del Rey N. Señor D. Felipe IIII el grande* (Mexico City, 1666).
Courtesy of the Getty Research Institute, Los Angeles (84-B8199)

does not own the coats of arms, the banners of victory, or the family trees. Perhaps he borrowed it all from Constantine?[86]

In this way, the deeds and virtues of Philip became intrinsically linked to those of Constantine in whose footsteps he trod as a Catholic Emperor. Surrounding Constantine's *labarum* on the eighty-four-foot tall *túmulo*, there were also statues of Alexander, Charlemagne, Prometheus, Theseus, Jason and Janus, alongside a statue of Philip himself. These too contributed to the chain of exemplary figures to which Philip and Del Puerto's audience were the heirs. Philip, the orator declared, had earned the title "the Great" (*el Grande*) by being more clement than Constantine, more munificent than Alexander and more temperate than Leo the Great.[87] In this crescendo of *exempla*, the high-ranking ecclesiastics and office holders were thereby urged to outdo these great men, not in their achievements, but in their virtues, just as Philip IV had supposedly done.

Following the dictates of Christian humanism, to these classical *exempla* were often added those of biblical kings, especially King David and Solomon. In Oaxaca in New Spain, for instance, the funeral sermon was structured around Philip's Solomonic virtues: He was conciliatory, great, powerful, loveable and a defender of the faith.[88] Similarly, the second level of the *túmulo* in the cathedral of Mexico City featured a statue of Philip surrounded by four statues of Solomon, and looking down on them all stood the figure of faith, who was bathed in the light of a vast candle that stood at the top of the monument. These parallels between Philip and two biblical monarchs were then made even more explicit by the preacher's choice of theme, the so-called Psalm for Solomon, "Give to the king thy judgment, O God: and to the king's son thy justice" (Psalm 72.1). This led him to open the sermon in this way:

> Who is this? [The answer:] our David, in the opinion of the very Holy Fathers and the exegetes of this passage. It is David who asks for the virtues

---

[86] *Llanto del Occidente en El ocaso del más Claro Sol de las Españas*, fols. 113r: "E labaro Constantini, quod video, nec mei me dixisse paeniteat, sonant auribus haec verba: PHILIPPUS QUARTUS HISPANIARUM REX, INDIARUMQUE IMPERATOR SEMPER AUGUSTUS. Forsam Rex iste PHILIPPUS, aut Phasma, quod video, non ambit armorum stemmata, Trophaei vexilla, generis Philacteria; forsam haec omnia mutuatus a Constatino?"

[87] *Ibid.,*, fols 131r–v: "Emigrasti, o pia et generosa anima ex tuo corporis ergasterio, sed vivis o felix et fecunda anima inter celicolas hostia pacifica immolanda Christo, vivis o PHILIPPE, inter octodecim MAGNOS, quos usque fama provehit collaudandos, MAGNUS IN MEDIO an dicam MAYOR? An dicam, utrumque? An melius dicam, vivis MELIOR. Vivis LEONE PRIMO temperantior. Vivis CONSTANTINO clementior. VIVIS CAROLO PRIMO mitior. Vivis ALEXANDRO LIBERALIOR. Vivis quinque FERDINANDIS moderatior. Vivis duodecim ALPHONSIS humanior. Vivis tribus PHILIPPIS pior."

[88] Antonio Lascari, *Real Panteón, Oratorio Fúnebre: Sermón que el Sr. Antonio Lascari Beneficiado del Partido de Tututepec, en el Obispado de Oaxaca* (Mexico City, 1667), fols. 2v–3r.

and outstanding features necessary to exercise with skill the juridical power of a king for himself and for Solomon, his son and successor in power.[89]

Moving into a close reading of the biblical passage, Poblete continued:

> The title and the commentary to this psalm assure me of the novelty of my thought ... "for Solomon," "according to Solomon," "to Solomon," and even better, in the words of St Jerome, "dedicated to Solomon." These meanings are united in the four Solomons of this sepulcher. The argument and subject matter is the kingdom of David to whose throne Solomon succeeded as the heir and son of his royal power.[90]

Combining biblical exegesis with virtue-driven panegyric, Poblete linked Philip with King David and Charles II with Solomon, whose exemplary actions, past and future, became a byword for the virtuous exercise of power that his audience were meant to imitate.

Although officials were usually left to reason by analogy about exactly how they might imitate their monarch's virtues, on some occasions very particular advice was given. In Mexico City, Poblete lauded Philip IV explicitly as a protector of the poor and helpless, before quoting a *real cédula* published by the famous jurist Juan de Solórzano Pereira (1575–1655) that chided the viceroy and *audiencia* of New Spain for not showing due diligence in protecting the loyal *indios* of the Americas:

> Since it is against God and against me, and highly damaging to these kingdoms, the native inhabitants of which I esteem, I wish that they be treated as befits vassals who have rendered such services to the monarchy and have so extended it and brought it honor.[91]

Not only did Poblete take pains to show that Philip had been just and charitable as befitted a monarch, but he also underlined that he had given his ministers in New Spain explicit guidelines on how they might do the same. These came in the form of precise instructions about how to treat the indigenous population, which the Habsburg monarch had personally

---

[89] *Ibid.*, fol. 137r: "¿Quién será éste? Nuestro David, en sentir de los más santos padres y expositores de este lugar. Pide para sí como rey, y para su hijo Salomon sucesor de su reino, las virtudes, y excelencias necesarias para exercer con acierto la judiciaria potestad de Rey."

[90] *Ibid.*, fol. 137v: "El título, y sobreescrito de este Psalmo, me asegura el discurso en la novedad de mi pensar ... *In Salomonem, pro Salomone, ad Salomonem,* y mejor S Geronimo: *Salomoni dicatus.* Aí están en uno significados los quatro Salomones de este sepulchro. Argumento, y materia es del reino de David, en cuyo Throno sucedió Salomon, como hijo heredero de su Regia potestad."

[91] *Llanto del Occidente en El ocaso del más Claro Sol de las Españas,* fol. 142r: "'Por ser contra Dios, y contra mí, y en total destruición de estos reynos, cuyos naturales estimo, quiero sean tratados como lo merecen vasallos, que tanto sirven a la monarchia, y tanto la ha engradecido e ilustrado.'" Here, Poblete is quoting from: Juan de Solórzano Pereira, *Política Indiana* (Madrid, 1648), 58.

Figure 2.6   Emblem, "The Pious and Merciful King" (*Llanto del Occidente en el ocaso del más claro sol de las Españas*, fol. 53r).
Courtesy of the Getty Research Institute, Los Angeles (84-B8199)

added "in his royal hand" (*de su real mano*) in the margin of an earlier draft of the *real cédula* sent to him by the Council of the Indies. In this way, Poblete sought to encourage the highest standards of personal and professional conduct among the local officials in his audience. Those who might otherwise have been tempted to behave tyrannically had to be left in no doubt that the king would intervene to preserve the social contract between himself and his indigenous subjects. This was a message that was reiterated in one of the emblems on the *túmulo* that showed Philip IV as an eagle expelling the cuckoo-like "bastard" (*bastarda*) from its nest in order to protect its brood (Figure 2.6).[92]

This important social function of reminding Philip's vassals of the underlying moral obligations of those in positions of authority and the standards that could be expected by the ruled meant that there was little resistance to the performance of *exequias*. Authorities in Naples admittedly delayed a few months, but this was only because they had to check how

[92] *Llanto del Occidente en El ocaso del más Claro Sol de las Españas*, fol. 53r.

exactly they had performed the *exequias* for his father, Philip III, in 1621.[93] In some places, certain dioceses also struggled to collect a sufficiently large "donation" (*donativo*) from local congregations to pay for these events, as in Nueva Cárcares in the Philippines where there was a famine, and Sucre in the *real audiencia* of Charcas where despite the proximity of the mines of Potosí funds were scarce.[94] External events might also intervene, as in Durango in New Spain where the funeral sermon was not delivered after the orator was held up by "barbarian Indians."[95] Disputes also occasionally arose. However, these did not center on whether to perform the *exequias*, but were usually caused by competition between the bishop and the town council (*cabildo secular*) as to whose *exequias* should take precedence, as happened in both Puebla and Guadalajara.[96]

At the same time, there is evidence not from royal *exequias* per se but from similar occasions that local officials were often less than happy about uses of the classical rhetorical tradition as a "technology of negotiation" to criticize those among their number who had undermined the King's duty of care. For instance, when the learned Franciscan and former holder of the chairs of grammar, humanities, rhetoric and theology at the University of San Marcos in Lima, Buenaventura de Salinas y Córdova (1592–1653), delivered a vituperative epideictic sermon in Cuzco in 1635, he faced accusations of sedition and fomenting rebellion.[97] Salinas himself claimed that he was merely highlighting the plight of the *indios*. As he reported later in life, on his way to Cuzco he had observed a group of 300 barefoot and naked *indios* tied together at the neck with ropes each carrying sacks of grain and accompanied by *fiscales* and *mestizos* who whipped them like beasts of burden. The grain they had grown and were transporting, he was told, was to be sold at a great profit in Cuzco by the priests who were

---

[93] "Breves y cartas de pésame por la muerte de Felipe IV," AGS, Estado Roma, 3038.

[94] AGI, Filipinas, 330, L.6, fol. 207r–v; AGI, Charcas, 416, L.6, fol. 42r–v.

[95] Juan de Echevarria, *Fúnebre Memoria de la Muerte del Rey N Señor D. Felipe Quarto el Grande. Piadosa Seña de la Gloria en que Descansa su Magestad Cesárea. Panegírico Cenotaphio en las Exequias, que la S. Iglesia Cathedral de Durango, y Reyno de la Nueva Vizcaya le Consagraron a sus Cenizas Reales* (Mexico 1667), fol. 4r: "que se avía de seguir a la oración fúnebre, que faltó porque el beneficiado a quien se avía encargado, no pudo venir por impedírselos los Indios bárbaros, que tenían cogidos los caminos."

[96] AGI, Guadalajara, 230, L.3, fol. 309r–v. Puebla, Biblioteca Palafoxiana, ms. 2733, fol. 5r–v.

[97] According to his accusers Salinas had described Philip IV of governing "tyrannically," and sending corrupt officials who were not "fishers [of men]" (*pescadores*), but "hunters" (*cazadores*) bent on taking all the riches of the Indies back to Europe and stripping the heirs of the conquistadors of their wealth. This incident is studied in: Masaki Sato, "Revisando a Criollos y al Criollismo en el Virreinato Peruano del Siglo XVII: el Caso de Fray Buenaventura de Salinas y Córdova," *Historia y Cultura* (Lima), 27 (2015), 83–114.

meant to be preparing them for eternal life. Salinas then came across another group of *indios* carrying baskets of chickens. This group, he learned, had been forced by their *corregidor* to travel with little or nothing to eat and drink despite the summer heat, while their womenfolk had to stay at home and spin and weave cloth to enrich the same *corregidor*. In the context of such injustices, Salinas underlined, the preacher took on a special role in reminding the *indios* that it was not the king but his selfish servants (*interesados*) who were the cause of their problems. The sacred orator played the role of a loyal dog, he explained, keeping watch, barking loudly and attacking those who threatened the tranquility of the Hispanic Monarchy![98]

It is clear then that the oratory performed within the context of the *exequias* and elsewhere was far from an expression of an inflexible and merely top-down imperial culture. While a just monarch who was "a subject of the laws" reigned and virtue was the standard by which all conduct was measured, there was always the possibility of correcting and even replacing tyrannical officials (if not the monarch) if they broke their covenant with the ruled by overtly governing in their own interest, rather than for the common good.[99] Philip may have been presented as Spain's "sun king," the brightest star in the sky that cast its rays across every continent.[100] However, he also sat at the center of overlapping systems of pre-Enlightenment rights and privileges, in which authority was balanced with liberty, both individual and corporate.[101] This was not a mere legal formality, but a widely believed and much touted point of pride in each of the constituent kingdoms of the Hispanic Monarchy. Royal commands that were contrary to divine and natural law, or against conscience, the Church or the faith, or uttered in anger, were of no force, and could be

---

[98] Buenaventura de Salinas y Córdova, *Memorial, Informe, y Manifiesto* (Madrid, 1646), fol. 35v–47v.

[99] Giacomo Lubrani, *L'Anfiteatro della Constanza Vittoriosa Oratione Funerale del P. Giacomo Lubrani della Compagnia di Giesù. Detta nel Duomo di Palermo per le Solenni Essequie Celebrate alla Cattolica Maestà di Filippo IV il Grande re delle Spagne e di Sicilia* (Palermo, 1666), 22: "Non cadde in queste secche FILIPPO, re nell'ingegno, suddito nelle leggi, tutto arrendevole agli ammonitori verdici, niente incorrigibile a' decreti del meglio, e si scrupolo in qualunque minutia convenente al ben publico." Robert Bireley, *The Counter-Reformation Prince: Anti-Machiavellianism or Catholic Statecraft in Early Modern Europe*, 36–37. Although few went this far, Juan de Mariana famously argued that if a monarch ruled tyrannically, he could be deposed: Guenter Lewy, *Constitutionalism and Statecraft during the Golden Age of Spain: A Study of the Political Philosophy of Juan de Mariana, S.J.* (Geneva: Librairie E. Droz, 1960), 152–160.

[100] Virgilio Bermejo Vega, "Acerca de los Recursos de la Iconografía Regia; Felipe IV, de Rey Sol a Nuevo Salomón," *NORBA-ARTE*, 12 (1992), 163–186.

[101] Maravall in fact recognized this in a later less well-known study: José Antonio Maravall, *Teoría del Estado en España en el Siglo XVII*, 319–359.

resisted, leading to the famous maxim, "I obey but I do not comply" (*obedezco pero no cumplo*), a delaying tactic that could be used while appealing to the Council of Castile or the Indies. "Resistance" could thus be couched in terms of "obedience" and appeals be made to the King's justice or his mercy through various channels. It was this political culture of "negotiation" that was celebrated in the *exequias*, rather than the absolutism identified by Maravall.[102]

The Language of Virtue beyond the *Exequias*

The orations and sermons delivered for the *exequias* represented one of the most detailed and widely experienced articulations of a virtue-driven political culture that ultimately played out in the legal system. This was a bureaucracy punctuated by several layers of judges and officials descending from the king that served less to enforce written law in any mechanical way, than to defend widely accepted standards of fairness within the context of a system that prized social hierarchy and corporate privileges. Here, justice was the paradigmatic virtue, defined as it had been by the Roman jurist Ulpian as "giving each his own" (*suum cuique tribuere*). Just like the funeral orations for Philip IV, the ultimate aim of the legal system was thus to maintain an idealized status quo, in which subjects and representatives of the monarch all behaved according to generally accepted standards of virtuous behavior.[103] This larger understanding of justice was reinforced during the legal proceedings, not only by the words of the advocates and judges, but by the buildings themselves. For instance, we know that when the *audiencia* in Quito was reestablished in 1722, the entrance to the main courtroom featured two statues of anonymous Romans pointing to Latin legal maxims "give each his own" (*suum cuique tribuere*) and "each suffers for what he has done" (*quod quisque fecit patitur*) and in order to pass into the next room one had to pass beneath a painting of the theologian and Church Father, St. Jerome, which stood alongside the paintings of famous battles fought by the Kings of Castile. In some courtrooms, the particular virtues that judges were meant to police were

---

[102] Ruth MacKay, *The Limits of Royal Authority: Resistance and Obedience in Seventeenth-Century Castile* (New York: Cambridge University Press, 1999), 1–4.

[103] *Institutiones*, 1.3; *Digesta*, 1.1.10. This refers mainly, but not exclusively to the *justicia* (i.e. final court of appeal) and *gobierno* (i.e. responding directly to petitions from vassals) functions of the royal bureaucracy at both the viceregal and the Crown level: Adrian Masters, "A Thousand Invisible Architects: Vassals, the Petition and Response System, and the Creation of Spanish Imperial Caste Legislation," *Hispanic American Historical Review*, 98 (2018), 377–406 (381–383).

also made explicit visually, as in the case of Granada where the entrance to the main courtroom in the Royal Chancellery was decorated with statues representing justice, fortitude, prudence and moderation.[104]

Since the legal system was moralist and socially embedded, rather than positivist and objectivist in conception, the division between private and public law was loose. Similarly, great emphasis was placed on the need for officials to possess a moral compass and to be socially influential enough to enforce judgments. Consequently, learned judges (*letrados*) did not necessarily have to possess a degree in civil law, but could also hold bachelor's degrees, doctoral degrees or licentiates in related subjects, such as canon law or theology. This gave them the authority to judge cases according to a combination of their conscience and their command of learned authorities on the "law," be it natural, divine, civil, canon or customary. This was possible because it was widely believed that all good laws were ultimately in harmony. Judges might not even be degree holders at all, if they were suitable in other respects. This is not to say, of course, that positive law and knowledge of it was irrelevant. Rather, it was considered the product of, and to exist within, social hierarchies and an overarching Christian (and neo-Roman) framework.[105]

It should come as no surprise, then, that the language of virtue described regularly permeated legal documents throughout the Hispanic Monarchy, be they in Castilian or other languages. Whether filing a petition to a local court or writing to an *audiencia*, the Council of the Indies, or directly to the king himself, litigants referred occasionally to particular laws or decrees, but the underlying patterns of thought relied on a virtue-driven language of praise and blame. If we take the denunciations sent to the Council of the Indies from the Philippines as our starting point, we find that they rarely say that a person or group has disobeyed a particular law, but rather that they have acted in contravention of the norms of good

---

[104] Tamar Herzog, *Upholding Justice*, 183–184 and n. 11. The second maxim is taken from Seneca, *Hercules Furens*, 735.

[105] Charles Cutter, "The Legal System As a Touchstone of Identity in Colonial New Mexico," in Luis Roniger and Tamar Herzog, *The Collective and the Public in Latin America: Cultural Identities and Political Order* (Portland, OR: Sussex Academic Press, 2000). 57–70; Tamar Herzog, "¿Letrado o Teólogo? Sobre el Oficio de la Justicia a Principios del Siglo XVIII," in Johannes Michael Scholz (ed.), *Fallstudien zur Spanischen und Portugiesischen Justiz (16.–20. Jahrhundert)* (Frankfurt: Rechtsprechung, 1994), 697–714; *eadem, Upholding Justice: Society, State, and the Penal System in Quito (1650–1750)*, 3–8; Brian Owensby, *Empire of Law: Indian Justice in Colonial Mexico*, 7; Víctor Tau Anzoátegui, *Casuismo y Sistema: Indagación Histórica Sobre el Espíritu del Derecho Indiano* (Buenos Aires: Instituto de investigaciones de historia del derecho, 1992), 29; Bianca Premo, *The Enlightenment on Trial: Ordinary Litigants and Colonialism in the Spanish Empire* (New York: Oxford University Press, 2017), 23.

behavior and should be punished. For instance, in 1671 the Dominican friar, Juan de Santa María, wrote to denounce an *oidor*, Fernando Escaño, for bribery and corruption. Importantly, his letter did not open with a description of the events, the precise nature of his venality, or even the amount of money that changed hands. Rather, it consisted of a character sketch. Escaño was by his very nature a troublemaker whose dissoluteness put the whole Spanish Philippines at risk. He lacked virtue and desired only to enrich himself and his sorry band of followers.[106] Similarly, an Augustinian, Diego de Herrera, wrote to the Council of the Indies in 1570 to complain that the Spaniards in the Philippines were pillaging the islands and enslaving the local population, and justice (*justicia*) had fallen victim to license (*licencia*). The remedy for this was to send well-born and moral people (*gente de calidad*) who could govern the islands in the interests of the local population and the larger Hispanic Monarchy.[107]

This epideictic frame of reference also influenced the petitions by indigenous litigants in the Philippines. While such documents were usually mediated through Spanish ecclesiastics, they represent summations of real conversations, in which indigenous elites learned the language of virtue, if they had not already acquired it by listening to sermons or inherited from analogous local traditions.[108] For instance, the *indios* of the village of Silang near Manila wrote to an *oidor* named Pedro Calderón in the wake of the famous Tagalog Agrarian Revolt of 1745 asking him to accept their apology for their role in the uprising. The crown must understand, they wrote, that their actions were the result of the "hardship and misery" (*desgracias y miserias*) that they had suffered at the hands of the Dominicans and the Recollects who had seized the land that they had possessed since their conversion to Christianity in the "distant past" (*tiempos antiguos*). It was this misconduct that had led them into "error" (*yerro*), for which they sought royal clemency. Their intention had never been to revolt against their "natural lord" (*señor natural*), the king. Rather, they had merely hoped to put an end to the actions that were "troubling our hearts" (*perturbar nuestros corazones*) and to avoid starvation and their womenfolk having to sell their bodies. The petitioners then

---

[106] AGI, Filipinas, 86, n. 31, fol. 1: "subjeto tan fácil benal y borascoso que con çismas y cavilaciones de su vario inquieto natural, tiene inquieta de nueba esta republica, y a riesgo de perderse esta tierra porque luego que entró en ella con muger y seis hijos desnudos y con muchos empeños con animo de salir dellos y hacerse muy presto ricos y poderosos y temer de todos."

[107] AGI, Filipinas, 84, n.1.

[108] On the issue mediation in legal sources, see Brian Owensby, *Empire of Law and Indian Justice in Colonial Mexico*, 53.

concluded in the conventional way by swearing that their intentions were pure (*juramos no proceder de malicia*). This was a petition, like most others regardless of its writers, that presumed a certain understanding of virtue, vice and the importance of adhering to tried and true patterns of Christian behavior.[109] This is the same worldview that we also find echoed in the far briefer petitions for privileges (*gracia*) in reward for service to the Crown. Importantly, these were given not only to ethnically Spanish conquistadors, but also to the many indigenous and mixed-race military leaders who helped expand and defend the territories of the Hispanic Monarchy in the Philippines and elsewhere. In exchange for showing loyalty and valor, as well as for dutifully baptizing their children, these non-Spanish elites were judged "worthy" (*merecedores*) to receive grants of land, labor (*encomiendas*), pensions and other benefits that in some cases could become hereditary.[110]

Such documents written at the behest of and in collaboration with indigenous subjects, in turn, mirror the virtue-driven complaints directed by ethnically Spanish critics against royal officials and missionaries who mistreated the non-elite indigenous population. Indeed, when Salvador Gómez de Espinosa y Estrada (*c.* 1600–1660) attacked the abuses of the system of obligatory native labor at the hands of both local officials and missionaries in a short treatise published in Manila in 1657, he couched his discussion of the legal status of the native population in terms of the authorities' need to respect royal decrees meant to regulate native labor "according to the most rigorous interpretation of justice and the strictest demands of their conscience." Here, the king was understood to be the defender of the natural liberty of the native population, and all God-fearing and loyal officials had to obey his directives, which were themselves always in keeping with natural law and the most orthodox theology. The missionaries whose conduct had been called into question, of course, saw

---

[109] AGI, Filipinas, 261, n.1, fols. 1227r–1228v. The 1745 revolt is discussed in: Nicholas P. Cushner, *Landed Estates in the Colonial Philippines* (New Haven, CT: Yale University Southeast Asian Studies, 1976), 59–64.

[110] These petitions are discussed in: Antonio García-Abásolo, "Mestizos de un país Sin Mestizaje. Mestizos Españoles en Filipinas en la Época Colonial," in Marta Maria Manchado López y Miguel Luque Talaván (eds.), *Un Mar de Islas, un Mar de Gentes. Población y Diversidad en las Islas Filipinas* (Córdoba: Editorial Universidad de Córdoba, 2014), 223–246; Stephanie Mawson, "Philippine Indios in the Service of Empire: Indigenous Soldiers and Contingent Loyalty," *Ethnohistory*, 63 (2016), 381–413. A particularly good example is that of Juan Macapagal (d. 1683), a Pampango military leader from Arayat: AGI, Filipinas, 43, n. 27.

things differently and proceeded to deliver vituperative sermons against Gómez de Espinosa and even denounced him before the Inquisition.[111]

In the Philippines, an advantage for native subjects of remaining vassals of Philip IV seems to have been the stability (*pax*) it offered and the advantages of having an external arbiter to judge local disputes. This also seems to have been a factor in the Americas, where following a period of violent conquest or mutually beneficial alliance in the conquest of other indigenous groups native populations were slowly drawn into a legal and political system that provided an external point of reference for resolving their differences.[112] *Indios* in New Spain quickly learned to navigate the Spanish legal system, and indeed positively swamped the Crown with petitions in the late sixteenth century. This quickly led to the foundation of the General Indian Court (*juzgado general de indios*), which was envisioned as a means to regulate disputes within indigenous communities and in cases when Spaniards sued *indios*. While in theory the *audiencia* dealt with cases in which *indios* sued *españoles*, there were particular procedural ruses that could be employed to have such cases heard in the General Indian Court allowing indigenous petitioners to push back more effectively against the ongoing threat of settler colonialism. Access to this legal avenue goes a long way toward explaining why rebellions among the sedentary peoples of the Americas were vanishingly rare, and, when they did happen, they usually took the form of what James Lockhart has called "self-assertion," a defense of rights by a single *pueblo* or local ethnic state within the larger context of convergence in cultural norms between the multiethnic populations of New Spain. When these took the form of violent revolts (*tumultos*), they were most often the culmination of a process of petitioning and represented the peak of legal attention-getting, when arguments on paper proved unsuccessful.[113]

Due to exposure to Hispanic legal culture, sermons, funeral orations, devotional and doctrinal texts, and other articulations of virtue politics, when *indios* in New Spain sought to resolve disputes through legal

---

[111] James S. Cummins and Nicholas P. Cushner, "Labor in the Colonial Philippines: 'The 'Discurso Parenetico' of Gomez de Espinosa," *Philippine Studies*, 22 (1974), 117–203 (148): "en punto rigurosísimo de justicia y términos estrechísimos de conciencia."

[112] Felipe Fernández-Armesto, "The Stranger-Effect in Early Modern Asia," *Itinerario*, 24 (2000), 80–103; Susan Kellogg, *Law and the Transformation of Aztec Culture, 1500–1700*; Brian Owensby, *Empire of Law and Indian Justice in Colonial Mexico*, 32–33, 43–44. On the General Indian Court, see Woodrow Wilson Borah, *Justice by Insurance: The General Indian Court of Colonial Mexico and the Legal Aides of the Half-Real* (Berkeley: University of California Press, 1983).

[113] James Lockhart, "Receptivity and Resistance," in *Of Things of the Indies: Essays Old and New in Early Latin American History* (Stanford, CA: Stanford University Press, 1999), 304–332.

channels, they invariably relied on this framework. For instance, when *procuradores* petitioned for an *amparo* (i.e. legal protection pending a hearing by a local judge), they frequently described the seizure of land or the illegal gathering of firewood as acts of "wrong and damage" (*mal y daño*), in what Brian Owensby has called "legal morality tales," which pitted a virtuous plaintiff against an unethical defendant with only ornamental references to particular laws.[114] It is no wonder then that the legal system of the Hispanic Monarchy has been compared to casuistry.[115] This language was also used in claims by non-elite *indios* against the indigenous nobility who frequently trampled on the rights of their subordinates. For example, in 1615 Juan Cano Montezuma, the alcalde mayor of Otucpa and a direct descendant of Montezuma II, was accused of flying into a rage when he learned that some local people had gone to Mexico City to complain about his arbitrary conduct and his alleged assertion that he was the "natural lord" (i.e. hereditary ruler) of the region because he was a descendant of the emperor Montezuma, "the heir of all of New Spain and not a parvenue like those from Castile." They also censured him for various other unlawful *cum* immoral acts, including excessive use of violence against non-elite *indios* without due cause. His *lèse-majesté* thus fitted into a broader pattern of vice and at times even licentiousness.[116] This was exactly the sort of person against whom the orators at the *exequias* were trying to inoculate society.

Colonialism and the Limits of "Virtue Politics"

Across vast swaths of the Hispanic Monarchy from Manila to Madrid, virtue politics was the primary frame of reference. There, panegyrics of Philip's virtue were seemingly sufficient to justify his crown and his position as a model to be imitated, while leaving space open for institutionalized resistance to misrule. However, there was one part of the Hispanic Monarchy where a more heavy-handed approach was required to iron out the creases in Philip's perceived legitimacy and to underline that any injustice attributable to the Crown was the fault, not of the king, but of his iniquitous subordinates. Interestingly, this was not the case in the Americas. Rather, it was in the

---

[114] Brian Owensby, *Empire of Law and Indian Justice in Colonial Mexico*, 49–89.

[115] Víctor Tau Anzoátegui, *Casuismo y Sistema: Indagación Histórica Sobre el Espíritu del Derecho Indiano*.

[116] Quoted in: Brian Owensby, *Empire of Law and Indian Justice in Colonial Mexico*, 384–386, 233–239.

Spanish Netherlands that we find orators having to defend the King's "just title" to rule in more legalistic terms.[117]

In most respects, the funeral orations from Flanders are identical to those from other parts of Philip IV's global monarchy in that they were delivered by humanistically educated clerics and imagined as part of a long tradition that ran from Ancient Greece and Rome to their own day. However, in contrast to the orators in the Americas who if they mentioned conquest and colonization at all spoke of it in highly generalized providential terms, those in the Spanish Netherlands, like Iodocus Houbraken (*c.* 1619–1681) who delivered a Latin funeral oration in Antwerp Cathedral, addressed the legitimacy of the Habsburg rule head-on.[118] Here, virtue politics was necessary, but not sufficient. To create a compelling argument in Flanders, it was seemingly necessary to explain the legal basis of Philip's sovereignty. As Houbraken put it:

> And what deserves the highest admiration and glory is that there is no province at all in this vast empire, which has not been inserted into the crown of Spain by inheritance, or by union, or through marriage, or by donation, or through some legal testament, or finally through sale or some other just title.[119]

Similarly, in his learned French sermon delivered in Brussels, Charle-François Amounet de Hailly (1625–1667) took pains to underline that the Habsburgs had acquired their global empire legally, just as Alexander the Great had done:

> No, no, sirs, there is no pearl or diamond in the crown of Philip the Great, which does not belong to him either by succession, or by alliance, or by very just accession as in the Indies. In what follows, I will give a number of

---

[117] For a parallel, if polemical, argument, see: Jorge Klor de Alva, "Colonialism and Postcolonialism As (Latin) American Mirages," *Colonial Latin American Review*, 1 (1992), 3–23; *ibid.*, "The Postcolonialism of the (Latin) American Experience: A Reconsideration of 'Colonialism,' 'Postcolonialism,' and 'Mestizaje,'" in Gyan Prakash (ed.), *After Colonialism: Imperial Histories and Displacements* (Princeton, NJ: Princeton University Press, 1994), 241–275.

[118] For example, Juan Antonio de Palma, *Lágrimas en las Honras que a la Magestad Real de N Rey y Señor Filipo IV el Grande Celebró el Real Acuerdo de Lima, Gobernando en Vacante, en su Santa Iglesia Metropolitana en 17. Días del Mes de Septiembre de 1666* (Lima, 1666), fol. 32v: "Juzgavan algunos, que por la expulsión se minoravan los vasallos, y permitió Dios, que entonces se abriesse camino a la navegación de Christoval Colón, para el descubrimiento de las Indias Orientales, y que después se rindiessen estas Occidentales, en que se le acrecentó a la corona tanto número de vassallos, que voluntariamente hincan la rodilla al Crucificado. Por quatro judiguelos, que salieron de España, aumentó Dios a la corona un número sin número de Católicos."

[119] Iudocus Houbraken, *Oratio Funebris in Exequiis Philippi IV., Hispaniarum ac Indiarum Regis Catholici* (Antwerp, 1666), 9–10: "Quodque admirationem maximam meretur et gloriam, nulla omnino est in hac imperii amplitudine provincia, quae non vel legitima haereditate, vel affinitate, vel connubii iure, vel donatione, vel testamento, aut denique emptione vel alio iusto titulo Coronae Hispanicae sit inserta."

summary proofs of this from among the large number of them carefully researched and outlined by the learned jurist Solórzano.[120]

Here, "virtue politics" was not enough to placate an audience that obviously considered the legality of Philip's claim to Flanders something of an open question. This may have been at least partly the result of a long-standing propaganda campaign by the Dutch Republic, which had for over a century portrayed Philip as a foreign tyrant. In the Netherlands, the colonization of the Americas too required an explanation. This Hailly attributed to the desire on the part of Philip's ancestors to spread Catholicism.[121] Indeed, while elsewhere it was common for orators to claim Philip for their particular kingdom or viceroyalty, so keen was Hailly to counter the claims of the Dutch Republic that he went to the other extreme, going as far as to downplay the monarch's connection to Spain. Borrowing the words of Cardinal Baronius, the author of the most erudite history of the Church written in an age of crushing erudition, Hailly reminded his listeners that all Catholics should mourn Philip as the "father of the world" (*pater orbis*), just as Charlemagne's death had been greeted by universal sorrow. Within the context of a Catholic ecumene threatened by Protestant forces to the north, this identification of the Spanish Habsburgs as universal protectors and with a Holy Roman Emperor from northwestern Europe made perfect sense.[122] However, Flandrians should mourn him in particular, Hailly continued, because Philip was fundamentally, perhaps even exclusively a Flandrian. Certainly, they should not consider him primarily "Spanish."[123] In the other parts of the Hispanic Monarchy, such as the Viceroyalty of Peru, Philip IV was happily celebrated as both their king and that of multiple other kingdoms in the "Two Spains" and beyond. By contrast, in Flanders the need to obviate the risk of the Habsburgs appearing "foreign" meant that the connection between Philip and Spain had to be finessed.[124]

---

[120] Charle-François Amounet de Hailly, *Harangue Funebre Prononcée aux Exeques de Philippe le Grand Roy Catholique des Espagnes et des Indes*, 19–20: "Non, non, Messieurs, il n'y a aucune perle ny diamant a la Couronne de PHILIPPE LE GRANDE qui ne luy appartienne, ou par succession, ou par alliance, ou par un très-juste acquét, comme est celuy des Indes: et en voicy quelques preves sommières entre une infinité d'autres très-bien recherchées et établies par le docte Jurisconsulte Solorzan."

[121] *Ibid.*, 20.

[122] Judith Pollmann, *Catholic Identity and the Revolt of the Netherlands, 1520–1635* (Oxford: Oxford University Press, 2011).

[123] *Ibid.*, 40: "Mais nous, mes chers Compatriotes, ne le devons nous pas pleurer comme ses fils aînez? Puis que c'est de nos Pays-Bas qu'il a pris son origine, et que nous le regardons en qualité de Flamand, avant que de le considérer 'Español.'"

[124] Juan Antonio de Palma, *Lágrimas en las Honras que a la Magestad Real de N Rey y Señor Filipo IV el Grande Celebró el Real Acuerdo de Lima, Gobernando en Vacante, en su Santa Iglesia Metropolitana en 17. Días del Mes de Septiembre de 1666*, fols. 27v–28r "¿Filipo Gótico? ¿Filipo Austríaco? ¿Filipo

In the exceedingly elegant Latin inscriptions by Jean Gaspard (1593–1666) that graced the *túmulo* in Antwerp, Philip's association with the Iberian Peninsula was similarly deemphasized. While this close friend of Rubens who had collaborated with the artist to produce the famous ephemeral architecture for the triumphal entry of Ferdinand of Austria in 1635 gave Philip his title of the "Catholic King of the Spains and the Indies," the focus of the Latin inscriptions centered on his position as a Habsburg and the heir to the Dukes of Burgundy. Indeed, peninsular Spain is notable for its absence in the iconography of the *túmulo*. Of the rivers that crisscrossed the vast structure representing Philip's mourning provinces, none were Iberian. Instead, they included Arethusa in Sicily, Maddalona near Naples, the Indus, Río de la Plata, the Danube, the Tiber and of course the nearby Seine and Scheldt. Unlike in the urban contexts of the New World, a connection to "Spain" (a potential watchword for tyranny in the Low Countries) had to be minimized in this celebration of the Hispanic Monarchy.[125]

This need to defend Philip's sovereignty was born out of the strikingly different circumstances of the Spanish Netherlands and the Americas. In the main urban centers of Spanish America and beyond much of the population from the elites downward shared a lingua franca in Spanish, a common religion and many common Hispanic cultural traits by the mid-seventeenth century. As a result, few attempts to rid the Americas of the "Spanish" came from within this increasingly Hispanized society. Reform was always on the agenda, occasionally even revolts, but the Crown and Hispanic Catholicism remained strong rallying cries.[126] In contrast, the Spanish Netherlands featured a very different elite vernacular, distinct cultural traits and the enticing prospect of joining a flourishing competing polity to the north, whereas in the Americas there was no obvious political alternative. Furthermore, whereas the main urban centers of New Spain and Peru enjoyed relative peace and prosperity in the seventeenth century, the Spanish Netherlands was wracked by ongoing wars with the United Provinces in the territory's former northern half, and threatened from the

---

Hispánico? ¿Filipo Lucitánico? ¿Filipo Itálico? ¿Filipo Índico? ¿En qué ha parado toda ésta grandeza?"

[125] Iudocus Houbraken, *Oratio Funebris in Exequiis Philippi IV., Hispaniarum ac Indiarum Regis Catholici*, 29–41.

[126] Ryan Dominic Crewe, "Brave New Spain: An Irishman's Independence Plot in Seventeenth-Century Mexico," *Past and Present*, 207 (2010), 53–87. Not that all was well in New Spain in this period, but it appears that central urban areas did enjoy greater stability than many parts of contemporary Europe: Jonathan Israel, "Mexico and the 'General Crisis' of the Seventeenth Century," *Past and Present*, 63 (1974), 33–57.

south by an increasingly assertive Louis XIV. Without an army of occupation 70,000 or more strong that fought for Spain annually in the Netherlands in the seventeenth century, it is unlikely that Philip would have remained monarch for long.[127] In such a pressed context and with the reduced circumstances of Antwerp, it is no wonder that orators felt the need to justify in legalistic terms why they were praising a king who might easily be construed as a tyrant and a "foreign imposter" whose rule was based on little more than brute force bankrolled by American silver.

Long-standing accusations of tyranny in the "colonial" Netherlands also meant that orators needed to draw more overt attention to the possibility of institutionalized resistance offered by the virtue-driven idea of kingship. The king, Houbraken made clear, was the paradigm of virtue. However, not all his subordinates lived up to this ideal. In praising the King's munificence, Houbraken contrasted royal virtue with noble vice, citing a currency crisis in 1639 when Philip melted down his own silverware to bolster the supply of money. Despite having a ready *exemplum* to follow, the Spanish nobility did not follow the example of their king.[128] As long as the king remained the personification of justice, his vassals could appeal to him in the case of injustices by nobles and officials and, Houbraken urged, they should not allow such complaints to develop into a dissatisfaction with the monarch and the Hispanic Monarchy as a whole.

One of the few parallels to this careful parsing of the virtues of the king and his inadequate underlings is to be found in the funeral oratory for the death of Philip III in another "colonial" context, the Kingdom of Portugal during the Iberian Union. According to the Trinitarian priest who delivered the funeral oration for Philip III in Lisbon, the deceased monarch's only fault was that he expected his *válidos* and ministers to be as virtuous as he was. Overflowing with virtue himself, the king could not imagine that his subordinates would lie to him. All the long-suffering population had to do was bring these miscarriages of justice to the king's attention, and he would set things right again.[129] In the "colonial" contexts of Flanders and

---

[127] Geoffrey Parker, *The Army of Flanders and the Spanish Road 1567–1659: The Logistics of Spanish Victory and Defeat in Low Countries' Wars* (Cambridge: Cambridge University Press, 1972), 10–21; *ibid.*, *The Dutch Revolt* (Ithaca, NY: Cornell University Press, 1977), 253–266; *ibid.*, "Crisis and Catastrophe: The Global Crisis of the Seventeenth Century Reconsidered," *The American Historical Review* 113 (2008), 1053–1079.

[128] Iudocus Houbraken, *Oratio Funebris in Exequiis Philippi IV., Hispaniarum ac Indiarum Regis Catholici*, 18: "Puduit Magnates non imitari Regis exemplum; et ideo certatim aurum et argentum undique in eandem officinam conferebatur, non efferendum, nisi omnium usibus adaptatum."

[129] Baltezar Páez, *Sermão que Fez o Doutor Fr. Baltezar Páez Provincial da Orden da Santissima Trinidade no Convento da Mesma Orden Desta Cidade de Lisboa. Em hum Officio, que os Irmãos*

Portugal, legitimacy was at a premium, and so the opportunity for insti-tutionalized resistance to royal officials had to be underscored to unify an audience around the Habsburg cause.

"Virtue Politics" in the Indigenous Republic

In the semi-autonomous indigenous republic of Tlaxcala in New Spain, virtue politics seems to have been sufficient to reassure local elites that they had a way to defend their autonomy and privileges by appealing to the king's justice. Indeed, this political philosophy was particularly attractive in Tlaxcala, which had long enjoyed unique privileges within the Hispanic Monarchy, and so was especially invested in the rule of law and good governance within the status quo. Having supported Cortés in his con-quest of Tenochtitlan and provided forces for the later expansion of the Hispanic Monarchy, the Tlaxcalans successfully petitioned Charles I for legal privileges, including self-governance and the title of "very noble and very loyal city" (*muy noble y muy leal ciudad*) for their new capital, the City of Tlaxcala.[130] Recognizing this dynamic, in recent times discussions of Tlaxcala's position within the Hispanic Monarchy have moved from "resistance" toward "negotiation." However, few have realized that virtue-driven panegyrics with their parenetic function were an important expression of this culture of "negotiation."[131] On few other occasions was the position of Tlaxcala as a self-governing city-state and the sort of

da Irmandade de Todos os Sanctos dos Officiaes e Criados de sua Magestade Fizerão, Conforme ao su Compromisso. Pela Magestade Catholica del Rey Dom Philippe II de Portugal (Lisbon, 1621), fol. 8r–v: "Em razão disto, não faltou quem se atrevesse a notar neste nosso grande Monarcha os defeitos, faltas e queixas que houve de seus Validos, e ainda dos mayores ministros seus ... Nesta calumnia e nota imposta ao Nosso Rey e com que os criticos pretendem deslustrar suas grandes, e reays virtudes entendo, que nenhũa razão tem, antes me parece que a mayor prova da bondade, e virtude de /fol. 8v/ sua magestade, he a maldade de seus validos, e ministros ... Não ha gente mais facil de enganar, que mais sancta, porque como jugaõ aos outros por sua virtude, e por sua verdade, não entendem, que os podem enganar, porque nem elles o sabem fazer." For a more overtly nationalist interpretation of these Portuguese funeral sermons, see João Francisco Marques, *A Parenética Portuguesa e a Dominação Filipina* (Porto: Imprensa Nacional Casa da Moeda, 1986), 255–257, and for a general introduction to the Mirrors for Princes genre in Portugal, see Ana Isabel Buescu, *Imagens do Príncipe: Discurso Normativo e Representação (1525–49)* (Lisbon: Edições Cosmos, 1996).

[130] Charles Gibson, *Tlaxcala in the Sixteenth Century* (Stanford, CA: Stanford University Press, 1967), 158–169. On preconquest Tlaxcala, see James Lockhart, *The Nahuas after the Conquest: A Social and Cultural History of the Indians of Central Mexico, Sixteenth through Eighteenth Centuries* (Stanford, CA: Stanford University Press, 1992), 21–23.

[131] R. Jovita Baber, "The Construction of Empire: Politics, Law and Community in Tlaxcala, New Spain, 1521–1640," (Ph.D. Dissertation, University of Chicago, 2005), 263–277.

virtuous governance under which it could retain its historical privileges celebrated so enthusiastically and so publicly.

This is no better illustrated than in the rich and vivid Nahuatl account of the funeral *exequias* for their *tlatoani* ("ruler") by Juan Buenaventura Zapata y Mendoza (dates unknown), which offers insights into the Tlaxcalans' engagement with the tradition of "virtue politics," and which is worth recounting in detail. As Zapata tells us, on the afternoon of the royal vespers, the viceroy of New Spain Antonio Sebastián with his wife doña Leonor, Tlaxcalan elites, the local religious orders and Spanish officials set out from the *cabildo* hall. At the head of the procession was the Spanish *gobernador* accompanied by beadles carrying a black standard. Zapata himself carried a red cushion on which rested a golden crown wrapped in black cloth alongside a scepter and a sword. Arriving at the church of San José, he placed the crown, scepter and sword before the *túmulo*. At the end of the mass, the young son of a former *gobernador* went up to the pulpit and delivered a sermon in *laticopa* ("Latin"), the text of which unfortunately does not survive.[132] The next day, a smaller procession traveled the same route for the *honras fúnebres* themselves. Throughout the subsequent mass, two indigenous *pipiltin* ("nobles") dressed as kings stood at the foot of the *túmulo* representing Tlaxcala's participation in the Hispanic Monarchy as an autonomous aristocratic republic. As the mass ended, Francisco de Linares y Urdanivia (dates unknown), a "son and resident" of the republic, arose to deliver the Castilian funeral sermon.[133] Having received a late humanist education, probably in one of the Jesuit colleges in nearby Puebla, and as a speaker of Nahuatl and perhaps other indigenous languages, Linares was in a unique position to channel the sentiments of the indigenous *altepetl* ("city state"), combining, as Isidro Sarinaña, a learned priest from the parish of Veracruz in Tlaxcala, put it in the preface to the published version, "all the skills of

[132] Juan Buenaventura Zapata y Mendoza, *Historia Cronológica de la Noble Ciudad de Tlaxcala*, Luis Reyes García and Andrea Martínez Baracs (eds.) (Tlaxcala: Centro de Investigaciones y Estudios Superiores en Antropología Social, 1995), 361–377. This is discussed in Kelly S. McDonough, *The Learned Ones: Nahua Intellectuals in Postconquest Mexico* (Tucson: University of Arizona Press, 2014), 75–81.

[133] AGN, vol. 24, exp. 89, fols. 52v–53r: "porque el gobernador, alcaldes principales y officiales de República de la ciudad de Tlaxcala me ha representado que de próximo están para celebrar las exequias y honras del Rey nuestro Señor que está en gloria y tienen comendado el sermón de ellas al licenciado Francisco de Linares y Vrdaniubia attendiendo a ser hijo y patrimonial de aquella ciudad, abogado de la Real Audiencia, Teólogo y predicador en ambas lenguas de las partes y erudición que es público y notorio en todo el Reyno."

oratory with an assessment of the virtues of his Majesty."[134] This took the form of a sermon focused on the biblical passage "And he did that which was right in the sight of the Lord, and walked in the ways of David his father, and declined neither to the right hand, nor to the left" (2 Chron. 34), which Linares used to praise Philip IV for his "heroic virtues" of justice, prudence, constancy, faith, piety, religiosity and love.[135]

Following the conventions of humanist epideictic oratory, in his sermon Linares equated nobility with virtue, and argued that inherited nobility was only valid if it was accompanied by a degree of virtue equal or greater to that of one's noble ancestors.[136] As the Tlaxcalan nobles listened, Linares reminded them that Philip IV was a model of behavior for his vassals and a "mirror for the republic," since a king "should shape his kingdom more by his example than by the exercise of his power."[137] Just like his imagined Roman predecessors, Philip was the ultimate protector of the rights of the indigenous republic, but his life also served a parenetic function as a model for Tlaxcalans, indigenous and Spanish, noble and plebian, as well as for the Spanish officials who could then be held to account for their actions according to this standard.

This virtue-driven panegyric was also framed within the context of a celebration and full-throated defense of the privileged position of Tlaxcala, which was presented as a sister city to Jerusalem and the archetypal Republic, Rome.[138] Indeed, Tlaxcala's unique mixed constitution and proven military prowess had long been portrayed as echoing the Roman

---

[134] Francisco de Linares Urdanivia, *Oración Fúnebre … en las Exequias que Celebró a la Sacra y Real Magestad de Nuestro Catholico Rey y Señor D. Felipe IV. El Grande* (Mexico City, 1667), fol. §§2r: "He leydo esta oración fúnebre, que en las exequias, que celebró a la Catholica Magestad del Rey N. Señor Don Felipe Quatro el Grande, que Dios aya, la muy leal Ciudad de Tlaxcala, dixo el Bachiller Francisco Linares Urdanivia, cuya erudición logrando todos los primores a la oratoria, pondera tan bien las virtudes de su Magestad, que consigue en sus Basallos, los consuelos, que imaginaba impossibles el sentimiento."

[135] *Ibid.*, fol. 7r. Which particular virtues were included under the rubric of the "heroic virtues" could vary considerably in this early period.

[136] *Ibid.*, fol. 2v: "que el buen príncipe no ha de aspirar tan solo a heredar de sus progenitores el mando; ha de ser una definición essencial de sus proessas, en el imperio; que el nacer en magestosas cunas, es dicha; no degenerar de las reales fajas, es gloria."

[137] *Ibid.*, fol. 2r: "dichoso Rey, que disciplinó mas con el exemplo, que governó con el poder a su reyno; que a de ser espejo de la republica, el que manda, por ser el coraçon de quien reciben vida los que govierna."

[138] *Ibid.*, fol. 1r: "Por esto pues, viste lutos, exala suspiros, vierte lagrimas, se dedica a sollozos, manifiesta profundo dolor, y publica unívocos sentimientos, esta ilustre Ciudad de Tlaxcala, que a emulación de la embiodiosa corrupción del olvido, merece aclamaciones de insigne, goza epítetos de leal, y obtiene aplausos de noble, en rescriptos con que le indultan, y privilegios con que le favorecen sus católicos reyes." On Tlaxcala as Jerusalem, see *ibid.*, fols. 2v–3r.

Republic. As Peter Martyr (1499–1562) had noted a century and a half before:

> First of all, the city, as I mentioned above, is partly democratic, but partly also aristocratic, like the Roman Republic before it became a violent monarchy, having nobles (as I said already), but shunning monarchs. Cortés writes and those that have been there tell us that it is much larger, more densely populated and more abundant in foodstuffs than the city of Granada.[139]

The Tlaxcalans themselves quickly embraced this flattering portrait. Tlaxcala was a Christian Rome in the New World, as was clear, Linares argued, from the city's coat of arms, which he described in an extended *ekphrasis*:

> If in the past the imperial and triumphant city of Rome had a coat of arms as evidence of its nobility and so that the world would recognize it as its master, drawing on it a pyramid or a single column, not with stripes, sashes, bands, flowers, eagles, castles, lions, squares or boxes, rather with the five letters of the name "Caesar," the city of Tlaxcala, as the city's coat of arms shows, as a glorious sign of its loyalty and eternal possession of its nobility inscribed the initials of three venerable names on its own: a "J" in memory of the most serene Queen Juana; a "K," which in Aramaic is the first letter of the name Carlos, the fifth of this name as Holy Roman Emperor, first both in valor and in our two Spains; and thirdly a "P," which records the three Philips who succeeded them, so that the world may know for ever more and always celebrate the fact that these most outstanding princes, with the arms of this city and with the exertions worthy of undefeated athletes and brave champions of this Republic, united such a monarchy to its empire and brought numerous provinces under its crown.[140]

---

[139] Peter Martyr d'Angleria, *Opera*, Erich Woldan (ed.) (Graz: Akademische Druck und Verlagsanstalt, 1966), 165: "Hoc primum, ut supra tetegi, democratiae partim, partim vero aristocraticae uti aliquando respublica Romana, priusquam ad violentam monarchiam deveniret, patitur proceres (uti iam dixi), dominos fugiunt. Scribit Cortesius aiuntque venientes, civitatem esse urbe Granata multo maiorem, populisque frequentiorem et rerum omnium ad victum adundantem."

[140] Francisco de Linares Urdanivia, *Oración Fúnebre*, fol. 1r–v: "Como la manifiesta el Escudo de sus Armas, que si allá la Imperial, y triunfante Ciudad de Roma, para executoria de sus proesas, y que el mundo la reconociesse señora, pautó las suyas en un pirámide, o descollada columna, no con Barras, faxas, bandas, flores, aguilas, castillos, leones, Xaqueles, ni Escaques, si con cinco caracteres, que contenían el nombre de Cesar; la Ciudad de Tlaxcala en las suyas, por gloriosa divisa de su lealtad, y padrón perpetuo de su nobleza, grava tres letras iniciales, de tres augustissimos nombres, una J. en memoria de la Serenissima Reyna Doña Juana, una K, que da principio, en el idioma / fol. 1v/ Armenico, al apellido de Carlos, por el quinto de este nombre, en el Imperio, y primero, assi en el valor, como de este cognomento en nuestras Españas; y la tercera una P. en que se recuerdan los tres Philippos sus successores, para que conosca el mundo en la posteridad, y celebre por eternas duraciones la fama, que estos preclarissimos príncipes a fuerças de las armas de la Ciudad, y a esfuerços de invictos atletas, y valerosos campiones de esta Republica, unieron tanta Monarchia, a su Imperio, sujetaron numerosas provincias a su corona."

Drawing on Theodor Zwinger's famous encyclopedia *Theatrum vitae humanae* (1565), Linares then explained how, just as Rome had lost Caesar yet still became a great power, Tlaxcala, despite losing Philip IV, could look forward to a glorious future under Charles II whose initial ("K") already appeared in its coat of arms.[141] Indeed, the Habsburgs had the advantage of being Christian monarchs in contrast to the early Roman emperors:

> We also have confidence that [the soul of] his Catholic father, our deceased monarch, has ascended to heaven, not to become a god, as some wrongly imagined Caesar did, but to enjoy the presence of God for all eternity, as a reward for the piety of his soul, for the reverence of his heart, for the firmness of his faith, for the equality of his justice, for the strength of his virtues, for the generosity of his deeds, which joined his piety and linked his prudence to the strength of his love and the example of the cult of the Empress of Heaven, the Queen of the Angels, Mary, the Mother of God, and our Lady.[142]

Therefore, Linares stressed, Tlaxcala was the New World heir to both Rome and a Jerusalem, in which its orator, the son of a Tlaxcalan "senator" (*conscripto padre*), played the role of a new Jeremiah who had to address his fellow "citizens and residents" (*republicanos y vecinos*) after the death of Philip IV, the indigenous republic's Josiah.[143] In Tlaxcala, the orator thereby seamlessly weaved together indigenous political structures, colonial privileges and models, both Greco-Roman and biblical, into a virtue-driven epideictic sermon, which provided a vocabulary to defend the interests of the *altepetl* within the Hispanic Monarchy.

[141] *Ibid.*, fol 1v: "Vizarreaba pues jactanciosa la Ciudad de Roma, con el nombre de Cesar, en su Escudo: quando emula una nube de sus dichas (que no perdonó la embidia a las menores glorias) asombrando essa vagarosa región a estrallidos, alborotando los ayres a estruendos, bostezando llamans, y respirando centellas, asertó con una a borrar la letra inicial, que es una C. dexando ilesas las quatro, que le subsiguen, y componen el termino ESAR. Apelaron los Romanos a sus Agoreros, y consultaron supersticiosos, a los oráculos, y respondieron, que semejante prodigio, y tan pasmoso portento, era presagio fatal para el mundo, y un auspicio favorable para Cesar, porque desvanecer el rayo la C. que es el numero ciento, en la arismetica, pronosticaba, que dentro de bien días moriría, como murió, el Emperador, y quedar intacto el termino ESAR, era prenuncio, que ibra a descansar con los Dioses, y a eterniçarse, como uno de ellos respecto de que fuena lo proprio, que Dios, la palabra ESAR."

[142] *Ibid.*, fol. 2r: "Quedandonos tambien las esperanças, de que su Catholico Padre, y nuestro ya difunto Monarca, subió a los cielos, no a ser Dios, como fingió aquella quimera de Cesar, si a gozar eternamente de Dios, en premio de lo piadoso de su animo, de lo religioso de sup echo, de la firmeza de su Fe, de la igualdad de su justicia, de la consistencia de sus virtudes, y de lo generoso de sus proessas, que eslabonó su piedad, y compaginó su prudencia, con lo fervoroço de su amor, lo fino de su voluntad, lo ardido de sus afectos, lo acendrado de su devoción, y lo exemplar de su culto a la Emperatriz de los cielos, a la Reyna de los Angeles MARIA Madre de Dios, y Señora nuestra."

[143] *Ibid.*, fol. 3r.

In contrast to the Spanish Netherlands where consensus could only be maintained with reminders of the legal underpinnings of royal rule and explicit references to the opportunities for institutionalized resistance, in Tlaxcala the policing of virtue was accepted as the primary means to defend the city-state's particular status. Indeed, the Tlaxcalans were seemingly so invested in the virtue-driven, negotiated system of the Hispanic Monarchy that, as we learn from Zapata, there was great rejoicing in February 1668 when a letter arrived from the Queen Regent thanking the *cabildo* for performing the *exequias*, a sign that royal favor was forthcoming to those who valued virtue and practiced loyalty.[144]

Virtue Politics and Non-imperial Spaces

In constructing their narratives of the *exequias* as technologies of political domination, Maravall and Rama concentrated on those performed in Spain and Spanish America, respectively, regions where Philip IV was monarch. However, they did not realize that almost identical ceremonies were also performed outside the Hispanic Monarchy. This included in Genoa, a satellite republic of the Habsburgs, as well as in the Papal States and the Grand Duchy of Tuscany, which were tied to Philip IV by bonds of alliance and shared interests, although conflicts did arise from time to time. These polities received no *cédulas reales* commanding them to memorialize their monarch "in the usual fashion." Instead, they voluntarily held elaborate funeral commemorations with towering ephemeral architecture, royal imagery and erudite funeral orations that celebrated their ties to the Hispanic Monarchy as allied Catholic polities and put forward an ideal of public and private behavior grounded in late humanist virtue politics around which their citizens could similarly rally. Like the *exequias* in Mexico City and Madrid, their function was primarily parenetic and expressed a desire for social cohesion. The very fact that polities like the Papal States, which had a sometimes rocky relationship with the Spanish Habsburgs, celebrated *exequias* for Philip IV definitively shows that these multisensory displays were not by default the violent technologies of class or colonial domination that they have been presumed to be, and were certainly not seen as such by local elites, artisans and intellectuals.

---

[144] Juan Buenaventura Zapata y Mendoza, *Historia Cronológica de la Noble Ciudad de Tlaxcala*, 395–396.

Instead, they were means for negotiated social improvement and the expression of collective identity within these polities, which found themselves simultaneously part of both Philip IV's "empire of influence" and his "empire of eloquence."

This "influence" was, of course, political in some sense.[145] For instance, Genoa, an independent republic headed by a Doge, had tied its fortunes to the Spanish Habsburgs since the time of Charles I and reaped the rewards. Genoese bankers had grown rich by extending loans to the crown, while the city's merchants had capitalized on privileged access to markets across the pacified western Mediterranean. As the dominant Catholic power in the region, Habsburg Spain also offered protection for its coreligionists against incursions by both the Turks and Protestant powers. In other words, the Genoese knew which side their bread was buttered on, and acted accordingly. In light of this, the funeral oration delivered in the Church of San Lorenzo by the senator and well-known orator in Latin and Italian Orazio della Torre (1620–1675) took as its structuring rationale two particularly relevant virtues of Philip IV: his piety and his dedication to securing peace.[146] Philip did not have to be monarch in Genoa to be praised as a protector of Christendom and its shared interests.[147] A Habsburg eagle above the main portal of the cathedral had other meanings beyond vassalage. The statues representing Spain, America, Flanders and Naples spreading flowers from the top of the *túmulo* did not necessarily serve as a "technology of empire" or even a celebration of political union per se. Rather it was a self-interested celebration of common aspirations and values that all Genoans could and should uphold with more than a hint of *do ut des*.

The situation was very similar in Papal Rome. Within a month of Philip IV's death, the news had reached the Spanish ambassador in the city who sent his manservant by horse to Castel Gandolfo on Lake Albano to inform Pope Alexander VII of the death of the "most Catholic monarch" (*rex*

---

[145] Lauren Benton and Adam Clulow, "Empires and Protection: Making Interpolity Law in the Early Modern World," *Journal of Global History*, 12 (2017), 74–92.

[146] Pietro Giovanni Calenzani, *Descrizione del Funerale Fatto dalla Serenissima Republica di Genova al Catolico Filippo Quarto* (Genoa, 1666), 7–8. Manuel Herrero Sánchez, "Republican Monarchies, Patrimonial Republics: The Catholic Monarchy and the Mercantile Republics of Genoa and the United Provinces," in Pedro Cardim, Tamar Herzog, José Javier, Ruiz Ibáñez and Gaetano Sabatini (eds.), *Polycentric Monarchies: How Did Early Modern Spain and Portugal Achieve and Maintain a Global Hegemony?*, 181–196.

[147] Pietro Giovanni Calenzani, *Descrizione del Funerale Fatto dalla Serenissima Republica di Genova*, fol. 1r: "la commune perdita di tutto il Christianesimo."

catholicissimus).[148] Early modern Rome was built with Spanish money, its population swelled by Spaniards, its Italian, European and global prestige bolstered by Spanish successes. This said, Rome remained a battleground for influence between the French Bourbons and the Spanish Habsburgs, which only swung back in the latter's favor in the 1650s.[149] When Philip IV died some fifteen years later, four commemorative ceremonies were organized: in the church of Santiago de los españoles by the Spanish Ambassador; in the Church of San Carlo del Curso by the Milanese nation; in the church of Santa Maria Maggiore by the canons of the same church; and by the Pope in the Pauline Chapel of the palazzo Quirinale. Like those in Genoa, these Roman *exequias* were celebrations of shared values and aspirations, which espoused behaviors that primarily served local interests, while recognizing Habsburg patronage in the city.

In Santa Maria Maggiore, the canons did not owe Philip IV political allegiance, but they did owe him a vote of thanks, as he had contributed vast sums for the Basilica's construction and upkeep. Alongside the contractual aspect of the ceremony, as the author of the festival book printed to record the event put it, the particularly rich *exequias* had a parenetic function: "so that the living might receive life from the dead, and from cold cadavers bright light might shine to break the ice of vice, which often freezes our souls, so as to make them more inclined to right action."[150] As a result, when they passed through the main entrance, which was decorated with Philip's coat of arms and skeletons representing death, visitors to Santa Maria Maggiore were greeted by a *túmulo* constructed by the famous architect Carlo Rainaldi (1611–1691). This featured a painting of Philip IV beneath a model of his crown coated in silver and shining with the light of some 1,000 white candles set against the black drapes that covered much of the Basilica's white and gold interior. Atop the vast octagonal structure was an orb with a cross on it representing Philip's efforts to spread Catholicism throughout the world. Here, the message was that Philip was no different from his Habsburg predecessors whose divinely sanctioned mission was to bring the whole world into the warm

---

[148] Antonio Pérez de Rúa, *Funeral Hecho en Roma en la Yglesia de Santiago de los Españoles à 18 de Diciembre de 1665: a la Gloriosa Memoria del Rei Catolico de las Españas Nuestro Señor D. Felipe Quarto el Grande en Nombre de la Nación Española*, 15–16.

[149] Thomas James Dandelet, *Spanish Rome, 1500–1700*, 202–214.

[150] *Relatione delle Sontuose Esequie Fatte dall'Illustriss. e Reuerendiss. Capitolo, e Canonici della Sacrosanta Basilica di S. Maria Maggiore in Roma, alla Gloriosa Memoria di Filippo Quarto, Re delle Spagne: con Alcune Osseruationi sopra i Particolari del Funerale* (Rome, 1666), 20 "che i vivi ricevano vita dai morti, e che dai freddi cadaveri escano fiamme, che distemprino il gielo de' vitii, che suole rapprendere gli animi nostri, e renderli inetti al bene operare."

embrace of Catholicism, a mission shared by the inhabitants and ecclesiastics of Rome, whether they were Spaniards or not.[151] In the Latin funeral oration, the Jesuit professor of humanities at the *collegio romano*, Ignazio Bompiani (b. 1612), also constructed an idealized image of Philip IV, which served very local interests. While the ornate decoration of the church bespoke Philip's magnificence, Bompiani told his listeners, the oration would concentrate on his magnanimity, a virtue worthy of emulation by all those present.[152] Piety combined with generosity to the Church and a willingness to give funds to this church in particular, was to their advantage and to that of Rome as a whole. By presenting an idealized image of "the most Catholic monarch," their true aim was not to bolster his temporal power in the city, but to encourage others to follow in his footsteps.

This was also reflected in the oration delivered in the Pauline chapel of the palazzo Quirinale in the presence of the Pope by Blasio Peinado de Santaella (dates unknown), canon of the church of Sacro Monte de Granada. Pontifical ritual dictated that no Latin oration could exceed 3,000 characters in length, so it was with great brevity that Philip was portrayed as the bulwark of Christianity in life and the example of Christian behavior in death.[153] The Pope had no interest in being the creature of the Spanish monarch. Instead, he wanted the papal court and the differing interests from across the Catholic world that it represented to defend the papacy, just as Philip was portrayed as having done.

Similarly, self-interest led Ferdinando II de' Medici, the Grand Duke of Tuscany – a relative by marriage of the Spanish Habsburgs – to stage funeral *exequias* in his family church, the Basilica of San Lorenzo in Florence. The Grand Duchy of Tuscany had long been closely allied to the Hispanic Monarchy and like Genoa hid behind Spanish military might. It also bordered Spanish territories. After the defeat of Siena at the hands of the Medici and Charles I in 1557, Siena's former port cities

---

[151] *Ibid.*, 7–8.

[152] Ignazio Bompiani, *Philippus Quartus Catholicus Hispaniarum Rex Magnanimus, laudatus inter Solemnes eius Exequias in Basilica S. Mariae Maioris* (Rome, 1666), 3: "Quoniam vero maiestas regitur divinitatis arbitrio et ipsa potentiae damna sunt divinae beneficia providentiae, interest quoque sapientiae temperare dolorem tum religione per hanc sacrae maestitiae umbrum splendidum et honorarium, tum recordatione quadam virtutum, quibus Rex tantus excelluit, ut qui profuit imperio dum vixit; post quam vixit, prosit exemplo."

[153] Antonio Pérez de Rúa, *Funeral Hecho en Roma en la Yglesia de Santiago de los Españoles à 18 de Diciembre de 1665: a la Gloriosa Memoria del Rei Catolico de las Españas Nuestro Señor D. Felipe Quarto el Grande en Nombre de la Nación Española* (Rome, 1666), 107: "Merito, beatissime pater, in hoc summo religionis Catholicae sacello Apostolica pietas parentat Philippo Quarto Hispaniarum Regi magno, cuius vita, et praesidium fuit Romanae fidei et Christianae virtutis exemplar."

(*lo stato dei presidi*) on the Tuscan coast and the Tuscan archipelago came under Spanish control, serving to safeguard the communication between Milan and Naples, and Spanish interests in Italy more generally.[154] As an allied state (*amicus*), Tuscany's commemoration of Philip had little to do with applying "shock and awe" tactics to repress a subject population or with making the king present.[155] He was not the King of the Tuscans, and the large Habsburg coat of arms placed above the nave of the Basilica did not have the political valiancy that has been attributed to it in Spain and the Americas.[156] Instead, Philip was an exemplary figure whose vast power had allowed him to exercise his virtues with great efficacy, something the Tuscans wished to encourage among their own elites alongside a sense of goodwill toward their powerful ally.

Habsburg interests in Italy also overlapped substantially with Tuscan interests. Although the oration delivered on this occasion by a young playwright named Mattias Maria Bartolommei Smeducci (1640–1695) does not survive, the classicizing Latin inscription that was placed above the main entrance to the Basilica gives us a sense of the virtue-driven panegyric that was delivered:

TO PHILIP IV
SON OF PHILIP III AND GRANDSON OF PHILIP II
GREAT-GRANDSON OF HIS IMPERIAL MAJESTY CHARLES I
CATHOLIC KING OF THE SPAINS AND THE INDIES, ETC.
PIOUS, JUST, CLEMENT, MAGNANIMOUS,
OUTSTANDING CULTIVATOR OF PIETY
MOST STAUNCH DEFENDER OF RELIGION
DEFENDER OF JUSTICE
CUSTODIAN OF PEACE
PURE IN FAITH AND OPEN IN HAND
TO HIS CLIENTS
AND TO HIS ALLIES

---

[154] Giuseppe Caciagli, *Lo Stato dei Presidi*, 2nd ed. (Pisa: Arnera, 1992), 60–62.

[155] *Esequie di Filippo IV. Cattolico Re di Spagna: Celebrate in Firenze dal Serenissimo Ferdinando II. Gran Duca di Toscana Descritte da Giovanni Batista Borgherini Canonico Fiorentino* (Florence, 1665), 4: "Perchè qual gente è così barbara, e per così lungo tratto di mare disgiunta dal nostro Mondo, la quale, o per titolo di vassallaggio, o per vicinanza di confini, o per conformità d'interessi, o per ragione d'amicizia, o d'altra simile aderenza, o finalmente per via di commercio non fosse in un certo modo vicina, e pronta a cogliere i frutti della Pietà, della Magnificenza, e della Magnanimità del Re, il quale con amplissimi Stati stendeva il suo dominio per entro tutte le quattro parti del Mondo? . . . Ferdinando Secondo Gran Duca di Toscana . . . quanto più egli era col morto Re per somiglianza di virtù, e per doppio vincolo di sangue, e di stretta benevolenza congiunto."

[156] *Ibid.*, 11.

WITH GENEROUS INDULGENCE
LOVING EVEN TO ENEMIES
FERDINAND II THE GREAT DUKE OF TUSCANY
THE FOREMOST SUPPORTER
OF HIS UNPARALLELED RELATIVE
AND IN PUTTING ON THESE FUNERAL RITES
ACCORDING TO HIS MERITS
HE LEAVES A SIGN OF HIS MOURNFUL AND COMPLIANT HEART[157]

Entering the Basilica, Tuscan grandees were greeted by an even longer inscription that illustrated the virtues of Philip IV, "crowned with a wreathe of virtue and might."[158] If the oration had been structured according to his biography, the attention of the audience might have been drawn to the statues and images on the *túmulo* that showed the pursuits for which he had showed particular "aptitude and affection," including horsemanship, music, painting and poetry. His nobility, the ephemeral architecture seemed to argue, did not come from his lineage alone, but was earned through his virtue and ability, and through his patronage of the arts.[159] Had the oration been structured around Philip IV's "heroic virtues," then they might have noticed that between the arches that separated the nave from the aisle, there were emblems representing his piety, his role as a defender of Catholicism and his devotion to spreading Christianity in the Americas.[160] The Florentines had no interest in

---

[157] *Ibid.*, 9:

PHILIPPO IV.
PHILIPPI III. FIL., PHILIPPI II. NEP.
IMP CAES. CAROLI I. AUG. PRONEP.
CATHOL. HISPANIAR., INDIARQ; REGI, &c.
PIO, IVSTO, CLEMENTI, MAGNANIMO,
PIETATIS CVLTORI INCLYTO,
RELIGIONIS VINDICI ACERRIMO,
IVSTITIAE CONSERVATORI,
PACIS CVSTODI,
INCORRVPTA FIDE, AC PROFVSA
BENEFICENTIA CLIENTIBUS,
A T Q U E A M I C I S
GENEROSA INDVLGENTIA VEL
PERDVELLIBUS CARISSIMO,
FERDINANDUS II. MAG. DUX ETRURIAE
AFFINI INCOMPARABILI, ET FAVT. MAX.,
AC DE SE OPTIME MERITO
EXEQUIARUM IVSTA FACIENS MOESTISS.
ET OBSEQVENTISSIMI ANIMI EXHIBET
MONUMENTUM

[158] *Ibid.*, 12–14.
[159] *Ibid.*, 37.   [160] *Ibid.*, 15–24.

inculcating loyalty to this foreign monarch. Instead, driven by pragmatic self-interest, they wanted to celebrate their role as "allies" (*amici*) of a powerful relative and neighbor, and remind elites and non-elites alike of their shared Christian and neo-Roman values. As in the Hispanic Monarchy itself, the *exequias* primarily served a morally exhortative function, celebrating personal virtue and evenhanded government. Local populations seem to have embraced the politics of virtue as their best, perhaps only hope for protection against the powerful.

Conclusion

Just as artisans sweated, furiously sewed, hammered and painted to build the towering ephemeral *túmulos* that graced the cathedrals of Philip's global monarchy, the learned clerics chosen to deliver the funeral orations and sermons in Castilian and Latin labored over piles of books, paper and ink, straining every scholarly sinew to compose suitably erudite and eloquent memorials to the king. In contrast to the traditional accounts given by Maravall and Rama, these orations and sermons were not heavy clubs to beat the local population into submission. Instead, they were multisensory celebrations, legible to the lettered and the unlettered alike, of an idealized vision of the Hispanic Monarchy's political system that left space for institutionalized resistance or "negotiation" by appealing to models of royal and personal behavior codified in epideictic rhetoric and humanist "virtue politics."

Deeply embedded in the classical rhetorical tradition as revived in the Renaissance and expressed clearly in the funeral oratory for Philip IV, virtue politics was a widely espoused political ideology, perhaps even the "default" political ideology of the Hispanic Monarchy. This has not been recognized to date partly because one of the most useful sources for analyzing the political thought of this patchwork polity, namely its funeral oratory, has remained untapped, and partly because the model of politics that it espoused was less institutional and more personal than we may be used to today. For late humanist thinkers, political virtues were personal traits, governance was very much the product of men, and justice and social harmony were not impersonal and mechanistic, but the result of individual acts of conscience. In this way, classical and Christian currents bound together the day-to-day governance of the polity with the future of the souls of the community in the next life, serving as the basis for a social contract that held together disparate and diverse peoples on five continents. As the most effective means to exhort society's leaders to virtue and local populations to hold their leaders accountable, eloquent and erudite oratory in Latin and the vernacular was the "technology of negotiation" par excellence.

CHAPTER 3

A Japanese Cicero Redivivus

On the sixth day before the Ides of May 1585, Hara (原) Martinho (*c.* 1568–1629) became a Roman. Standing in the *palazzo senatorio* overlooking the ruins of the Republican forum and surrounded by Renaissance Rome's senators and other magistrates dressed *all'antica*, Hara and the three other leading members of the Tenshō Embassy each received a certificate of Roman citizenship presented to them on a silver platter. This meant Hara could now claim membership in a guild that included Caesar, Pliny and, of course, Marcus Tullius Cicero. Yet, Roman citizenship was not the only thing that united Hara and the personification of ancient eloquence. He was also an orator, and a Latin orator at that, having received at great expense of time and labor on the part of his Jesuit teachers in Japan and Europe the Renaissance incarnation of Cicero's own education under Greek and Roman grammarians, rhetoricians and philosophers. Although born at the opposite end of Eurasia from the Eternal City, this young Jesuit humanist could nonetheless lay claim to the title of Japan's first *Cicero redivivus*, "Cicero brought back to life."

Clutching the vellum document written in Latin and weighed down with a heavy gold seal as wide as a man's palm and as thick as a finger, the embassy's most blue-blooded (although not necessarily most intellectually adept) member, Itō Mancio (*c.* 1569–1612), then expressed the Japanese ambassadors' gratitude through a translator with words that greatly impressed the listeners. It was a great honor to receive Roman citizenship, since Rome, having once held sway over a vast empire, could now lay claim to even greater glory as the capital of the Catholic world, which included lands and peoples entirely unknown to the inhabitants of the ancient Mediterranean.[1] These words, although to some extent hyperbolic, were

---

[1] *Relationi della Venuta Degli Ambasciatori Giaponesi a Roma Fino alla Partita di Lisbona: con le Accoglienze Fatte Loro da Tutti i Principi Christiani per Doue Sono Passati* (Rome, 1586), 97. Guglielmo Berchet, *Le Antiche Ambasciate Giaponesi in Italia* (Venice: Visentini, 1877), 25–26,

no doubt sincere, since the Japanese ambassadors were aspiring members of Catholicism's vanguard, the Society of Jesus.

Riding on the coattails of Iberian commercial and military expansion across the Atlantic and the Indian Oceans to the Americas, India, China and Japan, the Jesuits directed wave after wave of missionaries in all directions in the service of their single goal: the souls of all of humanity in this life and the next. Their aims thus overlapped with those of Iberia's stridently Catholic monarchies, which provided them with resources, manpower and synergistic support. This meant that the Jesuits frequently became conscious or unconscious drivers of Iberian expansion, initially in cultural and religious but ultimately also in political terms. This is not to say, however, that the Jesuits should be considered simple tools of Iberia's monarchies. Right up until its suppression at the hands of reforming monarchs and enlightened bureaucrats in the second half of the eighteenth century, the Society of Jesus remained a separate entity with its own ambitions, hierarchy and identity, independent from European political structures and with considerable autonomy even within the Catholic Church. They were, in this sense, close allies, rather than agents. Their network of colleges, seminaries and professed houses also represented a coherent, if not hermetically sealed Jesuit world both within and beyond the Iberian World, which was not only connected by a constant ebb and flow of people, goods and correspondence, but also united by shared intellectual standards, including Renaissance humanism.[2] This was the Jesuit context, frequently Iberian or Iberianizing, always Neo-Roman, and increasingly global, in which Hara and his companions moved, and which shaped their interaction with the classical rhetorical tradition.

By charting the lives and educations of Hara and his companions, this chapter will show how the Jesuits and their students (both European and non-European) used their humanist oratorical skills to push back the boundaries of Iberianized Catholicism, and thereby the Iberian World. Whereas most treatments of humanist culture in Iberian Asia specifically address its role in the genesis of the Jesuits' "accommodation" strategy (i.e. the practice of adapting Christianity to local cultural norms that drew inspiration from ancient rhetorical theory), this chapter demonstrates that the classical rhetorical tradition was also conceived of and applied by European Jesuits and their Asian students as a tool to further their

68–69. Francesco Boncompagni-Ludovisi, *Le Prime Due Ambasciate Dei Giapponesi a Roma (1585–1615)* (Rome: Forzani & Company, 1904), L–LI.

[2] Anthony Grafton, *Worlds Made by Words: Scholarship and Community in the Modern West* (Cambridge, MA: Harvard University Press, 2009), 160–175. Paula Findlen, Suzanne Sutherland Duchacek and Iva Lelková, "A Jesuit's Letters: Athanasius Kircher at the Edges of His World," forthcoming *American Historical Review*.

expansionist evangelizing mission. This was a process highly reminiscent of the "spiritual conquest" of the Americas that Robert Ricard first identified in the 1930s, the acknowledgment of which has driven the interest among Americanists in the role of missionaries in creating stable Iberianized Catholic societies.[3] In other words, this is a process that took place, *mutatis mutandis*, in both the Americas and Asia, contexts that have historically been studied separately for disciplinary and especially linguistic reasons.

As we shall see, this "spiritual conquest" was cheered on in classicizing orations that exhorted missionaries to greater acts of derring-do. Therefore, there is perhaps some merit to the older militaristic image of the Jesuit Christian soldier armed not with a sword or a matchlock, but with a humanist education, a metaphor that appears prominently in Hara's own oratory.[4] Following in Hara's footsteps, in this chapter we shall also see how the humanist curriculum was repackaged for Japanese seminarians in an effort to train a native priesthood that was Catholic, classicizing and Iberianizing, but also distinctly Japanese. Although the Jesuits' underlying aim in Japan was not large-scale territorial conquest (nor could it realistically have been, given the geopolitical reality), nonetheless for a few decades during the Renaissance Nagasaki and other parts of southern Kyūshū came to participate, albeit in a limited way, in many features of an Iberian World that crisscrossed maritime Asia. This was an Iberianizing religious expansionism that offers a parallel, but subtly different (and thereby very telling) case to compare with the Americas.

Humanism at the Arima Seminary

From Francis Xavier's arrival in 1549, the Jesuit missions in Japan had produced a particularly rich harvest of souls despite crippling financial problems, a fact that was not lost on the Jesuit *visitador*, Alessandro

---

[3] Robert Ricard, *La "Conquête Spirituelle" Du Mexique* (Paris: Institut d'Ethnologie, 1933). On Jesuit "accommodation," see John O'Malley's *The First Jesuits* (Cambridge, MA: Harvard University Press, 1993); Stephen Schloesser, "Accommodation As a Rhetorical Principle: Twenty Years after John O'Malley's *The First Jesuits* (1993)," *Journal of Jesuit Studies*, 1 (2014), 347–372. Although it is true that O'Malley contributed to the strength of the accommodation narrative and linked it firmly with Renaissance humanism, the term was already in common use among scholars of Christian missions: Johannes Thauren, *Die Akkommodation Im Katholischen Heidenapostolat; Eine Missionstheorethische Studie. Teil I. Inaug.-diss* (Münster: Aschendorff, 1926). The poster boy for Jesuit accommodation is usually Matteo Ricci, see Ronnie Hsia, *A Jesuit in the Forbidden City: Matteo Ricci 1552–1610* (New York: Oxford University Press, 2010).

[4] This view is common in Anglophone scholarship from the early modern period until about 1980, for example: Herman W. Konrad, *A Jesuit Hacienda in Colonial Mexico: Santa Lucía, 1576–1767* (Stanford, CA: Stanford University Press, 1980), 109–110.

Valignano (1539–1606). Soon after his arrival in Japan in 1579, the tall Neapolitan aristocrat conceived of the idea of a diplomatic mission that would travel from Nagasaki to Rome and back again and thereby kill two birds with one stone. First, by presenting the four noble Japanese seminarians as a "living letter" (*carta viva*) to the Pope and other European princes, he would be able to convince them of the spiritual returns of funding the Jesuits' efforts in Japan. Second, by taking these well-bred intermediaries on a tour of the flourishing cities of southern Europe, he would be able to convince the Japanese elite of the rewards of pledging loyalty to the Catholic God.[5]

When it came to finding suitable recruits, Valignano looked to the students in the recently opened Jesuit seminary at Arima, which was housed in an abandoned Buddhist monastery in the shadow of the Hinoe Castle near Nagasaki.[6] He eventually chose four students, all of them closely connected to leading Christian *daimyō*. The two principal ambassadors were to be Chijiwa Miguel (1569–1633), the cousin of Dom Protasio (1567–1612), *daimyō* of Arima and the nephew of Dom Bartolomeu (1533–1587), *daimyō* of Ōmura, and Itō Mancio who, although not directly related to Dom Francisco the former *daimyō* of Ōtomo (1530–1587), was charged with representing this most fervent of the Jesuits' protectors. To these, Valignano added two attendants, the future humanist orator, Hara whose sister had married into the House of Ōmura and whose brother seems to have been the castellan of an important fort in the Ōmura domain, and Nakaura Julião (1568–1633) who was of minor Samurai stock.[7]

When the embassy departed Nagasaki in early 1582, the Arima seminary had been open for less than two years and so the Japanese seminarians, all aged around 14, were probably only acquainted with the rudiments of Latin grammar, which they had studied alongside Japanese literature, music and Christian doctrine. The seminary was part of Valignano's grand strategy to create a trilingual clergy that could understand Christian texts in Latin and Portuguese, as well as write and preach eloquently in Japanese. This native priesthood was to make up for the

---

[5] J. A. Abranches Pinto and Henri Bernard, "Les Instructions du Père Valignano pour l'Ambassade Japonaise en Europe. (Goa, 12 Décembre 1583)," *Monumenta Nipponica*, 6 (1943), 391–403 (400).

[6] Joseph Moran, *The Japanese and the Jesuits: Alessandro Valignano in Sixteenth-Century Japan* (New York: Routledge, 1993), 12. Hubert Cieslik, "The Training of a Japanese Clergy in the Seventeenth Century," *Studies in Japanese Culture* (1965), 41–78 (44–45).

[7] J. S. A. Elisonas, "Journey to the West," *Japanese Journal of Religious Studies*, 34 (2007), 27–66 (34–35).

shortcomings of European-born Jesuits who were both few in number and usually failed so miserably at their attempts at learning Japanese that they had to rely heavily on Japanese coadjutors (*dōjuku*) as interpreters for preaching, and even for hearing confessions. The Jesuits also faced other hurdles. The long and uncertain lines of communication with the rest of Catholic Christendom meant that there were constant and chronic short-ages of funds, manpower and books. These logistical obstacles were only compounded by the unwillingness of some Europeans to countenance the idea of Japanese priests, and the aversion among many of the Japanese Christians to learning an obscure and peculiar language like Latin, prefer-ring instead to concentrate on the Jesuits' Christianized version of the Sino-Japanese humanities, which commanded greater prestige beyond the walls of the seminary.[8] Yet, Valignano was not to be discouraged and set about founding a network of seminaries and colleges in Japan, where well-bred Japanese boys were trained in both the European and East Asian humanistic traditions under the watchful eyes of their Jesuit schoolmasters.

Thanks to Valignano's penchant for writing exhaustive lists of instruc-tions on every possible topic, we can reconstruct Hara's probable early exposure to the *studia humanitatis* in the Arima seminary in some detail. A typical day for the youngest students like Hara likely involved rising at 4:30 a.m., putting on their handsome blue kimonos and white shoes (being careful always to distinguish outside wear from inside wear) and attending mass before studying lists of Latin vocabulary or basic grammar between 6 a.m. and 7 a.m.[9] Although we do not know which printed or manuscript textbooks were used by Hara and his companions, we do have copies of the schoolbooks that were printed in the decades after the return of the Tenshō Embassy, which give a sense of both the methods used in the Arima seminary and the motivations for the tremendous expenditure of time and money in training Japanese students in the European humanities.

For instance, later Japanese students building their Latin vocabulary could turn to an abridged Latin-Portuguese-Japanese version of Ambrogio Calepino's famous Latin dictionary reprinted in 1595 in the Jesuit college

---

[8] Alessandro Valignano, *Sumario de las Cosas de Japón (1583); Adiciones del Sumario de Japón (1592)*, José Luis Álvarez-Taladriz (ed.) (Tokyo: Sophia University, 1954), 170. Tadao Doi, "Das Sprachstudium der Gesellschaft Jesu in Japan im 16. und 17. Jahrhundert," *Monumenta Nipponica*, 2 (1939), 437–465 (446–450).

[9] Joseph Moran, *The Japanese and the Jesuits*, 182. Josef Franz Schütte, *Valignanos Missionsgrundsätze für Japan*, 2 vols. (Rome: Edizioni di storia e letteratura, 1951–8), I.2, 485–486.

on the islands of Amakusa off Kyūshū. In the prologue, the compiler explained the motivations behind teaching Latin to Japanese students:

> The Jesuit fathers thought it was a suitable and advantageous way to achieve this [i.e. the conversion of Japan], if they not only imbued the Japanese boys with a knowledge of orthodox Catholicism from a malleable age (since they possessed, they recognized, exceptional and outstanding talent), but also instructed them with examples of virtues and finally put them through their paces in the gymnasium of Latinity, so that they could more easily drink of the many things that flow, like from subterranean springs, from Latin books, and which are good for an upstanding life and the spreading of our faith.[10]

Latin then was not only the liturgical language and the key to accessing the concrete theological precepts needed to spread orthodox Christianity, but also opened the way for texts that would inculcate intangible standards of thinking and behavior (*integritas morum*). In practice, this meant that Hara's early exposure to Latin was intended as the gateway to a fully fledged humanist education, which wrapped models of virtuous behavior in the finely woven cloak of elegant Latin prose.

The *lemmata* included in the Amakusa dictionary also make it clear that Japanese seminarians were expected to encounter texts of a humanist nature. Although heavily abridged in comparison to European editions, the dictionary included a wide range of classical and post-classical Latin vocabulary on a variety of themes. This suggests that Japanese students were being prepared to read not just devotional works like Ignatius de Loyola's *Spiritual Exercises*, which was printed at Amakusa in 1596, but might reasonably also have expected to encounter texts on silk dresses from the island of Cos (*coa, -orum*) or tragic actors (*tragicus, -i*).[11] Furthermore,

---

[10] *Dictionarium Latino-Lusitanicum ac Japonicum ex Ambrosii Calepini Volumine Depromptum* (Amakusa, 1595), fol. 2r: "Patres Societatis IESU ... idoneam et salutarem rationem ad hunc finem consequendum arbitrati sunt, si pueros Iaponenses, in quibus egregiam quandam et praeclaram indolem esse cognoscebant, a flexibili illa aetate non solum peculiari orthodoxae fidei cognitione imbuerent, sed etiam virtutum documentis ad omnem honestatem erudirent, ac denique in latinitatis palaestra exercerent, quo facilius multa, quae et ad morum integritatem et fidei nostrae propugantionem plurimum valent, e libris Latine conscriptis tamquam reconditis e fontibus possent haurire." Although I concentrate here on use of the dictionary by Japanese students of Latin, it was also intended for Europeans learning Japanese. For a detailed comparison of the Japanese "Calepino" to European editions, see: Emi Kishimoto, "The Adaptation of the European Polyglot Dictionary of Calepino in Japan: *Dictionarium Latino Lusitanicum, ac Iaponicum* (1595)," in Otto Zwartjes and Cristina Altman. (eds.), *Missionary Linguistics II/Lingüística Misionera II: Orthography and Phonology* (Philadelphia: John Benjamins Publishing Company, 2005), 205–223.

[11] St. Ignatius Loyola, *Exercitia Spiritualia* (Amakusa, 1596). A copy is preserved in the Tōyō Bunko with a photostat copy in the Kirishitan Bunko, Sophia University, Tokyo.

the Amakusa dictionary also retained not only the single *lemmata*, but also many of the examples of usage found in Calepino's original, which were all faithfully translated into a formal Japanese. It was clearly the intention of the Jesuits that Japanese seminarians read not just more advanced Latin texts, but ones which treated topics well beyond the standard missionary fare, for which the entries under *senatus*, such as "to shut down the senate" (*senatum extinguere*) and "to promote someone to the senate" (*in senatum legere aliquem*), might have been useful.[12]

After studying vocabulary at first light, Hara would have then moved onto the second Latin class of the day between 7:30 a.m. and 9 a.m., followed by a period of recreation and further classes in music and Japanese composition in the afternoon. Students ended their day by reviewing their Latin lessons between 6 p.m. and 8 p.m. before heading to an early bed. Hara and his companions probably spent many of these late-night review sessions in the repurposed Buddhist monastery at Arima puzzling over Latin declensions and conjugations. This is suggested by the Japanese edition of Manuel Álvares' *De institutione grammatica* to which Jesuit grammarians made several important additions on the basis of their experience teaching in Japan: "so that the novices in this corner of the world do not lose heart due to the irksomeness of the foreign language."[13] The declensions of Latin nouns had clearly presented students with problems, and so the Jesuits added a section with the declined forms of the noun *dominus* glossed with the relevant Japanese particles that showed their function in the sentence.[14] Similarly, the conjugations of Latin verbs presented a challenge, so in addition to the Portuguese verbal paradigms, which had, for instance, graced the Lisbon 1572 edition, the Jesuits at Amakusa included the analogous verbal patterns of Japanese, as well as

---

[12] *Dictionarium Latino-Lusitanicum ac Japonicum ex Ambrosii Calepini Volumine Depromptum*, 125, 832, 734. Tadao Doi, "Das Sprachstudium der Gesellschaft Jesu in Japan im 16. und 17. Jahrhundert," *Monumenta Nipponica*, 2 (1939), 437–465 (450): "Was das Japanisch angeht, ist es zwar in der Schrift- und nicht in der Umgangsprache gehalten."

[13] Manuel Álvares, *De Institutione Grammatica Libri Tres. Coniugationibus Accessit Interpretatio Iapponica*, Carlos Assunção and Masayuki Toyoshima (eds.) (Tokyo: Yagi Bookstore, 2012), fol. 3v: "Cum iis, qui in Iapponia, latino idiomati operam impendunt, Patris Emmanuelis Alvari grammatica institutio necessaria sit in eaque verborum coniugationes Lusitana lingua huius insulae hominibus ignota vertantur, ne tyrones in ipso limine peregrini sermonis imperitiae taedio animum desponderent, superioribus visum est, ut (ordine quo liber ab auctore editus est, nihil immutato) verborum coniugationibus Iapponicae voces apponerentur, aliquaque scholia praeceptoribus ad latinarum et Iapponicarum loquutionum vim facilius dignoscendam maxime conducentia, attexerentur. Vale."

[14] *Ibid.*, fol. 3v: "Nominativo, Dominus, Aruji, aruiua, arujiua, ga, no, yori . . . Particulae Iapponicae, qua numero plurali latino respondent, huiusmodi sunt, Tachi, xu, domo, ra. Item eiusdem nominis repetitio, ut sitobito, cuniguni, etc."

scholia comparing Latin and Japanese tense, aspect and mood, alongside translations into Japanese of some of the examples of classical Latin usage, such as Plautus' use of the subjunctive.[15]

Humanism on Deck

With some vocabulary and the rudiments of Latin grammar under their belts, Hara and his companions boarded the black carracks that brought the *nanban* (南蛮, "southern barbarian") trade to Japan, and set sail for Europe to visit the Pope in Rome. They were not, of course, to make this journey alone. Valignano accompanied them as far as Goa, from where their safety and education was entrusted to a small entourage, including a young Jesuit named Diogo de Mesquita (1553–1614) who was to act as their Latin tutor, and three Japanese attendants, including the Japanese Christian brother (*irmão*) Jorge de Loyola (1562–1589) who was to instruct them in Japanese during their time away.[16] There were also several slaves on board, including a Japanese slave named Damião (d. 1642) who belonged to the ship's captain, Ignácio de Lima (dates unknown).[17] During the multiple voyages over two and half years that it took to reach Europe, when the conditions on board permitted they kept a similar routine to that of the seminary in Arima with regular prayers, litanies and study.[18] As one of the Japanese interlocutors described it in the dialogue, *De missione legatorum Iaponensium ad Romanam curiam* (1590), drafted by Valignano and then translated into Latin by the able humanist Duarte de Sande (1547–1599) to preserve the story of the embassy for later generations of Japanese seminarians:

> If there were tempests and storms, the voyage passed with difficulty and the hardest labor. However, if the sea was flat and the wind favorable, there were many distractions to while away the hours. We ourselves passed the time by applying ourselves to Latin, playing our musical instruments,

[15] *Ibid.*, fols. 12v–52r (fol. 16v): "Hae voces praesentis temporis (Dearŏca? Iyŏzuca?) cum interrogatione sunt pronunciandae Plaut. Amph. *Vir ego tuus sim?* Vareua nangiga votto dearŏca?"

[16] Diego Pacheco, "Diogo de Mesquita, S. J. and the Jesuit Mission Press," *Monumenta Nipponica*, 26 (1971), 431–443 (431–432). Duarte de Sande, *Japanese Travellers in Sixteenth-Century Europe: A Dialogue concerning the Mission of the Japanese Ambassadors to the Roman Curia (1590)*, J. F. Moran (trans.), Derek Massarella (ed.) (London: Routledge, 2012), 50, n. 2.

[17] Lúcio de Sousa, *The Portuguese Slave Trade in Early Modern Japan: Merchants, Jesuits and Japanese, Chinese, and Korean Slaves* (Boston: Brill, 2019), 466–467.

[18] Pedro Frois, *La Première Ambassade du Japon en Europe*, J. A. Abranches Pinto, Yoshitomo Okamoto, Henri Bernard (eds.) (Tokyo: Sophia University, 1942), 23–24.

fishing for a variety of fish and losing ourselves in conversations with our fellow travelers, without forgetting of course the usual prayers to God and the saints.[19]

Despite initial bouts of severe seasickness, which affected all the boys except Itō who heartlessly laughed at his companions' misfortune, they continued to make headway in their studies.[20] With each of the boys following essentially a personalized version of the humanist curriculum, they all progressed to at least what the later *Ratio studiorum* (1599) would call the "humanities class." This prescribed the reading of longer extracts from good classical and contemporary authors, and the production of eloquent prose and verse based on the best models, a skill that would then be perfected in the "rhetoric class," which Hara, the most precocious of the four, may have reached during the voyage.[21]

As humanist eloquence had a practical application in their newfound role as ambassadors, Mesquita set them composition exercises with this end in mind. He instructed Hara to compose and memorize a Latin oration to be delivered to the Jesuit Superior General in Rome, while he charged Itō, the more senior member of the delegation, with producing a shorter oration for the Pope. Hara seems to have accomplished this with relative ease and with little outside assistance, whereas Itō's oration required some corrections when they arrived in Évora, either because he was less able than Hara or because any oration delivered before the Pope had to be of the very first water.[22] It is also possible that the boys were

---

[19] Duarte de Sande, *Diálogo Sobre a Missão dos Embaixadores Japoneses à Cúria Romana*, Sebastião Tavares Pinho and Américo da Costa Ramalho (eds.), 2 vols. (Coimbra: Imprensa da Universidade de Coimbra, 2009), I, 129: "Tempus navigationis, si tempestatibus et procellis sit infestum, difficile et cum summo labore transigitur. Si tamen adsit serenitas et secundorum ventorum flatus, multa sunt quibus navigantes distineri possunt, quo minus aegre temporis diuturnitatem ferant. Quod praecipue nobis usu venit, nonnumquam linguae Latinae operam dantibus, interdum instrumenta musica pulsantibus, denique non raro piscatu variorum piscium, sive dulcissima aliorum vectorum consuetudine animos relaxantibus, non tamen solitis ad Deum divosque precibus omissis." On Duarte de Sande and *De missione*, see Charles Burnett, "Humanism and the Jesuit Mission to China: The Case of Duarte de Sande (1547–1599)," *Euphrosyne*, 24 (1996), 425–471.

[20] *Diálogo Sobre a Missão dos Embaixadores Japoneses à Cúria Romana*, I, 59, 61.

[21] "Ratio atque Institutio Studiorum Societatis Iesu [1599]," in *Monumenta Paedagogica Societatis Iesu*, Ladislaus Lukács (ed.), 5 vols. (Rome, 1965–1986), V, 355–454 (430–433).

[22] Pedro Frois, *La Première Ambassade du Japon en Europe*, 24: "e fizerão bom progresso no Latim conforme a penuria do tempo: Dom Martinho se poz a compor hũa oração em Latim, e depoes a decorar para a ter diante de nosso Padre Geral, e Dom Mancio fez outra mais breve, que hum Padre nosso lhe emendou depões em Evora em algũas palavras, e como tem muito boa memoria, e habilidade, a tem ja quasi estudada para a recitar diante do Papa." Unfortunately, there is not mention of Martinho delivering this oration when they met the General: *Relationi della Venuta Degli Ambasciatori Giaponesi a Roma Fino alla Partita di Lisbona: con le Accoglienze Fatte Loro da Tutti i Principi Christiani per Doue Sono Passati*, 80–81.

charged with composing Latin epistles, a common exercise in the early stages of any humanist education and a skill that Itō and Chijiwa would apply in the decades after the return of the embassy when writing letters to the Pope from the college at Amakusa.[23]

We also know that by this stage the Japanese boys had a good understanding of Latin poetics, since during the voyage Mesquita set Chijiwa and Nakaura the task of composing epigrams in praise of His Holiness.[24] Although not absolutely necessary to perform the liturgy or to read theology in Latin, versification was intrinsic to the *studia humanitatis*, and this was no less the case in Japan than elsewhere. After having learned the principles of Latin prosody in the Arima seminary, perhaps from the third book of Álvares' grammar that treated syllable length as well as poetic feet and figures, while on board the boys probably moved on to reading passages of classical or Christian poets.[25] Indeed, this attention to both prose and poetry seems to have been a constant feature of Jesuit education in Japan. Although Chijiwa and Nakaura's epigrams do not survive, we do have a later example composed by Gotō Miguel (dates unknown), a student of the Arima seminary who later found himself exiled to the Philippines alongside numerous other Japanese Christians, and whose four elegiac couplets were included in the prefatory material to an Ilokano *Doctrina Christiana* printed in Manila in 1621. If we are to judge from this later example, Chijiwa and Nakaura probably produced competent verses of the sort that any Jesuit seminarian in the Iberian World would have been proud:

> As the golden light expels the dark shadows with its brilliance,
> And kindly cherishes all things in its warm embrace,
> So this book frees minds from murky ignorance,
> And with a divine fire moves sluggish hearts.
> So arise, Ilocanos, if you wish to glimpse the light,

---

[23] ARSI, Jap. Sin. 33, fols. 38r–67v. Other contemporary Latin epistles by Japanese seminarians are edited in: Akihiko Watanabe, "Diego Yūki no 1615-nen 8 tsuki 2 hidzuke Kuraudio akuavu-ĩvu-a ate shokan (ARSI Jap. Sin. 36. 245 R. - 246 V.): Ratengo genbun to chūkai" (ディエゴ結城の1615年8月2日付クラウディオ・アクアヴィーヴァ宛書簡(ARSI Jap.Sin. 36.245r.-246v.): ラテン語原文と注解), *Otsuma Journal of Comparative Culture* 大妻比較文化 : 大妻女子大学比較文化学部紀要, 14 (2013): 94–112; *ibid.*, "Neo-Latin in 17th Century Japan: Two Epistles from Japanese Seminarians to the Jesuit Superior General (ARSI Jap. Sin. 75, 78)," *Japan Studies in Classical Antiquity*, 2 (2014), 137–154. Professor Watanabe also informs me that there are further letters of Itō preserved in the Archivio Segreto Vaticano in Rome.

[24] Pedro Frois, *La Première Ambassade du Japon en Europe*, 24: "os outros tres fizerão cada hum seo epygrama em louvor de S. Santidade."

[25] Manuel Álvares, *De Institutione Grammatica Libri Tres*, fols. 137v–170v.

And desire to kindle your cold breasts with flames.
If you take up this book, read it day and night,
It will be a light and flame for you forever.[26]

Humanist Education in Renaissance Japan

As Mesquita's floating humanist school bobbed its way across the Indian Ocean, the four Japanese seminarians studied longer Latin texts and eagerly read whatever they could get their hands on during their hours of recreation to pass the time in the featureless maritime landscape. For students who had advanced beyond basic grammar and shorter introductory texts, the traditional humanist curriculum prescribed the reading of the best authors of antiquity. However, like Tertullian before him, Valignano was deeply concerned about the effects of exposing his recruits to the heritages of both Jerusalem and Athens. In Europe, Christianity had grown up in the shadow of the Roman Empire with its high regard for pagan eloquence and philosophy, so these were naturally intrinsic to a Christian education in Spain, Portugal and Italy. In contrast, in Japan the pagan classics were much less necessary or desirable. Since Aristotle and Cicero were not names to conjure with, so Valignano reasoned, they might have to be excluded in order to obviate the risk that the views of pagan philosophers (which were, he thought, dangerously reminiscent of Buddhism) might lead the Japanese into heresy. The picturesque world of Roman religion was also to be hidden from the Japanese seminarians, lest they be attracted to paganism and vice. As a result, in his instructions for Mesquita he made it abundantly clear that on no account should they bring back from Europe works by Ovid or Virgil, which might arouse in

---

[26] Reproduced in: Hiroshi Harada, *Kirishitan Shisai Goto Migeru no Latengo no Shi to Sono Insatsusha Saisho Migeru wo Megutte* キリシタン司祭後藤ミゲルのラテン語の詩とその印刷者税所ミゲルをめぐって (Tokyo: Kindaibungeisha, 1998), 13:

"In commmendationem Libri Epigramma de D. Miguel Goto Xapon Sacerdote.
　　Aurea lux veluti caecas fulgore tenebras
　　　　Pellit, et alma suo cuncta calore fovet:
　　Sic liber hic mentes caligine liberat atra,
　　　　Igneque divino frigida corda movet.
　　Ergo age gens Illoca, cupis si cernere lucem
　　　　Et tepidum flammis urere pectus aves
　　Si capis, hunc legito noctesque, diesque libellum
　　　　Hic tibi perpetuo lux erit, ignis erit."

Later students in the Jesuit seminaries in Japan also copied Latin poetry, for example: *Compendium Catholicae Veritatis*, 3 vols. (Tokyo: Sophia University, 1997), I, fols. 430r–431r.

the Japanese seminarians an unhealthy interest in Venus and the sins of Dido.[27] As we shall see, however, while the humanist education of Hara and later Japanese students reflected these concerns, it nonetheless embraced many classical Latin authors, including some initially deemed dangerous by Valignano.

In truth, we do not know which books Mesquita packed for his students, whether from the seminary at Arima or from his own personal library.[28] Yet, if we are to judge from Valignano's choice of textbooks for the Japanese seminaries printed in Macau after their return, Hara and his companions were not entirely shielded from pagan antiquity. Instead, they were fed on a diet of expurgated, but always eloquent classical and humanist culture, similar to the fare served up in Jesuit schools in Europe, where the mandate of the later *Ratio studiorum* that most classical authors were permitted "only if they are purged of all obscenity" held sway.[29] For example, if we peruse the 1588 Macau edition of Juan Bonifacio's *Christiani Pueri Institutio*, first printed in Salamanca in 1575, we find that, although some of the longer poetical extracts had been removed and the sections showing the moral character of animals redacted, it retained essentially the same pious excerpts from Scripture, as well as patristic, classical and humanist authors as its earlier editions. This included an extract from a letter from the Florentine humanist Angelo Poliziano (1454–1494) to Pico della Mirandola (1463–1494) on the literary talents of a young member of the Orsini clan, and another from Cicero's *De senectute* regarding the Spartans' respect for their elders. Even the long extracts from authors that Valignano had explicitly condemned were retained, including Horace, Juvenal and even Ovid.[30] Indeed, it

---

[27] Alessandro Valignano, *Sumario de las Cosas de Japón (1583); Adiciones del Sumario de Japón (1592)*, 171–172. Josef Wicki (ed.), *Documenta Indica*, 18 vols. (Rome, 1948–88), XIII, 761–762.

[28] The Jesuits were careful to supply all their missions with books, and as early as 1554 transferred collections from Goa to Japan, a shipment, which included devotional books, the works of Plato, Aristotle's Ethics and a herbal: *Documenta Indica*, III, 201–205. On the earliest Jesuit books in Japan, see Jesus Lopez-Gay, "La Primera Biblioteca de los Jesuitas en el Japón (1556). Su Contenido y su Influencia." *Monumenta Nipponica*, 15 (1959), 350–379. For the cases of China and Ethiopia, see Noël Golvers, *Libraries of Western Learning for China: Circulation of Western Books between Europe and China in the Jesuit Mission (ca. 1650–ca. 1750)* (Leuven: Leuven University Press, 2012); Kristen Windmuller-Luna "*Guerra com a Lingoa*: Book Culture and Biblioclasm in the Ethiopian Jesuit Mission," *Journal of Jesuit Studies*, 2 (2015), 223–247.

[29] "Ratio atque Institutio Studiorum Societatis Iesu [1599]," in *Monumenta Paedagogica Societatis Iesu*, V, 355–454 (430): "modo sint ab omni obscaenitate expurgati."

[30] Juan de Bonifacio, *Christiani Pueri Institutio (1588): Fac-simile da Edição (Existente na Biblioteca da Ajuda) do Mais Antigo Livro Impresso Pelos Missionários Europeus na China* (Lisboa: Centro de Estudos do Livro e da Edição, 1988). Shinzo Kawamura, "Humanism, Pedagogy, and Language: Alessandro Valignano and the Global Significance of Juan Bonifacio's Work Printed in Macao

seems that the passages chosen for European youth, already selected for their moralizing character, were suitable examples of good Latinity for Japanese Christians and required little modification.[31]

The four boys were probably also encouraged to keep commonplace books with passages from texts they had read, arranged according to subject headings, which would be easily accessed and applied in their compositions. These manuscripts have, of course, long since vanished, but if they were anything like the commonplace book, entitled *Flosculi ex veteris ac novi testamenti, Sanctorum Doctorum et insignium philosophorum floribus*, printed at the Jesuit college in Nagasaki in 1610, they contained memorable phrases from scripture, the Church Fathers, notable Christian authors and "from outstanding men both Greek and Latin" (*ex viris illustribus tam Graecis quam Latinis*). Naturally, this final category was probably more expansive in the later printed work than in Hara's commonplace book, since access to classical authors was probably limited during the voyage. However, later Japanese students composing their declamations could certainly choose from *dicta* by a vast array of classical authors, including Cicero, Seneca, Valerius Maximus, Virgil, Demosthenes, Plautus, Ovid, Horace, Lucan and Caesar.[32]

All this said, despite having much in common with Jesuit education in other parts of the Iberian World and beyond, the humanist curriculum in the Arima seminary was, by its very nature, restricted. In Europe and the

---

(1588)," in *O Humanismo Latino e as Culturas do Extremo Oriente* (Treviso: Fondazione Cassamarca, 2006), 143–155. Cf. Juan de Bonifacio, *Christiani Pueri Institutio* (Salamanca, 1575).

[31] Juan de Bonifacio, *Christiani Pueri Institutio (1588)*, 45v–47v, 144r–145v. In the sixteenth century, Poliziano was a popular intermediate-level author in schools and universities: Alejandro Coroleu Lletget, "Angelo Poliziano in Print: Editions and Commentaries from a Pedagogical Perspective (1500–1560)," *Cahiers de l'Humanisme*, 2 (2001), 191–222.

[32] *Flosculi ex Veteris ac Novi Testamenti, S. Doctorum et Insignium Philosophorum Floribus Selecti per Emanuelem Barretum Lusitanum Presbyterum Societatis IESV (Nagasaki, 1610)* (Tokyo, 1978), fol. iir ("Autor ad lectorem"): "Si aliquando, prudens religioseque lector, aureum illud opus, quod flores Bibliae appellant, diligenter attenteque legisti, facillimo quidem negotio iudicabis sententias omnes in hoc opusculo contentas ad sacram paginam spectantes iuxta vulgatam editionem fideliter correctas fuisse. Quanta vero diligentia id factum fuerit ex numeris, qui post capita adiecti sunt, aliqua ex parte cognosces. Numeri autem quanto adiumento sint ad omnia, quae optaveris, brevi et sine ulla difficultate reperienda, nemo est, qui ignoret. Ordinem etiam librorum tam veteris, quam novi testamenti, quoad fieri potuit, servavimus, ne longa alicuius sententiae inquisitione defatigareris, multumque in eo temporis aliquando sine fructu consumeres. Vale, et hoc nostro qualicumque labore fruere." On Barreto, see Josef Franz Schütte, "Christliche Japanische Literatur, Bilder und Druckblätter in einem Unbekannten Vatikanischen Codex aus dem Jahre 1591," *AHSI*, 9 (1940), 226–280 (233–236). On European commonplace books, see Ann Moss, *Printed Commonplace Books and the Structuring of Renaissance Thought* (Oxford: Clarendon Press, 1996), 186–207.

Americas, seminarians could easily acquire the full texts of Cicero's philosophical works or Ovid's *Metamorphoses*, which circulated in cheap
editions. In Japan, such things were simply not available. This was, of
course, not without its advantages from a missionary perspective, since any
interest in Pythagoreanism or the deities worshiped in ancient Rome
sparked by reading the *Christiani pueri institutio* would have been impossible to pursue. The Jesuits could therefore be safe in the knowledge that
when in the 1590s they printed a selection from the works of Virgil for use
in the seminaries, there was no chance that their students could have access
by other means to the more problematic books of the *Aeneid* and the
Eclogues.[33]

Whereas Valignano was probably keen to exclude Cicero's philosophical
works for their accounts of Stoicism and Epicureanism, he nonetheless
ultimately agreed with the authors of the *Ratio studiorum* who considered
Cicero "the only model of oratory," and so essential for the upper echelons
of the Latin classes in Japan as well.[34] Similarly, Hara and his companions
probably read, recited and analyzed several of Cicero's orations in their
seaborne humanist classroom, perhaps with the help of a basic introduction to rhetoric, like Cipriano Soáres' *De arte rhetorica* (1562), or simply
with Mesquita as their guide to the orations' important linguistic, historical and rhetorical features.[35] As Cicero's orations were simultaneously
indispensable for a humanist education and largely free from heretical
ideas, Hara and his companions may have also had a chance to read them
in some of the fine editions that were produced in the period, which are
known to have circulated in Asia.[36] Around 1592 Valignano also had the
Japanese mission press produce an edition of Cicero's orations. As no copy

[33] Biblioteca da Ajuda, Lisbon, 49-IV-59, fol. 10: "imprimiose mais de nossa letra hum livro de
interiore domo de São Bernardo com as suas meditacoens e tambem hum Virgilio para os
estudantes do seminario por perecer o numero delles, e haver falta de livros de humanidade."

[34] "Ratio atque Institutio Studiorum Societatis Iesu [1599]," in *Monumenta Paedagogica Societatis Iesu*,
V, 355–454 (426): "De primo satis dictum est regula prima; unus enim Cicero ad orationes, ad
praecepta praeter Ciceronem Aristoteles adhibendus est."

[35] *Ibid.*, 430: "Gradus huius scholae est, postquam ex grammaticis excesserint, praeparare veluti solum
eloquentiae; quod tripliciter accidit: cognitione linguae, aliqua eruditione, et brevi informatione
praeceptorum ad rhetoricam spectantium ... Divisio temporis haec erit. Prima hora matutina
memoriter recitetur M. Tullius et ars metrica apud decuriones."

[36] This is suggested by from the presence of a 1578 Venetian folio edition of Cicero's orations in the
former Jesuit seminary, now St. Joseph's Seminary, Macau. Nothing is known of its provenance,
although the title page bears the name "Jose Maria d'Oliveira e Lima" in a later hand. The only
discussion of this volume is: Helen Ieong Hoi Keng, "An Exploration of Documents from Catholic
and Buddhist Sources in Macao Libraries," *Revista de Cultura (Macau)*, 5 (2003), 6–25 (18). On the
seminary itself, see Michael Hugo-Brunt, "The Jesuit Seminary and Church of St. Joseph, Macao,"
Journal of the Society of Architectural Historians, 15 (1956), 24–30.

survives, it is impossible to say for certain which orations were deemed
suitable for a Japanese student to study, although, as we shall see, Hara
almost certainly knew *Pro Archia*, which was also one of the dozen or so
orations most commonly read by students in Renaissance Europe.[37]

Jesuit Eloquence in Europe

After a voyage of over two and a half years, the carrack *cum* humanist
school finally rounded the Cape of Good Hope and successfully docked in
Lisbon. Unable to accompany them after receiving instructions from the
Superior General to stay in Goa, Valignano had left strict instructions that
the boys be greeted without excessive ceremony as they passed through the
Iberian Peninsula and on to Rome. This directive was largely respected at
the court of Philip II in Madrid, although by the time they reached Italy,
Valignano's directive seems to have been forgotten.[38] However, this over-
sight was an unexpected boon for Hara, as the diplomatic pomp and
circumstance in papal Rome and elsewhere allowed the budding
Japanese humanist to see fantastic displays of humanist acrobatics within
their full ritual context. No longer were elegant Latin periods and carefully
constructed figures merely the stuff of his small, isolated seminary in Japan
or Mesquita's academy on the high seas. At last, Hara could see the
application of this powerful persuasive tool in its full glory.

   This was nowhere more the case than in Rome itself. After a triumphal
horseback procession through the streets of the city followed by a 300-gun
salute at Castel Sant'Angelo, the ambassadors, in full Japanese dress and
carrying Japanese swords and daggers, were guided through the Apostolic
Palace by an entourage of bishops and archbishops to the *sala regia*, a space
usually reserved for meeting kings and emperors. After the boys had paid
homage to the Pope, letters from the leading Christian *daimyō* were read
out in Japanese then translated into Italian. Then, a Portuguese Jesuit
arose and began his elegant Latin offensive.[39] Here, it is important to
remember that eloquent Latin oratory from the mouth of a diplomat, or an
"orator" (*orator*) as they were called in this period, was an essential part of

---

[37] Biblioteca da Ajuda, Lisbon, codex 49-IV-56, fol. 143v. "Ratio atque Institutio Studiorum
   Societatis Iesu [1599]," in *Monumenta Paedagogica Societatis Iesu*, V, 355–454 (430).
[38] Printed accounts of their passage through the capitals of Europe are collected in: Adriana Boscaro,
   *Sixteenth Century European Printed Works on the First Japanese Mission to Europe: A Descriptive
   Bibliography* (Leiden: Brill, 1973).
[39] Nakaura was not present, as he was gravely ill: Duarte de Sande, *De Missione Legatorum
   Iaponensium ad Romanam Curiam* (1590), II.457–471.

diplomatic ritual. These orations also served a practical purpose beyond the requirements of ritual and courtesy, namely to set the tone for later more in-depth negotiations and to clothe in subtle and elegant words the aims of the embassy.[40] Given these pressures, the original plan to have Itō deliver the oration was abandoned. The Latinity and delivery had to be flawless, and Itō was probably not quite up to the task. Neither was Hara, but for reasons of protocol. As a mere attendant, he could only sit on the steps of the papal throne rather than at the Pope's side during the following days' ceremonies. Instead, Gaspar Gonçalves (1540–1590), a humanist, theologian and lawyer who had accompanied them from Portugal, was chosen to bear the oratorical burden. Luckily for the embassy, Gonçalves was an expert in the sort of rhetorical heavy lifting required for such a role. Frequently asked to deliver orations for the arrival of dignitaries and to give his opinion on pressing canonical matters, like the status of marriages between *índios* in Brazil, Gonçalves represented the peak of scholastic and humanistic learning that the Society of Jesus so prized.[41]

In the midst of all this pageantry, Gonçalves delivered an oration that aimed to move first the heart and ultimately the purse strings of the Pope. They had not come so far and at such expense on a courtesy call. Rather, this was an opportunity to present the Jesuits' efforts in Japan in the most positive light and move the listeners who included not only the Pope but also the cream of the curia to offer financial and institutional support for their missionary efforts. To this end, much of the oration consisted of a careful panegyric of Japan and the embassy, before subtly moving into an exhortation to send more money to the Japanese mission.

Confident that the cause he was upholding was respectable (*honestum*), Gonçalves got straight to the point (*principium*), as classical rhetorical theory demanded, and for the sake of clarity structured his *exordium* around the subject of the oration (*de re*), Japan itself.[42] Since this archipelago on the other side of the Eurasian landmass was largely unknown to

---

[40] Garrett Mattingly, *Renaissance Diplomacy* (London: Jonathan Cape, 1955), 38–39, 236–237; Raphaële Mouren, "La Rhétorique Antique au Service de la Diplomatie Moderne: Piero Vettori et l'Ambassade Florentine au Pape Jules III," *Journal de la Renaissance*, 1 (2000), 121–154; Brian Maxson, *The Humanist World of Renaissance Florence* (Cambridge: Cambridge University Press, 2014), 85–106.

[41] Gonçalves' extensive production is preserved in numerous manuscripts in Portugal and Italy, which are partly listed in: Friedrich Stegmüller, *Filosofia e Teologia nas Universidades de Coimbra e Évora no Século XVI* (Coimbra: Universidade de Coimbra, 1959), 57. To these can be added: Hispanic Society of America, New York, ms. HC411/53, fols. 149r–150r (*Oratio ad eundem [legatum Petrum da Sylva]*), 154r-176 (*Dialogus qui inscribitur Gloria*). The early Jesuits did not see any contradiction between "humanism" and "scholasticism": John O'Malley, *The First Jesuits*, 226.

[42] Cipriano Soáres, *De Arte Rhetorica Libri Tres* (Madrid, 1597), 93–96.

the audience, the Jesuit orator took care to describe its location, painting a picture of a land that abounded with cities and civilized and sophisticated inhabitants who lacked nothing, except, of course, the word of God.[43] As the oration continued, the arrival of ambassadors from this distant corner of the world was repeatedly couched in the most common *comparatio minorum* in Jesuit humanist oratory delivered in and about Asia: The extent of ancient Roman military power was nothing compared with the influence of Renaissance Rome as the capital of a triumphant global Catholicism.[44] Comparing the Tenshō Embassy to the delegation sent by the Indian King Poros to Augustus in the first century CE, Gonçalves declared:

> Rome once thought herself fortunate during the reign of Caesar Augustus, since under his rule, the name and reputation of the Roman empire was extended so far and wide that some people in India were so impressed by its magnitude that they sent ambassadors to seek her friendship. But go on, compare that delegation from India to this one from Japan, if you like! Has it not travelled farther? In order even to reach India, it had first to traverse the great distance from Japan to Macau, then to Malacca, before finally arriving in India, and only then traveling on to Portugal and faraway Spain so that it might reach Pope Gregory in Rome after a full three years spent traveling across land and sea.[45]

As well as being quantitatively greater, the journey of the Japanese ambassadors was also qualitatively more impressive. Not only had the Japanese boys, unlike the ancient "ambassadors," undertaken their journey for the sake of the true religion, but the Pope could rightly claim that he has

---

[43] *Acta Consistorii Publice Exhibiti a S.D.N. Gregorio Papa XIII Regum Iaponiorum Legatis Romae, Die XIII Martii MDLXXXV* (Rome, 1585), 7: "Iaponiorum insulas tanto locorum ac marium intervallo a nostris regionibus natura disiunxit, ut tenuissimo nominis vestigio paucissimis ante cognitas, cetera omnibus ignotas, nunc etiam nonnulli, ut esse credant, vix adduci posse videantur. Sunt tamen, Pater Beatissime, et sunt numero multae, magnitudine amplissimae, urbibus frequentes, hominum ingeniis ac militaribus studiis usque adeo praestantes, ut qui eas viderunt, ceteris illius caeli regionibus longe antecellere, nostris vero ut comparari possint, nihil illis aliud quam religionem, qua carebant, ac verae fidei lucem deesse credant."

[44] Cipriano Soáres, *De Arte Rhetorica Libri Tres*, 38–39.

[45] *Acta Consistorii Publice Exhibiti a S.D.N. Gregorio Papa XIII Regum Iaponiorum Legatis Romae, Die XXIII Martii MDLXXXV*, 8–9: "Beatam se quondam ac felicem Caesare Augusto imperatore Roma esse credidit, quod eius principatu Romani imperii nomen ac fama, longe adeo lateque propagata erat, ut eius amplitudine commoti nonnulli Indiae populi, amicitiae compondendae gratia legatos ad Caesarem destinassent ... Sed age, iam legationem illam Indorum cum hac Iaponensium legatione, si placet, conferamus. Erat illa quidem ex remotissimis terrarum oris, at haec quanto ex remotioribus? Cum longissimo primum tempore ex Iapone ad Sinarum portus, inde ad auream Chersonesum, mox in Indiam veniendum fuerit, ut ex India tandem in Lusitaniam navigari, ex Lusitania vero, Hispania quam longa est, peragrata, toto triennio partim in itinere, partim in navigatione posito, Romam ultimo ad Gregorium Pontificem Maximum posset perveniri."

surpassed Augustus in that they had come not merely in a spirit of friendship, but one of obedience.[46] Here, we also find the martial metaphors so beloved of the Jesuits used to describe the Pope's efforts in Asia: "today in their country they willingly admit defeat at the hands of the invincible arms of the Roman faith, which is Christian and Catholic, as soon as they glimpse the conquering standard of Christ sent forth at Gregory's command."[47] Furthermore, this victory for Catholicism in Asia was not only a source of pride for an expansionist Church, but also acted as a salve for Catholicism's open wound, the loss of large parts of Europe to Protestantism. Indeed, the acquisition of this territory in Asia more than made up for the loss of minor European possessions. The trivial island of Britain could be forgotten now that the Catholic Church held sway among the numerous islands, kingdoms and peoples of Japan.[48]

As the oration developed, the motivations behind this extended panegyric of the mission became even clearer. In yet another *comparatio minorum*, Gonçalves declared that if great princes were like the sun shining the light of their beneficence (*beneficentia*) into the deepest recesses of their kingdoms, then the Pope was the greatest prince, since his beneficence was not confined to Italy, Hungary, Germany or Greece, but reached beyond China and India to far-off Japan. This support, he argued, came in the form of the Pope's financial contributions to the seminaries in Japan. It was for this reason that the embassy had traveled so far: to give thanks to

---

[46] *Ibid.*, 11: "Enimvero philosophum nescio quem, hominem alioqui vanissimum, tamen ob insignem discendi cupiditatem longinqua peregrinatione suscepta, quantum adeo omnis antiquitas mirata est, quantum omnis posteritas commendavit? Intravit ille Persas, pertransivit Caucasum, Albanos, Scythas, Massagetas (ut Hieronymi verbis dicam) et opulentissima Indiae regna penetravit, ut Hiarcham in throno sedentem aureo, inter paucos discipulos de natura, de siderum motu, de dierum cursu docentem audiret. Magnum et inusitatum sed tamen inutile ac vanum unius hominis discendi studium. At in his quanto admirabilior religionis amor, quanto fidei cupiditas ardentior, quibus hac una de causa tanto longinquior suscepta est peregrinatio." *Ibid.*, 9: "Amicitiam a Romanis Indi ut socii flagitabant, non obedientiam offerebant, foedus ab imperatore quasi pares, non tamquam a superiore vivendi leges postulabant."

[47] *Ibid.*, 9: "illi in suis hodie regionibus victricia Christi signa Gregorio duce explicata intuentes, invictissimis se armis Romanae fidei, hoc est Christianae ac catholicae, superatos esse libentissime confitentur."

[48] *Ibid.*, 9–10: "Et quidem quod ad Ecclesiam attinet, multum illa quondam suae felicitate ac gloriae accessisse existimavit, cum Gregorii Magni temporibus Sanctissimi illius Pontificis industria ac opera amplissimam Angliae insulam, et toto, ut ait ille, divisos orbe Britannos, ad Christi fidem adiunctos esse vidit, sed quantum illo pontifice gloriae unius insulae accessione acquisisse videbatur, tantum suis ornamentis illius postea defectione detractum esse maerebat. Sed ecce tibi alterius Gregorii diligentia ac felicitate summa (ne quid illa suae gloriae deesse doleat) unius insulae loco insula altera, immo vero insulae plures ac regna, et toto a nobis orbe, toto mari divisae gentes magno numero ad Ecclesiam accesserunt, ut praeterito illo damno, quod sane fuit maximum, non minore fortasse lucro, spe vero etiam maiore cumulatissime compensato, pristinum animi maerorem novo gaudio et incredibili ecclesiae totius iucunditate levare liceat."

the Pope for his generosity and in the hope that, as "new legions of soldiers would spring up from these seminaries daily," more would join the faith thanks to the Pope's beneficence.[49] The final periodic sentence of the oration with its interlaced subordinate clauses, then promised that:

> Thus, soon it will happen, Holy Father, that, with the Almighty listening to the prayers of your Holiness and supporting the works of this humble Society of ours, you will hear that not just a few Japanese cities have taken on the Christian faith, not just a few kingdoms (which we offer you today as the first fruits of the fertile field) have done so, but such a large number of kingdoms, of which that region is filled, and such multitude of people that they cannot be counted, have done so.[50]

The Pope, as Gonçalves portrayed it, need only give his blessing to the Jesuits and their victory was assured. This was a tempting prospect for a counterreformation Church that was only just coming to terms with the rise of Protestantism in Northern Europe. While the Pope and the cardinals listened, the erudite and eloquent Jesuit tried to convert their admiration for the embassy and the missions in Japan so skillfully glorified in his panegyric into a desire to act and direct funds to Valignano's ambitious plans in Japan. In this grand diplomatic ritual, humanist oratory from the mouth of a learned Jesuit thus became a vehicle for bolstering the Jesuit cause in Asia in Catholicism's heartland. This is a mantle Hara would later take up.

Homeward Bound

Although the Japanese seminarians begged to be allowed to stay in Rome to complete their education at the *collegio romano*, their Jesuit mentors heeded Valignano's instructions and pressed on with the return journey. Passing through Venetian and Genoese territory, they returned to the Iberian Peninsula, visiting the great Jesuit center at Évora, before embarking at Lisbon to begin the long return journey to Japan. After an unplanned delay in Mozambique due to unfavorable winds, the delegation finally arrived in Goa, the capital of the *estado da Índia*, in late May 1588, where, as Itō described in his Latin epistle to Sixtus V, they were reunited

---

[49] *Ibid.*, 15–17.
[50] *Ibid.*, 16: "Ita brevi futurum est, Pater Beatissime, ut Deo Optimo Maximo Sanctitatis tuae votis et minimae Societatis nostrae laboribus favente, non iam paucas Iaponis urbes, non regna pauca (quae tibi hodierna die quasi quasdam fecundissimi agri primitias offerimus), sed plura alia, quibus amplissima illa regio distincta est, et tantam hominum multitudinem, quae numero facile comprehendi nequeat, ad Christi fidem audias accessisse."

with their patron, Valignano.[51] In Goa, they were housed in the recently completed Jesuit College of St. Paul, the foremost center of humanist learning in Asia where generations of Jesuit missionaries destined for Japan or China completed their training. It was here, where around a decade before Valignano himself had established St. Paul's first rhetoric class and Matteo Ricci had taught Demosthenes' *First Philippic* in the college's short-lived Greek class, that Hara would publicly show his gratitude to Valignano in a Latin panegyric.[52] This was, however, not only an opportunity to massage the Neapolitan's ego, or for Hara to showcase his considerable progress in the *studia humanitatis*.[53] It was also an occasion to exhort his fellow students to reaffirm their commitment to extending the reach of Iberianized Catholicism. Like all academic oratory, the form and content of Hara's oration was to some extent predictable. In this sense, it was no different from the annual panegyrics for the *santa rainha* at Coimbra, or the orations for the inauguration of the academic year at every college and university in the Iberian World.[54] However, this does not mean it did not serve a serious purpose, containing as it did a powerful call to action.

[51] Duarte de Sande, *Diálogo Sobre a Missão dos Embaixadores Japoneses à Cúria Romana*, II, 703. Itō's epistle is very reminiscent of Martinho's later oration: ARSI, Jap. Sin. 33, fol. 38r–v.

[52] *DI*, X, 718–719; XII, 152; Josef Wicki, "Zum Humanismus in Portugiesisch-Indien des 16. Jahrhunderts," in *Studi sulla Chiesa Antica e sull'Umanesimo: Studi Presentati nella Sezione di Storia Ecclesiastica del Congresso Internazionale per il IV Centenario della Pontificia Università Gregoriana, 13–17 Ottobre, 1953* (Rome: Universitatis Gregorianae, 1954), 193–246; Duarte de Sande, *Diálogo Sobre a Missão dos Embaixadores Japoneses à Cúria Romana*, II, 705: "MICHAEL: non defuerunt nobis solitae bonarum artium exercitationes iucundaque et commoda vitae oblectamenta, quibus tempus illud breviter labi nobis visum est ... MANCIUS: inter honestas literariasque exercitationes numerare possumus eam, quam suscepit Martinus noster orationem quandam de nostra navigatione et eius fructibus latino sermone elaborate compositam coram patre visitatore et ceteris colegii Goënsis venuste et eleganter habens. MARTINUS nescio an velis, charissime Manci, diurnitatem huius colloquii istis veluti salibus aspergere, meamque in dicendo insultatem irridere. IULIANUS nequaquam id de Mancio credendum est, manifestum sit testimonium."

[53] Martinho's authorship of the oration has been questioned: Michael Cooper, *The Japanese Mission to Europe 1582–1590: The Journey of Four Samurai Boys through Portugal, Spain and Italy* (Folkestone: Global Oriental, 2005), 145–147, 187; Joseph Moran. *The Japanese and the Jesuits*, 186–188; Diego Pacheco, "Diogo de Mesquita, S. J. and the Jesuit Mission Press," *Monumenta Nipponica*, 26 (1971), 431–443 (440). However, Martinho composed Latin orations both before and after delivering the panegyric of Valignano, so it is perfectly within the realms of possibility that he was largely responsible for the composition of this oration. This is not to deny that it may have benefited from some polishing at the hands of others. My view echoes that of Akihiko Watanabe, "Hara Maruchino no Varinyāno Raisan Enzetsu: Koten Juyō no Ichirei toshite" (原マルチノの ヴァリニャーノ礼讃演説 ―古典受容の一例として―), *Otsuma Journal of Comparative Culture* 大妻比較文化: 大妻女子大学比較文化学部紀要, 13 (2012): 3–19.

[54] Charles Burnett, "Humanism and the Jesuit Mission to China: The Case of Duarte de Sande (1547–1599)," *Euphrosyne*, 24 (1996), 425–471 (433).

Delivered in the church of St. Paul's College in Goa, Hara's classicizing oration had a suitably classicizing setting. Entering through a portal in the shape of a Roman triumphal arch set in a facade decorated with pairs of composite orders and geometric designs, the listeners were presented with an interior painted so gleamingly white, it was said, that a single candle was enough to illuminate all three barreled vaults, which soared over the Manueline naves.[55] Borrowing an image from Seneca's *De beneficiis*, Hara's *exordium* too reworked classical material for contemporary ends:

> Not without due cause, most reverend father, the ancients left to posterity that image of the Graces fashioned to show them with joyful faces and linked hands, dancing with each other in turn in a circle. By means of this image, those most learned and high-minded mortals sought to emphasize two laws above all, which must be observed in giving and receiving favors, namely that the givers should have a smile on their faces and once the favor has been received, the recipients must then immediately return the favor with interest.[56]

This pagan mythological imagery, which had clearly not been entirely hidden from the young Japanese seminarian during his education, offered a model of behavior for Hara and his companions. Indeed, Valignano had shown them such favor that the only way they could adequately repay him ("return the favor with interest") was if they admitted that they owed more to him than to their parents "from whom we received life and spirit."[57] Valignano's namesake, Alexander the Great, who would appear again in the *peroratio*, provided a further classical *exemplum* that both raised

---

[55] Cesar Guillen-Nuñez, *Macao's Church of Saint Paul: A Glimmer of the Baroque in China* (Hong Kong: Hong Kong University Press, 2009), 33–44; António Nunes Pereira, *A Arquiectura Religiosa Cristã de Velha Goa: Segunda Metade do Século XVI – Primeiras Décadas do Século XVIII* (Lisbon: Fundação Oriente, 2005), 175–180.

[56] Hara Martinho, *Oratio Habita a Fara D. Martino Iaponio, suo et Sociorum Nomine, cum ab Europa Redirent ad Patrem Alexandrum Valignanum Visitatorem Societatis IESU, Goae in D. Pauli Collegio Pridie Non. Iunii Anno Domini 1587* (Tokyo: Yushodo Booksellers, 1978), fol. 10v: "Non immerito, reverende admodum pater, veteres celeberrimam illam gratiarum picturam posteris ita effigiatam reliquerunt, ut praecipuam in earum vultu hilaritatem ostenderent et implexis manibus chorum ad se invicem redeuntium exhiberent: qua icone sapientissimi mortales et alta quadam mente praediti duas potissimum leges innuere voluerunt, quae in conferendis et accipiendis beneficiis observari debent, ut et conferentium vultus hilares sint, et post acceptum beneficium cum usuris gratiarum ii, qui acceperunt, quam primum revertantur." Cf. Seneca, *De Beneficiis*, I.3.2–5.

[57] Hara Martinho, *Oratio Habita a Fara D. Martino Iaponio*, fol. 10v: "Beneficium tu quidem in nos contulisti ita magnum et excellens, ut eius ponderi et magnitudini hac sola ratione satisfacere posse videamur, si tibi uni longe maioribus nominibus quam ipsismet parentibus, a quibus vitam et spiritum accepimus, obligatos nos esse fateamur."

Valignano to the position of Aristotle, the Macedonian conqueror's teacher, and offered the listeners another model of virtuous conduct:

> What is more, if Alexander of Macedon declared that he owed no less to Aristotle, to whom he had been given to be educated as a child, than to his father Philip, since although his father had given him life, his teacher had taught him how to live, how much more just is it then for us to confess frankly our gratitude to you who chose us in particular to join the embassy to that part of the world, where, by channeling the laws of good living and piety as if from their source, that undeveloped nature given to us by our parents could flower into something more beautiful, refined and polished?[58]

What had begun as a panegyric of Valignano quickly revealed itself to be a panegyric of the Jesuit evangelizing project in Asia that the Visitor had spearheaded, and the happiness that Hara described Valignano displaying at their return in the rhetorical figure of *chiasmus* ("you would not want to hide if you could, nor could you if you wanted to") morphed into joy at the onward march of Christianity and its Jesuit missionaries.[59]

The more expert among his audience might also have recognized another feature of classicizing oratory that Hara employed to urge on his fellow Christian soldiers: quantitative prose rhythm (*numerus*). In antiquity, this had been an essential part of formal public speaking. Although the rules for rhythmic prose were less strict than for poetry, certain combinations of long and short syllables, especially at the end of phrases (*clausulae*) were considered the most effective way to communicate certain sentiments.[60] As Cicero had explained in his dialogue *De oratore*:

> All people are accordingly moved, not only by carefully arranged words, but also by prose rhythm (*numerus*) and the sound of the orator's voice. How few are those that understand the science of rhythm and metrics! Yet, if in

[58] *Ibid.*, fol. 10v–11r: "Enimvero si Alexander ille Macedonum imperator Aristoteli, cui puer informandus traditus fuerat, non minus se quam patri Philipo debere affirmabat, quod a patre vivendi, a praeceptore bene vivendi initium accepisset, quanto nos maiori iure decet hanc erga te ingenuam grati animi confessionem usurpare, qui nos potissimum ad eam orbis partem cum legatione abire voluisti, ex qua et bene vivendi legibus et pietatis observandae normis tanquam e fonte delibatis, rudis a parentibus natura data, longe pulchrior, humanior ac limatior, evaderet."

[59] Ibid., fol. 11r: "Sed gaudes tandem proculdubio, pater amatissime, quatuor his filiis felicissime receptis atque ita guades, ut hanc animo tuo exundanti laetitiam nec possis dissimulare, si velis, nec velis, si possis." Cipriano Soáres, *De Arte Rhetorica Libri Tres*, 183–185 (under *conduplicatio*).

[60] In antiquity, prose rhythm was largely based on the length of syllables with word stress, and perhaps even pitch, also playing minor roles: W. Sidney Allen, *Accent and Rhythm: Prosodic Features of Latin and Greek* (Cambridge: Cambridge University Press, 1973), 86. The best account of ancient prose rhythm remains: Adolf Primmer, *Cicero Numerosus. Studien zum Antiken Prosarhythmus* (Vienna: Bohlau, 1968).

these matters the smallest offence be given by an actor, so that any sound is made too short by contraction or too long by extension, whole theatres burst into uproar. Does not the same thing also happen in the case of musical notes, so that not only whole groups and bands of musicians are turned out by the multitude and the populace for varying one from another, but even single performers for playing out of tune?[61]

With the wholesale revival of classical rhetoric and oratory in the Renaissance, this stress on quantitative prose rhythm returned, although in a slightly modified form, since vowel quantity was no longer a feature of spoken Latin.[62] As Soáres explained, *clausulae* normally consisted of two or three feet (four to nine syllables), for which choreos [-u] or spondees [--] were particularly suitable, as well as double choreos (called dichoreos) [-u-u], *dochmii* [u--u-], or cretics [-u-], which might be duplicated or combined with anapests [uu-].[63] In the face of this intimidating array of possibilities, Soáres consoled his readers that:

> However, this ability to speak properly and according to the rules of prose rhythm is not as much work as it appears. Nor is it treated by the leading men in such a way that an oration, which must be well received and flow, grows torpid by counting feet and weighing syllables. Rather, what an orator requires is practice to be able to speak properly and in rhythmic prose extemporaneously.[64]

This was advice that Hara seems to have taken to heart. Like many of his Jesuit-educated contemporaries, he made liberal use of the famous Ciceronian *clausula* -uuu- (*esse videātur*), which appears a total of five times in the oration. Like Gonçalves who ended his first sentence with this *clausula*, Hara underlined the purpose of his oration, namely to show gratitude to Valignano, by framing it within two such figures:

---

[61] Cicero, *De Oratore*, III.196: "Itaque non solum verbis arte positis moventur omnes, verum etiam numeris ac vocibus. Quotus enim quisque est qui teneat artem numerorum ac modorum? At in eis si paulum modo offensum est, ut aut contractione brevius fieret aut productione longius, theatra tota reclamant. Quid, hoc non idem fit in vocibus, ut a multitudine et populo non modo catervae atque concentus, sed etiam ipsi sibi singuli discrepantes eiciantur?"

[62] Ronald G. Witt, *In the Footsteps of the Ancients: The Origins of Humanism from Lovato to Bruni*, 509–514; Eduard Norden, *Die Antike Kunstprosa: vom VI. Jahrhundert v. Chr. bis in die Zeit der Renaissance*, 2 vols. (Berlin: Nabu Press, 1915), II, 763–809; Juan María Núñez González, "Las cláusulas métricas Latinas en el Renacimiento," *Latomus*, 53 (1994), 80–94.

[63] *Ibid.*, 250–251.

[64] *Ibid.*, 265–256: "Haec autem facultas apte atque numerose dicendi, non est tanti laboris quanti videtur. Nec ideo haec tractantur a summis viris, ut oratio, quae ferri debet ac fluere, dimetiendis pedibus, ac perpendendis syllabis consenescat. Satis enim in hoc oratorem formabit multa scribendi exercitatio, ut ex tempore etiam apte numeroseque dicat."

You did us such a great and exceptional favor that we can only seem to do justice to its magnitude if we admit that we owe more to you alone than to our very parents, from whom we received life and breath.

Beneficium tu quidem in nos contulisti ita magnum et excellens, ut eius ponderi et magnitudini hac sola ratione satisfacere posse videamur (-uuu–), *si tibi uni longe maioribus nominibus quam ipsismet parentibus, a quibus vitam et spiritum accepimus, obligatos nos esse fateamur* (-uuu–).[65]

This was by no means the only time Hara used prose rhythm to add weight to a certain phrase, or to nod to the more expert in his audience, showing a preference for many of the same *clausulae* as the leading orator of the day in Rome, Marc-Antoine Muret (1526–1585).[66]

Important passages also featured other related sorts of rhetorical features. For instance, in order to praise the selfless efforts of the Jesuits in bringing the true faith to Japan, Hara made very clear the depths of superstition into which the Japanese had sunk. This he clothed in an *amplificatio de definitionibus conglobatis* in the form of a *tricolon abundans*, which with its increasing number of syllables in each clause swells the Jesuit missionary efforts to heroic proportions:

you have taken us from darkness into the light (8)
    from slavery to freedom (10)
        at once from ignorance to knowledge of the true faith (23).[67]

To rescue the Japanese from eternal damnation, Valignano, their spiritual father in their new post-baptismal lives, had entrusted their education to the Society of Jesus whose regimented program of prayer and study in the Arima seminary then took on almost heroic proportions. Rather than just schoolmasters, the Jesuits were for Hara like the proverbial "Spartan nursemaids" so sought after in Athens who like their ancient predecessors

---

[65] Hara Martinho, *Oratio Habita a Fara D. Martino Iaponio*, fol. 10v.

[66] Although Martinho's oration is too short to constitute a statistically significant corpus, nonetheless if we apply the widely used "internal method of comparison," we find a preponderance of evidence that he was applying prose rhythm with a similar degree of frequency as his contemporary, Marc-Antoine Muret: Hans Aili, *The Prose Rhythm of Sallust and Livy* (Stockholm: Almqvist & Wiksell international, 1979), 30–50; Miller Stanley Krause, "Prose Rhythm in the Orations and Epistles of Marcus Antonius Muretus" (Masters Thesis, University of Kentucky, 2009).

[67] Hara Martinho, *Oratio Habita a Fara D. Martino Iaponio*, fols. 11v–12r: "Iacebamus paucos ante annos et quidem /fol. 12r/ errorum caligine sepulti misere iacebamus depravatae legis superstitioni mancipati et aeternae perfitionis laqueis irretiti, cum tu citra menita nostra solo amore ductus miserrimam sortem nostram miseratus a caligine in lucem, a servitute in libertatem, a perfidia nos subito in verae fidei cognitionem vendicasti." Cipriano Soáres, *De Arte Rhetorica Libri Tres*, 46–47.

brought up their charges under a regime of iron discipline.[68] Like nurse-maids too, the Society of Jesus eventually had to give its Japanese charges back to their mother, a rather apt analogy that allowed Hara to interweave seamlessly the narrative of the Tenshō Embassy and these classical comparisons, since Rome as the seat of the Roman Catholic Church was "mother" to the new Christians in Japan, just as Valignano was their father.[69]

Hara then prepared the listeners for the ornate descriptions of papal Rome and the Jesuit professed house with a *captatio benevolentiae*, a feature more usually found in *exordia*. Asking Valignano's pardon for rejecting the bombastic language of the "orator," Hara vowed to employ the modest language of a "grateful witness to your kindness," and to give a "bare and artless account" of the Eternal City. This served to ingratiate the far from artless orator with his audience and to magnify the grand imagery that was to come.[70] For instance, he described their meeting with the Pope with an elaborate *comparatio minorum* with the meeting between the Queen of Sheba and Solomon. While Solomon had merely had servants, the Pope had the kings of Europe at his beck and call; Solomon's liberality to the Queen of Sheba was so inferior to that of the Pope that one might speak of the futility of comparing the human with the divine. The Japanese humanist then deployed a Roman example, only quickly and mercilessly to strike it down with another *comparatio minorum*: Cineas of Thessaly may have reported to Pyrrhus that the Roman Senate was like a council of kings, but the Japanese would learn that the College of Cardinals was like a heavenly host brought down to earth when compared to mere mortal monarchs.[71]

---

[68] *Ibid.*, fol. 12r: "Itaque nos primum sacro baptismatis lavacro renasci voluisti renatosque statim nutrici omnium officiosissimae, id est, almae Societati Iesu alendos instruendosque tradidisti atque ad hoc ab Europa saepe illam in Iaponem remotissimam toto orbe insulam evocasti, ut quemadmodum nutrices Lacedaemonias, quod caeteras in orbe foeminas in filiis educandis doctrinae ratione ac severitate antecellere credebantur, remotissimae gentes evocabant, ut earum disciplinae filios suos a primis incunabilis nutriendos, informandosque committerent, ita plane hanc venerabilem Societatem quae in animarum educatione caeteris facile palmam praerripere videtur, ab remotissimis terrarum partibus per inmensa marium spatia in Iaponem disiunctissimam insulam vel ut verius dicam alterum orbem enocatam nobis tanquam nutricem evigilantissam adhibuisti."

[69] *Ibid.*, fol. 13r.

[70] *Ibid.*, fol. 13r: "Postulabat hic locus, pater reverendissime, vim oratoris in dicendo maximam, ut quae nobis in hac longissime peregrinatione memoratu digna contigerunt, venuste eleganterque composita tuis auribus inculcarentur. Verum cum hic ego non tam oratorem agam, quam tuorum erga nos beneficiorum gratum professorem, dabis mihi hanc veniam, si quae dixero (dicam vero paucissima) non tam verborum prae se tulerint apparatum, quam nudam atque simplicem narrationem." Cf. Cipriano Soáres, *De Arte Rhetorica Libri Tres*, 90–91.

[71] *Ibid.*, fol. 14r–v.

This panegyric of papal Rome was, of course, not complete without mention of the Jesuit professed house. This time, however, it was not greater than any ancient institution. Rather, Hara compared it to the tree of Nebuchadnezzar, which "in height reached the heavens and in width the very edges of the earth, and due to the beauty of its leaves, the little birds of the sky merrily played on its branches, and with its superabundance of fruit, it fed all the creatures of the earth."[72] Like the vast tree described in the book of Daniel, the professed house in Rome reached up to heaven, from where it received its divine support and stretched to the ends of the earth. On the branches, there sung not birds but angels. The leaves with which it shaded the world were the leaves of virtue. Its fruit was so sweet that all lost souls were attracted to it and it satiated them and dispelled the hunger of their depravity.[73]

It was no wonder then, Hara argued, that kings and popes rushed to support this arboreal religious order. But what was truly astonishing was that despite its already vast dimensions it was growing:

> However, what amazed us in it was that it was not content with the dimensions it had already reached. So, sprouting new shoots every day, it grows taller and promises even more fruit in the future. When I consider the cause of this, it strikes me that it must be because it has running water (*aqua viva*) at its feet, which assists and nourishes it. What say you? Does the Society of Jesus not have Claudio Aquaviva (*Claudium Aquam Vivam*) in Rome as its General, by the plentiful waters of whose virtue and wisdom it sprouts forth new foliage and fruit?[74]

---

[72] *Ibid.*, fol. 16r: "proceritate sua caelum et latitudine terminos universae terrae contingeret ac propter foliorum pulchritudinem aviculae caelestes in ea festivissime luderent, fructuum vero exuberantia pasceret omnes terrae animantes."

[73] *Ibid.*, fols. 15v–16r: "Vidimus Roma nam illam domum quam vocant professam ubi primum Societas, tanquam arbor seminata, in tantam magnitudinem excrevit, ut iam illam Nabuchodonosor arborem et viriditate frondium et pomorum suavitate ac brachiorum longitudine et robore longe vincat. Nam si mi- /fol. Vii r/ rabilis illa propterea visa est Assyriorum regi, quod et proceritate sua caelum et latitudine terminos universae terrae contingeret ac propter foliorum pulchritudinem aviculae caelestes in ea festivissime luderent, fructuum vero exuberantia pasceret omnes terrae animantes; quis iam non videat Societatis in his omnibus praestantiam et excellentiam? Quae quantum divini amoris vi ad caelum usque atque adeo ad ipsum Deum extollitur, tantum amore proximorum ad ipsos orbis terrarum fines dilatatur. Virtutum vero folia tam gratam prae se ferunt ac tam viridem pulchritudinem, ut caelestes volucres, id est, Angeli in eius ramis non sine iucunditate consideant, ut suavissimos cantus certatim emodulentur. Iam doctrinae fructus ita exundat, ut et perditissimi homines longa scelerum fame enecti, plenissime satientur et ceteri pietatis ac virtutum amatores ad eius exemplum tanquam ad umbram gratissimam reficiantur." Cf. Daniel 4:8–9.

[74] *Ibid.*, fol. 16r–v: "Illud vero nobis in ea valde mirabile visum est, quod non ea magnitudine contenta, in quam excrevit, novis quotidie incrementis propagata vigeat ac fructum longe maiorem in posterum polliceatur. Et quidem huiusce rei causam mihi rimanti ea potissima visa est, quod aquam vivam ad pedem habet, qua continenter fo- /fol.16v/ vetur et irrigatur. Quid? Non

Despite its great dimensions, covering large parts of Europe, the Americas and Asia, the Society of Jesus had even greater ambitions, which it had the means to achieve, thanks to the nourishing presence of the General of the Order in Rome. Yet, although Aquaviva nourished the tree at its roots, growth was impossible without the Jesuit fathers themselves who brought the Christian message to all corners of the globe, thereby building a Jesuit Empire on which the sun never set:

> While the sun cannot illuminate us and the antipodes at once, the Society of Jesus casts its rays everywhere and shines a bright light even on us who occupy the other side of the world from Europe. This is the bright light of the fathers themselves who are the torchbearers of the Society.[75]

Seemingly overcome with joy at the prospect of the onward march of these Christian crack troops, Hara launched into a feverish praise of the missionaries being trained in Europe, imitating, as Akihiko Watanabe has noted, Cicero's exaltation of literature in his oration *Pro Archia*:

> [Hara] The vast and famous colleges are full, full too are the many professed houses, made rich and noble by their vows of poverty, full finally are the seminaries, which can all be observed and studied with the eyes, but in their dignity cannot be described or comprehended.
>
> [Cicero] Books are full of it, full too are the views of the philosophers, full also are the examples from history, which would never see the light of day, if they were not written down.[76]

Having clearly read and inwardly digested one of the most commonly studied of Cicero's orations, Hara was able to stand on the shoulders of the Roman statesman when building a balanced sentence with anaphora

---

Claudium Aquam Vivam praepositum generalem Romae habet, cuius virtutum ac sapientiae uberrimis aquis et nova frondium ac fructus ubertate pullulat?" Cf. John 7:38: "qui credit in me sicut dixit scriptura flumina de ventre eius fluent aquae vivae."

[75] *Ibid.*, 16v: "Itaque undique floret Societas sancta, undique tota lucida est et eximio Divini Solis, hoc est, Iesu Christi, a quo nomen accepit, splendore circum vestita unde fit, ut splendidior sit, splendore huius Solis, quem videmus. Iste quidem quo latius effunditur, eo magis infringitur; at societas quo longuis propagatur, eo lucidior efficitur. Ille nobis et antipodis simul lucere non potest; haec ubique suos spargit radios, ac nobis etiam qui adversa Europae vestigia urgemus mirabilem splendorem elargitur: splendorem inquam clarissimorum patrum, quibus ornata fulget."

[76] Discussed in: Akihiko Watanabe, "Hara Maruchino no Varinyāno Raisan Enzetsu: Koten Juyō no Ichirei toshite" (原マルチノのヴァリニャーノ礼讃演説 —古典受容の一例として—), *Otsuma Journal of Comparative Culture* 大妻比較文化：大妻女子大学比較文化学部紀要, 13 (2012): 3–19 (7–8). Hara Martinho, *Oratio Habita a Fara D. Martino Iaponio*, 16v: "Plena sunt collegia amplissima et celeberrima, plenae domus professorum multae ac ipsa paupertate nobiles ac divites, plena denique seminaria, quae omnia conspici ac lustrari possunt oculis, dici vero et excogitari pro dignitate non possunt." Cf. Cicero, *Pro Archia*, 14: "Sed pleni omnes sunt libri, plenae sapientium voces, plena exemplorum vetustas, quae iacerent in tenebris omnia, nisi litterarum lumen accederet."

(*repetitio*) of "full" (*plena*) within a *tricolon*.[77] In doing so, he was also appealing to the humanist connoisseurship of his audience whose ears would have pricked up when they heard this echo of a phrase that many of them had no doubt recited from memory in a Jesuit schoolroom.[78]

Cutting himself short in the typical self-aware fashion of a humanist orator, Hara brought his panegyric of the Society of Jesus to an end with a prayer that God might favor the Jesuits, leading into a series of exclamations typical of classicizing oratory:

> O glorious Society! O noble encampment of pious men! O guiding star of the Church! O well drilled battle line of forces! How the impious heretics cower in fear, how the terrible Styx dreads you, how the Tartarus trembles, that foul home to all the Furies![79]

After martial metaphors of the sort that appear again and again in Jesuit oratory, Hara returned to Valignano as he brought his panegyric to a close. Just like his panegyrics of Rome and the Society of Jesus, the final exhortatory *peroratio* was directed equally to Valignano and to the hordes of aspiring Jesuits who sat behind the tall Neapolitan aristocrat in the long nave of the college church. Idolatry was on the verge of defeat, and the Japanese and European seminarians need only follow their heroic general into battle to be assured of victory:

> That Alexander who was given the epithet "the Great" due his power, after he subdued a part of India, admiring the areas he had conquered by force of arms, that great general of noble bent is said to have wept. For Anaxagoras asserted that there was another world which no warrior could ever reach, a task for which even Alexander felt himself inadequate. Yet you, Alessandro, not merely "great" but far greater than the great one, have conquered and subdued almost all of India with the arms of Christ. Now Japan stands before you; it will not be easily brought to heel except by an Alexander. So now advance into Japan with the great army of almost heavenly warriors that you command; take the province by divine force; lay it low with virtue; rip our oppressed homeland from the hands of the savage enemy and restore it to true liberty! The Japanese call out to you and long for you, the wind is

---

[77] Cipriano Soáres, *De Arte Rhetorica Libri Tres*, 181–182.

[78] "Ratio atque Institutio Studiorum Societatis Iesu [1599]," in *Monumenta Paedagogica Societatis Iesu*, V, 355–454 (430): "Prima hora matutina memoriter recitetur M. Tullius et ars metrica apud decuriones."

[79] Hara Martinho, *Oratio Habita a Fara D. Martino Iaponio*, 16v–17r: "Hic iam mihi quoniam longius progredi dicendo non possum, exclamare ex intimis praecodiis liceat. O Societas gloriosa! O nobile pietatis contubernium. O lucidum ecclesiae iubar! O castrorum acies ordinatissima! Quam fidei deser- /fol. 17r/ tores impii verentur, quam styx horrenda extimescit, quam Tartarus ipse furiarum omnium sedes taeterrima exhorrescit."

at your back, the seas are calm, the doors are open; see, beloved father! Do not delay! *Marchons!*[80]

As Hara well knew, in humanist rhetorical theory, the peroration of a short panegyric oration need not rehearse the foregoing arguments (*enumeratio*). Instead, its full force could be applied to "opening the floodgates of eloquence" (*amplificatio*) to move the hearts of any remaining doubters in the audience.[81] With the image of Alexander the Great before them, Hara's listeners were to fall in line behind Valignano and lay siege to paganism's remaining citadels in Japan. This final *comparatio*, then, shows Jesuit academic oratory as more than ivory tower eloquence; it was a powerful megaphone to amplify the battle cries of expansionist Catholicism.

Whereas it has rightly become conventional to push back against the view of Protestant polemicists that the Jesuits were the Pope's crack troops who marched under the orders of their "general" in Rome, it is clear that militaristic language was not antithetical to Jesuit discourse either.[82] Indeed, Valignano in Hara's harangue was nothing less than a new Alexander commanding a multiethnic Jesuit "army" (*exercitus*) set on the conquest *cum* liberation of Japan. However, this is not to say that such martial metaphors were necessarily the result of an inbuilt Jesuit military tradition stretching back to Ignatius' soldiering days. Rather, they were partly necessitated by Hara's choice of the comparison with Alexander the Great, as well as an expression of the value attached to military exploits in the Iberian World and in the premodern world more broadly. Indeed, they may also have been a nod to the Japanese side of Hara's bicultural outlook. Elite culture in Sengoku-era Japan was equally if not more militaristic than

---

[80] *Ibid.*, fol. 17v: "Alexander ille, cui cognomen ex potentia magnus fuit, posteaquam partem aliquam Indiae subegit, cum cetera suis armis pacata circumspiceret, asserente Anaxagora, mundum esse alium, ad quem penetrare armatus nequaquam posset, illachrymasse dicitur, generosae mentis imperator, quod imparem se illo mundo opugnando sentiret. Indiam tu quidem fere totam o Alexander non iam magne, sed illo magno longe maior, Christi armis victam et pacatam habes. Nunc orbis ille Iaponius tibi restat; non facile expugnabitur, nisi ab uno Alexandro; transiens ergo in Iaponem magno cum exercitu tantorum ac paene caelestium militum quibus divinitus praees, expugna Provinciam divinis armis, vince beneficiis, assere ex atrocissimi inimici manibus in veram libertatem oppressam patriam nostram. Iaponii te vocant ac desiderant, arrident venti, maria tranquilla sunt, patent portus, eia Pater amatissime, rumpe moras omnes, proficiscamur." It was actually Anaxarchus who told Alexander about the Atomists' theory of multiple worlds: Plutarch, *De Tranquillitate Animi*, 4.

[81] Cipriano Soáres, *De Arte Rhetorica Libri Tres*, 138: "At hic, si usquam totos eloquentiae aperire fontes licet: hic denique efficiendum est oratori, ut non modo auditores qui sua sponte se dante, et quo impellit ipse, inclinant atque propendent, penitus incitentur, sed ut quietos etiam et languentes possit vi oratoris permovere."

[82] John O'Malley's *The First Jesuits*, 45.

in early modern Europe, such that the Jesuits were always keen to make sure Christianity was associated with military success.[83] For Hara, a vassal of the House of Ōmura (a military dynasty in constant conflict with neighboring *daimyō*), Alexander's exploits were therefore probably an attractive and natural frame of reference in which to couch his exhortation to missionary zeal.

Jesuit Eloquence in East Asian Languages

After a year spent in Goa, the embassy continued its return journey, finally arriving back in Japan in July 1590, almost eight and a half years after its initial departure. However, since then the prospects of Christianity in Japan had taken a turn for the worse. Not only had Dom Bartolomeu and Ōtomo Sōrin, the *daimyō* who had protected the Jesuits in Japan's changing political landscape, died, but Oda Nobunaga, the leading *daimyō* in the archipelago, had also died and been replaced by Toyotomi Hideyoshi (1537–1598) who on St. James' Day 1587 had officially banished the Jesuits from Japan. Although this banishment was not strictly enforced, never again would the Jesuits have the freedom to reap the same vast harvest of souls.

In the years following his return, Hara continued on his path to becoming a Jesuit, and in September 1608 he was finally ordained alongside his companions Nakaura Julião and Itō Mancio. The notable absence from this ceremony was the fourth member of the embassy, Chijiwa Miguel, who in 1603 had apostatized and would later die an adherent of Nichiren Buddhism. As a result, Chijiwa was the only one of the four to remain in his homeland after the final proscription of Christianity in 1614 in contrast to the other two surviving ambassadors who were either forced into exile, in the case of Hara, or into hiding, like Nakaura Julião who would later face arrest, torture and eventual martyrdom.[84]

Hara, however, with his skills in Japanese, Portuguese and Latin, was too valuable to be left to receive a martyr's crown. Between his return from the embassy and departure for Macau in late 1614, he taught Latin grammar to Japanese novices in Nagasaki where he also served as an ecclesiastical notary and labored on translations into Japanese of important

---

[83] Reiner H. Hesselink, *The Dream of Christian Nagasaki: World Trade and the Clash of Cultures, 1560–1640* (Jefferson, NC: McFarland, 2016), 3–4. On military culture in medieval Japan, see Stephen R. Turnbull, *The Samurai: A Military History* (New York: Routledge, 1977).

[84] Duarte de Sande, *Japanese Travellers in Sixteenth-Century Europe*, 28–30.

devotional works by Luís de Granada and Thomas à Kempis. His rhetorical skills were also not allowed to waste away, as Hara was frequently asked to deliver orations on important occasions, such as for the funerals of the vice-provincial of Japan, Pedro Gómez (1635–1600), and the bishop of Funai, Luis de Cerqueira (1551–1614).[85] Once safely ensconced in Macau, he spent the remaining years before his death in 1629 assisting João Rodrigues (1561–1633) with his monumental ecclesiastical history of Japan, teaching Latin at the Jesuit college and preaching to the Japanese community in this Christian enclave.[86] Indeed, the annual reports from the Jesuit college in Macau singled him out for praise as a preacher in Japanese, and the question naturally arises as to whether any part of his training in humanist rhetoric spilled out into this vernacular tradition.[87]

For instance, he may well have followed the surviving sets of rules for delivering simple doctrinal and epideictic sermons in Japanese drawn up by Valignano and Pedro Gómez in the 1590s.[88] However, there were other models available to Hara. Following the aforementioned "accommodation" strategy of presenting Christian ideas according to local rhetorical conventions, some contemporary Jesuits looked to Japanese Buddhist sermons when addressing Japanese Christians. Some even attended sermons in local temples with the aim of observing and codifying the precepts of Buddhist rhetoric so they could harness it for their own ends. Describing one such rhetorical reconnaissance mission, Luís Fróis tells us:

[85] Diego Pacheco, "Los Cuatro Legados Japoneses de los Daimyos de Kyushu Después de Regresar a Japón," *Boletín de la Asociación Española de Orientalistas*, 10 (1973), 19–58 (31–32, 44). Josef Franz Schütte, *Monumenta Historica Japoniae* (Rome: Monumenta Historica Soc. Iesu, 1975), 585. A document notarized by Hara is preserved in: Real Academia de Historia, Madrid, *Cortes*, 565 fols. 367r–368v. William J. Farge, *The Japanese Translations of the Jesuit Mission Press, 1590–1614: De Imitatione Christi and Guía de Pecadores* (New York: Edwin Mellen Press, 2002), 18–19, 75–86. Diego Pacheco, "Diogo de Mesquita, S. J. and the Jesuit Mission Press," *Monumenta Nipponica*, 26 (1971), 431–443 (442). The Japanese Jesuit called Martinho who gave an oration *in laudem scientiarum* in Macau in 1603 was not Hara Martinho, but Shikimi Martinho. *Cartas Ânuas do Colégio de Macau: (1594–1627)*, João Paulo Oliveira e Costa and Ana Fernandes Pinto (eds.) (Macau, 1999), 97: "o irmão Martinho cursante japão, o qual por ser o primeiro orador jappão que se ouvio em Machao satisfez muito ao auditorio." This other Martinho apostatized and probably died in prison in 1643: Charles Ralph Boxer, *The Christian Century in Japan: 1549–1650* (Berkeley: University of California Press, 1951), 390, 394, 447 n. 3.
[86] After the 1614 expulsion order he went to Macau, where he helped Joao Rodrigues with his history of the Japanese church and left marginal notes on the author's manuscript: *João Rodrigues's Account of Sixteenth-Century Japan*, Michael Cooper (ed.) (London: Routledge, 2001), 67, n. 2.
[87] Josef Franz Schütte, *Monumenta Historica Japoniae*, 601.
[88] Rômulo da Silva Ehalt, "A Difficult Enterprise: Rules for Preaching in Late Sixteenth Century Japan," *Bulletin of Portuguese/Japanese Studies*, ser. II, 4 (2018), 117–134.

[We observed that] the preacher was seated in a high chair so that everyone could see him and in front of him there stood a small table on which was placed a book. He was clothed in flowing silk vestments, the under-robe being white and the outer one colored, and he carried a golden fan in his hand. He was about 45 years of age and the paleness of his face made him look like a German; certainly he was one of the most handsome and engaging men I have ever seen, and they told me he was of noble birth. The soft and mellow voice and the gestures, which he made during the sermon were all worthy of note. His method of preaching was to read a passage from the book in front of him and then to explain it with such elegance that Father Gaspar Vilela (who could understand the sermon) and all the others present marveled at his great skill and technique. He gained no little profit from this outing and we learned a great deal about how to preach to the Christians in accordance with their liking and language.[89]

Although Hara had probably never entered an active Buddhist temple, he may have delivered sermons in Japanese on the basis of Gaspar Vilela's "reverse engineering" of Buddhist sermons. However, the surviving collections of Jesuit sermons from China present a further possible strategy that Hara might have employed.

Jesuit Eloquence in Early Modern China

Few in number and without the institutional support of Iberian monarchies, the Jesuits in Ming and Qing China could not, and did not roll out the *Ratio studiorum* on a large scale much beyond the Jesuit colleges in Macau and Beijing.[90] Nonetheless, the precepts and practices of the

---

[89] For a survey of rhetoric in pre-Meiji Japan, see Massimiliano Tomasi, *Rhetoric in Modern Japan: Western Influences on the Development of Narrative and Oratorical Style* (Honolulu: University of Hawaii Press, 2004), 25–42. *Cartas que los Padres y Hermanos de la Compañía de Jesús, que Andan en los Reynos de Japón* (Alcalá, 1575), 215–216: "El predicador sentado en una silla alta, para ser visto de todos, con una mesa pequeña delante de sí, y sobre ella un libro, y el vestido con unas ropas de seda largas, la de debaxo blanca, y la de encima colorada, con un ventalle de oro en la mano; podría ser hombre de quarenta y cinco años; y en su blancura de rostro parecía un alemán, por ser uno de los bien dispuestos y agraciados hombre que yo he visto. Dixeron nos que era de noble linaje. Su voz, madureza y blandura y actión, que tenía en el sermón, era cierto digno de ser considerado. La manera que tenía de proceder en su sermón, era de leer un passo por el libro que tenía delante de sí, y después lo explicaba con tanta gracia, que el padre Gaspar Vilela, que lo entendía, y los demás que allí se hallaron, venían admirados de su buen arte y modo. Y no aprovecho tan poco esta yda, que de allí no se tomassen algunas leciones, para mejor proceder con los Christianos en los sermones conforme a su gusto y lengua."

[90] On education in the Jesuit college in Macau, see *Cartas Ânuas do Colégio de Macau (1594–1627)*, 62, 68, 70–71, 88–89, 95, 97, 119–120, 125, 133, 139. Latin grammar and other parts of the Christian humanist curriculum were taught on a smaller scale in Beijing, including for the purpose of preparing Chinese ambassadors for missions to Russia: Antoine Gaubil, *Correspondance De Pékin: 1722–1759*, Simon Renée (ed.) (Geneva: Librairie Droz, 1970), 175, 349.

classical rhetorical tradition permeated the missionary activities of the small number of mostly, although not exclusively European-educated Jesuits in China. The most famous example, of course, is Matteo Ricci's (1552–1610) attempt to entice students preparing for the Chinese civil service examination to Christianity with a treatise on artificial memory. What better way to attract adherents from China's elite than to give them an edge in the examination that defined success in elite Chinese society? Unfortunately for Ricci, however, the techniques handed down by Quintilian and the anonymous author of the *Rhetorica ad Herennium* had a mixed reception in China, just as they had had in Europe, with complaints that it took as long to learn the system as it did to memorize the material through rote learning.[91]

In addition to Ricci, Giulio Aleni (1582–1649) tried to spread the word about the classical rhetorical tradition in China in an apologetic treatise on Christian learning, in which he described humanist rhetorical education in this way:

> As for the method of argument (*yilun zhi fa*, 議論之法), there are five steps. First to observe things, events, persons and the conditions of the times, and to seek the causes behind them; such are called the materials for discourse. Second, to deploy [materials and arguments] in good order: first this, then that. Third to adorn with flowers from ancient writers. Fourth, to commit to memory the finished discourse. If one is talented and good at memorization, there is a way to nurture it; or if one forgets things easily and is having difficulties in memorization, there is method of memorization. Finally, the student appears in a public hall in front of the examiners to recite his discourse, or mounts a platform for a disputation with wise and learned persons.[92]

As no parallel tradition of learned eloquence intended for delivery before large audiences existed in the Sinosphere, the emphasis in humanist education and practice on oratorical as opposed to written or conversational eloquence must have struck Aleni's learned Chinese readers as rather odd.[93] Indeed, Ricci observed that public speaking was a largely alien practice in China:

---

[91] Jonathan D. Spence, *The Memory Palace of Matteo Ricci*.

[92] The original is reproduced in: *Tianxuechuhan* 天學初函, 6 vols. (Taipei: Student Book, 1965), I, 28–29. The translation is adapted from: Bernard Lung-Kay Luk, "Aleni Introduces the Western Academic Tradition to Seventeenth-Century China: A Study of the *Xixue Fan*," in Tiziana Lippiello and Roman Malek (eds.), *"Scholar from the West." Giulio Aleni S.J. (1582–1649) and the Dialogue between Christianity and China* (Brescia: Fondazione Civiltà Bresciana, 1997), 479–518 (489).

[93] George A. Kennedy, *Comparative Rhetoric: An Historical and Cross-Cultural Introduction* (New York: Oxford University Press, 1998), 141–170; David Strand, "Citizens in the Audience and at the

It is generally agreed that this kingdom is unusual in that all its religions have spread their message not through sermons preached to the people, but rather through books ... I doubt that these people who are addicted to reading books would have been more easily persuaded by the preaching of our men – who are not always eloquent in foreign languages – than by what they had read in their leisure time.[94]

Although rhetorical handbooks usually made claims about the universal applicability of the classical rhetorical tradition, there were clearly some audiences, such as the Chinese *literati*, who were simply less receptive to its charms. It is no surprise then that when describing the humanist educational program Aleni went out of his way to justify the cultivation of the art of spoken eloquence as a way to ensure that important advice "not merely disappear into the void" (*bu tu fu yan san yu kongzhong eryi*, 不徒浮言散於空中而已) and cease to be useful knowledge.[95]

However, this is not to say that classicizing sermons were entirely absent from Jesuit missions in China. Indeed, there is evidence that classical epideictic models shaped the sermons delivered by Jesuit missionaries. Here, the audiences were diverse, but frequently united by their ability to understand Nanjing Mandarin, the lingua franca of the period, which was widely spoken or at least passively understood by those who had received any sort of education.[96] Many of these sermons were probably delivered in the Jesuit church in Fuzhou, a small wooden building in the traditional Chinese style made up of several halls and a courtyard. This was decorated on the outside with gilded Chinese characters, and on the inside with printed images of the Last Judgement and Purgatory, as well as painted panels depicting Jesus, the Virgin Mary and the Archangel Gabriel. In one corner also stood a clavichord that was the object of much curiosity for visitors.[97] There, to the light of red Chinese candles, the congregation heard sermons by the Jesuit missionaries, including one in honor of St. Ignatius Loyola delivered by Aleni in 1639, which began:

Podium," in Merle Goldman and Elizabeth J. Perry, *Changing Meanings of Citizenship in Modern China* (Cambridge, MA: Harvard University Press, 2002), 44–69.

[94] Matteo Ricci, *De Christiana Expeditione apud Sinas*, Nicolas Trigault (ed.) (Cologne, 1617), 537: "Quod huic regno peculiare est, satis constat, sectas omnes scriptis potius voluminibus quam habitis ad populum sermonibus fuisse evulgatas ... nam apud gentem libris legendis addictissimam nescio an efficacius lecta per otium persuadeantur, quam si a nostris minus semper facundis in sermone peregrino ad populum e loco superiore exponerentur."

[95] *Tianxuechuhan*, I, 30.

[96] *Kouduo Richao: Li Jiubiao's Diary of Oral Admonitions. A Late Ming Christian Journal*, Erik Zürcher (ed.), 2 vols. (Oxford: Routledge, 2007), I, 13. It is not impossible that on some occasions the sermons were delivered in one Sinitic language then translated into another.

[97] *Ibid.*, I, 35–36, 263.

In general, rites held in commemoration of a saint have three most important functions. First, we praise and thank the Lord of Heaven for having produced the saint as a compass (*zhinan*, 指南) for later generations. Second, we gratefully admire the good works and virtues displayed by the saint during his life. Thirdly, we imitate (*fangxiao*, 仿效) his virtuous conduct and try to make it our own. As regards his ears and eyes, his hands and feet, his speech and movement, his pacing and running, a saint is just like other people, but he differs widely from others in his determination and in his feats of self-cultivation. The Lord of Heaven has favored us with his birth, and the saint sets an example (*chuifa*, 垂法) for posterity. How would we be incapable of knowing whom to imitate?[98]

In other words, the members of the congregation were going to hear a typical epideictic sermon, which would give a glowing account of the life of St. Ignatius in order to encourage them to cultivate the saint's particular Christian virtues. These, we learn, were humility and deep love, which St. Ignatius expressed in his willingness to suffer severe pain to save the souls of others. At the same time, Aleni also warned his congregation that God's judgement was like "a sharp sword hanging by a single thread" (*ru xuan liren yu yilü zhi shang*, 如懸利刃於一縷之上). This was an oblique reference to the "sword of Damocles," a story recorded by Cicero in his *Tusculanae Disputationes* that was well known in early modern Europe.

There were also clear overlaps between humanist public speaking and some of the more overtly Sinicizing of the surviving Jesuit sermons from China, including those recorded in a diary that summarizes all the sermons delivered by an anonymous priest in 1690. These featured frequent references to canonical Chinese thinkers (Confucius, Mencius, Zhu Xi, etc.) whose *dicta* became Sino-humanist commonplaces. For instance, when condemning the sin of pride, especially intellectual pride, the unknown preacher referred to the famous Confucian maxim "The Master said, 'Learning without thought is labor lost; thought without learning is perilous.'" Similarly, when discussing the "way of the Lord" (*zhudao*, 主道), the preacher referred to sayings of both Confucius and Mencius on the importance of following the "way" (*dao*, 道), a key concept in several Chinese philosophical schools.[99] These and Aleni's

---

[98] Adapted from the translation in: *Kouduo Richao: Li Jiubiao's Diary of Oral Admonitions: A Late Ming Christian Journal*, I, 589–590 (VIII.12). On Aleni's *Kouduo*, see Gang Song, *Giulio Aleni, Kouduo Richao, and Christian-Confucian Dialogism in Late Ming Fujian* (Oxford: Routledge, 2018).

[99] *Faguo Guojia Tushuguan Ming-Qing Tianzhujiao Wenxian* 法國國家圖書館明清天主教文獻, 26 vols., Adrianus Dudink, Nathalie Monnet and Nicolas Standaert (eds.) (Taipei: Taipei Ricci Institute, 2009), XII, 158 (*Analects*, II.15); XII, 111 (Mencius, *Gaozi*, II, 22 and Zhongyong (Pseudo-Confucius), *The Doctrine of Mean*, 1.2).

sermon for the feast day of St. Ignatius were thus clear attempts on the part of missionaries to create consensus in their congregations about the best way to lead their lives as Christians using the tools of the classical rhetorical tradition frequently combined with methods borrowed from local learned culture and clothed in the best Chinese that they and the Chinese converts who assisted them could muster. These sermons, which in many ways mirrored the Indo-humanist sermons discussed in the next chapter, therefore throw light onto an approach to sermonizing that was also available to Hara who may have at least from time to time delivered Japanese panegyrics to his congregations in Nagasaki and Macau that borrowed from both the Sino-Japanese and Christian humanist learned traditions.

Christian Japan and the Iberian World

As is well known, the Tenshō Embassy was not the only Japanese mission to visit Rome during the Renaissance. In 1613, Hasekura Tsunenaga (1571–1622) and an entourage of samurai and other retainers set sail from Ishinomaki for New Spain where they stopped for several months on their way to Madrid and then Rome. As the Nahua annalist Chimalpahin recorded:

> It became known here in Mexico and was said that the reason their ruler the emperor in Japan sent this aforementioned lordly emissary and ambassador here is to go to Rome and to see the Holy Father, Paul V, and to give him their obedience concerning the Holy Church, so that all the Japanese want to become Christians; they are to be baptized, so that they will also be children of our mother the Holy Roman Church in matters of the holy sacraments and will always obey it in matters of divinity and faith. And when the great universal spiritual shepherd the Holy Father, our universal governor and caretaker, has accepted them, they too will be his sheep.[100]

Although the embassy's ultimate aim was stimulating trade between Northern Honshū and Renaissance Europe, Hasekura and his companions were considered by this *cacique* chronicler to be primarily seeking support for the wholescale conversion of Japan, which would enter the Catholic fold *alongside*, not *under* Iberia's various kingdoms and viceroyalties,

---

[100] Translated in: Domingo Francisco de San Antón Muñón Chimalpahin Cuauhtlehuanitzin, *Annals of His Time: Don Domingo De San Antón Muñón Chimalpahin Quauhtlehuanitzin*, James Lockhart, Susan Schroeder and Doris Namala (eds.), (Stanford, CA: Stanford University Press, 2006), 275–276. This event is discussed in: Miguel León-Portilla, "La Embajada De Los Japoneses En México, 1614. El Testimonio En Nahuatl Del Cronista Chimalpahin," *Estudios de Asia y Africa*, 16 (1981), 215–241.

including New Spain. This reflected the common Iberian perception of Japan, not as a future territory of the *estado da Índia* or as an extension of the Philippines, but as a prestigious missionary field analogous to Ming China, a sentiment we also find in the Jesuit drama of the period.[101] This was in no way accidental. Rather, it reflected the intentions and realistic goals of the vast majority of Jesuits and their European and Japanese allies in Japan during the "Christian Century."[102] This includes Hara who in his oration united evocative militaristic metaphors with a desire to spread Christianity that was fundamentally independent of any imperial project as we would understand it. Of course, this is not to say that Portuguese traders and Japanese Samurai did not regularly come to blows, especially in the 1550s and 1560s before the Jesuits succeeded in regulating the interactions between the Japanese and the blustering Portuguese, neither of whom much understood each other's cultural norms at the beginning.[103]

Nonetheless, Hara's Kyūshū underwent a rapid, although superficial and patchy, process of Iberianization at the hands of Portuguese missionaries and merchants who had the support of Catholic non-Iberians, most notably missionaries from the regions of the Italian Peninsula under Philip II, as well as the growing number of Japanese Catholics, both elite and non-elite. Here, the expansion of Catholic Christendom with Iberian characteristics was driven by economic incentives, opportunistic alliances and missionary persuasion, not direct territorial conquest. If one wanted to apply the word "empire" to Japan during this period, one would have to describe it as a very limited form of "informal empire," far more tenuous than anything seen in the late nineteenth century, with the carriers of Iberian culture, whatever their origin, by no means having the upper hand consistently.[104]

Although it is tempting to draw comparisons with the Americas here, the most analogous case for early modern Japan is really the contemporary

---

[101] Adrian Hsia and Ruprecht Wimmer, *Mission und Theater: Japan und China auf den Bühnen der Gesellschaft Jesu* (Regensburg: Schnell & Steiner, 2005).

[102] Stuart M. McManus, "Imperial History without Provincial Loyalty? Reading Roman History in Renaissance Japan," *KNOW: A Journal on the Formation of Knowledge*, 3.1 (2019), 123–157. For a somewhat different view, see: Reiner H. Hesselink, *The Dream of Christian Nagasaki: World Trade and the Clash of Cultures, 1560–1640*, 4: "Christianity as brought overseas in the fifteenth and sixteenth centuries, therefore, should be treated as an essentially ideological discourse that helped, expand, consolidate, and justify the newly acquired powers of Portugal and Spain."

[103] Reiner H. Hesselink, "The *Capitães Mores* of the Japan Voyage: A Group Portrait," *International Journal of Asian Studies*, 9 (2012), 1–41.

[104] John Gallagher and Ronald Robinson, "The Imperialism of Free Trade," *The Economic History Review*, second series, 6 (1953), 1–15.

Kingdom of Kongo, a context which is generally not brought into dialogue with either the Americas or Asia. Like Japan, Kongo was slowly integrated into the Iberian World, although not (in this period anyway) politically into the Kingdom of Portugal, through a gradual process of economic exchange, missionary efforts and a series of military alliances against the nearby Kingdom of Ndongo. The Jesuits did not come to Japan at the head of an army, but arrived alongside bands of Iberian merchant-pirates and supported Christian *daimyō* by sharing technology and tipping trade in their favor. This amalgam of exchange, evangelization and informal empire characterized at least the first century of contact, before Kongo and Japan parted ways from our perspective, and open conflict between Kongolese and Portuguese forces broke out in the seventeenth century with territorial conquest increasingly becoming the (largely unfulfilled) aim.[105]

These interactions had a significant cultural impact in Kyūshū. In particular, missionary efforts had wide-ranging effects. This was largely because the division between doctrine and cultural practices was decidedly muddy for both missionaries and converts. Hara and his companions perfectly exemplify this. For instance, as well as being baptized Hara took a Portuguese given name ("Martinho"), something we also find in other parts of the Iberian World, where Christian kings of Kongo were named Alfonso and elite *indios* like Chimalpahin took Christian names like Domingo. Just like his Iberianized contemporaries in Africa and the Americas, Hara's connection to Catholicism also had linguistic implications. He not only had a command of Latin, the language of the universal Church, but also spoke and wrote Portuguese, as well as probably dabbling in the other leading languages of the Iberian World, like Castilian and Italian. Dress was also not immune from influence. Whereas in Japan and during the embassy Hara and his companion wore traditional Japanese attire, on other occasions they are known to have donned garb typical of Jesuit novices. In this, they were not unique. Indeed, Iberian styles slowly came to influence the dress of Japanese Christians, as well as providing an exotic costume for non-Christians to dress up in, including Toyotomi Hideyoshi, the *daimyō* who would eventually become a scourge of the Christians.[106] Contact with Iberian and partially Iberianized Christians

---

[105] John Thornton, "The Development of an African Catholic Church in the Kingdom of Kongo, 1491–1750," *Journal of African History*, 25 (1984), 147–167; *ibid.*, "Conquest and Theology: The Jesuits in Angola, 1548–1650," *Journal of Jesuit Studies*, 1 (2014), 245–259.

[106] Charles Ralph Boxer, *The Christian Century in Japan, 1549–1650*, 207.

also had implications for diet, with the Iberian origins of tempura probably being the best-known example, although visitors to Nagasaki from other parts of Japan were also struck by the prevalence of wheat-based foods, such as Portuguese bread (*pão*).[107] This said, diet seems to have been something of a sticking point for the Jesuits and their Japanese students, partly because of the ongoing influence of Buddhist vegetarianism and partly because Valignano feared that Hara and his companions would fall ill if they were not able to eat rice.[108]

A further similarity between Kongo and Japan was that conversion to Christianity in Japan also seems to have frequently brought with it a certain attitude not only to the Pope who demanded respect verging on allegiance, but also to Iberia's monarchies who became favored allies, but not overlords.[109] As in Kongo, such attitudes stopped far short of political loyalty, which was still owed to their respective *daimyō*. This is perhaps best exemplified by Itō's 1587 letter to Pope Sixtus V, in which he referred only in general terms to Europe's "Christian princes" without singling out the Hispanic Monarchy for particular praise.[110] Similarly, writing in 1590 Chijiwa explicitly called the Christian *daimyō*, Dom Protasio (Arima Harunobu), his "Lord" (*dominus*), a term used to designate personal loyalty and territorial possession.[111] This attitude is mirrored in *De missione*, in which Philip II is described as the first among equals of Christian monarchs ("greatest and most supreme of all the kings of Europe"), to whom Christians owed respect, but not loyalty.[112] It was

---

[107] Reiner H. Hesselink, "*I Go Shopping in Christian Nagasaki*: Entries from the Diary of a Mito Samurai, *Ōwada Shigekiyo* (1593)," *Bulletin of Portuguese/Japanese Studies*, ser. II, 1 (2015), 27–45.

[108] J. A. Abranches Pinto and Henri Bernard, "Les Instructions du Père Valignano pour l'Ambassade Japonaise en Europe. (Goa, 12 Décembre 1583)," *Monumenta Nipponica*, 6 (1943), 391–403 (391–392).

[109] On Kongolese missions and attitudes to Rome, see Kate Lowe, "'Representing' Africa: Ambassadors and Princes from Christian Africa to Renaissance Italy and Portugal, 1402–1608," *Transactions of the Royal Historical Society*, 17 (2007), 101–128.

[110] ARSI, Jap. Sin. 33, fols. 38r: "Fuit praeterea non nobis solum, sed universae etiam Iaponiae emolumento maximo haec nostra ad te, pater beatissime, profectio, et ob eam causam a Deo et Christo Iesu servatore nostro patri visitatori in animum inducta, ut in Iaponiam reversi ipsius sanctae sedis Romae magnitudinem, magestatem ac charitatem, aliorumque regum et principum Christianorum magnificentiam; patrum quoque Societatis labores, quos in tam diuturna perferunt navigatione (quae omnia eam olim narrabantur, non incredibilia modo, verum aniles fabulae nostratibus videbantur) nunc uti testes vivi et praesentes ac (ut aiunt) oculati non solum suadere, sed persuadere etiam, Deo votis aspirante, nostris hominibus possimus."

[111] *Ibid.*, 33, fol. 55r: "non facile declarare possumus quibus gaudiis, qua animi exultatione nos exceperint dominus meus Protasius Arimae Rex et Sancius consobrinus meus, qui patri Bartholomeo in Omurensem principatum successit, ceterique principes Christiani et viri primarii ex finitimis regnis nos visendi studio accurrentes."

[112] Duarte de Sande, *Diálogo Sobre a Missão dos Embaixadores Japoneses à Cúria Romana*, I, 373.

for this reason that no oaths of allegiance were sworn to Philip II during the embassy's visit to Madrid, and when Hara and his companions were presented to him he is recorded as having responded in this way:

> [Philip II], when he had heard the letters read out in both Japanese and Spanish, answered the messages with a glad countenance, saying that he considered the Catholic kings and princes of Japan to be his allies by law. They were joined to him by a new bond of brotherhood, and written and etched on his breast such that he was delighted that they had sent him, as witnesses of their mutual benevolence, such fine and noble young men, and he hoped that in the future such most pleasing events would take place more and more often.[113]

Indeed, the political premise of the Jesuit mission in Japan in general, and the Tenshō Embassy in particular, was one of coequal Christian kingdoms, with diplomatic gifts exchanged, including Japanese armor. That to be a subject of an Iberian monarch required adherence to orthodox Christianity is undeniable, as the Spanish Habsburgs were the leading defenders of global Catholicism. However, being an adherent of Iberianized Catholicism did not require being a subject of an Iberian monarch.

Unfortunately for Hara, conflict would soon arise between his archipelago's new hegemon and the Christians of Kyūshū and their Portuguese allies. Unlike in Kongo, however, this involved the large-scale proscription and annihilation of Christianity, rather than relative religious continuity combined with interstate warfare. In this, Hideyoshi and his successors were largely, if not immediately successful. The reason usually cited for this policy was that the Jesuits were the vanguard of an Iberian invasion, a plan allegedly blurted out by a shipwrecked Spanish merchant in 1596. Admittedly, Gaspar Coelho, the Jesuit superior in Japan before Valignano, had contemplated inviting forces from the Philippines to intervene on the side of the Christian Ōmura clan.[114] This was, however, a passing fancy that was as unrealistic as it was unadvised, and was wisely never attempted.[115] The unfounded nature of Hideyoshi's suspicions comes into sharp focus if we consider that there was no realistic chance of the Jesuits, Portuguese merchants or any Japanese Christians regaining influence and defending their Iberianized Christian culture.[116] Hideyoshi's

---

[113] *Ibid.*, 385.
[114] *Ibid.*, 163–169; George Elison, *Deus Destroyed: The Image of Christianity in Early Modern Japan* (Cambridge, MA: Harvard University Press, 1988), 114–115, 136–141, 355–356.
[115] Donald Frederick Lach, *Asia in the Making of Europe*, 2 vols. (Chicago: University of Chicago Press, 1965), I, 746.
[116] Charles Ralph Boxer, *The Christian Century in Japan, 1549–1650*, 308–361.

growing polity was, as the Jesuits had implicitly understood, too militarily advanced, too organized and too far from the centers of Iberian power and culture to consider subjecting to an Iberian monarch.[117]

All this is obviously in contrast to the Americas and to some of the areas surrounding Goa in the *estado da Índia*, where conversion at the hands of a missionary loyal to a particular monarch was interpreted as an expression of loyalty on the part of the convert to the same monarch.[118] At the same time, it is well known that exhibiting Iberian religio-cultural markers, such as clothing, speech and behavior, could lead to people of non-Iberian descent being identified as "Spaniards," a legal category with wide-ranging political implications.[119] This said, the case of Renaissance Japan reminds us that conversion, cultural borrowing and conquest were linked, although not necessarily identical processes. This is an insight that already has some traction among readers of indigenous histories of New Spain, in which *cacique* authors stress the importance of processes of alliance and embrace of Christianity over submission to the crown.[120] Culture and empire, we must remember, were not identical, either for contemporaries or in historical reality. Similarly, military alliances may lead to one party engulfing the other, and this may well have happened in Japan, had events unfolded differently. However, this was not necessarily the inevitable or the intended outcome. It is therefore an error to buy into totalizing visions of Iberian expansion, which mask the gradual nature of political and cultural change, and overlook the lived experience of non-Iberians, like Hara who, as the title page of his oration clearly stated, was *Iaponius* not *Lusitanus*, despite being a Catholic and to some degree Iberianized.

Of course, Hara and other Japanese Christians were not always accepted with open arms and on equal terms by all Iberians. Rather, their position in the Iberian World was a function of their location on a three dimensional axis defined by perceived nobility, depth of connection to Catholicism and ethnicity. Hara and his companions therefore offer a

---

[117] This is obviously in constrast to other parts of the region, which were seen as fair game: Charles Ralph Boxer, "Portuguese and Spanish Projects for the Conquest of Southeast East, 1580–1600," *Journal of Asian History*, 3.2 (1969), 118–136.

[118] Tamar Herzog, *Frontiers of Possession: Spain and Portugal in Europe and the Americas*, 70–72. On the conversion in the *estado da Índia*, see Chapter 4.

[119] Tamar Herzog, "Can You Tell a Spaniard When You See One? 'Us' and 'Them' in the Early Modern Iberian Atlantic," in Pedro Cardim, Tamar Herzog, José Javier Ruiz Ibáñez and Gaetano Sabatini (eds.), *Polycentric Monarchies: How Did Early Modern Spain and Portugal Achieve and Maintain a Global Hegemony?*, 147–161.

[120] Louise M. Burkhart, "2014 Presidential Address: Christian Salvation As Ethno-Ethnohistory: Two Views from 1714," *Ethnohistory*, 63 (2016), 215–235. The current concensus is best exemplified by: Matthew Restall, *Seven Myths of the Spanish Conquest*.

richly documented parallel case to the students at the Franciscan College of Tlateloco, the indigenous priests of eighteenth-century New Spain and the noble Filipino curate-scholar, Bartolomé Saguinsín, discussed elsewhere in this book. Like them, Hara and his companions rose to prominence in the Iberian World thanks to their noble lineages and deep knowledge of and dedication to Catholic culture, a central element of which was Christian humanism. Yet, ethnicity continued to matter. Indeed, concerns about ordaining ethnically Japanese priests undeniably hindered Hara's path through the *cursus honorum* of the Society of Jesus. In this, he was not alone. Another Jesuit novice Fabian Fucan (*c.* 1565–1621) seemingly chose to apostatize (and later compose a treatise in which he used his detailed knowledge of Christianity to attack the Jesuits!) precisely because of their unwillingness to let Japanese Christians advance through their ranks at the same rate as their European peers.[121] Japan, therefore, also reminds us that what we today call "race" mattered everywhere in the early modern Iberian World, but that it was not the sole driver of human experience.

Conclusion

Like his fellow Roman citizen Cicero whose orations delivered over 6,000 miles away and a millennium and a half before his birth he grew up reading, Hara made a name for himself not through his victories on the battlefield, but by dint of his ability to move his listeners with words. This was, however, a persuasive process that mobilized classicizing military metaphors "for the greater glory of God" (*ad maiorem Dei gloriam*). If we follow Hara's career from the jubilation of the Tenshō Embassy to the sorrow of Christianity's proscription, we see the talented Japanese student grow from a seminarian and grammar student into Japan's leading humanist and Latin orator whose intellectual world was populated by erudite and eloquent Jesuit orators like Gaspar Gonçalves who shared his classicizing training and priorities.[122]

In the hands of these European and non-European Ciceronians, humanist rhetoric was no disinterested pursuit. It may indeed have inspired the Jesuits' pragmatic approach to converting non-Christian

---

[121] George Elison, *Deus Destroyed: The Image of Christianity in Early Modern Japan*, 154–155.
[122] Hara's skills as a translator of canonical works of Catholic devotion into Japanese were also widely praised: ARSI, Jap. Sin., 36, fol. 27v.

peoples known as "accommodation." Yet, the persuasive tools of the classical rhetorical tradition were also arms in the ongoing battle to conquer the world for Christ, a mission that overlapped with the interests of Iberian monarchies as part of a program of "spiritual conquest" reminiscent of that in the Americas. Be it in Latin, European vernaculars or Asian languages, classical rhetoric in its Renaissance incarnation was considered a versatile weapon in this struggle for souls.

Ultimately, of course, Hara's hopes were to be dashed. Alongside many of his Jesuit confreres and fellow Japanese Christians he was forced to leave Japan. He would end his days, not in Nagasaki, but in another Iberianized Christian city, Macau, where he died in 1629 and was buried in the Jesuit Church of St. Paul, the same place, perhaps fittingly, where Valignano had been interred some twenty years earlier. With him died Renaissance Japan's leading homegrown humanist.[123] The life and times of Hara Martinho therefore remind us that the success of "spiritual conquests" no matter how earnestly undertaken was not guaranteed, something that it is easy to assume if the process is studied from the perspective of the Americas alone.

---

[123] Diego Yuuki, *Os Quatro Legados dos Dáimios de Quiuxu após Regressarem ao Japão* (Macau: Instituto Cultural de Macau, 1990), 28.

CHAPTER 4

Indo-Humanist Eloquence

One Sunday in the first decades of the eighteenth century, the native inhabitants of the Jesuit mission (*reducción*) of Santa María La Mayor on the Uruguay River gathered to hear a sermon in Guarani in praise of the Japanese protomartyrs crucified at Nagasaki in 1597. Although delivered in Guarani, many of the structural and thematic conventions of the sermon by the learned Sicilian, Paolo Restivo (1658–1740), were those of Christian humanist epideictic. For instance, Restivo's sermon centered on a scriptural passage, "When you hear of battles and uprisings, do not be afraid" (Luke 21:9), and began with an "opening" (*salutatio*) that culminated in a communal recitation of the *Ave Maria*. Restivo then launched into an extended "line of argument" (*argumentatio*) and rounded off the sermon with a "conclusion" (*conclusio*), in which he eulogized the efforts of the Society of Jesus in Japan, and in particular the work of St. Francis Xavier, reassuring his listeners that whatever misfortunes Christians might suffer in this life they would always have ample rewards in heaven. In the course of this sermon, he followed the typical epideictic model closely, praising the virtues of an exemplary figure as a way to exhort listeners to similar feats.

On this occasion, one member of Restivo's almost 1,000-strong congregation, the *cacique* Nicolás Yapuguay (b. *c.* 1680), listened particularly attentively. When he returned home, Yapuguay transcribed what he had heard, smoothing over the rough edges in a sermon that was clothed in passable, if occasionally limping Guarani. He later added this polished panegyric of Xavier and the Japanese protomartyrs to a collection of Guarani sermons that in 1727 was sent up the Uruguay River and printed at the nearby *reducción* named after none other than Francis Xavier. Right up until the expulsion of the Jesuits from the Hispanic Monarchy in 1767, these printed sermons would serve as models for sacred oratory in the

missions, and may even have been recited verbatim by less able or experienced Jesuit missionaries or the indigenous catechists who assisted them.[1]

Although striking, the collaborative and synergistic scholarly mode of
Yapuguay and Restivo was far from unique in the Iberian World. Rather, it
was a typical manifestation of the "Indo-humanist" trend in the classical
rhetorical tradition.[2] Since the arrival of Iberianized Christianity in the
Americas in the sixteenth century, missionaries had relied on the assistance
of learned indigenous Christians to study and codify indigenous languages
and deliver sermons that combined elements of Christian humanist rhetoric and indigenous linguistic and literary norms. This was the front line
in what has been called the "invisible war" or the "spiritual conquest" of
the Americas that over time brought much of the Western Hemisphere
into the Catholic orbit.[3] For instance, with the help of his students at the
college of Santa Cruz de Tlateloco, Bernardino de Sahagún codified
Nahuatl *huehuetlatolli* into an Indo-humanist rhetorical system that served
as the basis for sermons and other Christian texts in the Valley of Mexico.[4]
Similarly, missionaries took inspiration from the classical rhetorical tradition to systematize the norms of pre-Columbian Zapotec ceremonial
oratory, which they then applied in sermons that replicated many of the
features of traditional Zapotecan stylistic ornamentation. The results of
this process of pragmatic blending were, of course, by no means uniform
even within language groups. Just like the myriad of local varieties of
Catholicism that grew up in the Americas, the Christian texts produced
there showed considerable diversity.[5] Not even the terminology used to
translate Christian vocabulary into local languages, such as Quechua and
Aymara, remained static, as missionaries and their collaborators

---

[1] The exact details of the collaboration between Yapuguay and Restivo is not documented by a
contemporary source, instead we must rely on the slightly confused account of José Manuel Peramás
writing around seventy years later: Nicolás Yapuguay, *Sermones y Exemplos en Lengua Guarani*,
Guillermo Furlong (ed.) (Buenos Aires: Editorial Guarania, 1953), V–IX. On life in the Guaraní
missions, see Julia J. S. Sarreal, *The Guaraní and Their Missions: A Socioeconomic History* (Stanford,
CA: Stanford University Press, 2014). On Yapuguay, see Bartomeu Meliá, *La Lengua Guaraní Del
Paraguay: Historia, Sociedad y Literatura* (Madrid: Editorial MAPFRE, 1992), 140.

[2] This was a product of "Catholic Orientalism": Ângela Barreto Xavier and Ines G. Županov, *Catholic
Orientalism: Portuguese Empire, Indian Knowledge (16th–18th Centuries)* (Oxford: Oxford University
Press, 2015).

[3] Robert Ricard, *La "Conquète Spirituelle" du Mexique*; David Eduardo Tavárez, *The Invisible War:
Indigenous Devotions, Discipline, and Dissent in Colonial Mexico* (Stanford, CA: Stanford University
Press, 2011).

[4] Mónica Ruiz Bañuls, *El Huehuetlatolli: Como Discurso Sincrético En El Proceso Evangelizador
Novohispano El Siglo XVI* (Rome: Bulzoni, 2009), 151–157.

[5] Mark Z. Christensen, *Nahua and Maya Catholicisms: Texts and Religion in Colonial Central Mexico
and Yucatan* (Stanford, CA: Standford University Press, 2013).

continually revised their approach in response to the changing cultural standards of post-conquest societies.[6] It was this continual interaction between the classical rhetorical tradition and local rhetorical traditions within the context of emergent Catholic societies that defined most if not all indigenous-language public speaking in the Americas.

This said, there were limits to such processes of scholarly syncretism. Elements of native rhetorical traditions that were too reminiscent of pre-Columbian religious beliefs were incompatible with the evangelizing aims of missionary Indo-humanists.[7] Similarly, important aspects of the classical rhetorical tradition were also excluded from indigenous-language sacred oratory in the Americas. For instance, Restivo and Yapuguay may have adhered to the basic structural scheme of late humanist sacred oratory, and perhaps even relied on some of the scholarly practices that usually accompanied the classical rhetorical tradition (e.g. commonplacing). Yet, they largely rejected other canonical aspects of humanist eloquence and erudition, most notably the continual appeals to classical, patristic and humanist texts, authorities and culture. This was, in fact, an aversion that we see across the Americas.[8] This omission might seem so predictable that it is hardly worth exploring. Surely, Socrates and Cicero were so particular to Europe and the hispanized urban regions of the Americas with their long-standing traditions of humanist education that they could not penetrate these "non-Western" indigenous contexts.[9] Indeed, the sixteenth century *mestizo* (i.e. mixed race) rhetorician Diego Valadés made it clear that the Bible and the Church Fathers were the only suitable sources for quotations in

---

[6] Alan Durston, *Pastoral Quechua: The History of Christian Translation in Colonial Peru, 1550–1650* (Notre Dame, IN: University of Notre Dame Press, 2007).

[7] For instance, many of the *huehuetlatolli* contained prayers to Mesoamerican dieties, which for obvious reasons did not find their way into sermons, since it was important to differentiate Catholic doctrine and religious practices from its pre-Hispanic counterparts: Thelma D. Sullivan, "*The Rhetorical Orations, Or Huehuetlatolli*, Collected by Sahagun," in Munro S. Edmundson (ed.), *Sixteenth-Century Mexico: The Work of Sahagún*, 86–88; María Sánchez Aguilera, "Jesucristo, 'Pontífice de los Bienes Futuros': Un Sermón en Náhuatl de Fray Bernardino de Sahagún," *Estudios de Cultura Náhuatl*, 48 (2014), 265–299.

[8] Here I have examined the following collections of sermons, albeit in Spanish translation, for humanist references: Juan de la Anunciación, *Sermonario en Lengua Mexicana* (Mexico City, 1577); *Doctrina Christiana en Lengua Española y Mexicana* (Mexico City, 1550); Susanne Klaus, *Uprooted Christianity: The Preaching of the Christian Doctrine in Mexico Based on Franciscan Sermons of the 16th Century Written in Nahuatl* (Markt Schwaben: Saurwein, 1999); Gérald Taylor, *Sermones y Ejemplos: Antología Bilingüe Castellano-quechua, Siglo XVII* (Lima: Instituto Francés de Estudios Andinos, 2002); Fernando de Avendaño, *Sermones de los Misterios de Nuestra Santa Fe Catolica, en Lengua Castellana, y La General del Inca: Impugnanse los Errores Particulares que los Indios Han Tenido* (Lima, 1648).

[9] An analogous line of argumentation is found in: Walter D. Mignolo, *The Darker Side of the Renaissance*, xii.

Nahuatl sermons.[10] But what if specifically local exigencies led to this approach, rather than a cultural specificity inherent to the classical rhetorical tradition? What if certain contingent features of the indigenous cultures of the Americas that go beyond a simple "European" vs. "non-European" dichotomy led to this rhetorical strategy? Luckily, there is a way to test this hypothesis.

As is well known, the process of Iberian political, cultural and demographic expansion in the Americas was not unique. Following a period of war in the Iberian Peninsula traditionally imagined as a "reconquest" (*reconquista*) of formerly Christian territories from invading Muslims, soldiers and merchants nominally loyal to the monarchs of the Kingdoms of Portugal and Castile set out into the world to trade and raid, forming alliances with local powers in the Americas and Asia dissatisfied with their current hegemons. From there, they succeeded in carving out commercial and territorial empires that at their height in the late sixteenth century literally encircled the globe. This was followed by the arrival of Iberianized Catholic missionaries with origins almost as often in the Italian as in the Iberian Peninsula who attempted to convert local populations in these territories and in so doing transformed Catholicism from a western European into a global religion. It was in this context that a little over a decade before the conquest of Tenochtitlán, the city of Goa in western India fell to soldiers under the command of Alfonso de Albuquerque (1453–1515) who like Cortés had not received explicit instructions to take the flourishing urban center and fought at the head of an army largely made up of local (i.e. non-Iberian) soldiers.[11] Of course, unlike the new capital of the viceroyalty of New Spain, Goa and the Salcete Peninsula to the south remained enclaves at the edge of powerful native polities. Rather than the seat of power of an extra-European Iberian kingdom (*reino*) that ended only where the ocean began, Goa was a beleaguered city-state connected to similarly isolated Iberian port cities in Asia by a fragile and sinuous maritime corridor. This meant that Catholic missionaries (largely but not exclusively Jesuits) in this part of India undertook their "spiritual conquest" in the face of continual threats from both land and sea in the form of the Sultanate of Bijapur, the Maratha Empire, the Ottomans and the Dutch.[12] Despite these challenges, they enjoyed considerable success

[10] Diego Valadés, *Retórica Cristiana*, Tarsicio Herrera Zapién (ed.), 125–127.
[11] João Paulo Oliveira Costa and Vítor Luís Gaspar Rodrigues, *Conquista de Goa, 1510–1512: Campanhas de Alfonso de Albuquerque* (Lisbon: Tribuna da História, 2008).
[12] In 1683, the Marathas invaded Salcete causing the Jesuits to flee to Goa: Dauril Alden, *The Making of an Enterprise: The Society of Jesus in Portugal, Its Empire, and Beyond: 1540–1750* (Stanford, CA: Stanford University Press, 1996), 187–202. On missionary culture in Portuguese Asia, see: Ângela

in this porous coastal zone. Mirroring contemporary events in New Spain, churches were soon built, pre-Christian religious objects and texts destroyed and sermons delivered, all with the blessing of Iberian monarchies, their representatives and the growing number of native Christians.

As Iberian global expansion and the "Empire of Eloquence" that was constructed in its wake simultaneously affected the Americas and large parts of southern coastal Eurasia, the ethnohistorian thus has the option to think in a connected and comparative way about the shared experiences of native peoples from across the Iberian World. Having been subject to attempts at persuasion grounded in the same classical rhetorical tradition, the Indian and *indio* audiences of these sermons represent what Tamar Herzog has described as "skewed mirrors" that only make sense when placed together.[13] In other words, Goa has the potential to tell us about the Guarani, and vice versa. Following this logic, this chapter seeks to globalize the ethnohistory of the Americas by placing it in the context of other native languages and peoples that were brought into the "Empire of Eloquence." Whereas global missionary history is a well-established genre, Latin American ethnohistory remains highly localized in focus, especially among the "New Philologists" (i.e. those who study indigenous-language sources). This is compounded by the tyranny of meta-geography that has permitted connected and comparative studies of speakers of Mayan and Mixtec, but not Quechua and Konkani.[14] By exploring the expansion of missions in Salcete and the codification of South Asian grammars and textual traditions at the hands of Jesuit missionaries and native converts (especially those associated with Konkani, one of the languages of western coastal India), this chapter explores the parallel processes that took place in India and the Americas. This will culminate in an analysis of the ways in which native audiences shaped and interpreted the classical rhetorical tradition as expressed in the Konkani panegyrics of Miguel de Almeida (1607–1683) whose oratory shows that high humanist erudition could appeal to non-European audiences given the right set of local exigencies. As we shall see, these centered on the desire of local Brahmins to maintain

---

Barreto Xavier and Ines G. Županov. *Catholic Orientalism: Portuguese Empire, Indian Knowledge (16th–18th Centuries).*

[13] Tamar Herzog, *Frontiers of Possession*, 11.

[14] Luke Clossey, *Salvation and Globalization in the Early Jesuit Missions* (New York: Cambridge University Press, 2008). For the nascent subfield of "global" ethnohistory, see Nancy E. van Deusen, *Global Indios: The Indigenous Struggle for Justice in Sixteenth-Century Spain* (Durham, NC: Duke University Press, 2015); José Carlos de la Puente Luna, *Andean Cosmopolitans: Seeking Justice and Reward at the Spanish Royal Court* (Austin: University of Texas Press, 2018).

an identity based on a privileged access to learning. This interaction between the Empire of Eloquence and a vernacular periphery of what Sheldon Pollock has called the "Sanskrit Cosmopolis" was thus premised on a factor independent of the "European" or "non-European" nature of the classical rhetorical tradition, and underlines the fact that local populations were not passive recipients of Iberian cultural forms, but played an active constitutive role in the cultural landscape of the Iberian World.[15]

Evangelization and Indo-Humanist Grammar in Goa and Salcete

In 1664, an Italian missionary in Salcete named Ignazio Arcamone (1615–1683) composed a Caesarean Latin commentary on the Jesuit missions in the peninsula that offers important insights into this neglected Iberian missionary context, and the interactions between missionaries and the native population.[16] Salcete itself, Arcamone reported, was separated from the terra firma by a series of interconnected rivers and directly connected to the mainland by a strip of land only three kilometers wide. Palm trees covered the region, and rice, wheat, beans and lentils grew in abundance alongside numerous varieties of local fruit trees that bore, among other things, the mangos that today are still called *ambē*. Unlike in Paraguay, there was no need to gather the native population into towns (*pueblos de indios*) for the purpose of evangelization, as Salcete was already divided into sixty-six villages. As elsewhere in premodern India, each of these villages formed a distinct political unit (or a *respublica* in Arcamone's account) led by the male members of a hereditary village nobility who were required to take all decisions unanimously. These were then recorded by a scribe from the Brahmin caste. Of these villages, the twelve largest contributed delegates to a deliberative body called by the Portuguese the "general assembly" (*câmara geral*), although it had local origins. Onto this traditional South Asian stem were then grafted various Iberian institutions, including a Portuguese judge who administered justice, not unlike in Tlaxcala in New Spain where indigenous offices and social structures existed alongside Spanish office holders.[17]

---

[15] Sheldon Pollock, *The Language of the Gods in the World of Men: Sanskrit, Culture, and Power in Premodern India* (Berkeley: University of California Press, 2006), 10–18, 259–280.

[16] On Arcamone, see Alberto Merola, *Dizionario Biografico Degli Italiani*, 81 vols. (Rome: Istituto della Enciclopedia Italiana, 1960–2014), III, 739–740.

[17] This was the system codified in the age of Albuquerque: Lagrange Fernandes, "Uma Descrição e Relação 'de Sasatana Peninsula' (1664) do Padre Inácio Arcamone," *AHSI*, 50 (1981), 76–120 (89–90); A. Kulkarni, "Marathi Records on Village Communities in Goa Archives," *The Indian*

Whereas the city of Goa had briefly been under the control of the Muslim Sultan of Bijapur and garrisoned by Ottoman forces, the vast majority of the population had remained Hindu. At the time of the Portuguese acquisition of Salcete, which along with Bardez (the area immediately north of the city of Goa) was given to the Crown of Portugal as a ransom for a rival claimant to the throne of Bijapur, the area possessed at least 280 Hindu temples. These, however, were destroyed in 1567 on the orders of the captain of the fort at Rachol, Diogo Rodrigues. In their place were built churches, chapels and twenty-four Jesuit houses.[18] This said, unconverted Hindus continued to live in Portuguese territory throughout this period, with those who provided the Portuguese population with goods and services receiving particularly lenient treatment.[19]

As in the Americas, in Iberian Asia conversion at the hands of a missionary loyal to a particular Iberian monarch was understood as an acceptance of loyalty to the same monarch on the part of the convert.[20] This was not a fact hidden from New Christians as Arcamone's description of the annual cycle of native baptisms makes abundantly clear. After receiving catechistic instruction at the Jesuit college in Rachol, the neophytes traveled by river to the island of Goa and lodged at the College of St Paul, where they were treated to a feast. At dawn the next day, they processed with great ceremony through the viceregal capital. The procession was accompanied by music and singing, and was headed by flagbearers who carried the banners of each of Salcete's villages. After lodging another night in Goa, the next day (the feast of the conversion of St. Paul) a similar procession took place back to the College of St. Paul. This time, however, they received a guard of honor from the local militia who wore their dress uniforms and fired their muskets into the air in celebration. Once in the collegiate church, they heard a sermon in Konkani before finally being baptized in the presence of the viceroy and many other Portuguese ecclesiastical and secular officeholders. In this way, native converts were brought fully into the fold of Iberianized Christianity and Iberian territorial empire in a ceremony that blurred the lines between the two.[21]

Economic and Social History Review 19, (1982), 377–385 (379–381). On Tlaxcala's very similar political system, see Chapter 2.

[18] Fernandes, "Uma Descrição e Relação," 94.

[19] Ângela Barreto Xavier and Ines G. Županov, "Ser Brâmane na Goa da Época Moderna," *Revista de História*, no. 172 (2015), 15–41 (36–37); Sanjay Subrahmanyam, *Three Ways to Be Alien: Travails and Encounters in the Early Modern World* (Waltham, MA: Brandeis University Press, 2011), 28–33.

[20] Tamar Herzog, *Frontiers of Possession*, 70–72.

[21] Fernandes, "Uma Descrição e Relação," 101–103.

In order to provide missionaries, local converts and Catholics from throughout Asia with instruction, the Society of Jesus founded two colleges in the region, one in the city of Goa and the other in the village of Rachol on the banks of the River Zuari in Salcete.[22] There, Jesuit missionaries worked with local Christians to codify the rhetorical-philological traditions associated with the native languages that they called "Konkani" (*canarim*) and "Marathi" (*marata*).[23] The former was commonly spoken along large stretches of western coastal India, while the latter predominated in the sultanates of the Deccan Plateau as well as serving as a high-caste lingua franca across the region.[24] In the case of both of these languages, Jesuit missionaries followed in the footsteps of missionaries across the Iberian World: They turned to native collaborators and also fell back on practices inherited from the ancient Mediterranean, which gave them both a model and a metalanguage for grammatical study. In Goa and Salcete, this latter technique produced particularly felicitous results, as Konkani and Marathi were Indo-European languages that had close affinities with the European classical languages. This fact did not escape missionaries like the English Jesuit Thomas Stephens (1549–1619) who noted in a letter to his brother: "This region has so many languages. Their pronunciation is not disagreeable, and their structure is not dissimilar to Latin and Greek."[25]

By grafting their growing understanding of Konkani and Marathi onto a humanist grammatical stem, missionaries like Stephens were able to build an extensive, if inevitably somewhat distorted understanding of the structure of the languages, and to couch their conclusions in a metalanguage familiar to other humanistically educated missionaries.[26] This meant that a

---

[22] On Goa College, see Charles J. Borges, "The College of St. Paul's and Jesuit Education in Goa," in Herman Castellino (ed.), *Jesuits and Education in India* (Anand: Gujarat Sahitya Prakash, 2005), 1–14. On the college at Rachol, see Mousinho de Ataíde, *Rachol: Jesuit College, 1610–1759* (Goa: Rachol Jesuit Seminary, 2012). The Jesuit provincial council of India in 1588 dictated that Rachol become a main center for the study of local languages: Josef Wicki (ed.), *Documenta Indica*, XV, 15.

[23] The division between Konkani and Marathi was largely the product of these missionaries, and has been the subject of intense debate ever since: José Pereira, *Konkani: A Language; A History of the Konkani Marathi Controversy* (Dharward: Karnatak University, 1971).

[24] The Jesuits had ambitions in the Deccan region, an area with which the Portuguese had considerable diplomatic and military interactions. Although the Portuguese relied heavily on Hindus, Muslims and Pharsis as diplomats, learned Jesuits like Arcamone and Almeida also served in Portuguese embassies in the Deccan, where their command of Marathi no doubt came in very useful: Directorate of Archives and Archaeology, Panjim, Goa, ms. 1422 (Regimento e Instruções, Instruções 1647–1657), fol. 64v.

[25] Josef Wicki,(ed.), *Documenta Indica*, XII, 825: "Linguae harum regionum sunt permultae. Pronunciationem habent non invenustam, et compositionem latinae graecaeque similem."

[26] The Jesuit codification of Konkani grammar is surveyed in: Stuart M. McManus, "World Philology: Indo-Humanism and Jesuit Indigenous-Language Scholarship in the Americas and

newly arrived missionary presented with an Indo-humanist grammar of Konkani, like the one written by Stephens and printed at Rachol in 1640, would have instantly recognized large parts of its form and content from his earliest days in a humanist classroom. For instance, Stephens outlined the Konkani "case system," which mirrored those of Latin and Greek. This was an imperfect but not unuseful way to understand a nominal system that is today more commonly described as having a morphology based on a dual system of "direct" and "oblique" forms that can be supplemented by a wide array of postpositions.

Indeed, although it would not be until the mid-eighteenth century that scholars began to hypothesize about the reasons for the close family resemblance between Konkani and the languages of Cicero and Demosthenes, the aforementioned Ignazio Arcamone went as far as to use Latin as a sort of pedagogical seedbed in which he planted these Indian vernaculars. Writing in a comparative grammar of Konkani and Marathi that circulated in manuscript at the college in Rachol, he noted that: "Konkani syntax hardly differs from that of Latin, but for a few additions."[27] A young Jesuit could, at least in the first instance, think in terms of Latin word order while speaking Konkani, and not go too far astray. This was a powerful time-saving trick to get missionaries into the field. However, Arcamone did not stop there. Once the missionary had constructed his knowledge of Konkani on these Latinate foundations, the same process of reasoning by analogy that stood at the core of the Indo-humanist grammatical method could also be applied to other South Asian vernaculars. Building on the comparative method outlined in his section on syntax, Arcamone proceeded to introduce his students to the closely related Indo-European language of Marathi, noting all the ways in which it differed from Konkani in terms of its morphology, syntax and vocabulary.[28] In this way, missionaries could advance quickly in their study of the "language of the Deccan" (*lingua Decanica*) using their knowledge of Konkani, which was in turn grounded in Latin, much in the same way as a modern student who has studied Latin might then pick up Spanish and then move on to Portuguese.

Asia," in Ines G. Županov (ed.), *Oxford Handbook of Jesuit History* (New York: Oxford University Press, 2019), 737–758.

[27] Arcamone's grammar survives in at least two copies: Biblioteca National de Portugal, Lisbon, cod. 3049; Biblioteca Nazionale, Naples, ms. I.F.60. *Ibid.*, fols. 50v–51r: "Syntaxis concannica fere non differt a latina nonnullis tamen apponendis."

[28] *Ibid.*, fols. 117v–126v.

How a Jesuit Missionary Read His *Mahābhārata*

While these grammars provided a grounding in the rudiments of Konkani and Marathi, this was far from sufficient for missionaries whose ultimate aim was to deliver eloquent sermons and produce other texts in local languages. To this end, missionaries composed more detailed normative works, such as the manuscript study of Konkani syntax by the Franciscan missionary Gaspar de São Miguel (*c.* 1595–1647), entitled *Most Copious Syntax of the Brahmin and Polished Language*, that offered a thorough treatment of word order and idioms, reflecting a level of competence in Konkani analogous to the Latin of the Jesuit "humanities" class.[29] However, as in the *Ratio studiorum*, this was only a first step to achieving true eloquence. It was also necessary to identify local traditions of eloquence to create something akin to the canon of classical and postclassical Latin orations and sermons that could provide the necessary models for creative imitation by sacred orators.

Across the Iberian World, different approaches had been taken to building a suitable canon. In the Valley of Mexico, the famous Franciscan friar Bernardino de Sahagún had collected and codified Nahuatl *huehuetlatolli* with the help of indigenous collaborators at the College of Santa Cruz de Tlatelolco who had at least secondhand knowledge of pre-Columbian public speaking. While Hindu religious practices continued in the areas surrounding Portuguese territories and to some extent in Salcete itself, there was no analogous oratorical genre to the sermon to deconstruct. This is not to say that there were no rhetorical traditions at all, far from it. Before the advent of Portuguese hegemony in Salcete, Brahmins in the region had copied and recited extended religious poems, including vernacular versions of canonical South Asian religious literature, such as the *Mahābhārata* and the *Rāmāyaṇa*, as well as Middle Marathi *bhakti* ("devotional") works, many of which were intended for public performance, albeit before selected audiences.[30] This latter genre in particular provided models for missionaries to compose their own devotional poetic works, such as the *Kristapurāṇa*, an extended poem composed by Thomas Stephens and his native collaborators in *ovī* verse. This drew heavily on the *Bhāgavata* of the sixteenth-century Marathi scholar-saint

---

[29] Jose Pereira, "Gaspar de S. Miguel's *Arte da Lingoa Canarim*, Parte 2a, *Sintaxis Copiossisima na Lingoa Bramana e Pollida,*" *Journal of the University of Bombay,* 36 (1967), 1–155.

[30] On the performance of *bhakti,* see: Jacqueline Jones, "Performing the Sacred: Song, Genre, and Aesthetics in *Bhakti*" (Ph.D. dissertation: University of Chicago, 2008).

Eknath whose account of the birth and life of Kṛṣṇa provided the perfect model for Stephens' poem on the life of Christ.[31] However, a *purāṇa* with its exacting metrical requirements and restricted performative context was unsuitable for the type of semi-spontaneous public speaking required of the sacred orator. As a result, the missionaries had to look elsewhere to create the textual base for their culture of Indo-humanist eloquence.

It was in this context that the missionaries turned to a group of unknown Christian Brahmins who provided a body of prose more suited to the needs of sacred oratory. This took the form of oral prose summaries of large sections of the *Rāmāyaṇa* and the *Mahābhārata* in Konkani with the latter showing considerable communalities with the Marathi version by the late sixteenth-century poet Viṣṇudās Nāmā with some influence from the thirteenth-century Marathi poet-saint, Jñāneśvar. These the Christian Brahmins recited orally, and the Jesuits duly transcribed, with copies now existing in two manuscripts held in the District Archive of Braga in Portugal alongside a third codex that contains short extracts from the same works in Marathi, as well as a Marathi translation of a section of the *Bhāgavatapurāṇa* attributed to Kriṣṇudās Ṣāmā, an early sixteenth-century Saraswat Brahmin from Quelossim in Salcete.[32]

Although the names of the native Christians who assisted in the production of these manuscripts are lost to us, it is possible to reconstruct something of their intellectual world. Between them, they certainly knew the *Rāmāyaṇa* and the *Mahābhārata* exceedingly well. Indeed, the Konkani manuscripts alone run to over 1,200 pages between them and contain summaries of ten of the eighteen "books" (*parvas*) of the *Mahābhārata*, some of which are preserved in multiple, slightly variant versions, including the all-important "first book" (*Ādiparva*) and "sixth book" (*Bhīṣmaparva*). As Rocky Miranda has noted, the texts also show some internal inconsistencies that suggest the existence of multiple overlapping mythological traditions in the region. In addition, there is evidence of the

---

[31] Hugh van Skyhawk, "'... In this bushy land of Salsette ...': Father Thomas Stephens and the *Kristapurāṇa*," in A. Entwistle, C. Salomon, H. Pauweis and M. Shapiro (eds.), *Studies in Early Modern Indo-Aryan Languages, Literature and Culture* (Delhi: Manohar Pubns, 1999), 363–378. The closest thing we have to a critical edition of the text is: Thomas Stephens, *Father Thomas Stephens' Kristapurāṇa: Purāṇa I & II*, Nelson M. Falcao (ed. and trans.) (Bengaluru: Kristu Jyoti Publications, 2012). All translations are taken from this edition.

[32] BPB, cod. 771 (Konkani prose version of the *Rāmāyaṇa*), 772 (Konkani prose version of the *Mahābhārata*), 773 (Marathi texts). On manuscript culture in premodern South Asia, see Sheldon Pollock, "Literary Culture and Manuscript Culture in Precolonial India," in Simon Eliot, Andrew Nash, Ian Willison (eds.), *History of the Book and Literary Cultures* (London: British Library, 2006), 77–94.

influence of folk tales common in what is now Gujarat and Karnataka, which points to intellectual connections not only with the inland Deccan Plateau, but also north and south along coastal western India. Finally, it bears mentioning that the main language of the manuscripts' intellectual milieu was not the classical language of South Asia, Sanskrit, but Marathi; the only Sanskrit in the Braga codices is a small number of garbled aphorisms.[33] This, then, was the context from which the South Asian component of Indo-humanism sprang.

With a representative corpus of texts in hand, missionaries at the Jesuit colleges at Goa and Rachol set about reading them. Given that the manuscripts provided them with both the bedrock of their rhetorical *inventio* and detailed accounts of the native religious traditions that the missionaries were seeking to undermine, such reading could not afford to be mere idle perusal. Rather, it necessarily involved what Anthony Grafton and Lisa Jardine called "purposeful reading." This entailed sitting quietly with the text and reading attentively with the evangelization mission of the Society of Jesus in mind. When the missionary reader came across words, phrases or information that could serve his ultimate aim, he would duly record the fact in the margin of the manuscript, sometimes by merely copying out the passage that had caught his attention verbatim (with or without a translation into Portuguese or Latin), other times by glossing or commenting on it in a marginal note that could run from a few words to short commentaries that dwarfed the original text.[34]

Some of the unknown readers of the Braga manuscripts probably also deposited the gems that they had mined from these Konkani versions of the *Rāmāyaṇa* and the *Mahābhārata* in rhetorical treasure troves known as "commonplace books," notebooks arranged under relevant headings that allowed the easy storage and retrieval of information gained from reading. If we are to judge from the influential treatise on note-taking by the Jesuit scholar and sacred orator Jeremias Drexel (1581–1638), such Konkani commonplace books were likely arranged under headings that emphasized the virtues and vices commonly found in Christian sermons. Virtue and vice, as Drexel noted, were the bread and butter of a sacred orator, a remark that would have come as no surprise to a Jesuit familiar with the constant alternation between praise and blame that characterized Christian

---

[33] Panduronga Pissurlencar, "A Propósito dos Primeiros Livros Maratas Impressos em Goa," *Boletim do Instituto Vasco da Gama*, 73 (1956), 55–79; Rocky Miranda, *The Old Konkani Bhārata* (Mysore: Central Institute of Indian Languages, 2011), 5–17, 242–266.

[34] Anthony Grafton and Lisa Jardine, "Studied for Action: How Gabriel Harvey Read His Livy," *Past and Present*, 129 (1990), 30–78 (32).

humanist epideictic. Yet, what precisely the Jesuit readers of the Braga codices noted under these headings is less clear, as commonplace books could take a number of forms. Some were lists of bare references to the page or chapter of the relevant section that required readers to have easy access to the original volume if they could not recall the exact wording. Others contained the passages copied out in their entirety, which maximized portability, but made the process of creating a commonplace book long, laborious and less economical in terms of paper. Whatever form they took, however, the aim was the same: to provide an indispensable aid to memory and a ready-made source of inspiration for creating original compositions, including sermons.[35]

The Braga codices are also particularly valuable for reconstructing the underpinnings of this Jesuit missionary *inventio*, since the variety of hands in the text and margins of the three manuscripts suggest that their copying, reading and annotation were undertaken not by a single, perhaps unrepresentative missionary, but by a number of Jesuits over the course of the seventeenth century.[36] An examination of these marginalia reveals that the interests of Jesuit readers were quite varied, while at the same time being focused on the job in hand. One reader used the margins to gloss particularly difficult words and phrases. Since most of these words do not appear in the contemporary Konkani-Portuguese dictionary by Diogo Ribeiro, it is reasonable to assume that these definitions were provided by native Christians.[37] Some of the marginal annotations also bespeak what we might call a "missionary-ethnographic" focus that prioritized understanding South Asian religion in order to refute it. For instance, in the course of reading the *Rāmāyaṇa*, one reader took pains to note a section that described the number of gods in Hinduism, while another was struck by a reference to the "giant" (*gigante*) named Kumbhakarna, Rama's evil adversary, who slept for six months and awoke ravenous.[38] Elsewhere, a Jesuit reader also noted a section on Indian funeral rituals (*exequiae*), and another on the phenomenon of gender variance in Hindu mythology, which he explained in a marginal note

---

[35] Jeremias Drexel, *Aurifodina Artium et Scientiarum Omnium: Excerpendi Solertia, Omnibus Litterarum Amantibus Monstrata* (Antwerp, 1641), 90–93, 291. On Jesuit commonplacing more generally, see Ann Moss, *Printed Commonplace-Books and the Structuring of Renaissance Thought*, 170–182; Ann Blair, *Too Much to Know: Managing Scholarly Information before the Modern Age* (New Haven, CT: Yale University Press, 2010), 72–73.

[36] Although the identity of the Jesuit readers of the Braga codices is unknown, the spellings of certain Latin words suggest that at least one of the annotators was Lusophone; e.g. BPB, cod. 772, fol. 77v: "filhius [*rectius* filius] non obediens patri."

[37] E.g. *Ibid.*, cod. 771, fols. 53r, 73v.   [38] *Ibid.*, cod. 771, fols. 67v, 21r, 12r.

Figure 4.1   Marginal annotation to the *Bhīṣmaparva* on Śikhaṇḍī (BPB, cod. 771 [PT/
UM-ADB/COL/M], fol. 21r).
Direitos da imagem: © Universidade do Minho/Arquivo Distrital de Braga

was akin to the Greek idea of the "hermaphrodite." For readers who
wished to know more, he also included a cross reference to the Marathi
text of the *Bhīṣmaparva*, which mentions Shikhandi, a combatant in the
Kurukshetra War who is born female but becomes male (Figure 4.1).[39]

This said, the majority of the marginal annotations focus directly on
passages that discuss particular virtues and vices that could easily be
repurposed in Christian sacred oratory and polemic. Indeed, if one were
to judge from the marginalia alone, one might be forgiven for thinking
that the *Rāmāyaṇa* and the *Mahābhārata* were as Christian as the sermons
of Leo the Great or St. Augustine's *Confessions*. The margins are positively
filled with notes that highlight examples of "wisdom," "duty" and "how to
go on pilgrimage," as well as portions of the text that could be used to
exhort listeners to "give thanks to God," and persuade them that "good

---

[39] *Ibid.*, fol. 35v. Ibid., fol. 21r: "Napushancu, neuter, hoc est nec mas nec faemina. Greci
Hermaphrodites sive androgynus, alio nomine marastice dicitur Xiqhanddio, a. Dadulo nhoe
anny balai nhoe. Vide Bhismaparva cap. 19."

works must be done" and "alms must be given to the poor."[40] The anonymous Jesuit readers also sought out passages to use in sermons in honor of the "virgin" and the "virgin and mother," terms that appear regularly in the margins.[41] Driven by the importance of praise and blame, however, by far the most sustained attention was paid to passages that could be used to compose epideictic orations. These included phrases that could be used to praise a king, a city or even God himself.[42] Once these had been transferred to a commonplace book, a Jesuit who needed to deliver a panegyric on a particular topic need only go to the section on "praises" (*laudes*) and find a ready-made selection of idiomatic phrases that he could use verbatim, imitate or simply echo in his sermon. In so doing, he was relying on an Indo-humanist culture of commonplacing that united Jesuit missionaries, canonical South Asian texts and native Christians in an expansionist Catholic intellectual project that had parallels across the Iberian World.

Konkani Sacred Oratory

The final product of such collaborative rhetorical-philological projects were the Konkani sermons delivered in Salcete every Sunday and feast day of the year.[43] While these sermons were largely the product of European-born missionaries who had been inducted into the region's local culture of Indo-humanist eloquence and erudition, indigenous collaborators may not have been absent even at the moment of delivery. Given the high mortality rate on the Portuguese route from Iberia to India, missionaries could be thrown into parishes before they had fully completed their training. In such cases, the actual delivery of indigenous language sermons might require the participation of indigenous Christians, as Henrique Henriques (1520–1600), a Jesuit missionary on the Tamil-speaking Malabar Coast, recounted:

> Since the pronunciation is really quite difficult and very different from ours, they do not always understand everything I say. Therefore, in most cases when I preach in the churches, I say the words in Malabar [i.e. in Tamil]

---

[40] E.g. *Ibid.*, cod. 772, fols. 10r (*officium*), 12r (*scientia*), 15v (*regis superbia*), 22v (*ira magna*), 32v (*obediendum maioribus*) 39v (*bona opera facienda*), 47v (*elimosina facienda pauperibus*), 50r (*gratia Deo reddenda*); 56r (*peregrinatio quomodo facienda*).

[41] *Ibid.*, cod. 771, fols. 75r, 148v; Cod. 772. fol. 7v.

[42] *Ibid.*, cod. 772, fols. 43r (*ornatus civitatis*), 70v (*laudes alicuius magni*), 89v (*laudes Dei*), 107r (*laudes regis*), 127v (*adulatioria verba*).

[43] Fernandes, "Uma Descrição e Relação," 103.

and have someone else repeat them after me like an interpreter of sorts, so that the people can understand it better. However, with the help of God I will only need an interpreter for a few more months, when I will be able to speak to them and they will all understand.[44]

There was one missionary, however, who certainly could address a native congregation without assistance: the Portuguese Jesuit, Miguel de Almeida (1607–1683).[45] Almeida had arrived in India at the age of sixteen, and had served first as parish priest in the villages of Quelossim and Benaulim, then as rector of the College at Goa and finally as Jesuit Provincial Father. In addition to these pastoral and administrative activities, he earned the praise of Ignazio Arcamone for having "composed many books in the elegant language of this land and published volumes of sermons, catechisms and even histories in a quite learned and impressive style."[46] This was no understatement, as Almeida was responsible for the largest surviving collection of Konkani sermons, entitled *Garden of the Shepherds Put into the Language of the Brahmins*, printed in Goa in five volumes between 1658 and 1659.[47] The surviving three volumes of the larger work contain sermons for every possible occasion during the liturgical year with a particular focus on feast days of saints. Of course, as with all texts that purport to record acts of public address in a written form, we cannot be sure that the printed text represents what was actually delivered. What is certain, however, is that they were meant to serve as models for priests in Goa and Salcete who could either use them as a basis for creative

---

[44] Josef Wicki (ed.), *Documenta Indica*, I, 287: "porque la pronunciación della es muy dificultosa y muy diferente de la nuestra, a las vezes no me entienden todos, y por lo tanto las más de las vezes, quando les hago platicas en la iglesia, digo las palabras en la misma lengua malavar y hago que las torne a dezir otro, que es como topaz, para que todos las entiendan mejor; pero daquí algunos meses con la ayuda del Señor no avrá necesidad dello, mas hablarles he que todos entiendan."

[45] Almeida was based at Benaulim in the early 1660s: Ignazio Arcamone, *Purgatorii Commentarium Concannice Compositum Mortuorum Christi Fidelium Immortalibus Animabus Purgatorii Poenas Patientibus* (Rachol, 1663), fol. 1r.

[46] Fernandes, "Uma Descrição e Relação," 118: "Pater Michael de Almeida, lusitanus, ex oppido Govea, patris Ignatii Martines in Lusitania celeberrimi proximus cognatus, plurimos libros terrae huius eleganti lingua composuit et in lucem edidit concionum et cathechismi, quin etiam historiarum, satis docta et clara loquela."

[47] Miguel de Almeida, *Jardim dos Pastores*, 5 vols. (Goa, 1658–1659). A copy of volume I is currently in an unknown private collection in India but was published in a Devanagari transcription in V. B. Prabhudesai, "Vanavāḷyāñcô Maḷô by Father Miguel de Almeida," *Nagpur University Journal (Humanities)*, 21 (1970–1971), 1–110; volume III is preserved in Goa Central Library, Panjim and partly transcribed in Devanagari in Olivinho J. F. Gomes, *Konkani Manasagangotri: An Anthology of Early Konkani Literature* (Chandor: Konkani Sorospot Prakashan, 2000), 200–280; volume V is preserved in two copies, one at the School of Oriental and African Studies, University of London and the other at the Bibliothèque National de France in Paris.

imitation or recite them verbatim to their native congregations.[48] They offer, then, a guide, albeit an imperfect one, not only to Almeida's sacred oratory, but also to the sermons heard by native congregations across Salcete and Goa during the seventeenth and eighteenth centuries. As such, they are a plausible starting point for understanding the interaction between the classical rhetorical tradition and native audiences, and when placed in the context of similar moments in the Americas for a connected and comparative ethnohistory of the Iberian World.

If we turn to the three surviving volumes of *Garden of the Shepherds*, we find that the sermons contained therein are far from uniform. Instead, they contain two distinct varieties of sacred oratory. The first and the third volumes contain explanatory doctrinal sermons (*práticas*). Instead of a tripartite structure (*salutatio-argumentatio-conclusio*) and the extensive rhetorical ornamentation of Yapuguay and Restivo's sacred panegyrics in Guarani, these offered plainer narratives and discussions of the events of the feast day and their meaning. This is not to say that they were without eloquence or entirely devoid of erudition. For instance, in a sermon dedicated to St. Matthew that aimed to provide Christian consolation to those suffering, Almeida made occasional references to the Church Fathers, including St. Augustine, whom he quotes first in Latin and then translates into Konkani.[49] In another sermon, this time for Our Lady of the Pillar probably first delivered in the Church devoted to her in Seraulim, Almeida played with the possible Konkani and Marathi etymologies of the town's name. There were three possible interpretations, Almeida argued. Seraulim could be derived from the words for "knife" (*sury, ie*), "sun" (*surio, iâ*) or "heaven" (*suru, â*), which led him to exhort his listeners to reject the "knife" as a symbol of sin, and embrace heaven and the "sun." This was because, as he noted, it was widely accepted that "Christ is the sun of justice" (*Christus sol justitiae*).[50] This was a self-consciously skillful, although not necessarily identifiably classicizing strategy, even if it is true that etymological figures of speech do appear in both ancient and humanist rhetorical handbooks.[51]

[48] Miguel de Almeida, *Jardim dos Pastores*, V, fol. IIv: "Antes julgo ser obra mui proveitosa pera os Christãos desta terra, e a inda mais pera os parachos e pregadores destas novas Christandades. Por onde julgo que se pode e deve de imprimir."

[49] *Ibid.*, III, fols. 92v–99v.

[50] Discussed in: Antonio Pereira, *The Makers of Konkani Literature* (Goa: Pilar, 1982), 90–99.

[51] Nicolas Caussin, *Eloquentiae Sacrae et Humanae Parallela Libri XVI*, 174–176. In this sense, Almeida's doctrinal sermons followed the pattern visible in other *práticas* delivered in both European languages and Konkani, as is clear from Arcamone's small collection of model "sermons" (*conciones*), printed at Rachol in 1668, which also show occasional flashes of Christian humanist erudition in the form of examples taken from the Church Fathers and other authoritative

However, direct if not entirely artless doctrinal sermons were not the only way to address native converts in Salcete. As we learn from the fifth volume of *Garden of the Shepherds*, Almeida composed and probably also personally delivered full sacred panegyrics in Konkani that made extensive use of the Indo-humanist form of the classical rhetorical tradition, including allusions to ancient Mediterranean history and culture, as well as appeals to ancient, patristic and humanist authorities. In this regard, his panegyric sermon for the Decollation of John the Baptist, likely delivered in the eponymous Jesuit church at Benaulim during the 1640s or 1650s, proves particularly illustrative.[52]

This sermon was delivered within the context of a religious ritual, which included a sung mass, a procession around the inside of the church, confessions and opportunities to take communion.[53] Toward the end of the celebrations, Almeida ascended to the gilded baroque pulpit, and addressed the native Christians and assembled Jesuits in a style that would have been recognizable across the Iberian World:

> Seneca speaks in praise of the constancy (satvadhiru) of Socrates, in terms of the greatness of the courage of this unfortunate sage. In other words, when in plain sight he withstood being thrown into prison because of evil and envy on the part of his enemy. However, thanks to his constancy of courage he could not be troubled, nor his sensations descend into the realm of pain in that place, and he happily entered into prison.[54]

Christian figures. For instance, in a sermon on the crowning of Jesus with thorns (John 19:2), Arcamone included a number of learned references as part of his larger argument that Christ had taken on the crown of thorns in order to save mankind. In so doing, Arcamone was following the view of the theologian Theodoret of Cyrrhus that the evergreen nature of the Juniper tree pointed to Christ's desire to "cure you with all my might, protect you from every ill and terrify the enemy, so to speak, with some thorns," which Arcamone cited first in Latin and then translated into Konkani. Ignazio Arcamone, *Conciones per Annum Concannice Compositae* (Rachol, 1668), fols. 12r–15r (fol. 13v): "omni studio curabo, ab omni pernicie tutum efficiam et invadentem quasi quibusdam aculeis perterrefaciam."

52 Fernandes, "Uma Descrição e Relação," 99. The church itself was notable for its mannerist style, central oculus and fleur-de-lis alettes on the facade, and played an important role in religious life in Salcete, as it was situated close to a hilltop chapel dedicated jointly to St. Anthony of Padua and Francis Xavier. It was also the starting point for an important procession undertaken on the first Sunday of Lent, which went from the church to the aforementioned chapel, covering a distance that was said to be identical to that between the house of Pontius Pilate and Golgotha. On the church, see José Lourenço, *The Parish Churches of Goa: A Study of Façade Architecture* (Margao: Amazing Goa Publications, 2005), 55.

53 ARSI, Goa 45, 1, fols. 302v–303r. As Arcamone tells us, eponymous saints' days were particularly important occasions in Salcete when Jesuit missionaries and native Christians from across the Salcete gathered to hold processions, attend mass, hear a sermon and in some cases watch firework displays: Fernandes, "Uma Descrição e Relação," 104.

54 Miguel de Almeida, *Jardim dos Pastores*, V, fol. 48r: "Socratas mhall*a*lea zannateachea nirvannachy vhaddiuy, satuadhiru, Seneca vaqhannitâ mhannata, quy zavalli tacheâ drustiâ manani vaittive, va neduqhachara nimiti bandaqhanni ghaluncheaca taca dharlo, tavalli to, teachi niruannachea

Almeida then quoted a Latin commonplace taken from Seneca's *Consolatio ad Helviam matrem*, in which the Stoic philosopher attempts to console his mother in the wake of his own exile by giving an account of the steadfastness of Socrates at the prospect of an ignominious death after being convicted of corrupting the youth: "when he entered the prison, he took away the infamous character of the place, for no place that contained Socrates was truly a prison."[55] Almeida then translated this into Konkani and briefly explained its significance, before underlining that if Seneca had praised the wisdom of Socrates' actions in this case, then his congregation should venerate John the Baptist for the same reason.[56] In this "opening" (*salutatio*), he also criticized Herod's marriage to his brother's wife, which as John the Baptist had insisted, was against "God's law" ("Devachie sumurty"). This then culminated in an argument for the necessity of "divine grace" ("Devacrupechy garza") and an invocation of the Virgin in the form of an *Ave Maria* ("Namo Mariye" in Konkani), the typical closing gesture in a Christian humanist *salutatio*.

As his Konkani-speaking audience listened, Almeida then continued in the same Indo-humanist vein in the *argumentatio*, making extensive use of arguments from learned authorities to praise John the Baptist whose constancy he carefully contextualized and put forward as a model for imitation in line with the conventions of panegyric oratory.[57] He first compared the prophet's constancy in the face of violence to the well-known biblical account of Balaam's donkey. As the Book of Numbers narrates, the diviner berated his steed for stopping in its tracks at the sight of an angel sent to communicate God's displeasure with its master for agreeing to curse the Israelites. Balaam threated the donkey: "if only I had a sword, so that I could kill you" (*utinam haberem gladium, ut te percuterem* [Numbers 22:29]). As Almeida noted, the poor beast was fortunate as God did not give Balaam a sword, citing the words of the first century-CE Hellenistic Jewish philosopher, Philo of Alexandria, who concluded that we should give: "great thanks to the Creator who knowing the madness of folly did not give it to him like giving a sword to a madman who would

---

satuadhira vhaddivena veacullu nazatâ, achava duqhichy matra qhunna tache tthaî drustty napaddota, harquita muqhî bandaqhannintu rigalo, *carcerem intravit ignominiam ipsi loco detracturus, neque enim poterat carcer videri ubi Socrates erat.*"

[55] Seneca, *Consolatio ad Helviam Matrem* (=*Dialogi* XII), 13.4
[56] Miguel de Almeida, *Jardim dos Pastores*, V, fol. 48r.
[57] Nicolas Caussin, *Eloquentiae Sacrae et Humanae Parallela Libri XVI*, 196–197.

then use it to do great harm to all who crossed his path."[58] This reference to the madman was, of course, borrowed from the discussion of justice in Plato's *Republic*, a fact that may have been known to Almeida, although most likely not to his congregation.[59] Returning to the Gospel narrative, Almeida then reminded his native and Jesuit listeners that, unlike Balaam, Herod did have access to a sword in the form of his executioner. Yet, in spite of the threat of violence, John the Baptist remained strong in the knowledge that he had righteousness on his side, thereby, in the words of the Church Father, Tertullian, allowing "his virtue to shine all the brighter" (*ut eius virtus splendidior elucescat*).

Moving back and forth between the story of John the Baptist and other biblical examples, Almeida then argued that Jezabel's death threats against the prophet Elijah for ordering the execution of the priests of the pagan deity Baal proved that the mere fact of receiving a threat of violence from a monarch was a sign that justice was on the saint's side. The story of Cain and Abel was another example of an individual favored by God who met an unfortunate end.[60] In closing his panegyric sermon, Almeida quoted a Latin letter from a sixteenth-century Jesuit theologian, Alfonso Salmerón to Stefano Tucci, the Jesuit orator, dramatist and theologian. In it, Salmerón argued that pride of place in heaven belonged to Mary and "glorious St John, the soul that was a heroic soul and an example of immeasurable greatness."[61] According to Almeida, the Virgin sat at God's right hand, while Christ's cousin sat on the left, a privileged position given to him as a reward for his unwavering constancy. As Almeida took pains to underline in the *conclusio* of this virtue-driven epideictic oration: "your virtue (sagunnu, a) is deserving of all things, your good deeds (punne, ea) deserve the richest rewards."[62] Having proven that John was the embodiment of Socratic, Senecan and Old Testament satvadhiru and the mirror of the Virgin Mary, Almeida hammered home his message in a series of parallel noun phrases in which he praised these two biblical figures whose virtuous actions were a model for the Konkani-speaking congregation. Looking up at the Jesuit preacher in his gilded pulpit, Almeida's

---

[58] Miguel de Almeida, *Jardim dos Pastores*, V, fol. 49v: "Philo xastrapravinnu mhautami zapadita: *gratia maxima conditoris qui sciens imprudentiae rabiem non dedit illi tanquam furenti gladium ne quoscumque obvios magna claude conficeret* [Philo, *On the Cherubim*, 32–33]."

[59] Plato, *Republic*, 331c.   [60] *Ibid.*, V, fol. 52v.

[61] *Ibid.*, V, fol. 54r: "Mugtivanta Bhagta Ioaõ, ho manu zo assa vhaddu manu, aparampari vhaddivy." On Tucci, see Mirella Saulini, "Tra Erasmo e Cicerone: l'Eclettismo Oratorio di Stefano Tuccio, S.J. (1540–1597)," *AHSI*, 78 (155) (2009), 141–221.

[62] *Ibid.*, V, fol. 54r: "tuzeã sagunnanca hê sarua phaua; sarua tuzea punneachea bhanddarantu sambhavata."

congregation must have been left in no doubt that constancy was a path to God and John the Baptist one of its leading exponents.

As well as being erudite in the traditional sense of the word, Almeida's sermon was also stylistically sophisticated. Indeed, it brimmed with rhetorical figures recognizable from Jesuit rhetorical handbooks. For instance, after a series of rhetorical questions regarding why John was doomed to be beheaded, Almeida began his answer with an emphatic *tricolon abundans* with *variatio*, in which the sum of the syllables in the first two coda approximated that of the third:

> Vlairām, bolatā, xastra sangatā.
> "I speak, I say, I preach the law."[63]

Such figures of parallelism abounded in the sermon from start to finish, particularly in the *conclusio*, where Almeida praised John the Baptist in a series of clauses that each began with the pronoun "you" ("tû ... tû ... tû"). Although Almeida was probably initially inspired to use this figure by his training in humanist rhetoric, the mere fact that it fitted the pattern of the classical rhetorical tradition does not mean that it would necessarily have grated on the ears of even the most recent converts among his congregation. Indeed, the passage may have sounded just as harmonious to the first-time hearer of a Konkani sacred panegyric as to a native listener who had heard hundreds of sermons, albeit for different reasons. This was because analogous figures existed within South Asian literary traditions, most notably dīpaka ("repetition of syntactical category") and āvrtti ("repetition of a word or sense"), although in the *alaṃkāraśāstra* tradition (i.e. Sanskrit poetics and aesthetics) they were codified and conceptualized in ways that differed significantly from ancient Mediterranean rhetorical theory.[64] Nonetheless, this was a convenient overlap in rhetorical-philological traditions that, whether present by design or not, enhanced Almeida's persuasive power.

On the face of it, then, Almeida's sermon for the feast of the Decollation of John the Baptist stands in contrast to the indigenous-language sermons delivered in the Americas in that it shows all the familiar features of

---

[63] *Ibid.*, V, fol. 51v. Cf. Cipriano Soáres, *De Arte Rhetorica Libri Tres*, 46–47.

[64] On figures featuring repetition, see: Edwin Gerow, *A Glossary of Indian Figures of Speech* (The Hague: Walter de Gruyter, 1971), 65–70. It has been observed that the syntax of Almeida's sermons is particularly Latinate: Olivinho J. F. Gomes, *Old Konkani Language and Literature: The Portuguese Role* (Goa: Konkani Sorospot Prakashan, 1999), 117–118. On the rhetorical versus cognitive conceptions of Sanskrit tropes and figures, see Whitney Cox, "*Anantaprapañcā*: Thinking through Samāsokti with Ruyyaka," *Revista Degli Studi Orientali*, 90 (2017), 145–167.

humanist epideictic. This includes continual appeals to ancient Mediterranean history and culture, as well as classical, patristic and humanist authorities. Like Hara Martinho's epideictic oration for Valignano delivered in the nearby city of Goa (Chapter 3) and the funeral orations for Philip IV performed across the Hispanic Monarchy (Chapter 2), this was an erudite and eloquent panegyric that promoted John the Baptist and his classical and Old Testament antitypes, Socrates, Elijah and Balaam's donkey, as models for imitation by the Konkani-speaking congregation.[65] Indeed, if we take a Portuguese sermon given for exactly the same occasion in 1652 by Brazil's most famous sacred orator, António Vieira (1608–1697), we find many, if not all the same features. Delivered a few months before his departure for the Americas in the chapel of the women's convent of Odivelas in Portugal, Vieira's panegyric sermon similarly began in a highly classicizing fashion with a discussion of the ancient Greek, Roman and Hebrew practice of decorating tables with "riddles" (*problemas*), a practice, he argued, Herod was following when he displayed the head of John the Baptist. This "riddle" in turn became the "issue" (*problema*) of the sermon, namely whether a man's own wife or another man's wife is a more pernicious influence; Herodias was of course both, as she had been previously married to Herod's brother. This line of argumentation allowed Vieira to refer to numerous other biblical and classical women, including Helen of Troy, while proceeding through the typical *salutatio-argumentatio-conclusio* structure on his way to concluding that each was as disastrous as the other – although a man's own wife was usually worse, as her malign influence could more easily go unchecked. Whether this was good news for the chaste female members of the convent of St. Dennis where he gave the sermon is unclear.[66]

This said, there were also some notable differences between these roughly contemporary Portuguese and Konkani panegyrics of John the Baptist. Vieira's sermon was considerably longer than Almeida's, although this might be because the text that comes down to us is the product of revisions to his oeuvre that Vieira undertook in Brazil in the late 1670s. Despite its relative brevity, however, it is notable that Almeida's Konkani sermon is, if anything, slightly more philosophically sophisticated than Vieira's Portuguese effort, especially in the opening discussion of "constancy" (*satvadhiru*). This, as we shall see, may have been because such

---

[65] On contemporary Portuguese sermons, see João Marques, *A Parenética Portuguesa e a Dominação Filipina*.

[66] António Vieira, *Obra Completa*, João Francisco Marques (ed.), 30 vols., XI, 124–142.

learned themes had particular resonance for the largely Brahmin congregation in Benaulim whose role not only as an audience for Almeida's sacred panegyric, but also as "orators in the audience" who directly shaped the expression of the classical rhetorical tradition in this Indo-humanist context, is worth exploring in detail.[67]

"Orators in the Audience": Connecting Caste and Erudition

The majority if not all the Konkani-speaking Christians who crowded into the church at Benaulim on that unknown day were likely Brahmins, including the members of the church's confraternity devoted to the Virgin and the students of the local Jesuit school of reading and writing who, we know from contemporary accounts, likely wore garlands of flowers on this special occasion.[68] We are also reminded of the Brahmin character of the congregation by Almeida's words on the title page of *Garden of the Shepherds*, which states that the language of the sermons was specific to Brahmins. Indeed, Salcete in general and Benaulim in particular had a large population of Saraswat Brahmins who had been targeted for conversion by missionaries due to their high social status. This was accompanied by a compelling origin story.[69] It recounted that Benaulim ("village of the arrow") had been founded on the very spot where an arrow shot by Lord Parashurama (the sixth avatar of Vishnu) had landed to form the Konkan coast. It was here that his Brahmin followers settled and founded a temple that is widely believed to have stood on the original site of the church of John the Baptist.[70] This was an account that was well known to Jesuit missionaries in the seventeenth century, and is also to be

---

[67] This draws inspiration from the approach of: Shadi Bartsch, *Actors in the Audience* (Cambridge, MA: Harvard University Press, 1994).

[68] ARSI, Goa 45, 1, fol. 301r.

[69] Miguel de Almeida, *Jardim dos Pastores*, V, fol. Ar: "Cum enim quidquid ad Christianam sive Doctrinae, sive morum institutionem pertinet, Brachmanicae huius Indiae linguae tradiderim, Romana quidem Purpura hoc est totius orbis augustissima elegantia protegendam barbariem hanc nostram in urbem dimisi, ad culmen supremae maiestatis ascendere non permisi." ARSI, Goa 45, 1, fol. 297v: "Comprehende a jurisdição desta igreja tres aldeas. Entre as quais tem o primeiro lugar a aldea de Benaulim, assim por ser a mayor de todas como por ser de Bramenes gente mais nobre e principal, como tambem por estar a igreja fundada nella... A segunda aldea que abrange a jurisdição desta igreja chamase Canna; he pouvoada de charodos, gente que antigamente se exercitava nas armas e dizem descendere dos reis antigos gentios. A terceira e ultima aldea tem por nomem Adsulim; foi antigamente de bramenes descendentes dos sacerdotes e ministros dos seus pagodes."

[70] ARSI, Goa 45, 1, fol. 297v. On the temple see Anant Kakba Priolkar, *The Goa Inquisition: Being a Quatercentenary Commemoration Study of the Inquisition in India* (Bombay: Bombay University Press, 1961), 79.

found in early modern Marathi narratives, that recount a large-scale migration of Brahmins to Salcete sometime in the first millennium CE.[71]

As Arcamone described in his Caesarean commentary on Salcete, the Brahmins of the region were a self-identifying caste, or really a series of related castes, foremost among whom were the Saraswats who were employed in roles suited to their "razor-sharp intellects," such as scribes, priests and community leaders. This was a group, modern scholarship tells us, that in the nearby territories of the Sultanate of Bijapur and the growing Maratha Empire was in the process of solidifying its identity around learned and priestly pursuits, rejecting (in principle) those who engaged in commerce and agriculture as "un-Brahmin."[72] In the Portuguese enclaves along the Konkan Coast learning played no less an important role in this caste identity, which those Brahmins who remained after the destruction of the temples in the mid-sixteenth century sought to maintain in the new political circumstances. This desire to remain Brahmin while becoming Christian was given further impetus by the enduring connections between converts living in Portuguese territories and their non-Christian confreres along the coast and in the Deccan region, to whom they were tied by bonds of descent and (illicit) marriage.[73] In this context, it should come as no surprise that a learned tradition like Indo-humanism played an important role in bridging the gap between native caste politics and the Christian evangelizing mission. Indeed, its potential to facilitate interactions between missionaries and

---

[71] Candrakānta Keṇī and Murgaon Mutt Sankul Samiti, *Saraswats in Goa and Beyond* (Goa: Murgaon Mutt Sankul Samiti, 1998); Alexander Henn, *Hindu-Catholic Encounters in Goa: Religion, Colonialism, and Modernity* (Bloomington: Indiana University Press, 2014), 83–125; Urmila Rajshekhar Patil, "Conflict, Identity and Narratives: The Brahman Communities of Western India from the Seventeenth through the Nineteenth Centuries" (Ph.D. Dissertation, University of Texas at Austin, 2010), 177–204.

[72] Fernandes, "Uma Descrição e Relação," 88–89: "Brachmanum genus intellectus acie subtile nimis … inter Brachmanes genus quoddam praecipuum designator scilicet scribarum genus, alio nomine 'Sinay' [viz. saraswat] nuncupatum. Hi praeter caeteros mentis acie perspicaces, cuiusque territorii stabilia bona suis consignant scriptis, et iuxta scriptorum libros incolae gubernantur. Antequam Lusitani Indiae terras et peninsulae huius dominium obtinerent, inter Brachmanes aliud praestantissimum genus notabatur, scilicet falsorum numinum sacerdotes, vernacula lingua 'Botta' [viz. bhat] nuncupati. Verum postquam Lusitani hanc obtinentes peninsulam falsorum numinum templa diruerunt et superstitiosos cultus abolere coeperunt, huiuscemodi genus sub Brachmanum communi nomine latere coepit." On the construction of Brahman identity, see Rosalind O'Hanlon and Christopher Minkowski, "What Makes People Who They Are? Pandit Networks and the Problem of Livelihoods in Early Modern Western India," *The Indian Economic & Social History Review*, 45 (2008), 381–416.

[73] Ângela Barreto Xavier, *A Invenção de Goa: Poder Imperial e Conversões Culturais nos Séculos XVI e XVII* (Lisbon: Imprensa de Ciências Sociais, 2015); Paul Axelrod and Michelle Fuerch, "Flight of the Deities: Hindu Resistance in Portuguese Goa," *Modern Asian Studies*, 30 (1996), 387–421.

native high-caste converts was not restricted to Almeida's panegyric ser-
mons, but is perhaps best illustrated by the opening of Thomas Stephens'
Kristapurāṇa, a text that was known to have been recited by native
Christians in Benaulim.[74]

One Sunday, Stephens relates, the inhabitants of a village in Salcete were
sitting in church studying Christian "doctrine" ("dautrini"), presumably in
the form of Stephen's own Konkani catechism printed at Rachol in 1622.
After a while, a Brahmin approached the priest ("pādrī guru") and asked:

> But apart from this doctrine, if there is something else, some different, nice,
> sacred discourse ("śāstra-purāṇa") and that if you teach us it would be
> good.[75]

Stephens' Christian Brahmin was obviously eager for something meatier
than a simple list of the tenets of the Christian faith in a question-and-
answer format. Indeed, as he explained, without something more substan-
tial to get their teeth into, the Brahmins in Salcete might easily "forget the
way of devotion."[76] Other parts of Christendom have such books, the
Brahmin noted somewhat indignantly, but not Salcete. He continued:
"This is of great significance, please . . . you have removed the previous
religious books, so why do you not prepare other such books for us?"[77]
The priest who is then revealed to be Stephens himself, then agrees to
produce a "religious narrative book" ("śāstra-purāṇēṃ") on the life of
Christ that would replace the earlier pagan texts, and the Brahmin
quickly proclaims that all the high-caste households will rejoice to hear
it recited.

While obviously serving an important narrative role in the *Kristapurāṇa*,
Stephens' account of the Brahmin hunger for something akin to their lost
sacred texts probably reflected a real desire on the part of many upper caste
converts for access to scholarly traditions and educational opportunities in
keeping with their traditional role in society. This was something that the
Jesuits were more than happy to accommodate, both in the production of
Christian purāṇas and the founding of schools for native converts. For
instance, Stephens reported in 1608 that the children of Christian
Brahmins in nearby Margão flocked to the village's Jesuit school, while
sixty-two Brahmin students attended the Jesuit school in Benaulim.[78] It is

---

[74] ARSI, Goa 45, 1, fol. 299r. It has recently been studied by Ananya Chakravarti, *The Empire of Apostles: Religion, Accommodatio, and the Imagination of Empire in Early Modern Brazil and India* (Oxford: Oxford University Press, 2018), 178–227.
[75] Thomas Stephens, *Father Thomas Stephens' Kristapurāṇa: Purāṇa I & II*, 126 SDB–130 SDB.
[76] *Ibid.*, 142 SDB, 145 SDB.   [77] *Ibid.*, 143 SDB.   [78] ARSI, Goa 16, fol. 180; 45, 1, fol. 298r.

also important to note that the Brahmin presence in Jesuit schools was not limited to elementary studies, as the author of the 1674 Jesuit annual letter from Goa underlined. Railing against the misconception among many Europeans that Jesuit colleges in India did not educate the native population (*la gente naturale*), he wrote that "Goans" (*canarini*) outnumbered "whites" (*bianchi*) at the Jesuit College in the Portuguese capital of Goa by a factor of three-, sometimes even five-to-one. This was the case at every level, from the earliest grammar classes to the theology class.[79] Given their numerical superiority, we can only conclude that a contemporary Jesuit account of the successes of students at the college must have applied in large part to these aspiring native Indo-humanists: "I recognize, so to speak, many Soareses, I observe many Aristotles and I hear many Ciceros, although, to speak the truth, India does not exactly abound with humanists."[80] In fact, by the end of the seventeenth century Indo-humanism and indeed almost all higher learning was numerically a native (if high-caste) phenomenon, something that would find its full flowering in the Bardez-born founder of modern oriental hypnotism, José Custódio de Faria (1756–1819) who during his youth delivered a Latin oration in the presence of the Pope in 1775.[81] This, of course, belies the judgment of Alessandro Valignano that "all these dusky races are very stupid and vicious, and of the basest spirits," a statement made famous by Benedict Anderson who identified it as a precursor to modern racism.[82]

All this did not mean that Brahmins, however learned, were allowed to become Jesuits, unlike contemporary Japanese and Chinese Christians. Nonetheless, as elsewhere in the Iberian World, Portuguese India in the seventeenth century saw an explosion in the number of native secular priests, the difference being in India that the main criterion for admission

---

[79] ARSI, Goa 34, fol. 111v; 35, fol. 126r: "non parlo qui dell'essercitio delle lettere per essere commune a tutta la compania contarei solamente il numero dei scholari che studiano in queste scuole, acciò si sappia con quanto poco fondamente e raggione si disse costà in Europa che noi non ammettevamo nelle nostre squole la gente naturale dell'India. Nella theologia si contano 40 di ordini sacri, cioè adire sette bianchi e trentatre Canarini. Nella philosophia nove bianchi e settant'otto Canarini dodici de' quali hanno già gl'ordini sacri. Nella prima nove bianchi e ottantaquatro Canarini. Nella seconda quatordici bianchi e settantadue Canarini. Nella tertia tredici bianchi e trentasei Canarini. Questi scholari tutti cosi negl'oblighi dello studio, come nelle devotione della Congregatione sono molto pontuali."

[80] ARSI, Goa, 35, fol. 304r: "Multos, ut ita dicam, agnosco Suarios, multos contemplor Aristoteles, et multos audio Cicerones, quantumvis si vera loquar, circa humanioris artes India aliquantulum frigescat."

[81] José Custódio de Faria, *De Adventu Sancti Spiritus Oratio* (Rome, 1775).

[82] Benedict Anderson, *Imagined Communities: Reflections On the Origin and Spread of Nationalism*, rev. ed. (New York: Verso, 2006), 61–62.

was not nobility (as in the case of *cacique* priests in New Spain), but what we today would call "caste" status. This, the local church hierarchy thought, selected for dedication to learning and ensured that such priests would be well received by the native population.[83] Indeed, by 1705 there were 2,500 Brahmin secular priests.[84] This new class of native priests was also ambitious. Entirely excluded from the Society of Jesus and to a large extent from the higher rungs of the ecclesiastical hierarchy, in the 1680s a number of Saraswat priests turned to the Oratorians, and founded a Congregation of the Oratory in the church of Santa Cruz dos Milagres on the southern hill overlooking the city of Goa. These Brahmin Oratorians would play a significant role in the missions in Sri Lanka, most notably St. José Vaz (1651–1711), some of whose success in entering the priesthood may be attributed to the fact that his earliest years of Latin instruction in Benaulim overlapped with Arcamone's tenure as priest of the nearby Church of St. John the Baptist.[85] Others, like António João de Frias, the author of a learned treatise published in Lisbon in 1702, would provide the ideological justification for these missions as a continuation of both the Brahmins' general role as the historical priests of India, and their specific role as the original defenders of Christianity in the age of St. Thomas the Apostle.[86] As Frias noted, this inheritance continued to bear fruit in the form of the Brahmin bishops consecrated during the seventeenth century. The most notable among these was Matheus de Castro (1594–1679) from the island of Divar in the Mandovi River who attended the Franciscan College of Reis Magos before traveling to Rome via Jerusalem where he studied theology and was consecrated a bishop against the will of the Portuguese *padroado*. This started a conflict that would culminate in him publishing a pastoral letter in 1653 exhorting Brahmins to wrestle control of the local church away from the European Jesuits.[87] This was the sort of prestigious (although far from uneventful) career path made possible by the Indo-humanist learning that Almeida was subtly

---

[83] On concepts of indigenous nobility in New Spain, see: Margarita Menegus Bornemann, "El cacicazgo en Nueva España," in Margarita Menegus Bornemann and Rodolfo Aguirre Salvador (eds.), *El Cacicazgo en Nueva España y Filipinas* (Mexico City: Plaza y Valdes, 2005), 13–70.

[84] Carlos Mercês de Melo, *The Recruitment and Formation of the Native Clergy in India (16th–19th Century): An Historico-Canonical Study* (Lisbon: Agência Geral do Ultramar, 1955), 163–177.

[85] For an account of the missions in Sri Lanka written in Latin by Vaz, see: M. da Costa Nunes, *Documentação para a História da Congregação do Oratório de Santa Cruz dos Milagres do Clero Natural de Goa* (Lisbon: Centro de Estudos Históricos Ultramarinos, 1966), 289–293.

[86] António João de Frias, *Aureola dos Indios & Nobiliarchia Bracmana, Tratado Historico, Genealogico, Panegyrico, Politico, & Moral* (Lisbon, 1702).

[87] Giuseppe Sorge, *Matteo de Castro (1594–1677): Profilo di una Figura Emblematica del Conflitto Giurisdizionale tra Goa e Roma nel Secolo XVII* (Bologna: Clueb, 1986), 73–81.

dangling before his Brahmin congregation. In trying to understand precisely how Almeida's Indo-humanist oratory might have appealed to a
Brahmin congregation that was connected by bonds of caste and shared
interests to the Brahmin clergy, we might usefully begin by considering
what they would have made of the authoritative figures of Christian
humanism who populated his sermon. This was a world of proud and
purposeful native elites that can be usefully reconstructed using the
methods of the "New Philological" school of Latin American
Ethnohistory that has stressed the close reading of missionary texts with
regards to both European and pre-Conquest understandings.

    In this vein, it is likely that the native Christians of Salcete were familiar
with the figure of John the Baptist whom they could have encountered both
in iconographic sources, such as the famous Indo-Portuguese ivories, and in
textual and oral sources, such as catechisms, sermons and the *Kristapurāṇa*,
which included a detailed account of the decollation of John the Baptist.[88]
This said, it is highly unlikely that they would have been so familiar with
Socrates, the Church Fathers and contemporary Jesuit scholars, like Stefano
Tucci. In this context, native understandings of the terminology Almeida
used to describe these figures become important. Socrates, for instance, is
described as "zannato, -y," or a "sage" (*sabedor*), as the word is translated in the
Konkani-Portuguese dictionary compiled by Diogo Ribeiro in 1626 for use
by Jesuits in Salcete.[89] This is the Konkani cognate of the Marathi "jāṇatā,"
which in turn ultimately derives from the Sanskrit word "jñāna" ("knowledge").[90] This was a weighty but polyvalent term that was claimed by various
philosophical and yogic traditions. For instance, in the influential Old
Marathi commentary on the *Gita* by Jñāneśvar, it is used in the following way:

> So also those men who wisely ("jāṇatēna") serve their spiritual teachers
> thereby attain the object of their lives, just as when the roots of a tree are
> watered the branches begin to sprout.[91]

---

[88] The passages from this widely recited poetic text presented the narrative of the death of John the
Baptist including the legend that Herod was later punished by God and became a pauper, while his
daughter Salome, who had asked for John's head, would lose hers too: Thomas Stephens, *Father
Thomas Stephens' Kristapurāṇa: Purāṇa I & II*, II, 30/31SDB, 62.

[89] Diogo Ribeiro, *Vocabulario da Lingoa Canarim*, Tōru Maruyama (ed.) (Nagoya: Nanzan
University, 2005), 384.

[90] Shankar Gopal Tulpule and Anne Feldhaus, *A Dictionary of Old Marathi* (Mumbai: Popular
Prakashan, 1999), 255.

[91] Translation taken from *'Jnāneshvari (Bhāvārthadipikā)*, Vitthal Ganesh Pradhan and Hester
Marjorie Lambert (eds. and trans.), 2 vols. (London: Allen & Unwin, 1967), I, 26 (1.25). This is
the *locus classicus* given in: Shankar Gopal Tulpule and Anne Feldhaus, *A Dictionary of Old
Marathi*, 255.

In some cases, zannato could even connote precisely the virtue that Almeida had Socrates embody, as is apparent in a passage from the *Gita*:

> The best of these is the knower ("jñānī") whose discipline is constant and whose dedication is exclusive.[92]

It is no wonder then that Almeida turned to this word to describe Socrates' wisdom, just like Jesuits in the Madurai mission, like Roberto de Nobili and Constanzo Beschi, had relied on Tamil cognates of this word to express concepts ranging from God's wisdom to spirituality.[93] In short, although it is unlikely that many of the members of the audience had even heard of Socrates, his demeanor and philosophical stance probably seemed reassuringly familiar, even for those who had a closer relationship to the "Sanskrit Cosmopolis" than the "Empire of Eloquence."

If the particular wisdom that Socrates possessed was not necessarily rigidly determined by his status as a "sage," the Brahmin congregation was quickly informed that he was an icon of "constancy" (satvadhiru). This is the same virtue that John the Baptist is urged to cultivate when he hears the news of his imminent execution in the *Kristapurāṇa*:

> At that time, John sat in meditation contemplating the Lord. Gathering up all five objects of the senses, he was lost in meditation. Then the king's messenger called up John and said to him, "Why are you still so quiet? Your death has come seeking you. Take heart ('satvadhiru'), pure one."[94]

From the perspective of Almeida's early humanistic education, this satvadhiru was, of course, the neo-Stoic virtue that had shot to fame with the publication of Justus Lipsius' *On Constancy in Times of Public Calamity* (1584), and, as we saw in the last chapter, was beloved of Jesuit orators across the Iberian World. In Lipsius' Senecan dialogue, the virtue of "constancy" (*constantia*) was defined as the "upright and immovable mental strength, which prevents you from being elated or depressed by external or accidental things," and was required in a world in which

---

[92] Translated in: *Mahābhārata. Book Six. Bhīṣma*, Alex Cherniak (trans.) (New York: New York University, 2008), 227 (31.17). This passage does not seem to appear in the Braga manuscript.

[93] Bror Tiliander, *Christian and Hindu Terminology: A Study in Their Mutual Relations with Special Reference to the Tamil Area* (Uppsala: Religionshistoriska institutionen i Uppsala, 1974), 60–64.

[94] Thomas Stephens, *Father Thomas Stephens' Kristapurāṇa: Purāṇa I & II*, II, 30/31SDB, 42–43:
tava krupāthātēṃ pācāri rājadutu
mhaṇē ājhuni kāṃ gā nichitu
tuja kāḷa pātalā givasitu
hōī satva dhiru.

obedience to divine will (however horrific its results) was the path to true happiness and liberty.[95]

Yet, for the audience of local Brahmins, this Konkani *constantia* had none of these connotations. Etymologically, it was a compound of satva, -a, and dhiru, -a, translated in Ribeiro's dictionary as "virtue, strength, constancy" (*virtude, força, constancia*) and "mental strength, effort," (*grande animo, esforço*), respectively. These mapped roughly onto contemporary Marathi terminology, where "sattva" had the general meaning of "courage," "patience" and in some cases "consciousness," and "dhīra," "strength" or "fortitude." This equivalence was no less the case for other languages that were circulating in and around Portuguese India in this period, such as Kannada.[96] Furthermore, these terms also appear frequently in canonical texts in Sanskrit, the learned language from which this terminology was ultimately derived. For instance, in a passage of the *Gita* highly reminiscent of Seneca's Socrates and Almeida's John the Baptist, Krishna explains to Arjuna the route to immortality for those who possessed dhīra:

> Bull of a man, the wise man ("dhīram") whom these contacts don't disturb, to whom pain and pleasure are one and the same, is fit for immortality.[97]

"Satva" too had a particular meaning within the context of Sanskritic philosophical vocabulary. In rendering the defining feature of Socrates' wisdom as a derivative of the Sanskrit "sattva," Almeida was embedding neo-Stoicism within the philosophical context of the three "guṇa" or "constituents of nature," known in Sanskrit as: "sattva" ("goodness," "purity"), "rajas" ("passion," "energy") and "tamas" ("darkness" or "sloth").[98] These are also described in the *Gita* as the drivers of human action and generative of the four castes ("varna"), which are seen as a reflection of an individual's temperament and role in society.[99] Here, "sattva" is the virtue that dominates among the Brahmins whose perceived

---

[95] Justus Lipsius, *De Constantia Libri Duo, qui Alloquium Praecipue Continent in Publicis Malis* (Antwerp, 1584), 10: "Constantiam hic appello rectum et immotum animi robur non elati externis aut fortuitis non depressi."

[96] Shankar Gopal Tulpule and Anne Feldhaus, *A Dictionary of Old Marathi*, 706, 356. Cf. Ferdinand Kittel, *A Kannada-English Dictionary* (Mangalore: The Basel Mission Book & Tract Depository, 1894), 826, 1494–1495. On language circulation and use, see Sheldon Pollock, *The Language of the Gods in the World of Men: Sanskrit, Culture, and Power in Premodern India*, 20–21.

[97] *Mahābhārata. Book Six. Bhīṣma*, 183 (26.15).

[98] Varghese Malpan, *A Comparative Study of the Bhagavad-gītā and the Spiritual Exercises of Saint Ignatius of Loyola on the Process of Spiritual Liberation* (Rome: Gregorian & Biblical Press, 1992), 75–77.

[99] *Mahābhārata. Book Six. Bhīṣma*, 273–275 (38.5–18).

steadfastness in the pursuit of virtue is used to justify their social position.[100]

As such, Almeida's native congregation may have interpreted Socrates not just as the embodiment of one of the most desirable forces in nature, but also as the archetypical Brahmin who provided a high-caste gloss for the story of John the Baptist. If the congregation did indeed view Socrates in this way, they may have been drawn to him as a figure who had the potential to cement their caste status by providing a model for certain Brahmin virtues and the associated learned virtuosity. Furthermore, Socrates may have been interpreted as a mirror for a very particular Brahminical figure, namely, Lord Parashurama. As the Moses of the Saraswats, on the former site of whose temple Almeida delivered this particular sermon, Parashurama was (like Almeida's Socrates) an archetypal Brahmin who had gone as far as to take up his axe ("paraśu") to rid the world of the unruly warrior kings of the Kshatriya (i.e. warrior) caste whose "rajas" challenged Brahmin "sattva." Socrates, of course, provided a much meeker and milder *exemplum* than Parashurama, but one more suited to the New Christian context.[101]

It is likely that Almeida's congregation also interpreted other figures of the Christian humanist pantheon who appeared in the sermon in a similar way. For instance, the term consistently applied to learned Christian figures is "xastrapravinnu." This is a compound word formed of "xastra" ("law") and "pravinnu" ("learned"), which Ribeiro translated in his dictionary as "preacher" (*pregador*) and "learned in the law" (*douto na ley*).[102] This Almeida applied to a myriad of different authoritative figures, including Latin Church Fathers like Tertullian, Jewish philosophers like Philo of Alexandria and learned Jesuits like Alfonso Salmerón and Stefano Tucci whose works ranged from theology to humanist drama. Indeed, he described the very act of delivering sacred oratory as literally "to speak the xastra" ("xastra sangatã"), which in his dictionary Ribeiro had translated as "to preach" (*pregar*).[103] Saints, like Santiago, were also "preachers of the law" ("xastracathana").[104] In all this, Almeida was following

---

[100] Varghese Malpan, *A Comparative Study of the Bhagavad-gītā and the Spiritual Exercises of Saint Ignatius of Loyola on the Process of Spiritual Liberation*, 76, n. 19. Cf. *Mahābhārata. Book Six. Bhīṣma*, 297–299 (42.40–44).

[101] I owe this insight to Vijay Pinch. On Parashurama and the Brahmins of the Konkan coast, see: Candrakānta Keṇī and Murgaon Mutt Sankul Samiti, *Saraswats in Goa and Beyond*, 5–11. The importance of Lord Parashurama for Goan Saraswats is clear from eighteenth-century Marathi texts: Urmila Rajshekhar Patil, "Conflict, Identity and Narratives," 182–183.

[102] Diogo Ribeiro, *Vocabulario da Lingoa Canarim*, 262, 380.

[103] Miguel de Almeida, *Jardim dos Pastores*, V, fol. 51v.   [104] *Ibid.*, V, fol. 202r.

roughly contemporary usage among missionaries. In his sermon on the crown of thorns, Ignazio Arcamone had described both the Greek theologian, Theodoret of Cyrrhus, and the Greek Church Father, Clement of Alexandria, using the term xastrapravinnu.[105] Cognate terminology also appeared in the *Kristapurāṇa*, where the teachings of Jesus were described as the xastra, and his deeds as a "further narration of the law" ("xastra").[106] Stephens also used the term to gloss biblical prophets who were defined by their connection to the "xastra": "Victory to the patriarchs and prophets, the keepers of the law ('xastra'), the righteous ones."[107] This then is a term to which Almeida's congregation would have been drawn as they tried to ascertain the meaning of his sermon and of Catholic doctrine as a whole.

What then was this "law" (xastra), and what would Almeida's native congregation have made of it? To judge from his various other sermons, it was a multifaceted term. To some extent, of course, "xastra" was tied to Christian theology and sacred history. However, as Almeida's Socratic *salutatio* suggests, the xastra with which Jesuit missionaries tried to entice their Brahmin congregations was not purely "religious," in the modern sense of the word, but a Konkani reflection of the larger culture of Christian learning, including its more "secular" elements. For instance, when discussing the Sibyls who foretold the coming of Christ, Thomas Stephens mentioned the Hebrew "men of learning" (xastrapurussa) and pre-Christian ancients like Virgil in the same breath, or in this case, the same *ovī*:

> Those who were called the Greeks and the Latins and the Hebrew men of learning (*xastrapurussa*) greatly praised these virgins.[108]

---

[105] Ignazio Arcamone, *Conciones per Annum Concannice Compositae*, fols. 13r, 14r.

[106] Thomas Stephens, *Father Thomas Stephens' Kristapurāṇa: Purāṇa I & II*, II, 29/30SDB, 153, 156. This is in contrast to Almeida who referred to Elijah using the Portuguese loanword *propheta*. *Kristapurāṇa*, I, 1, 66 SDB:

> Jayā pātriārkāṃ prōphētāṃ
> śāstrapā/akāṃ nitivantāṃ...

[107] Miguel de Almeida, *Jardim dos pastores*, V, fol. 50v.

[108] Thomas Stephens, *Father Thomas Stephens' Kristapurāṇa: Purāṇa I & II*, I.35.95:

> Grega Latina zeyā mhannaty
> Anny Hebreua xastrapurussa ze hati
> Tem maha thori stuti carity
> Yā ancuuarinchy.

In early modern readings of the fourth *Eclogue*, the Cumaean Sibyl foretells the coming of Christ.

Indeed, it is likely the congregations that heard Almeida's numerous panegyrics would have become familiar to at least to some degree with the names of figures from the pre-Christian Mediterranean. This included not only philosophers like Socrates and Seneca, but also other canonical authors like the naturalist Pliny the Elder and the late antique historian Procopius, both of whom appeared in Almeida's sermons at different points.[109] Greco-Roman historical figures were also not absent from Almeida's sacred oratory. The Emperor Augustus appeared in the opening of a sermon on the Holy Sacrament as part of a discussion of the etymology of the month of August (*agosto*) and its other connotations "in the Latin language" (Latim bhassena), including "liberality" (*liberalitas*).[110] An allusion to a banquet organized by Cleopatra for Mark Antony, at which the queen famously dissolved and drank a valuable pearl, opened the *argumentatio* of the same sermon, which served as an entree into discussions of the Last Supper, which, Almeida argued, was much more spiritually valuable than Cleopatra's ostentatious feast.[111]

At the same time, Almeida's congregations were made aware that their preacher's knowledge of a particular ancient Mediterranean figure also came from a particular ancient source. For instance, in his sermon for the birth of the Virgin, Almeida mentioned that it was from Plutarch that he had gleaned his knowledge of Julius Caesar, the "emperor of the city of Rome" (Roma Xarantu Emperadoru), a city that his native audience might have recognized from *Kristapurāṇa*, in which Stephens mentions that: "Rome was not built in a day."[112] Similarly, the congregation that assembled to hear Almeida's sermon on St. Joseph would have heard the account of the birth of Alexander the Great to Philip of Macedon found in the work of the third-century-CE Christian writer, Sabellius. Interestingly, Alexander may have been the only Greco-Roman figure already familiar to the Konkani-speaking congregation, since Alexander (Iskandar) appears in the Qur'an as well as in other Syriac, Persian and Arabic texts that circulated widely in South Asia.[113]

Thus, when Almeida's native audience heard about the Christian "law" (xastra), they probably imagined the totality of Catholic learning, in which

---

[109] Miguel de Almeida, *Jardim dos Pastores*, V, fols. 83r, 122r.   [110] *Ibid.*, V, fol. 23r–v.
[111] *Ibid.*, V, fol. 25v.
[112] Miguel de Almeida, *Jardim dos Pastores*, V, fols. 68v–69r. Thomas Stephens, *Father Thomas Stephens' Kristapurāṇa: Purāṇa I & II*, I, 148 SDB.
[113] *Ibid.*, III, fol. 116v. On the Alexander tradition in Asia, see the essays in: Richard Stoneman, Kyle Erickson and Ian Richard Netton (eds.), *The Alexander Romance in Persia and the East* (Groningen: Barkhuis, 2012).

theology, history, philosophy, poetry and spoken eloquence (i.e. Christian humanism, as defined by the *Ratio studiorum*) all played important roles. Such an expansive definition of xastra likely came quite naturally, especially when we consider the contemporary Middle Marathi usage, according to which the term denoted "law" in the most general sense, and more specifically the myriad of didactic texts in Sanskrit and vernacular languages that stood at the heart of South Asia's long-standing intellectual traditions.[114] Transplanted into this learned Brahminical world, the canonical figures of Christian humanism thus became somewhat eccentric members of an alternative, yet authoritative learned tradition, in which figures with origins in the ancient Mediterranean World emerged dressed not in the *khitōn* (χιτών) of the Greek philosophers, but in the *dhoti* of Indian gurus. By adorning his Konkani panegyric of John the Baptist with the full array of humanist erudition glossed with South Asian philosophical vocabulary, Almeida was giving voice to the aspirations of his Brahmin congregation who sought an intellectually robust religious tradition as a way to preserve and advance a social status based on caste. This was a factor that was not at play in the Americas, where nobility was defined in different terms and the "orators in the audience" therefore shaped sacred oratory in subtly different ways.[115]

Conclusion

In their collection of Guarani panegyrics, Yapuguay and Restivo collaborated to produce epideictic sermons that combined native linguistic forms with elements of the late Renaissance incarnation of the classical rhetorical tradition. This collaborative and synergistic scholarly mode was common across the Americas, where missionaries and native Christians selected elements from each tradition on the basis of the expectations of local audiences and the exigencies of their evangelizing mission. In the Americas, this meant that pre-Columbian religious terminology and imagery had to be carefully filtered to avoid undermining the larger missionary

---

[114] Shankar Gopal Tulpule and Anne Feldhaus, *A Dictionary of Old Marathi*, 691. Lawrence McCrea, "Standards and Practices: Following, Making, and Breaking the Rules of Śāstra," in Yigal Bronner, Whitney Cox and Lawrence McCrea, *New Directions in South Asian Studies: Critical Engagements with Sheldon Pollock* (Ann Arbor, MI: Association for Asian Studies, 2011), 229–244. On other Christian uses of the term, see Bror Tiliander, *Christian and Hindu Terminology*, 69–70.

[115] On ideas of native nobility in New Spain, see Margarita Menegus Bornemann, "El Cacicazgo en Nueva España," in Margarita Menegus Bornemann and Rodolfo Aguirre Salvador (eds.), *El Cacicazgo en Nueva España y Filipinas* (Mexico City: Plaza y Valdes, 2005), 13–70.

project, while excessive humanist erudition had to be eschewed not because this sort of "European" learning could not penetrate these "non-European" indigenous contexts, but because it was not conducive to persuading these particular audiences. This is in stark contrast to Portuguese India, where humanist erudition had a particular rhetorical value in the context of a predominantly Brahmin audience who were attracted to such overt displays of learning. In Salcete, Christian recastings of Socrates, Seneca and Caesar became representatives of a learned tradition that was meant to substitute South Asian texts, practices and beliefs. The classical rhetorical tradition was thus far from homogenous across the Iberian World, but responded to indigenous agency. In other words, as this "Empire of Eloquence" expanded, native audiences were not passive subjects, but rather "orators in the audience," whose expectations played an active role in shaping the contours of this global cultural space.

CHAPTER 5

Centers, Peripheries and Identities in the Empire of Eloquence

Manuel Martí (1663–1737) loved Cicero. He loved Cicero so much that as he sat by the ruins of the orator's supposed villa at Tusculum near Rome in 1718 he was suddenly overcome by the majesty of the place and could not stop himself from crying out:

> Hail Cicero, immortal pinnacle of eloquence! I invoke your spirit! Set foot on this humble ground, smile upon us and fill me with the nectar of your divine mellifluousness![1]

Such invocations were in many respects unnecessary, as Martí (known to posterity by his title "the Dean of Alicante" or simply "the Dean") was by this point already one of the leading figures in Rome's foremost literary academy, the *Academia de la Arcadia*, where alongside like-minded scholars and clerics he cultivated a sparkling "neo-Renaissance" style in Latin, Italian and Castilian, rejecting, as he saw it, the turgid Gongorism of the previous century. To his powers of eloquence, Martí added considerable prowess as a scholar and antiquarian, composing philological notes on the poetry of Theocritus, a treatise on Roman drinking cups, a dialogue on Stoic philosophy, a hugely popular description of the Roman amphitheater at Saguntum near Valencia and also bringing to fruition Nicholas Antonio's (1617–1684) vast but unfinished *Bibliotheca Vetus Hispana*, a

---

[1] The full passage is as follows: Manuel Martí, *Epistularum Libri Duodecim*, 2 vols. (Madrid, 1735), II, 147–157 (154–155): "Perstat adhuc, obdurata adversus annorum insultus constantia, aedificium quoddam nobile ac vel semirutum majestatem quandam prae se ferens. Fama est eam fuisse M. Tullii villam. Vulgo appellant 'Ciceronis Scholas'. Illo ego animi causa saepius accedo, ac mira quadam voluptate perfusus memoria ac recordatione tanti viri, paene exsulto gaudio mihique videor illum disserentem audire ac divinas illas *Quaestiones Tusculanas* recitantem. Adeo ut mihi interdum temperare nequeam quin exclamem: 'Salve, Cicero, aeternum eloquentiae columen. Manes tuos invoco. Sic terram experiare levem, ades pacatus nobisque divini tui eloquii laticem instilla'. Eo nos rapit insaniae loci reverentia." On the traditions and archeology of Cicero's supposed villa at Tusculum, see Elena Castillo Ramírez, *Tusculum I: Humanistas, Anticuarios y Arqueólogos tras los Pasos de Cicerón: Historiografía de Tusculum (Siglos XIV–XIX)* (Rome: L'Erma di Bretschneider, 2005), 77–87.

bio-bibliographical work that listed all of the Iberian Peninsula's writers and their works from antiquity to the Renaissance. Thanks to his light-footed style in prose and verse, which he combined with intellectual curiosity, a lack of respect for authority and an acerbic wit, he won applause from his contemporaries throughout the Republic of Letters, and was considered by the discerning German historian of philosophy, Johann Jakob Brucker (1696–1770), among the most learned men of the age.[2] As one of the outstanding figures in the last generation of humanists in the Renaissance mode, the Dean thus had little need to invoke the orator from Arpinum, for he was already the personification of ancient eloquence and modern erudition.[3]

As well as being his place of residence for extended periods, Rome was Martí's spiritual home, in stark contrast to Spain, which, like the famous Enlightenment social critic Benito Feijóo (1676–1764), he considered an intellectual desert.[4] Characterizing the learned world of his compatriots as dominated by tedious scholastic philosophy (*scholastica crepitacula*), Jesuit teachers who skimped on grammar and rhetoric and men whose misplaced religious zeal led them to demolish Roman ruins, the Dean advocated a revival of Hispanic culture modeled on the world of Renaissance human-ists, like Juan Luis Vives (1493–1540).[5] As his fame grew, he amassed a small but dedicated group of followers, including the Enlightenment rhetorician, philosopher and jurist, Gregorio de Mayans y Siscar (1699–1781), whose deeply felt attachment to his mentor and the "neo-Renaissance" movement can be gauged by the busts of Martí and Vives that stared at each other across his library.[6]

Yet, Mayans' most ardent display of *pietas* was the publication of Martí's vast Latin correspondence, an act that, unbeknownst to either man, would

---

[2] Johann Jacob Brucker, *Pinacotheca Scriptorum Nostra Aetate Literis Illustrium, Exhibens Auctorum Eruditionis Laude Scriptisque Celeberrimorum, qui Hodie Vivunt, Imagines et Elogia* (Augsburg, 1741), 27r–30r.

[3] The standard biography is: Antonio Mestre Sanchis, *Manuel Martí, el Deán de Alicante* (Alicante: Gil-Albert, 2003).

[4] *Nova Acta Eruditorum* (Leipzig, 1738), 416: "veram eruditionem et ipse colit, et in aliis magni facit, libertatis in primis amans, qua sine frustra ad supremum scientiarum adspirari fastigium intelligit. Amoenus est in familiari colloquio, seriis admiscens iocos, eos salibus conditos ... Sophisticas Philosophorum disputatiunculas nihili ducit, in deliciis habens Philosophiam veram, sobriam, veritatis studiosam."

[5] Manuel Martí, *Epistularum Libri Duodecim*, II, 288.

[6] Gregorio Mayans y Siscar, *Emmanuelis Martini, Ecclesiae Alonensis Decani, Vita*, Luis Gil (ed.) (Valencia: Ayuntamiento de Oliva, 1977), 306: "Ego certe in meo museo habeo magni sapientissimique Jo. Ludovici Vivis, et Emmanuelis Martini, viri undequaque eruditissimi praestantissimique effigies; quas quoties intueor, vehementissime mihi animus accenditur ad sapientiam." Mayans also edited the Vives' *Opera omnia*, 7 vols. (1782–1790).

earn for Martí the sweetest of approbations and bitterest of censures. One letter in particular cast a long shadow. Writing from Rome in 1718, Martí addressed a young man named Antonio Carrillo (dates unknown) who was considering crossing the Atlantic. Martí, who saw in the young man some talent for study, was horrified by this idea, and in one of his typically stylish but irreverent epistles, attempted to dissuade him from swapping Europe for the Americas:

> To whom among the Indians will you turn in such a vast desert of letters? I won't ask to which teacher will you go from whom you might learn something, but will you find anyone at all to listen to you? I won't ask whether you will find anyone who knows anything, but anyone who wants to know anything at all, or, put simply, anyone who does not despise letters. Indeed, which books will you leaf through and which libraries will you peruse? … So ponder this: what does it matter if you are in Rome or Mexico City, if you just want to haunt the avenues and street corners, to gaze at the magnificence of the buildings, to be idle and to waste away while you schmooze with all and sundry like a slimy politician?[7]

If Martí had little respect for the Peninsular Spanish branch of the Republic of Letters, he had even less for that of the Indies, which he considered an intellectual backwater of a decrepit cultural sphere and, in line with the European stereotype of the day, an Eldorado only for those who sought wealth, not culture. Instead, Martí advised the young man to join the priesthood, which could provide financial and domestic freedom, and to make his way to Rome where men of letters were still held in high esteem.[8]

Of course, the sentiments expressed in Martí's letter to Carrillo did not go down well with the learned men of Mexico City, such as Juan José de Eguiara y Eguren (1696–1763), Vicente López (1700–1757), Cayetano Javier de Cabrera y Quintero (c. 1700–1775) and Juan Gregorio de Campos y Martínez (b. 1719). The offending letter seems to have first

---

[7] Manuel Martí, *Epistularum Libri Duodecim*, II, 38–39: "Quo te vertes apud Indos in tam vasta litterarum solitudine? Quem adibis, non dicam magistrum, cuius praeceptis instituaris, sed auditorem, non dicam aliquid scientem, sed scire cupientem, dicam enucleatius, a litteris non abhorrentem? Ecquosnam evolves codices? Ecquas lustrabis bibliothecas? … Ita tamen cum animo tuo reputa, non te idcirco urbem petiisse, ut vias et compita tereres, ut aedificiorum magnificentiam admirarere, ut inertem vitam ageres, ut in salutationibus, ceterisque candidatorum officiis contabesceres. His enim artibus quid refert Romaene sis an Mexici?"

[8] The larger controversy is discussed in: Stuart M. McManus, "The *Bibliotheca Mexicana* Controversy and Creole Patriotism in Early Modern Mexico," *Hispanic American Historical Review*, 98.1 (2018), 1–41.

come to the attention of Eguiara and López in April of 1745, probably after they had sought out an edition of Martí's letters, which had been reviewed favorably in the *Nova Acta Eruditorum*, a popular Latin periodical from Leipzig.[9] López initially vented his anger to Eguiara in their Latin correspondence, and by the end of the summer the Dean's letter seemed to be common knowledge in the city, perhaps due to Eguiara's central position in the *academia eguiarense*, a pious learned circle that met at the local university.[10] The ensuing controversy was fierce and long lasting, with responses to Martí from scholars in Mexico City, Habana and elsewhere appearing several decades after the original publication of the letter.[11] Since university-based scholars like Eguiara remained particularly wedded to late humanist practices, which in turn were bolstered by the widespread influence of Martí's neo-Renaissance aesthetic, the most notable early responses also appear in archetypal late humanist genres. These include: a brilliant Latin oration delivered by Campos at the inauguration of the academic year in Mexico City in October of 1745 (Figure 5.1);[12] a Ciceronian dialogue by López set in a garden in Mexico City where the

---

[9] Despite living only a few streets from each other in the shadow of Mexico City's cathedral, the two men corresponded in elegant Latin epistles in the same manner as their contemporaries Martí and Mayans, with whom they shared a dedication, if not quite such an exclusive one, to the practices of late humanism. BNM, ms. 329, fols. 125r–130r (127r–v): "Accusamur quod non veterem orbem evisceramus; non laudamur quod novum eruditis omnibus et antiquitati ipsi aperuimus ... Sed maiores sunt Emmanueli cum Antiqua /fol 127v/ quam cum Nova Hispania contentiones et lites." Juan José Eguiara y Eguren, *Bibliotheca Mexicana, sive Eruditorum Historia Virorum, qui in America Boreali Nati, vel Alibi Geniti, in Ipsam Domicilio aut Studiis Asciti quavis Lingua Scripto aliquid Tradiderunt. Eorum Praesertim qui pro Fide Catholica et Pietate Amplianda Fovendaque Egregie Factis et quibusvis Scriptis Floruere Editis aut Ineditis Ferdinando VI Hispaniarum Regi Catholico Nuncupata* (Mexico City, 1755), fol. 7ar: "quos non absque egregia animi voluptate combibere incepimus, et gravate licet ea tulerimus, quae in scholarum professores nonnunquam scribit, et in Hispanorum dedecus, quod ad rem litterariam spectat, haud semel iacit, pergebamus tamen et inchoatam lectionem persequebamur; haerere vero coacti sumus et morosius circumspicere chartam, ubi ad Epistolam 16 lib. 7 offendimus, quam tamen iterum et iterum non sine bili et stomacho deglutivimus, lectam recogitare placuit et memoria tenere atque in ipsam serio pacateque inquirere ... Totus in ea epistola Martinus est, ut adolescentem illum in novum orbem traiecturum, ab hocce consilio removeat, et aptum natum capessendis litterarum studiis, Romae constituat et a Mexiceis oris quam longissime abducat." Ibid., fol. 7br: "Scilicet, cum latissime Indiae Occidentis extendantur et pateant, nec dum Martinus in epistola sua insulam, urbem, pagum aut oppidulum stylo signasset, quo se Antonius apud Indos conferre vellet, Mexicum tandem indigitavit, postremam, si Superis placet, totius orbis barbariem."

[10] The Academy gathered regularly to hear panegyric orations, defend theological theses and compose *tituli* (Latin epigrams): Stuart M. McManus, "The Art of Being a Colonial *Letrado*: Learned Sociability and Urban Life in Eighteenth-Century Mexico City," *Estudios de Historia Novohispana*, 56 (2017), 40–64.

[11] José Martín Félix de Arrate y Acosta, *Llave del Nuevo Mundo, Antemural de las Indias Occidentales. La Habana Descripta: Noticias de su Fundación, Aumentos y Estados*, 4th ed. (Havana: Comision Nacional Cubana de la UNESCO, 1964), 144–145.

[12] Juan Gregorio Campos y Martínez, *Oratio Apologética* (Mexico City, 1746).

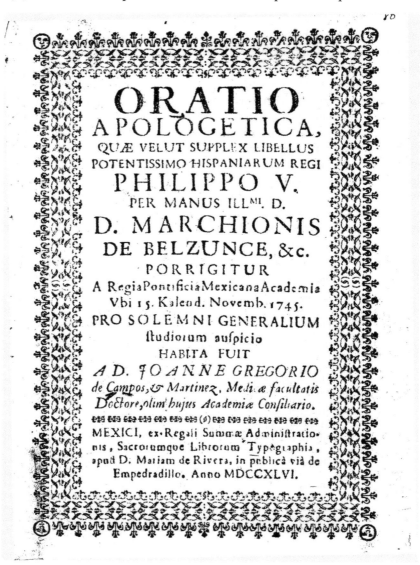

Figure 5.1   Title page of Juan Gregorio Campos y Martínez, *Oratio apologetica*
(Mexico City, 1746).
Courtesy of the Bancroft Library, University of California, Berkeley

interlocutors debated Martí's critiques of both "Old" and "New" Spain;[13] and Eguiara's famous *Bibliotheca Mexicana* (1755), a vast unfinished bio-bibliographical work akin to the *Bibliotheca Hispana Nova* compiled with the help of Eguiara's correspondents throughout New Spain, which aimed to crack the nut of Martí's letter with a several-thousand-folio-page Latin hammer.[14]

The normal story we are told about the controversy started by Martí's letter is that it was one of the most important expressions of an intellectual current called "creole patriotism," with "creole" (*criollo*) being the term used by historians and some contemporaries to refer to those of pure Spanish descent born in the Americas. Presuming a binary distinction between "metropolitan" Spain and "colonial" Mexico, scholars have interpreted this dispute as an early milestone in the development of Mexican national identity, which was forged in the ongoing struggle between proud local-born scholars on the one hand, and haughty European armchair philosophers and colonial administrators on the other. This embryonic nationalism found cultural expression in the creole appreciation of the American landscape, pre-Columbian antiquity and the cult of the Virgin of Guadalupe, and ultimately formed the backdrop for the nationalist ideology of the Wars of Independence.[15] Although some have begun to

---

[13] Vicente López, *Diálogo de Abril: Acerca de la Bibliotheca del Señor Doctor Juan José de Eguiara y del Ingenio de los Mexicanos*, Silvia Vargas Alquicira (ed.) (Mexico City: Universidad Nacional Autónoma de México, 1987).

[14] This transatlantic humanist dispute was by no means unique. A century earlier, Diego de León Pinelo (d. 1671), a professor of canon law at the university in Lima, had composed a 400-page Latin treatise condemning the famous classical scholar Justus Lipsius (1547–1606) who had neglected to mention Peru's leading seat of learning in his account of the universities of the world. Diego de León Pinelo, *Hypomnema Apologeticum pro Regali Academia Limensi in Lipsianam Periodum* (Lima, 1648); Antonello Gerbi, *Diego de Leon Pinelo contra Justo Lipsio; una de las Primeras Polémicas sobre el Nuevo Mundo*, 2 vols. (Lima: Editorial Lumen, 1945–1946).

[15] The literature on creole patriotism in Mexico and elsewhere is vast. Representative studies include: Solange Alberro, *Del Gachupín al Criollo: O de cómo los Españoles de México Dejaron de Serlo* (Mexico City: El Colegio de Mexico, 1992); Benedict Anderson, *Imagined Communities: Reflections on the Origin and Spread of Nationalism*, 47–65; Bernard Lavallé, *Las Promesas Ambiguas: Ensayos sobre el Criollismo Colonial en los Andes* (Lima: Pontificia Universidad Católica del Perú, 1993); Severo Martínez Peláez, *La Patria del Criollo: Ensayo de Interpretación de la Realidad Colonial Guatemalteca*, 4th ed. (Guatemala City: Fondo de Cultura Económica, 1976). The Martí controversy is addressed directly in: David A. Brading, *The Origins of Mexican Nationalism* (Cambridge: Centre of Latin American Studies, University of Cambridge, 1985), 13–14; idem, *The First America: The Spanish Monarchy, Creole Patriots, and the Liberal State, 1492–1867*, 389–90; Jorge Cañizares-Esguerra, *How to Write the History of the New World: Histories, Epistemologies, and Identities in the Eighteenth-century Atlantic World* (Stanford, CA: Standord University Press, 2001), 209–212; José Carlos Rovira, *Entre dos Culturas. Voces de Identidad Hispanoamericana* (Alicante: Universidad de Alicante, 1995), 45–62; Roberto Heredia, "Eguiara y Eguren, las Voces Concordes," *Literatura Mexicana*, 8 (1997), 511–549; Jacques Lafaye, "Literature and Intellectual Life in Colonial Spanish America," in Leslie Bethell (ed.), *The Cambridge History of Latin America*,

suggest that New Spain's creole patriotism was just one example among many of pan-Hispanic local patriotism (*foralismo*), which stressed the autonomy and traditions of each constituent kingdom (*reino*) and its right to a reserve of officials drawn from local residents, it remains the framework through which the dispute between Martí and his Novohispanic contemporaries is understood.[16]

In contrast, this chapter shows that while the dispute certainly touched a patriotic nerve, the Mexican responses to Martí's letter were not expressions of "proto-nationalism" in any meaningful sense of the word. Rather, they articulated an ethnically charged sense of belonging in the Hispanic and Catholic branches of the Republic of Letters, an identity that was centered on a flourishing urban center (Mexico City) and a Hispanic pseudo-kingdom (New Spain), but which was inseparable from larger imperial and religious conceptions of belonging. This Russian doll of complementary identities emerged as early as the first public reaction to Martí's letter in Mexico City: the largely unknown Latin judicial (i.e. courtroom-style) oration delivered by Juan Gregorio de Campos y Martínez at the inauguration of the academic year at the Royal and Pontifical University in 1745.[17] Indeed, we should take Campos' speech particularly seriously, since as an epideictic oration in judicial garb, it was meant to mirror quite closely the views of the assembled university community, to elicit nodding applause even as it made a pointed intervention in a scholarly controversy. As a result, it is most likely highly

---

11 vols (Cambridge: Cambridge University Press 1984), II, 663–704 (698); Walter D. Mignolo, *The Darker Side of the Renaissance: Literacy, Territoriality, and Colonization*, 63, 163, 165; Anthony Pagden, "Identity Formation in Spanish America," in Nicholas Canny and Anthony Pagden (eds), *Colonial Identity in the Atlantic World, 1500–1800* (Princeton: Princeton University Press, 1987), 51–93.

16 For revisionist scholarship, see Fred Bronner, "Urban Society in Colonial Spanish America: Research Trends," *Latin American Research Review*, 21, (1986), 7–72 (43); Cornelius Conover, "Reassessing the Rise of Mexico's Virgin of Guadalupe, 1650s–1780s," *Estudios Mexicanos*, 27 (2011), 251–279; Tamar Herzog, "Los Americanos Frente a la Monarquía: el Criollismo y la Naturaleza Española," in *La Monarquía de las Naciones. Patria, Nación y Naturaleza en la Monarquía de España*, 77–92; eadem, *Defining Nations: Immigrants and Citizens in Early Modern Spain and Spanish America*; I.A.A. Thompson, "Spain, Castile and the Monarchy: The Political Community from *Patria Natural* to *Patria Nacional*," in Richard L. Kagan and Geoffrey Parker, *Spain, Europe and the Atlantic World: Essays in Honour of John H. Elliot* (Cambridge: Cambridge University Press, 1995), 125–159.

17 My argument is indebted to the work of: Antonio Mestre Sanchis, *Manuel Martí, el Deán de Alicante*, 295–306; Andrew Laird, "Patriotism and the Rise of Latin in Eighteenth-Century New Spain: Disputes of the New World and the Jesuit Constructions of a Mexican Legacy," *Renaessanceforum*, 7 (2012), 163–193; Ernesto de la Torre Villar, "Prólogo," in Juan José de Eguiara y Eguren, *Biblioteca Mexicana*, 5 vols. (Mexico City: Universitdad Nacional Autónoma de México, 1986–1989), I, CCLVII.

representative of the views of Mexico City's intelligentsia. Reading Campos' oration, we also learn that what might appear to be an ivory-tower debate had political overtones. Learning was a precondition for self-rule, without which "foreigners" (i.e. royal officials born or domiciled in other kingdoms) might rightfully be sent to govern this corner of the Hispanic Monarchy. To possess academic standards was to deserve political autonomy.

Following the rolling periods and harsh invective of Campos' oration, which was made possible by his late humanist education at the hands of Jesuit teachers, we become aware of the plasticity of the classical rhetorical tradition in the Iberian World. When brandished by a trained orator, even academic oratory (a largely ignored genre that this chapter introduces in some detail) could become a nifty rapier suitable for fighting any number of battles. These might include bolstering the Hispanic Monarchy and creating space for imperial negotiation (Chapter 2), as well as in this case defending local traditions against a detractor within the context of the larger learned world of the Republic of Letters.

Finally, by setting out the "Mexican" case against Martí's defamatory letter, Campos made an implicit meta-geographical argument. Namely, he inadvertently defined the relationship between New Spain, Peninsular Spain, the Hispanic Monarchy and the rest of the world, as he and his audience understood it. Here, his conception was to some degree "polycentric," in that New Spain was no periphery and Castile no center in any binary sense, although the Iberian Peninsula was the seat of ultimate political and judicial authority, which Campos and his contemporaries like Eguiara considered the origin point of much of their Hispanic culture. Therefore, a more accurate way to describe it might be "hierarchically polycentric." Peninsular Spain held a special place politically and cultur-ally, but this did not preclude significant cultural autonomy and local pride. Nor did it not stop Campos and Eguiara interacting intellectually with other parts of the Hispanic Monarchy, and other parts of the early modern world, including Protestant Europe. In other words, it is abso-lutely true that the early modern Hispanic Monarchy, and arguably the Iberian world as a whole, cannot usefully be described only in terms of a series of bilateral relationships between the Crown and its subject terri-tories. Rather, the various kingdoms and provinces of the Hispanic Monarchy were numerous points in a three-dimensional space. While these may have clustered around the Iberian Peninsula and the monarch that resided there, they also possessed deep and lasting connections with the other so-called peripheral parts of the Monarchy, as well as with other parts of the early modern world as a whole. In this regard, it bears underlining that to at least some extent both Campos and Martí viewed themselves as living in a mere province of the true metropole of the Catholic Republic of Letters, Italy. Finally, from the perspective of individual actors like Campos and Eguiara, no set of relationships was ever static, and even membership in one of these communities (i.e. citizenship) was not preordained, but an emergent property that could be acquired by various means, including birth, residence and education. This was a situation that mirrored that of the Roman Empire whose legal system the Iberian world in general and the Hispanic Monarchy in particular had inherited.[18]

The Making of a Late Humanist Orator

Before examining Campos' oratorical performance itself, it is necessary to appreciate the late humanist culture in New Spain that produced a young man capable of delivering such an impressive piece of classicizing Latin oratory in Mexico City in 1745. Although by the early eighteenth century the Renaissance was over in many respects, there were nonetheless considerable continuities in both rhetorical education and the institutional culture surrounding public speaking. This was especially true within that bastion of late humanism, the Society of Jesus, although its classrooms were not immune from the move to post-humanist rhetorical culture. Like many of the scholars at the Royal and Pontifical University of Mexico City, be they professors of law, theology, rhetoric or medicine, Campos was a product of the Jesuits' network of colleges that spanned every major urban center in New Spain from Havana to Manila. Born in Veracruz, Campos studied grammar at the Jesuit college in the port city in the late 1720s and 1730s, where the heavily humanist *Ratio studiorum* (1599) continued to dictate the curriculum.[19] This is not to say that every student who attended these colleges was molded into the sort of late humanist orator that Campos became – far from it – but they had to jump through the same hoops, even if they did not do so quite as gracefully.

---

[18] Pedro Cardim, Tamar Herzog, José Javier, Ruiz Ibáñez and Gaetano Sabatini (eds.), *Polycentric Monarchies. How Did Early Modern Spain and Portugal Achieve and Maintain a Global Hegemony?* For a critique of this model, see the review by Jorge Cañizares-Esguerra in *Estudios Interdisciplinarios de America Latina y el Caribe*, 26 (2015), 138–140.

[19] Ignacio Osorio Romero, *Colegios y Profesores Jesuítas que Enseñaron Latín en Nueva España (1572–1767)*, 337–340.

After his elementary studies, the young Campos would have turned to the rudiments of Latin grammar, which was supplemented by the reading of simple Latin texts both ancient and modern, alongside a variety of vernacular works, principally of a pious sort.[20] Students then took a year of "humanities," which involved the reading of more extended and advanced passages from classical authors, anthologies of Roman history and a basic introduction to rhetorical theory, perhaps from one of the two textbooks printed in Mexico City for this purpose, Cipriano Soáres' *De arte rhetorica* or the later but very similar handbook of François Pomey.[21] At this stage, the rules of prosody and some basic Greek were also introduced.[22] Students' knowledge of rhetorical theory was also supplemented by the reading of selected orations of Cicero, which were often printed alongside Soáres' handbook.[23] Students then tried their hand at composing basic texts such as "prose descriptions" (*ekphrasis*) of churches or gardens, epistles or epigrams, usually with a pious bent.[24] From this point on, Latin was at least in theory the only language permitted to be spoken by students, although it is impossible to gauge to what extent this convention was still followed in Campos' day.[25]

Having forged his Latinity, Campos would then have set about sharpening it in the rhetoric class, where, through theory and practice, students

[20] Students often seem to have copied out their Latin grammars rather than relying on a printed textbook, for example: BNM, ms. 1421, fols. 1r–19v. Notes on grammar from students who resided in the *Colegio de San Ildefonso* in Mexico City can be found in: Archivo Histórico de la Universidad Nacional Autónoma de México, Mexico City, caja 54, exp. 34.

[21] "Ratio atque Institutio Studiorum Societatis Iesu [1599]," in *Monumenta Paedagogica Societatis Iesu*, V, 355–454 (430–433). *M. Tullii Ciceronis Orationes Duodecim Selectae … quibus Accesserunt Compendium Rhetoricae R.P. Cypriani Soarii S. J. et Lachrymae Sancti Petri R. P. Sidonii Hoschii* (Mexico City, 1756); François Pomey, *Novus Candidatus Rhetoricae Praecepta* (Mexico City, 1726). Examples of good prose were printed in: *Solutae Orationis Fragmenta* (Mexico City, 1641). The surviving theoretical works on rhetoric from New Spain are cataloged in: Osorio Romero, *Floresta de Gramática, Poética y Retórica en Nueva España (1521–1767)*.

[22] The only active Hellenist in Mexico City at this time was Cayetano de Cabrera who wrote Greek verse: Lia Coronati, *Obras Poéticas Latinas de Cayetano de Cabrera y Quintero: Catálogo* (Mexico City: Universidad Nacional Autónoma de México, 1988).

[23] "The Ratio atque Institutio Studiorum Societatis Iesu [1599]," in *Monumenta Paedagogica Societatis Iesu*, 430 suggests *Pro lege Manilia Pro Archia poeta*, *Pro Marcello* and "the other orations given to Caesar," which was broadly reflected in the speeches normally printed with rhetorical handbooks in Mexico City: *Pro lege Manilia*, *In Catilinam I-II*, *Pro Archia poeta*, *Ad Quirites post reditum*, *Post reditum in senatum*, *Pro Milone*, *Pro Marcello*, *Pro Ligario*, *Pro rege Deiotario*, and *Philippicae I and IX*.

[24] An eighteenth-century *ekphrasis* and practice epistles from the Jesuit College at Tepotzotlan are preserved in: "Descriptio sacelli Tepotzotlanensis," BNM, ms. 1421, fols. 66r–v, 68r–v; BNM, ms. 1420, fols. 99v–104v.

[25] "Ratio atque Institutio Studiorum Societatis Iesu [1599]," in *Monumenta Paedagogica Societatis Iesu*, 41 (*Latine loquendi usus*).

brought their abilities in persuasion to a point.[26] The rhetoric curriculum he would have followed appears to have been almost entirely focused on expression in Latin, which was still considered by Jesuit pedagogues the archetypal form of eloquence. To this end, the orations of Cicero previously studied were the subject of more detailed historical and linguistic scrutiny, memorization and, of course, recitation to practice the art of delivery. The reading of these orations with attention to structural and linguistic features highlighted in Soáres' handbook then led into classroom exercises, which taught students how best to structure individual parts of an oration, with further examples of openings (*exordia*) and arguments (*confirmationes*) being provided as models.[27] With an eye to their own compositions, students were expected to keep a commonplace book of notable passages from texts they had read for the purpose of later citation or imitation.[28] All this culminated in exercises in oratorical composition and delivery (*declamatio*).[29] Verse composition was also part of the rhetoric and humanities curriculum, and textbooks were printed in Mexico City to aid its teaching, although it is unclear whether Campos' dedication to hexameters and pentameters ran as deep as it did for his contemporary Jose Mariano de Iturriaga (b. 1717) who as an exercise composed an 810-line epyllion on the conquest of Baja California, known today as the *Californiada*.[30]

Late humanist culture was not limited to the classroom, as college life still brimmed with occasions for classicizing oratory in Latin. At the beginning of the school year, students were treated to a Latin inaugural oration, while the Jesuit colleges frequently organized public shows and competitions in eloquence, both in Latin and the vernacular.[31] Students were also introduced to models of Latin sacred oratory either in textual form or actively on feast days, which offered the students further models of classicizing eloquence put to pious ends, the importance of which lay in

---

[26] *Ibid.*, 424–430. Some logic was also to be taught alongside rhetorical theory: *Ibid.*, 424–425 (*Gradus*).

[27] "Analysis prolusionis pro qualibet grammaticae classe," BNM, ms. 1421, fols. 60r–65v. Examples of *exordia* and other structural features can be found in: BNM, ms. 1420, fols. 120v–130r.

[28] An example of such a commonplace book is BNM, ms. 1473.

[29] "Ratio atque Institutio Studiorum Societatis Iesu [1599]," in *Monumenta Paedagogica Societatis Iesu*, 427 (*Argumentum scribendae orationis*), 428 (*Publica declamatio*), 428 (*Nostrorum exercitatio*).

[30] Assistance in verse composition came in the form of: *Epigrammata Aliqua ad Faciliorem Epigrammatis Componendi* (Mexico City, 1641). Jose Mariano de Iturriaga, *La Californiada*, Alfonso Castro Pallares (ed.) (Mexico City, 1979).

[31] "Ratio atque Institutio Studiorum Societatis Iesu [1599]," in *Monumenta Paedagogica Societatis Iesu*, 403 (*Declamationes a quo probandae*), 408 (*Scholarum disputationes; Academiae*), 414 (*Praemiorum numerus*).

the fact that the most common application in later life of all this rhetorical training would be in preaching.[32] Campos was probably also exposed to classicizing vernacular oratory on feast days (*oraciones panegíricas*), of the sort delivered for the royal exequies discussed in Chapter 2, which would have both bolstered the rhetorical theory he had learned in the classroom and pointed to its practical applications.

After this training, Campos went to study at the colegio de san Ildefonso in Puebla, which was the viceroyalty's main center for the next stage of the Jesuit arts curriculum: philosophy.[33] Beyond studying Aristotelian logic, physics and metaphysics, we do not know how he occupied his time in Puebla. However, we do know that humanist culture did continue in Puebla in the 1730s and 1740s, with local clerics regularly corresponding in Latin, and of course Latin oratory remaining a feature of college life.[34] Furthermore, we know that the city boasted libraries associated with its four Jesuit colleges, which were probably significantly larger than what Campos had had access to in Veracruz. As well as the full gamut of classical authors, normally found in high quality northern European editions from Amsterdam, Cologne and (in the case of the famous Ad usum Delphini editions) Paris, the library of the colegio de san Ildefonso contained a variety of works by popular Renaissance authors, such as Justus Lipsius, John Barclay, Polydore Virgil, Lorenzo Valla, Marc-Antoine Muret, Antonio Strada and Juan Luis Vives.[35] The nearby colegio del Espíritu Santo also had rich collections, which, although dominated like all Jesuit libraries by books of sermons, saints' lives and theology, contained several sixteenth-century folio editions of Cicero's *opera omnia*, as well as works by earlier Jesuit humanists.[36] These readily accessible stores of elegant Latinity

---

[32] An oration for the Feast of the Assumption is preserved in BNM, ms. 1421, fols. 71r–78r.
[33] Ernesto de la Torre Villar, *Historia de la Educación en Puebla (Época Colonial)* (Puebla: Universidad Autónoma de Puebla, 1988), 44–58.
[34] A number of eighteenth-century Latin epistles and orations from Puebla is preserved in: Biblioteca Lafragua, Puebla, MF 329.
[35] "Libreria del colegio de San Ildefonso," Biblioteca Lafragua, Puebla, ms. 48282. The college's 1724 annual letter describes the library containing over 2,000 volumes thanks to the generosity of José de Luna, an oidor in Mexico City: Archivo General de la Nación, Mexico City (henceforth AGN), Jesuitas III, 16, exp. 13. Pedro Rueda Ramírez, "Libreros y Librerías: la Ofera Eultural en el Mundo Moderno," in Marina Garone Gravier (ed.), *Miradas a la Cultura del Libro en Puebla: Bibliotecas, Tipógrafos, Grabadores, Libreros y Ediciones en la Época Colonial* (Mexico City: Gobierno de Puebla, 2012), 377–400.
[36] The nearby *Biblioteca Palafoxiana* (completed 1773), which received a large number of books from the city's Jesuit colleges after the dissolution of the Society of Jesus, contains a vast number of edition of Cicero's orations and humanist texts, which give a sense of the ready availability of such books in Puebla in Campos' day. For example, the *Biblioteca Palafoxiana* preserves an edition of the popular *Conciones, sive, Orationes ex Graecis Latinisque* (Paris, 1570) (Biblioteca Palafoxiana, Puebla,

and urbane wit might have kept a student like Campos entertained when not reading Aristotle or engaging in logical disputation.

If late humanism and the classical rhetorical tradition had played an important, albeit probably declining, role in the Jesuit colleges of Puebla, their profile was considerably higher in Mexico City where Campos arrived around 1740. This was at least partly a result of the university having a long-standing chair of rhetoric, a position contested twice by Campos (both times unsuccessfully) and many of his contemporaries, including Eguiara and Cabrera.[37] With upwards of thirty aspiring rhetoricians vying for the role, the competition was intense and the selection process both rigorous and, for our purposes, highly illustrative of the state of the classical rhetorical tradition in New Spain in the early eighteenth century.[38] When the chair became vacant, a call was put out in Mexico City and nearby Puebla for scholars to present themselves, and each applicant was then assigned a time to deliver his "job talk" (*lección de oposición*) of an hour and a half. This involved analyzing a passage from the third volume of Cicero's collected orations, which included the most commonly studied examples such as *Pro Caelio* and *Pro Balbo*.[39] So that scholars could not influence which passage they would comment on, it was selected at random by a child less than twelve years old (*i.e.* one who would not possibly have begun to study rhetoric yet and be familiar with the text) who opened the volume at three pages with a knife (again to avoid preselecting passages), from which the *opositor* chose a single passage. As in the competitions for the chair of Nahuatl and Otomí, in which candidates had to deliver sermons in both languages to show their practical linguistic skills, aspiring professors of rhetoric were expected to possess the eloquence they claimed to understand at the level of theory. As a result, their lecture had to take the form of a classicizing oration, as well as providing a summary of the content and historical context of the Ciceronian extract.[40]

N.L. 16362), which belonged to the *colegio de San Juan* de Puebla and which was even corrected by the Inquisition. María del Carmen Aguilar Guzmán, "Hacia una Reconstrucción de la Librería del Colegio del Espíritu Santo de Puebla: Inventario de sus Libros, Siglos XVI–XVIII" (Thesis for the *Licenciada en Historia*: Benemérita Universidad Autónoma de Puebla, 2006), 197, 233. My thanks to the author for providing me with a copy of her excellent thesis.

[37] AGN, Ramo Universidad, 129, fols. 275r–277r. On Cabrera, see Introduction.

[38] Ignacio Osorio Romero, *Tópicos sobre Cicerón en México*, 55–112. AGN, Ramo Universidad, 82, fols. 780r, 813r.

[39] It is unclear which edition was used.

[40] Jesús Yhmoff Cabrera, *Una Muestra de los Actos Académicos en el Virreinato de la Nueva España* (Mexico City: Universidad Nacional Autónoma de México, 1979), 17. Campos' 1750 lecture is preserved in BNM, ms. 23, fols. 110r–118v, and reproduced in Ignacio Osorio Romero, *Tópicos sobre Cicerón en México*, 96–110; Cabrera's lecture from 1721 in BNM, ms. 27, fols. 78r–84v; and

In 1750, Campos delivered a lecture on the passage "But why do I keep you here longer, judges?" (*Sed cur diutius vos, iudices, teneo?*) from Cicero's well-known oration in defense of Caelius, a wealthy Roman equestrian who had been accused of violent conduct (*vis*) and of attempting to poison the infamous Roman matron, Clodia.[41] In his lecture, Campos was careful to underline his technical understanding of the oration, highlighting its various rhetorical features, including its notable use of prosopopoeia, a device we will see him applying in his own orations.[42] To stress his command of the Ciceronian idiom, Campos carefully, but not slavishly, imitated the Roman orator's text, reworking Cicero's judicial oration to fit contemporary Christian norms.[43] The lecture also made several concessions to the ritual context of delivery. Aware that a panel of scholar-clerics in Mexico City had different sensibilities from a jury in late Republican Rome, he had, of course, to tread carefully around the Roman orator's defense of a flagrant adulterer. Following the conventions of academic oratory at Catholic institutions, he also included an invocation of Mary and the angels, the "guardians of our Republic of Letters" (*nostraeque litterariae Reipublicae custodes*). Furthermore, the occasion demanded he earn the affection of the judges, which he attempted to do by employing the relevant classical instruction for the opening of an oration, a *captatio benevolentiae*, saying that he had been concerned they might not like his lecture as the passage was chosen by chance, but their kind gazes have put him at ease.[44] Although unsuccessful in his bid for the prestigious, although poorly remunerated, chair of rhetoric, Campos continued to deliver orations on ceremonial occasions at the Royal and Pontifical University. These included panegyrics in praise of St. Paul, the Virgin and St. Thomas.[45] Yet, his finest hour was to come early: Just a few

---

Eguiara's lecture from 1721 in BNM, ms. 329, fols. 44r–50r, and reproduced in Osorio Romero, *Tópicos sobre Cicerón en México*, 84–94.

[41] Cicero, *Pro Caelio*, 55.   [42] Osorio Romero, *Tópicos sobre Cicerón en México*, 99.

[43] *Ibid.*, 96 "Quis nunc, auditores, existat Academiae nostrae legis ignarus, miretur profecto quae fuerit mihi mens quod ipsis feriarum diebus, publicis supplicationibus omnibus scholaribus institutis omissis, unam hanc dicendi provinciam suscepissem, nec dubitet quin tantae gravitatis causa versetur, ut nostra maxima intersit de ea vos hodierno vespere iudicare." Cf. Cicero, *Pro Caelio*, 1: "Si quis, iudices, forte nunc adsit ignarus legum, iudiciorum, consuetudinis nostrae, miretur profecto, quae sit tanta atrocitas huiusce causae, quod diebus festis ludisque publicis, omnibus forensibus negotiis intermissis unum hoc iudicium exerceatur, nec dubitet, quin tanti facinoris reus arguatur, ut eo neglecto civitas stare non possit."

[44] *Ibid.*, 97.

[45] Campos' orations for the Virgin and Saint Thomas are preserved in BNM, ms. 23, fols. 92r–97v, 104r–109v. Another example from the 1740s is preserved in: BNM, ms. 1607, 157–168.

months after he received his medical doctorate in 1745 he was asked to deliver the oration for the inauguration of the academic year.

Tradition and Innovation in Campos' 1745 Oration

When Campos mounted the rostrum to address the viceroy and assembled members of the university in October 1745, he began his oration with a recognition of its place within the larger tradition of academic oratory. Not only, he reminded them, was it a tradition of their own university, but one common to the "whole world of universities" where it had been the custom since time immemorial.[46] Indeed, Campos' vague gesture toward the antiquity of the tradition was not misplaced. Classicizing oratory had been a feature of academic life in Northern Italy since the turn of the fifteenth century, where the nascent humanist movement began to influence academic ceremony at great centers of learning like Padua and Bologna. By the sixteenth century it had become a feature of university and college life in all corners of the Republic of Letters, and a particularly large number of these orations survive from New Spain.[47] Some of these orations even enjoyed fame beyond their immediate delivery and printing, such as the 1644 inaugural oration by Baltasar López (1610–1651), the onetime professor of rhetoric, philosophy and sacred scriptures at Mexico City's colegio de San Pedro y San Pablo who offered a highly ornate discussion of "keenness of wit" (*acumen ingenii*) that was later reprinted in Mexico City as a model for aspiring late humanist orators.[48]

---

[46] *Oratio*, 1: "Etsi veteri consudetudine iam inde a primis repetita temporibus atque optimis non huius tantum celeberrimi scientiarum domicilii, sed omnium totius orbis Academiarum institutis, sic hoc, auditores, sancitum, ut pro novis studiorum auspiciis ea prima constituatur oratio, qua studiosae iuventutis hortatus cum Academiae laude iungatur."

[47] The earliest examples of classicizing academic oratory I have been able to find come from Bologna in the second decade of the fifteenth century: Biblioteca Riccardiana, Florence, Italy, 784 (M IV 32). On early humanist academic oratory: Maurizio Campanelli, "L'Oratio e il 'Genere' delle Orazioni Inaugurali dell'Anno Accademico," in *Lorenzo Valla, Orazione per l'Inaugurazione dell'Anno Accademico 1455–1456. Atti di un Seminario di Filologia Umanistica*, Silvia Rizzo (ed.) (Rome: Roma nel Rinascimento, 1994), 25–61. Katherine Elliot van Liere, "Humanism and Scholasticism in Sixteenth-Century Academe: Five Student Orations from the University of Salamanca," *Renaissance Quarterly*, 53 (2000), 57–107. A good, if not complete, finding list of humanist academic orations from New Spain is provided in Osorio Romero, *Tópicos sobre Cicerón en México*, 115–150.

[48] Baltasar López, *Oratio pro Instauratione Studiorum Habita in Collegio Mexicano Societatis Iesu* (Mexico City, 1644). Joaquín Rodríguez Beltrán, "La Agudeza del Ingenio Vista por un Humanista Novohispano: Estudio, Edición y Traducción de la *Oratio pro Instauratione Studiorum* de Baltasar López" (Master's Thesis, Universidad Nacional Autónoma de México, 2012).

The recipe for such orations was fairly simple: open with a request for patience for what was a well-worn genre of public speaking; gain their good will of listeners (*captatio benevolentiae*); praise the university, the city and the relevant local potentates; provide a panegyric of learning and good letters; and end with an exhortation to study. This rather predictable dish was usually served with a good helping of piety, with the orator under-lining the importance of God's favor for the flourishing of good letters and the need for good letters to understand God's creation. The surviving orations from New Spain confirm this pattern. For example, an 1596 ora-tion for the university's inaugural course in civil law opened with the news that this was the first time an oration was being given in Mexico City in praise of jurisprudence, thus avoiding the need for an apology for the genre, before praising the value of jurisprudence to the state (*respublica*) and the stability of human communities (*societates*) in general. The orator then gave a brief a history of law from its mythical origins, through Athens and Rome to their own day, before again praising the good effects of jurisprudence, including its positive influence on charitable efforts for poor widows and *indios*, and ending with a final exhortation to its study.[49] As educational institutions in New Spain were dominated by clerics, academic oratory could also be highly pious. For instance, in an oration delivered in Guatemala City in 1703, the learned priest praised the students for their efforts, peppering the discourse with commonplaces from classical authors, while all the time stressing that it is God who allowed human reason to penetrate so far.[50]

However, in 1745 the circumstances did not permit Campos to offer the usual felicitous combination of praise of the university and an exhor-tation to study. Word, it seems, had spread of Martí's letter, and so, Campos explained, the usual conventions had to be cast aside.[51] Rather than laudatory commonplaces, what was needed was justice, perhaps even vengeance![52] In rhetorical terms, what he was proposing was turning this epideictic academic oration into a judicial oration, moving the symbolic

---

[49] Juan Bautista Balli, *Oración en Elogio de la Jurisprudencia*, Daniel Kuri Breña and Salvador Ugarte (eds.) (Mexico City: Editorial Jus, 1950), 80.
[50] Pedro de Ocampo, *Prolusio pro Studiorum Instauratione Habita Guatamalae* (1703), in Archivo Histórico de la Provincia de los Carmelitas Descalzos en México, Mexico City, Libros manuscritos de doctrina 27 (microfilmed in Mexico City, CEHM, fondo CCCLIII, rollo 38, carpeta 1674).
[51] *Oratio*, 1.
[52] *Oratio*, 1–2: "Quare cum in hac versemur tempestate, auditores, qua non vos laudibus, sed iustitiae; non honoribus, sed exactae vindicatae; non venturae gloriae, sed debitae oppugnantium ultioni velificari debeatis."

locus of delivery from the imperial court, where the art of praise and blame in Latin had first been perfected, to the forum, where Cicero had spoken in criminal cases. As both ancient and contemporary rhetorical handbooks noted, epideictic and judicial oratory were not necessarily antithetical genres, as both could include encomia or invectives directed toward particular individuals, acts, places and things.[53] Campos, with his background and interest in humanist rhetorical theory, was well aware of this close association, stating "all praise, esteem and ornament will be wrapped up in punishing injustice (*iniuria*) and subduing the enemy."[54] In this way, by successfully "prosecuting" Martí he could praise the university and return it to its rightful place of honor in the imagined community of the learned.

Although set-piece courtroom oratory was relatively uncommon in the early modern period and humanist judicial oratory almost unknown, Campos had plenty of examples from Cicero's orations of how to construct a forensic oration. With these in mind, he argued for Martí's conviction for *iniuria*. However, by prosecuting Martí for *iniuria* Campos had chosen a complicated delict. First codified in the XII Tables (449 BCE) as a law pertaining to assault against another person and usually requiring the payment of an equivalent fine, or in the case of a maimed limb (*membrum ruptum*) the equivalent corporal punishment, by the first century BCE, *iniuria* had come to include all manner of personal injuries both physical and to reputation (*infamia*) committed against individuals or vicariously against family members, and in some cases even against slaves. This unwieldy conglomerate then found its way into the Justinianic corpus, and later became the standard frame of reference for later legal systems in the Iberian World and beyond.[55] Not intimidated by the legal complexity or discouraged by his lack of formal training in the law, Campos armed himself with legal texts and commentaries, and set to work. Having placed the oration in its ritual context and justifying the change of genre in the *exordium*, Campos wasted no time in the *narratio* in presenting Martí's letter as a clear case of *iniuria*, stating in a rolling *tricolon* that Martí's

[53] Nicolas Caussin, *Eloquentiae Sacrae et Humanae Parallela Libri XVI*, 543 (*De invectiva*): "Etsi ad demonstrativum genus magis pertinere videtur invectivae tractatio, quando tamen huic generi frequenter immiscetur, et a nonnullis in eo collocatur ordine, non pigebat hic aliqua de eadem ascribere."

[54] *Oratio*, 2: "ut omnis laus, omnis commendatio ac decor in puniendis iniuriis, simulque comprimendis hostibus claudatur."

[55] Justinian, *Institutes* IV tit. 4 *de iniuriis*. Matthias Hagemann, *Iniuria: von den XII-Tafeln bis zur Justinianischen Kodifikation* (Cologne: Böhlau, 1998).

action was a willing attack and that the reputation of Mexico City's scholars had been damaged:

> For you know how fiercely Manuel Martí the Dean who exceeds only in his sarcasm those in the Mexican commonwealth (*respublica*) whom he has offended, sharpened his pen while piling up insults against you; you feel how you are now scorned by others because of his words; you realize that there are many who, if they could, would banish us from the public sphere.[56]

In Roman law, extreme cases of *iniuria* could also fall under the category of *atrox iniuria*, especially if the injury caused death, was committed against an individual of high standing or was committed in a public place or in the presence of an important office holder. Campos was quick to characterize the Dean's letter as such and to demand the requisite punishment. Not only had Martí attacked men of high station, including Mexico City's learned ecclesiastical hierarchy, but due to his reputation and the wide circulation of his published letters he had spread these lies to all four corners of the earth. Not content with this basic legal argument, Campos built on it rhetorically (*amplificatio*), subtly blending the language of *iniuria* as defamation with the associated idea of *iniuria* as physical violence, applying a topic of invention that he would have met in the rhetoric class of his Jesuit college in Veracruz, the "comparison of equal things" (*comparatio parium*),[57] alongside the rhetorical question ubiquitous in the orations of Cicero:

> Would you not have justly and legally gone after the Dean of Alicante, had he skewered such men with a stake, beaten them around the head, and finally bludgeoned them with an axe? Since he has pierced the flesh of your reputation with the scourge of his insults, disfigured the beauty of your genius with heavy verbal blows, assassinated your character with the sharp blade of his invective, do you not think that he should be silenced?[58]

He then employed another rhetorical comparison, this time a "comparison of greater things" (*comparatio maiorum*): If it is right to demand legal

---

[56] *Oratio*, 2: "Scitis enim quam acriter Emmanuel Martí Alonensis Decanus omnes Mexicanae reipublicae infensos dicacitate superans, vestri dedecoris compendium efficiens calamum exacuerit; sentitis quanto in hominum despectu transigatis aetatem; advertitis plures esse, qui cum illo communem lucem, si possent, prorsus eriperent."

[57] Cipriano Soáres, *De Arte Rhetorica Libri Tres*, 39–40.

[58] *Oratio*, 9–10: "An, si Alonensis Decanus tales homines sude perfodisset, alapis cecidisset, securi denique contrucidasset, in eum iure ac iudicio peteretis? Quia vero gravibus conviciorum flagriis famae corpus affecit, taetris verborum alapis ingenii faciem deturpavit, acuto maledicti mucrone honoris vitam ademit, diem illi dicendi potestate interdictum vobis esse credatis?"

satisfaction when someone calls you an "ass," should not Martí be punished more harshly, since he called all the inhabitants of Mexico City
"more stupid than asses"? If Roman law stated that it was considered an
offense to call someone blind, should not Martí be considered a
worse offender, since he said that *Mexicani* were blinded by the mere
sight of learning? If, according to the same laws someone who falsely
accused another of being insolvent in front of his creditors could be
prosecuted for *iniuria*, should not Martí be prosecuted to the full extent
of the law, since he alleged that they were penniless when it came to good
letters?[59]

Just as Cicero had made constant reference to historical precedents in
his orations, so Campos lined up examples of severe punishments doled
out to criminals: The Romans punished sedition by throwing the perpe-
trators from the Tarpeian rock, the Greeks believed in "an eye for an eye"
(*lex talionis*), the Lombards cut off noses, the Emperors Justinian and
Hadrian had tongues cut out and the famously cruel Domitian and the
"degenerate Muslims" were equally severe.[60] Campos calls up a similar cast
of historical characters to justify his argument that the publication of
"libelous books" (*libri famosi*), the Roman equivalent of "libel," could fall
under the category of *atrox iniuria*, and so incur the death penalty![61]
Among the ancients, it was generally thought that such books should be
burned. Nero ordered slanderous wills burned, while Ptolemy II
Philadelphus of Egypt went a step further, having the satirist Sotades
locked inside a lead chest along with some verses he had written about
the king's incestuous relationship with his sister.[62] He even rolled out the
corpse of Justus Lipsius, the famous Flemish humanist and author of an
oration on fake accusations (*Oratio de calumnia*) whom he called as an
expert witness to examine the fate of Sotades and the others.[63] Campos
then drew on modern history and contemporary legal codes in demanding
the punishment, which in the end was not as severe as his historical
examples might have led the listeners to imagine. Instead of throwing
Martí from the Tarpeian rock and letting him tumble down to the bottom,
Campos demanded a simple retraction. Considering that Martí was already
dead, however, this was still quite a demand![64]

---

[59] *Oratio*, 12. Cipriano Soáres, *De Arte Rhetorica Libri Tres*, 37–38.   [60] *Oratio*, 10.
[61] Atonius Pichardus, *Commentariorum in Quatuor Institutionum Iustinianearum Libri*, 2 vols.
(Salamanca, 1620), II, 105–106 (*ad Institutiones* IV.4, *De iniuriis*): "Praeterea adverto atrocem
iniuriam esse, cum famoso libello bona alicuius fama laeditur, siquidem a gravitate poenae atrocem
esse iniuriam iudicamus. Est enim adversus libellum famosum facientem poena capitalis sancita."
[62] *Oratio*, 11.   [63] *Oratio*, 11–12.   [64] *Oratio*, 11.

Taking Martí's "neo-Renaissance" prose style as a model, Campos strained every sinew to compose an oration that adhered more strictly to the conventions of classical oratory than had been typical in the seventeenth century. This did not mean, however, that the oration was a mere antiquarian exercise divorced from contemporary legal culture. Indeed, if we compare Campos' frame of reference to early modern prosecutions for *iniuria*, *infamia* and *libri famosi* from New Spain, we find significant common ground.[65] As in the Roman world, assault could be prosecuted under *iniuria*, as apparent in an 1808 case of a dragoon musician from Michoacán who was accused of throwing stones at the commissioner of the mayor who in turn was forced to seek refuge in a nearby bakery.[66] Defamation too remained part of *iniuria* and was the delict for which José Francisco de Izaguirre, a public notary from Maravatío, was hauled up before the magistrate in 1741 accused of breaching his marriage contract after he discovered that his fiancée was not a true maiden (*doncella*).[67] There were also prosecutions for *atrox iniuria*, especially in the case of *iniuria* against individuals of high rank, as in the case of a soldier Joaquin de Amorrosta who in 1783 was imprisoned for six months in the castle of San Juan de Ulúa in Veracruz for insulting an officer.[68] The authors of defamatory texts were also regularly prosecuted provided that their identities could be ascertained, with an especially large number of such cases arising in New Spain's Pacific outpost in the Philippines, where libelous manuscripts, such as the *Bascoana*, a satire on José Basco y Vargas (1733–1805) the governor general of the Philippines, appeared with some frequency.[69] Such cases were not exclusive to secular courts, as it seems that the Inquisition took a special interest in *libri famosi*, investigating attacks on the church, as well as seditious and libelous material more generally. In 1738, for instance, a manuscript was found to be circulating in Manila that mocked the ecclesiastical and secular hierarchy in a macaronic language that mixed classical sources, like the opening of Cicero's first oration against Catiline ("How long will you try our patience, Catiline?") with passages from the Vulgate Bible to make an irreverent

---

[65] There is also a special category of academic defamation described by the rector, Dr. Ignacio Rodriguez Navarijo, in his letter to the King of Spain published with the oration. *Oratio*, vii–viii. Winfried Stelzer, "Zum Scholarenprivileg Friedrich Barbarossas (Authentica 'Habita')," *Deutsches Archiv für Erforschung des Mittelalters*, 34 (1978), 123–165.

[66] AGN, Real Audiencia, Criminal, 615, exp. 15.

[67] AGN, Indiferente Virreinal, caja 985, exp. 4.

[68] AGN, Gobierno virreinal, correspondencia de diversas autoridades, 38, exp. 35.

[69] Archivo General de Indias, Seville, Filipinas, 337, L.20, fols. 345r–6v.

textual patchwork. This so offended one of the investigating clerics that he declared *libri famosi* to be a "mortal sin" (*peccatum mortale*).[70] Within this context, Campos' theatrical prosecution of Martí for defamation, although highly reminiscent of the Roman forum, used a legal framework that would have been familiar to those with knowledge of legal practice.

Since the Roman courtroom permitted a range of nonjuridical arguments including ad hominem attacks on the accused, witnesses or even the opposing counsel, Campos had considerable room for both praise and vituperation, which he fully exploited in his effort to combine a panegyric of the university with a defense of their learned community. To this end, Campos imitated Cicero's harsh courtroom invective, belittling Martí and arguing that the "Mexican youth" (*iuvenes Mexicani*) were much more accomplished than him. Relying on the information in Mayans' biography, Campos stressed that if the Dean had grown up in New Spain (*Mexicana respublica*), his achievements, while celebrated by scholars everywhere, would not have seemed so exceptional. From his earliest years, Campos proclaimed, the Dean was a mediocre student: To have finished the study of grammar at the age of thirteen would have garnered him no praise in Mexico City, while his progress through the other parts of curriculum were equally unimpressive.[71] Martí may have been praised for his precocious talent for Latin versification, a task on which he expended considerable effort, but the youth of Mexico City, Campos argued, achieved such feats in their spare time, while devoting the bulk of their early years to more serious pursuits. Similarly, translating a Greek author or two into Latin, for which Martí was lauded by Mayans, was regarded as child's play in New Spain. Even his antiquarian studies, which Mateo Delgado, professor of theology at the university, had rightly described as "digging up the filthy and putrid cadavers of antiquity," were nothing to write home about.[72] The scholars of Mexico City achieved even greater feats though they rightly prioritized philosophy and theology and certainly did not boast about it like the puffed-up Dean. While Martí was busy "whoring," the *Mexicani iuvenes* were excavating pre-Columbian monuments and studying the religious rites of the Mexica without presuming to call themselves "defenders of antiquity."[73]

[70] AGN, Inquisición, 986, n. 4, fol. 56r.   [71] *Oratio*, 14–15.   [72] *Oratio*, xvii, 15, 17–18.

[73] *Oratio*, 16: "Tu, quod illos puderet, in muliebri corona profudisti; illi cum huius regni monumenta eruerint, Indorum ritus ac sacrificia noverint, se antiquitatis patronos non appellant." It is likely that he is referring specifically to the early archaeological work of Carlos de Sigüenza y Góngora: Daniel Nemser, "Archaeology in the Lettered City," *Colonial Latin American Review*, 23 (2014), 197–223.

Prosopopoeia and Patriotism

Among the many figures of speech transmitted in the classical rhetorical tradition, prosopopoeia (the act of channeling a person or a personification of a place) was one of the most grand and emotive.[74] This was most famously employed by Cicero in his first oration against Catiline, when he had the *patria* berate him for not dealing with the traitor more swiftly and severely. Given prosopopoeia's prominence, there is no doubt the assembled clerics and scholars immediately recognized it in action when Campos had their Mexican *patria* declare:

> What is more humane . . . than to prosecute him, so that you can rescue your community (*civitas*), your class and all those of good will from that terrible fate? In this way, you will be able to release the *patria*, the shared mother of all, so that she might enjoy honor again. Having been struck down in these recent controversies, she cries out distraught and in tears, seeming to address you thus: "What are you doing, noble citizens and dearest sons? What are you doing? Will you not restrain the man who has cast the splendor of my name into darkness and seeks to smother it with a thick fog of words? Will you suffer these slanders to circulate any longer? Will you not see to it that they are consigned to the flames? I have borne, as much as I could, many insufferable insults from other pygmies. Every time I was abused by their jeers, I stood silent as they tormented me and trampled me in their wake. Now I place myself at your feet, you to whom has been entrusted the glory, honor and reputation of all the citizens. Have these outsiders not torn at my flesh enough, unless they carry off my good name, which is all that remains? Will they not be restrained by gold, silver and riches, which I give them in abundance, and leave me alone? What pretext do you have for delay? Many years have already passed; why have you not said something in your defense? Arise before it is too late and come to the aid of your injured and banished mother. Bury the rage of the enemy in eternal silence; if you do not see to this, you will never live up to my expectations![75]

---

[74] Cipriano Soáres, *De Arte Rhetorica Libri Tres*, 210–211: "Prosopopoeia est personarum ficta inductio, vel gravissimum lumen augendi haec et adversariorum, et nostros cum aliis sermones et aliorum inter se credibiliter introducimus, et suadendo, obiurgando, quaerendo, laudando, miserando personas idoneas damus. Quin mortuos excitare in hoc genere dicendi concessum est. Urbes etiam, populi vocem accipiunt, in quibus hoc modo mollior fit figura. Etenim *si mecum patria, quae mihi vita mea multum est charior, si cuncta Italia, si omnis respublica sic loqueretur: M. Tulli, quid agis? Etc.* Sed magna quaedam vis eloquentiae disideratur. Falsa enim et incredibilia natura necesse est, aut magis moveant, quia supra vera sunt, aut pro vanis accipiantur, quia vera non sunt. Formas quoque fingimus saepe, ut famae Virgilius, ut voluptatis ac virtutis (quemadmodum a Xenophonte traditur) Prodicus, ut multarum aliarum rerum Ovidius." See also Nicolas Caussin, *Eloquentiae Sacrae et Humanae Parallela Libri XVI*, 349, 292, 277. Cf. Cicero, *In Catilinam*, I.17–9.

[75] *Oratio*, 13: "Quid humanius . . . quam contra unum ire, quo totam civitatem, vestrum ordinem ac omnes denique bonos, a turpissimo interitu vindicetis, ut patriam communem omnium matrem in honoris libertatem asseratis, quae propriis ingemit afflicta querelis ac flens ac verecunda vobiscum ita loqui videtur: 'Quid agitis ingenui cives, carissimi filii, quid agistis? Vosne eum, qui mei nominis splendori tenebras offundit et densa litterarum caligine nititur obscurare, non actutum coercebitis?

By appealing simultaneously to his audience's sense of patriotism and compassion, Campos sought to galvanize them into action. In this compelling prosopopoeia, he had no need to delineate specifically the *patria* he had made the mouthpiece of the common grievances of the *iuvenes Mexicani*, as this was presumably obvious to his audience. Since, however, it is not necessarily self-evident to us today, it is worth exploring in detail.

Although Martí had attacked the Americas in general and Mexico City specifically, the community Campos defended did not overlap perfectly with either of these. Rather, it consisted of a classicizing polity that he called the "Mexican republic" (*Mexicana respublica*). Despite the modern connotations of the word "republic," this choice of terminology did not necessarily preclude it being ruled by a monarch. This was a "republic" in the sense of a legitimate, coherent and constitutionally ordered commonwealth, to be contrasted not with "monarchies" (since most ancient and early modern "republics" had a monarch) but with "tyrannies." Indeed, this was the terminology of choice for all the other kingdoms, viceroyalties, dukedoms, captaincy generals and city-states under the Hispanic Monarchy, which imagined themselves as corporate entities with their own political and legal traditions.[76]

On this issue, further context is provided by Eguiara in his *Bibliotheca Mexicana* (1755), in which Campos' colleague at the Royal and Pontifical University of Mexico City defined and defended their shared community. Geographically, this was described as being located in North America (*America septentrionalis*) and being roughly coterminous with the Viceroyalty of New Spain (*America Mexicana*), which he contrasted with South America (*America meridionalis*), in other words the Viceroyalty of Peru (*America Peruana*).[77] Despite its dubious legality, Eguiara considered both Americas to be kingdoms (*regna*) analogous to Castile and Aragon,

---

Has[ne] diutius in hominum manibus versari feretis? Ut flammis mandentur, non impetrabitis? Plurima iam non ferenda aliorum homuncionum, ut potui, pertuli convicia, audivi probra, toties eorum vocibus lacerata et proculcata conticui. Nunc vero me totam sententiis vestris committo; vobis omnium civium gloria, decus et fama concreditur. Parumne mea viscera exteri hactenus diripuere, nisi nomen, quod solum supererat, auferrent? Sint auro, argento et divitiis, quarum copiam illis facio, contenti, hoc unum mihi relinquant. Quid amplius moras nectitis? Plures iam anni transiere, quin aliquid pro vobis diceretis? Exurgite aliquando atque afflictae et obscuratae genitrici sucurrite, infestorum furorem perpetuo comprimite silentio, hac nisi ratione consulere velitis, nunquam satis meo desiderio facietis.'"

76   On the early modern republicanism, see James Hankins, "Exclusivist Republicanism and the Non-nonarchical Republic," *Political Theory*, 38 (2010), 452–482.

77   Juan José Eguiara y Eguren, *Bibliotheca Mexicana*, I, fol. 33av. Despite its separate existence as part of the Viceroyalty of New Granada from 1717, Caracas is also included in *America Mexicana* due to its position in the ecclesiastical administration: Juan José Eguiara y Eguren, *Bibliotheca Mexicana*, I, fol. 34br. On humanism in New Granada, see José Manuel Rivas Sacconi, *El Latín en Colombia:*

with territories in North America that were under different kings such as New England and New France naturally falling outside of this. Geopolitics, however, was only part of the puzzle. An equally important factor in delineating Eguiara's *Mexicana respublica* within the Americas seems to have been the circulation of books and his personal correspondence network, which reached only as far south as Caracas. Indeed, one of the main reasons he gives for not including Peru is that it was not possible for someone from *America Mexicana* to have good knowledge of the books printed in *America Peruana*, as ships from Peru only reached Guatemala once a year, while the Philippines, despite being a constituent part of the Viceroyalty of New Spain and having a vibrant print culture was excluded, presumably due to the difficulty of obtaining books printed there.[78] This then was a community shaped by geopolitics and the administrative patterns of the Hispanic Monarchy, but one that also reflected the individual lived experiences of its members and the frequency of their interactions with each other.

This community, partly real and partly imagined, was, however, no protonation state. Rather, as Eguiara described it, it appears more like an expansive city-state modeled on Renaissance Milan than the France of Richelieu. As Eguiara explained, *America Mexicana* was so named because of its principal city, and all the surrounding regions were measured by their connection to this central city.[79] Even when defining those who were to be considered *Mexicani* by birth, he privileged Mexico City over the region as a whole, defining as *Mexicanus* someone who was born in "either Mexico City or Mexican America."[80] This was also reflected in Eguiara's view of the history of *America Mexicana*, as for him it was the fall of Mexico-Tenochtitlan to Cortés, "the glorious general and man above all praise," that marked the beginning of the history of the Mexican "republic" and

Bosquejo Histórico del Humanismo Colombiano, 3rd ed. (Bogota: Instituto Caro y Cuervo, 1993), 207–211.

[78] Juan José Eguiara y Eguren, *Bibliotheca Mexicana*, I, fol. 34br.

[79] To summarize Eguiara's usage: *Mexicani* refers to all the territories associated with Mexico City and is roughly synonymous with the Viceroyalty of New Spain; *Mexicus* (locative *Mexici*) refers to Mexico City; *mexicanensis* to a resident of the city; and *mexiceus* is a poetical adjective sometimes referring to Mexico City, other times to the larger territories, and, in historical contexts, specifically to the Mexica empire. Juan José Eguiara y Eguren, *Bibliotheca Mexicana*, I, 33av: "ad Mexiceas oras." Cf. Ignacio Osorio Romero, *El Sueño Criollo: José Antonio de Villerías y Roelas (1695–1728)* (Mexico City: Universidad Nacional Autónoma de México, 1991), II.110–1:

> Mexicei partier totius cernitur ingens
> Imperii series; seraque ab origine gentis
> Progenies, priscique duces, veteresque tyranni.

[80] Juan José Eguiara y Eguren, *Bibliotheca Mexicana*, I, fol. 34av: "et insimul Mexicani natione, quippe natale solum Mexicum habeant, aut Mexiceam Americam."

inaugurated the Christian culture that Eguiara and Campos held so dear.[81] The formation of their community was therefore providential with the increasingly popular local Marian apparition, the Virgin of Guadalupe, also playing an important role in the formation of this city-state, as Campos had made clear in a 1756 oration delivered in the medical faculty:

> Yet, some will respond: what about that great immortal hero Hernán Cortés who, envious of the fictional Jason, brought back the American Golden Fleece? And, they might ask: had not his followers and those who were inspired by his great deeds already brought the true faith and religion to this land where the sun sets, overturned the temples of daemons and set up the standard of the cross, a decade before the Guadalupe stood witness to the triumphant truth with the famous appearance of her image? It is very difficult to pass judgment on such matters, dear listeners, since the truth is hidden from us by the veil of divine providence. Yet, I grant to those men [i.e. Cortes and his followers] a greatness of spirit, no small expertise in military matters, bravery in the face of adversity, and joy when they overcame it. But I contend that things would not have fallen into their lap as they did, and they would not have succeeded in their planned conquest in two years, had the Guadalupan mother not provided mystical reinforcements.[82]

Campos, a devotee of the Virgin of Tepeyac throughout his life, clearly shared Eguiara's positive view of Spanish colonialization, which for him was tightly linked to its homegrown Marian cult and the foundation of *America Mexicana*.[83]

Defining Citizenship in the "Mexican" Branch of the Republic of Letters

When Campos defended the traditions of learning by the "Mexican people" (*Mexicanus populus*), he was not referring to all the inhabitants

---

[81] *Ibid.*, I, 1–2.

[82] BNM, ms 23, fols. 65v–67v (66r–v): "Sed dicet aliquis: quid heros ille immortalis Herdinandus Cortesius, qui ad ementiti Iasonis invidiam aureum Americae vellus reportavit suorumque facinorum aemulatores et socii nonne iam veri numinis cognitionem et fidem ad hanc usque occidentis solis metam attulerant, Daemonum delubra postraverant, vexilla crucis erexerant decennio ante quam Guadalupana mater triumphantem iam veritatem praesentissimae suae imaginis exhibitione firmasset [sic]? Est quidem in hoc versari perdifficile, auditores, cum arcano divinae providentiae obveletur sipario, sed esto magnis illis viris tribuam animi magnitudinem, non adimam disciplinae militaris peritiam, in adeundis periculis fortitudinem, in superandis felicitatem; illud tamen in illorum Manium pace con- /fol. 66v/ tendam numquam illos designatam oppugnationem tanta felicitate biennio perfecturos, nisi Guadalupana parens arcanis praesidiis auxiliatrices manus contulisset."

[83] For instance, Campos endorsed a 1789 work on the veracity of the Guadalupan apparition: Ernesto de la Torre Villar and Ramiro Navarro de Anda (eds.), *Testimonios Históricos Guadalupanos* (Mexico City: Fondo de Cultura Económica, 1982), 600.

of New Spain. Indeed, in the early modern Iberian World (and arguably much, if not all of the premodern world), membership in a political or intellectual community was a restricted and highly regulated status based on a number of factors, from ethnicity to residency, and from wealth to education. Being born within the geographic bounds of the *Mexicana respublica* was clearly an important criterion in this regard. Yet, this was not sufficient, as Iberian ethnocentrism set limits on access to, and the status incurred by learning.[84] For instance, although "pure-blooded" *caciques* were in theory permitted to take a degree on equal footing with Spanish *hidalgos*, in practice they usually made up a relatively small proportion of graduates and did not advance to the higher degrees, with the first *indio* receiving a doctoral degree in 1772. Of the scholars addressed by Campos in 1745, there were therefore probably few, if any, *indios*, as the epidemic that raged in the 1730s seems to have meant that no indigenous students graduated in arts at all between 1732 and 1753, in contrast to the years before and after when at least one graduated per year. This said, there was a small number of *indio* scholars among the *Mexicani* noted by Eguiara in the *Bibliotheca Mexicana*, in particular during the sixteenth century whom Eguiara took care to differentiate from "Spaniards."[85] There were also scholars of mixed parentage despite the prohibition against them matriculating at the university, most notably the Jesuit Antonio del Rincón (1566–1601) who appeared in both the *Bibliotheca Mexicana* and the *Bibliotheca Hispana Nova*.[86] Those of African descent were not so fortunate and were entirely excluded from both the university and the *Bibliotheca Mexicana*, as were both slaves (whatever their ethnicity) and freedmen.[87]

---

[84] María Elena Martínez, *Genealogical Fictions: Limpieza de Sangre, Religion, and Gender in Colonial Mexico*.

[85] E.g. Juan José Eguiara y Eguren, *Bibliotheca Mexicana*, I, 329: "D. Augustinus de la Fuente, natione Mexicanus, parentibus Indis, in ea Imperialis nostrae urbis regione natus est, quae Tlatelolco etiamnum audit." *Bibliotheca Mexicana*, I, fol. 34av: "Mexicanos natione quos legeris, scito Hispanos esse in America natos, nisi conceptis verbis expressum videris ab Indis parentibus illos esse procreatos." On Indian student numbers, see Margarita Menegus Bornemann and Rodolfo Aguirre Salvador, *Los Indios, el Sacerdocio y la Universidad en Nueva España, Siglos XVI–XVIII*, 78–80, 91–93.

[86] Nicholás Antonio, *Bibliotheca Hispana Nova*, 2 vols. (Rome, 1672), I, 123. Cf. Juan José Eguiara y Eguren, *Bibliotheca Mexicana*, I, 265–266; Alegambe Filipp, *Bibliotheca Scriptorum Societatis Iesu* (Antwerp, 1676), 43.

[87] Juan de Palafox y Mendoza, *Estatutos y Constituciones Hechas con Comisión Particular de su Magestad* (Mexico City, 1688), 45: "Ordenamos que cualquiera que hubiere sido penitenciado por el Santo Oficio, o sus Padres o Abuelos tuviere alguna nota de infamia, no sea admitido a grado alguno de esta Universidad, ni tampoco los Negros, ni Mulatos, ni los que comúnmente se llaman Chinos morenos, ni cualquiera genero de esclavo, o que lo haya sido: porque no solo no han de ser

As a result of these restrictions, the learned community that Campos defended on that October day in 1745 consisted almost exclusively of the viceroyalty's highest caste, the "Spaniards" (*Hispani*), a transregional group that shared a common origin in Peninsular Spain, which Campos alluded to when he addressed his speakers as the "offspring of Europe" (*Europaea progenies*). Like all elite inhabitants of the Iberian World, they also possessed a common language in the Romance dialects of the Iberian Peninsula, a common religion in Catholicism and certain shared Iberian cultural practices.[88] Although the bonds of pan-Hispanism were strong, it is undeniable that some of Campos' contemporaries subdivided Spaniards of "pure-blood" (*limpios de sangre*) according to whether they were born in Europe or the Americas. The latter group were sometimes referred to as creoles, a term originally used to designate African slaves born in the Americas. However, this was by no means universally accepted usage and is nowhere to be found in Campos' oration. Some like Andrés de Arce y Miranda (1701–1774), Eguiara's learned correspondent in nearby Puebla, even openly rejected the term because of its associations with African slavery, preferring instead "Spaniards born in the Americas," and Eguiara seems to have taken his friend's advice.[89] Even if this distinction was not hugely important to Campos and Eguiara, as American-born Spaniards, they were no doubt aware of the view of some scholars that those of Iberian stock born in the Western Hemisphere were degenerate in comparison to their European cousins. Indeed, this was an issue Eguiara chose to address head-on in the *Bibliotheca Mexicana*. Echoing Benito Feijóo's defense of *criollos*, Eguiara argued that the American climate has little effect on Spanish blood lines, piling up quotations in support of his arguments from scholars who had firsthand experience of the Americas, while taking care to appear objective by excluding evidence produced by American-born scholars, as the impartiality of such "suspicious witnesses" might reasonably be doubted.[90]

admitidos a grados, pero ni a la matricula; y se declara, que los Indios como Vasallos libres de su Magestad, pueden y deben ser admitidos a matricula y grados."

[88] *Oratio*, 6.

[89] Efraín Castro Morales, *Las Primeras Bibliografías Regionales Hispanoamericanas: Eguiara y sus Corresponsales* (Puebla: Ediciones Altiplano, 1961), 33. *Idem*, "Los cuadros de castas de la Nueva España," *Jahrbuch für Geschichte von Staat, Wirtschaft, und Gesellschaft Lateinamerikas*, 20 (1983), 671–690 (679).

[90] Juan José Eguiara y Eguren, *Bibliotheca Mexicana*, I, fols. 18br–21av. *Ibid.*, I, fol. 18br–v: "ne suspectis et repellendis iure testibus rem agamus, natos in America viros hac in causa tacitos praeteribimus; credimusque a sapientibus viris auditum non iri eos qui, Andabatorum more, clausis oculis, quos in Americam minime conievere, nec probatis instructi monumentis aut auctoribus eruditi, iaculis nos impetere et de nobis iudicare tentaverint. Reliquum est ergo, ut

Although the *criollos* were certainly a large part of the intellectual community whose honor Campos and Eguiara rushed to defend, it would be more accurate to describe membership in their branch of the Iberian World as being defined along similar lines to contemporary citizenship (*vecindad*). "Citizenship" (*vecindad*) and "nativeness" (*naturaleza*) in cities and kingdoms in the Hispanic Monarchy were more than just statuses conferred on those who were born within each political unit's generally accepted borders. Following Roman precedents, Spanish law recognized a number of ways by which individuals could become natives, with birth or ten years of residence being the primary criteria, and vassalage, nurture, knighthood, marriage, inheritance, rescue, emancipation, conversion and owning property all playing minor roles as well.[91] In defining his scholarly community, Eguiara, consciously or subconsciously borrowed this framework. As he wrote of the hundreds of learned *Mexicani* whose lives and works he catalogued: "they are all bound together by a single political and scholarly community."[92] As early as the title page of his magnum opus, he spelled out the criteria for inclusion in their number:

> *The Mexican Library dedicated to Ferdinand VI, the Catholic King of the two Spains, or the History of the erudite men, who, having been born in North America or elsewhere and given citizenship there by virtue of their residence or studies, committed something to letters in any language, and above all of those who distinguished themselves by their deeds or writings, either published or unpublished, for the cause of the Catholic faith and piety.[93]*

Although the scholars he listed were born in cities in Spain, Italy, New Spain and Peru, they were all considered *Mexicani*, whether by birth

---

idoneis usuri testibus, viros doctos et graves audiamus, qui apud Europam nati, in consuetudinem nostrum venerint, et longo Americanarum rerum usu et experimentis res ipsas imbiberint, mox alios optimis usos testimoniis et fide dignis instrumentis, parce exhibeamus." Cf. Jorge Cañizares-Esguerra, *How to Write the History of the New World: Histories, Epistemologies, and Identities in the Eighteenth-Century Atlantic World*, 211–212.

[91] Tamar Herzog, *Defining Nations: Immigrants and Citizens in Early Modern Spain and Spanish America*, 68–70.

[92] Juan José Eguiara y Eguren, *Bibliotheca Mexicana*, I, fol. 34ar: "iam vero cur in Bibliotheca Mexicana et natos apud Americam nostram viros et alibi genitos atque domicilio et studiis in ipsam ascitos comprehendimus, non una nobis ratio est, nam et Alonensis decanus una omnes calumnia impetivit et una eos omnes politica societas et respublica litteraria coniungit, et, quod caput est, Hispani in America geniti ut stirpem et genus ducimus ab Hispanis apud Europam natis, ab ipsis itidem litteras primum traximus et doctrinam, cum Universitati Mexicanensi condendae operam dantibus, tum religiosis ordinibus constituendis, fidei iuxta ac pietatis et litterariae quoque rei causa." The term *respublica litteraria* is used by Eguiara and Campos in both a general sense (the "Republic of Letters"), and a specific sense (their branch of that community).

[93] Juan José Eguiara y Eguren, *Bibliotheca Mexicana. Thesaurus Linguae Latinae*, 11 vols. (Leipzig: Teubner, 1900–2012), II, 764, l. 29–42 (*adscisco, ad civitatem*).

(*natione*), long-term residence (*domicilio*), his studies (*studiis*) or office-holding (*munere*).[94] This was because membership in the community was not an intrinsic, but an emergent characteristic. For Eguiara, who was keen to expand citizenship to its reasonable limits, it was not even really necessary to know the place of a scholar's birth, if there was solid evidence of their studies or residence in Mexico City or a dependent territory, which automatically bestowed membership, while those whose residence was insufficient to merit this were excluded as foreigners (*hospites*).[95]

To grasp fully how Campos and his audience understood who was a member of their community, it is important to understand the main addition that Eguiara made to the neo-Roman citizenship paradigm, the criterion of "studies" (*studiis*). In defining what was primarily an intellectual community, it is perhaps unsurprising that they put great store by an association with educational institutions, a view Campos expressed openly in his oration when he declared that it was equally, if not more important to defend one's intellectual honor as one's family honor.[96] Indeed, it appears again that they were defending a city-state, but one centered not so much on Mexico City as on the Royal and Pontifical University in Mexico City. In the case of Eguiara's bio-bibliographical encyclopedia, its reliance on this model of a learned *respublica* appears as early as the first entry of the encyclopedia. Beneath images associated with Mexico City and its place in the Hispanic Monarchy (the coat of arms of Castile and Leon, the Virgin of Guadalupe and an eagle sitting on a cactus holding a snake), Eguiara recounted the familiar story of Cortés' conquest of the Mexica capital and Charles V's subsequent foundation of a university for the propagation of the Catholic faith, to which students flocked from both near and far (*exteri confluentes et incolae*).[97] The story of the foundation of the *academia Mexicanensis* thus became the foundational moment for the intellectual history of New Spain, and so membership of the university

---

[94] E.g. Juan José Eguiara y Eguren, *Bibliotheca Mexicana*, I, 16, 62.

[95] *Ibid.*, I, 27: "Illustrissimus D. F. Alphonsus de Benavides, natione Mexicanus an Hispanus, scire adhuc non potuimus, S Francisci Regulam in Provincia Sancti Evangelii sequutus, variisque distentus officiis, custos, ut dicitur, in Novam Mexicum destinatus regionem illam a veteri Mexico, primaria Americae septentrionalis urbe, quadrigentas non minus leucas distantem invisit." Juan José Eguiara y Eguren, *Bibliotheca Mexicana*, I, fol. 34ar–v: "Hinc aliquos missos facimus in Bibliotheca nostra, de rebus Americae nostrae praeclare scribentes, quos hospites potius habuimus quam cives."

[96] *Oratio*, 5. Here, he cites: Barthélemy de Chasseneuz, *Catalogus Gloriae Mundi* (Cologne 1692), X.7 (351–353): "Scientia utilis est, quod exemplis probatur, cum multi ex scientia et doctrina habiti sunt in magno honore et pretio."

[97] Juan José Eguiara y Eguren, *Bibliotheca Mexicana*, I, 1–2.

(*studiis*), which also usually involved a considerable period of residence, rightly bestowed membership in their branch of the Republic of Letters.

This more flexible model of citizenship that went beyond *ius soli* and *ius sanguinis* was probably also reinforced by a number of intellectual currents. The first was Roman law mediated not only through medieval and early modern Spanish law, but also through the humanist educational program and the study of the civil law at universities throughout the Iberian World. This was a tradition well known to Eguiara, and which he described in detail in his *lección de oposición* for the chair of rhetoric in 1721, when he spoke on a passage from Cicero's *Pro Balbo*, an oration in which the Roman orator defended Balbus from accusations of having falsely claimed Roman citizenship. In his summary of Cicero's argument, Eguiara reminded his audience that, although born in Gades (Cádiz), Balbus was entitled to Roman citizenship thanks to his service to the Roman state and his virtuous behavior while a resident in Rome, and ridiculed the idea that Rome, the "common fatherland of all peoples" (*patria omnium gentium communis*), would have rejected individuals who could have contributed to its glory (*civitatis ornamentum*).[98] Secondly, this way of defining membership in an intellectual community was reminiscent of the way authors of other *Bibliothecae* had treated their regional or political communities.[99] For example, Eguiara's criteria aligned perfectly with those of another city-state, Milan, which gave scholarly citizenship (*civitas*) to those born there, long-term residents and those who had studied at the university in nearby Pavia.[100] Whether this is an example of influence or convergence is not clear, but the conventions followed by Eguiara seem to be in line with those applied elsewhere. There was, of course, the temptation to push the

---

[98] Osorio Romero, *Tópicos sobre Cicerón en México*, 84–94 (92–94). cf. Justinian *Digest*, 50.1.33: "Roma communis nostra patria est." The Roman idea of citizenship and community is discussed in José Antonio Maravall, *Estado Moderno y Mentalidad Social (Siglos XV a XVII)*, 2 vols. (Madrid: Revista de Occidente, 1972), I, 457.

[99] According to Philippe Labbé, *Bibliothecae Bibliothecarum* (Rouen, 1672), 30–31, *Bibliothecae* could be organized according to the following principles: places, people (e.g. the Bodleian), rulers, religious orders, subjects, arrangement or circumstances. Tamar Herzog, *Defining Nations: Immigrants and Citizens in Early Modern Spain and Spanish America*, 164–200.

[100] Filippo Argelati, *Bibliotheca Scriptorum Mediolanensium, seu Acta, et Elogia Virorum Omnigena Eruditione Illustrium, qui in Metropoli Insubriae, Oppidisque Circumiactibus Orti sunt* (Milan, 1745), v–vi: "Ceterum si alii sint etiam scriptores veriori patriae restitudendi, quod non tam facile credam, non ob id ab Indice nostro sunt penitus expugnandi, sed ad classem eorum reducendi, qui literarum studiis, vel conscribendis libris in hac metropoli longam aetatem incubuerunt; unde si non origine, civitate saltem non minus, vere inter Mediolanenses censendi sint, ob eamque rationem ad instituti nostri modulum spectant, et servato cuique patriae iure, ob inchoatum studiorum cultum, quo renasci homines propremodum videntur, nemo negavit debitam cuique sedem in ea urbe, qua sit literarum copia nutritus."

envelope of citizenship in order to include particularly noteworthy indi-viduals, such as when the *Biblioteca Napoletana* claimed Cicero as a Neopolitan, and Eguiara was not immune from this tendency, claiming, among others, Christopher Columbus as a Mexican! However, he never abandoned the expanded neo-Roman citizenship framework, arguing that the explorer spent enough time in *America Mexicana* to qualify as a resident.[101]

The Meta-Geography of the *Mexicani*

As well as defending a distinct but not hermetically sealed community in his oration, Campos also inadvertently defined the relationship between the *respublica Mexicana* and the other *respublicae* of the Hispanic Monarchy (e.g. the kingdoms of the Iberian Peninsula, the Viceroyalty of Peru, etc.). This is worth reconstructing as the controversy started by Martí is conventionally seen as an intellectual fight-to-the-death between representatives of Spain and New Spain (proto-Mexico), polities that existed in a hierarchical colonial relationship of center and periphery. This is in contrast to the growing consensus that the Hispanic Monarchy was not "colonial" either in reality or conception, but politi-cally, legally and socially polycentric. That is to say, there were "many different interlinked centers that interacted not only with the king but also among themselves, thus actively participating in forging the polity."[102] So does Campos' meta-geography also fit into the polycentric mold?

Interestingly, the reality is far more complex than either framework suggests, and can be modeled in at least three ways. These fluctuated in prominence depending on the particular exigencies of the moment. First, Campos and his audience lived at the center of multiple concentric circles: the university, the pseudo-city-state of New Spain, the Hispanic Monarchy and the Catholic Republic of Letters. Second, their community existed within a larger constellation of communities in the Republic of

---

[101] It was claimed that in a forest near città de Santovica, there was an inscription that marked the site of Cicero's tomb: Nicoló Toppi, *Biblioteca Napoletana et Apparato a Gli Huomini Illustri di Napoli e Del Regno, delle Famiglie, Terre, Città, e Religioni, che Sono nello Stesso Regno, dale Loro Origini per Tutto l'Anno 1678* (Naples, 1678), 202–203. *Bibliotheca Mexicana*, I, 492: "D. Christophorus Columbus, natione Italus, patria Genuensis novi orbis detectione, quem ab Hispaniola auspicatus est insula, Mexicanus iure si quis alius, dicendus, scriptis quoque in America nostra litteris per utrumque, qua late porrigitur, orbem notissimus est."

[102] The *locus classicus* for this interpretation is: Pedro Cardim, Tamar Herzog, José Javier, Ruiz Ibáñez and Gaetano Sabatini (eds.), *Polycentric Monarchies: How Did Early Modern Spain and Portugal Achieve and Maintain a Global Hegemony?*

Letters, with which they interacted to different degrees and in different ways.[103] Many of these were part of the Hispanic Monarchy (e.g. Peru, Castile and the Philippines), although some were not (e.g. Papal Rome, France and German-speaking lands). Even areas outside the Republic of Letters, like China, were not entirely absent. Third, the learned members of the *respublica Mexicana* had various bilateral, often hierarchical relationships with other individuals and institutions, some, although not all of which, fell along the conventional metropolitan-colonial divide. For instance, they undeniably looked to the Iberian Peninsula, the ultimate seat of political and judicial authority in the form of the king and the Council of the Indies. However, they also looked to Rome, and arguably Italy as a whole, as the religious and intellectual center of the Catholic world. These overlapping and constantly shifting frameworks formed the "hierarchically polycentric" meta-geography of Campos and contemporaries.

Of all these frameworks, the largest and the least appreciated by scholarship is surely the Republic of Letters (*respublica litteraria*). Just as Eguiara's monumental *Bibliotheca Mexicana* was addressed to the whole of the "Republic of Letters," whose judgment of the intellectual standing of the "Mexican" branch of their learned community he wished to influence, Campos used his oration to defend the reputation of the *Mexicana respublica* within the same Republic of Letters. The importance of this larger intellectual community lay not only in the benefits that accrued directly from acceptance within it, but, importantly for Campos' argument, also in the political implications of acceptance it had for a kingdom's standing in the Hispanic Monarchy. Citing the commonplace of Diogenes the Cynic that those who do not seek wisdom are not fully-fledged human beings (*homines*), Campos predicted that if the other members of the Republic of Letters came to accept the intellectual inferiority of the *Mexicani*, the Crown would no longer consider them worthy to hold offices in their native kingdom.[104] As one of the most carefully guarded rights of residents within the Hispanic Monarchy, the loss of office-holding privileges would be both a disgrace and a severe blow for local autonomy and community self-rule that could not be countenanced.[105] After all, they lived in a commonwealth (*respublica*), not a tyranny. Playing

---

[103] I have borrowed the word "constellation" here from: Byron Ellsworth Hamann, *The Translations of Nebrija: Language, Culture, and Circulation in the Early Modern World*, 121–122.
[104] *Oratio*, 19–20. Campos lifts the story of Diogenes from Alfonso de Azevedo, *Commentarii Juris Civilis in Hispaniae Regias Constitutiones*, 6 vols. (Lyon, 1737), IV, 37 (VI .2.70–71).
[105] *Oratio*, 19.

on the close relationship between reason, urban civilization and self-rule, Campos taunted his fellow *Mexicani*, asking what opinion they would hold of a people if they heard rumors about them like those spread by Martí. If Martí's slanderous comments were true, would it not be better, he asked, to send the *Mexicani* out of the city to live in the forest, where they could set up professorships of ploughing, since the study of theology and law would be wasted on them? Only the civilized could achieve self-rule and liberty from the passions through reason. The ignorant could and should not rule themselves or others. Thus, the importance of successfully prosecuting the Dean lay in the possible repercussions of his defamation, above all the subjection of the *Mexicani* to the "heavy yoke of servitude," which would be the ultimate calamity. New displays of erudition and eloquence of the sort valued in the Republic of Letters were now a political necessity.[106]

In this battle to avoid relegation to manual labor in the fields, Campos argued, they fortunately already had powerful allies among their fellow citizens of the Republic of Letters. In a string of Ciceronian *quid*'s (i.e. rhetorical questions), Campos maintained that his audience should not be afraid of losing face in the world of learning, since the ancient universities of Spain had already embraced the Royal and Pontifical University of Mexico City as their equal, something they would never have even considered if they shared the Dean's view that the "Mexican Minerva" was a "hovel out in the sticks" (*rusticum gurgustium*). Would Salamanca let the reputation of her sister university be besmirched? Never.[107] The *Mexicani* also had other powerful allies in the Republic of Letters who had similarly felt the sting of Martí's derision. They should remember that Rome would join Mexico City in the phalanx marching against the Dean who had insinuated that there was no one in the Eternal City apart from himself up to the task of completing the *Bibliotheca Hispana Vetus*. Although Campos and Eguiara do not seem to have held Martí's view that Spain was a miserable backwater in comparison to Italy, they both expressed a deep reverence for the undeniable center of ancient wisdom and modern learning. Indeed, in their intellectual meta-geography Italy

---

[106] *Oratio*, 20–21: "Quare, si hucusque inani studio laboratis, ut alii assequerentur, studuistis, nihil est iam in posterum, quod speretis; omnia mandatis atque imperio alienigenae implebunt, vos duro servitutis iugo subiacebitis. Per Deum immortalem, auditores, quo tandem animo estis aut haec quemadmodum concipitis? Utrum ego [d]ementia teneor et, plusquam expedit, discrucior in tanta urbis calamitate et pernicie? An vos quoque hoc acerbissimum reipublicae vulnus examinat ac interimit?"

[107] *Oratio*, 22.

stood alongside and at times even eclipsed the Iberian Peninsula. Considering it was the point of origin of the universal language of the Republic of Letters, the birthplace of its shared neo-Roman culture, the seat of the Papacy and the homeland of the systems of both civil and canon law by which they lived, Campos' choice to march out Italy, as opposed to say France or another possible ally, is perhaps not all that surprising.

While Campos explicitly mentioned Italy and the Iberian Peninsula in his oration, these were just particularly bright stars in a larger galaxy, with the perceived comradery of the other members of the Republic of Letters also contributing to a sense of belonging. Many of these politico-intellectual communities were parts of the Hispanic Monarchy. As already mentioned, Peru was firmly on Eguiara's and probably also Campos' radar, although the distance of its main intellectual center, Lima, meant that they had surprisingly little direct contact with it. Similarly, in the *Bibliotheca Mexicana* Eguiara treated the Philippines as a separate intellectual sphere (even though it was legally an extension of New Spain), and one that Eguiara knew at least something about, as his family had been involved in Basque trading networks that crossed both the Atlantic and the Pacific, and his personal library contained several books that discussed the Philippines in detail.[108] In addition, there were other kindred communities that were not part of the Hispanic Monarchy. For instance, we learn from the notes to the printed edition of Campos' oration that while preparing the text he had been reading a humanist history of Poland by Marcin Kromer (1512–1589).[109] If we turn to Eguiara's library for more context, we see that Campos' friend and confidant possessed books written and printed in Lyon, Paris and Coimbra, with many of these books being perhaps best described as products of the Jesuit branch of the Republic of Letters, of which both Campos and Eguiara were archetypal products.[110]

This said, it was not necessary to be a Catholic to be part of Campos' and Eguiara's intellectual world, although they doubtless preferred it that way. For instance, during his career in the Faculty of Medicine Campos was responsible for introducing the medical theories of the German

---

[108] E.g. Joseph Torrubia, *Disertación Histórico Política, en que Trata de la Extensión de el Mahometismo en las Islas Philipinas* (Madrid, 1736).

[109] *Oratio,* 11.

[110] Eguiara's library is catalogued and discussed in: Juan José de Eguiara y Eguren, *Biblioteca Mexicana,* Ernesto de la Torre Villar (ed.), V, 193–206; Stuart M. McManus, "The Art of Being a Colonial *Letrado*: Learned Sociability and Urban Life in Eighteenth-Century Mexico City," *Estudios de Historia Novohispana,* 56 (2017), 40–64 (51–52).

mechanist physician Frederick Hoffmann (1660–1742), a confidant of the English chemist Robert Boyle (1627–1691) who was so devoted to advancing the cause of Protestantism that he endowed a scholarship fund for aspiring indigenous ministers studying at Harvard College in Puritan Massachusetts.[111] Furthermore, the scholars of Mexico City were also at least aware of imperial China, the home of a neo-Egyptian humanistic tradition and the source of many of the luxury goods that they either owned or coveted, through the well-known *China illustrata* of the great Jesuit polymath Athanasius Kircher (1602–1680).[112] In other words, Campos and his contemporaries did not inhabit a Manichean intellectual world divided between a single metropolitan center and a colonial periphery, either in reality or in conception. Rather, they lived in an intellectual landscape that was expansive, diverse and hierarchically polycentric.

While Campos' Hispanic kingdom *cum* city-state was the center of his world and a co-equal part of a wider world that largely overlapped with the Catholic Republic of Letters, this is not to say that political hierarchies did not matter. Rather, they were not all that mattered, and when they did they were not always aligned in favor of the "strong" and against the "weak." Indeed, in his prefatory letter addressed to the President of the Council of the Indies and appended to the printed version of Campos' oration, the rector of the university, Ignacio Rodriguez Navarijo, made it clear that the scholars in Mexico City expected the political hierarchy to defend Mexico's honor.[113] Furthermore, in the oration itself Campos argued that his audience should take heart because they had the backing of the king whose paternal affection would not permit them to suffer such a demeaning fate at the hands of Martí:

> Here, if the cause itself compels you, your dignity and interests, the images of your ancestors exhort you. At the same time, the mighty King of Spain himself who *shall extend his power to the ocean, his glory to the stars*, bids you with most gentle compliments. You must firmly place your hope in him and can expect even greater results. For he is the one and only king who

---

[111] AGN, Ramo Universidad, 129, fol. 276r. On Hoffmann, see Johann Henry Schulz, *Commentarius de Vita Friderici Hoffmanni*, in Friederick Hoffmann, *Opera Omnia Physico-Medica*, 6 vols. (Geneva, 1761), I, i–xvi. On Boyle and Harvard Indian College, see Thomas Keeline and Stuart M. McManus, "Benjamin Larnell, the Last Latin Poet at Harvard Indian College," *Harvard Studies in Classical Philology*, 108 (2015), 621–642 (625).

[112] For Eguiara's discussion of Kircher's work on hieroglyphs that frequently mentions Chinese characters, see Juan José Eguiara y Eguren, *Bibliotheca Mexicana* (Mexico City, 1755), 9*r–11r. On Chinese goods in early modern Mexico, see Meha Priyadarshini, *Chinese Porcelain in Colonial Mexico*.

[113] *Oratio*, fols. §§br–§§dv.

delights in the name not of "master" but of "father." He is the king who lacks not diligence in adopting plans for your community, nor courage in protecting you from dangers, nor good faith in giving you credit for your merits, nor in improving your conditions, nor a propensity to be generous.[114]

Royal support for their cause was also suggested by the presence during the delivery of the oration of the King's representative, the viceroy, and later confirmed when the viceroy ordered the oration be printed.[115] Echoing the sentiment expressed by Eguiara in the dedicatory letter to his *Bibliotheca* that stressed the long-standing royal patronage of the University of Mexico City, Campos exhorted his fellow scholars to seek the fame brought by learning, while at the same time assuring them that they have the support of the highest earthly power in New Spain. While both Campos and his contemporaries in Mexico City conceived of their world as polycentric, there was also space for hierarchies, among the most natural and unquestioned of which was loyalty to their monarch whose role as a benevolent arbiter gave them the confidence to defend their own interests.

In short, Campos' Ciceronian rebuttal of Martí was not at its core a defense of the learning of New World patriots against a xenophobe from the Old. Rather, it was a scholarly controversy that pitted the Iberian Peninsula's leading late humanist against almost the entire Catholic branch of the Republic of Letters, a sprawling, polycentric community that was not without its hierarchies and that existed within a larger global context. The Republic of Letters, a term that Campos and Eguiara both used explicitly, was thus the court in which Martí was to be tried and in which the honor of the "Mexican" branch was to be redeemed. Campos' listeners should not doubt, he told them, that the judgment would be in their favor, as the jury was stacked with their supporters and even the defendant secretly wished the prosecution to be successful. The other members of this sprawling trans-Oceanic learned community may have been distant,

---

[114] *Oratio*, 21: "Ad quod certe si causa ipsa vos impellit, vestra dignitas et commoda cogunt, Majorum icones suadent, tum Hispaniarum ipse potentissimus rex *Imperium oceano, famam, qui terminet astris* [Virgil, *Aeneid*, I.287] lenissimis blanditiis invitat, in quo spem certissimam et eventum spe maiorem reponere debetis. Ille siquidem est ille rex, qui non domini, sed parentis nomine gloriatur. Ille rex, cui neque consiliis de vestra civitate capiendis diligentia, neque in periculis a vobis propulsandis animus, neque in gratia vestris pro meritis referenda fides, neque in fortunis vestris augendis, benefica animi proclivitas defuit, sed obstarunt tempora, obstarunt mali mores, obstitit invidia, verum nunc iam hoc ipso facto egregiam vestram indolem demirabitur atque alio tramite res agentur."

[115] *Oratio*, xv.

but for a moment, Campos made them present and unashamedly partisan. In a final hyperbolic flourish, Campos even argued that Martí himself would join them in demanding the destruction of the offending letter to Carrillo. Prefacing his assertion with the assurance that this is no mere rhetorical ploy (*oratorie loqui*) – itself a rhetorical figure common in classical oratory – Campos insisted that since Martí had been inducted into the ranks of those holding doctorates, which included many *Mexicani*, he would sooner or later recognize his duty to his fellow scholars and come to their aid.[116]

Conclusion

As one of the last true humanist orators in the "Mexican" branch of the Republic of Letters, Campos was able to call on his solid training in rhetoric at the Jesuit colleges in Veracruz and Puebla to craft a classicizing judicial oration that made the case for prosecuting Martí for defamation in both Roman and contemporary legal terms, while at the same time praising the university and exhorting its students to study, as the conventions of the academic ritual required. With moral support from the king who they believed would not let his loyal subjects be insulted and in solidarity with their contemporaries in Spain and Italy that Martí had also defamed, Campos defended his members of *Mexicana respublica* against the Dean who, as Vicente López would put it, had left them "no corner in the Republic of Letters" to call their own.[117]

If we place the oration within the context of the other Mexican responses to Martí, such as Eguiara's *Bibliotheca Mexicana*, it also becomes clear that their learned community, often considered by scholars to consist exclusively of the *criollos* of New Spain, is better understood as a learned branch of the Republic of Letters, a sprawling meta-geographical construct that included most of Catholic Christendom while remaining to some degree open to the best Protestant scholars, or their more useful works in particular fields at least. This *respublica Mexicana* was roughly coterminous with New Spain geographically and centered, like the city-states of Milan or Venice, on a grand metropolis, from which it took its name, where an ancient university nourished generations of pious students who came from

---

[116] *Oratio*, 22.

[117] Vicente López, *Diálogo de Abril*, 15: "Audiebat praeterea noster scriptor, legebat in famosis quibusdam libellis exagitari, proscindi saepius ac lacerari Americanos imo in ultimam aliquando barbariem relegari, ac ne angulum quidem illis in Republica literarum relinqui."

both sides of the Atlantic to devote themselves to the *studia humanitatis*, philosophy, theology and medicine. Far from being an invective directed at a "Spaniard" by a "Mexican," Campos' oration attacks Martí as a disgrace to Spain and Hispanic culture, as well as an enemy of the Republic of Letters as a whole. In this final burst of "neo-Renaissance" brilliance during late humanism's swan song in the second quarter of the eighteenth century, we see late humanist public speaking providing a powerful persuasive tool to defend local intellectual traditions. Informed by the same classicizing rhetorical culture that influenced the orators for the royal funeral *exequias* in Mexico City and elsewhere, Campos' oration shows the versatility of the classical rhetorical tradition, which could be put to a variety of ends, both conventional and controversial.

CHAPTER 6

The Republic of Eloquence

In 1844, Manuel Micheltorena (1802–1853), the Oaxacan governor of the *departamento de Californias* delivered an oration to celebrate the anniversary of the entrance of the Army of the Three Guarantees into Mexico City in 1827.[1] Standing before the *presidio* church in Monterey, the orator celebrated the struggle for *independencia o muerte* in a highly rhetorical style with constant reference to the Roman Republic. Turning his attention to Agustín de Iturbide (1783–1824), he praised the liberator of the nation's capital in this way:

> Almost all the parts of the Republic give irrefutable testimony of the valor and wisdom of that great general who in these virtues approached Caesar and Alexander, Pompey and the Prince of Condé. Those principles contained in the Constitution are certain proof of his lack of self-interest, and that without abusing his power he only used the free rein given to him by the nation in the Tacubaya agreement to do good and resist evil. Did not Regulus, Cicero and Trajan do the same in ancient Rome, and the great Washington in the modern United States?[2]

Such self-consciously classicizing praise of the liberators of "welcoming and leafy California" (*la hospitalaria y frondosa California*) was one of the final

---

[1] Micheltorena was a noted military officer and orator who also gave a similar oration in Mexico City in 1840: Manuel Micheltorena, *Discurso Pronunciado en México el Día 27 de Septiembre de 1840* (Mexico City: A. Diaz, 1840). His extensive learning, however, perhaps hindered him in worldly affairs. Antonio María Osio, *The History of Alta California: A Memoir of Mexican California*, Rose Marie Beebe and Robert M. Senkewicz (eds.) (Madison: University of Wisconsin Press, 1996), 210: "Even though the *californios* received very little formal education because there were no schools, they had a natural talent for assessing the capabilities of their governors at first sight. They viewed Micheltorena as a man of many theories, not a man of action. He would be better suited for a teaching position in a public school than a governorship, but even then, he probably would not have enough energy to punish the children who misbehaved."

[2] Manuel Micheltorena, *Oración Cívica que Elegido por la junta Patriótica de la Capital del Departamento de Californias Pronunció en Solemnidad del 27 de Septiembre, el exmo Sor. D. Manuel Micheltorena Actual Gobernador Comandante General e Inspector Ayudante General de la Plana Mayor del Ejército* (Monterey, CA, 1844), 3–4.

flowerings of the classical rhetorical tradition, a powerful tool not only for imperial unity and evangelization, but also for nation-building, even if California was not destined to remain part of Mexico.

This obvious continuity with earlier classicizing oratory (both secular and sacred) described in the preceding chapters goes against the standard narratives concerning the history of rhetoric and political thought in Mexico and the broader Iberian World in the modern period. For instance, we are normally told that revolutionary eloquence in Mexico grew up in the shadow of the colonial sermon, a purely religious genre of public speaking, from which it represented a sudden divergence toward "civic" oratory. Just as an enlightened, secular and republican order triumphed over the forces of monarchy and superstition, the classicizing oratory of the annual "September Orations" (*discursos septembrinos*) delivered between 1825 and 1871 marked an abrupt departure from the colonial sermon when faced with the need to celebrate the 1810 "battle cry" (*grito*) of Miguel Hidalgo y Costilla (1753–1811) on what would soon become Mexican Independence Day.[3]

It is, of course, easy to be taken in by an account that equates revolution and independence for the *Estados Unidos Mexicanos* with a radical break in the history of oratory, a practice long associated with republican politics. Yet, problems appear if we scratch below the surface. If the ceremonial oratory of the revolutionary and early republican periods really represented such a divergence from the norms of colonial preaching (understood narrowly, as it frequently is, as the less classicizing brand of the thematic sermon), it is surely remarkable that it deviated so quickly and so markedly from its source with such innovations as a lay Ciceronian speaker, new structural conventions not typical of thematic sermons and the use of ancient Mediterranean history and culture as the primary frame of reference. This view becomes even more difficult to maintain when we consider the continuities in rhetorical education and practice across the seventeenth and eighteenth centuries, which, as the preceding chapters have shown, were considerable. Indeed, since in the premodern Catholic world any distinction between "secular" oratory and "religious" preaching is by its very nature artificial and anachronistic, the conventions inherited from Mediterranean antiquity continued to influence the upper echelons of preaching into the eighteenth century and beyond, while also finding

---

[3] Carlos Herrejón Peredo, *Del Sermón al Discurso Cívico: México, 1760–1834* (Zamora: El Colegio de Michoacán, 2003), 356–357.

expression in academic and other sorts of "secular" ceremonial oratory. No, what we are really observing is another application of the classical rhetorical tradition, which had been continually reinterpreted and repurposed in the intervening centuries, but which never went away. Convinced of the effectiveness of this widely used tool of social ordering and encouraged by its newfound associations with republican government, orators therefore fell back on their training in Jesuit and onetime Jesuit colleges whose post-humanist and neoclassical rhetorical and oratorical cultures had long displayed many of the supposed "new" features of civic oratory to address the needs of their own day.

As such, this chapter will show how revolutionary ideas found expression through the post-humanist and neoclassical strands of the classical rhetorical tradition in the century after 1750. In particular, it will explore the neglected culture of "post-humanism," in which late humanist practices such as Latin declamation, the use of humanist rhetorical handbooks and the oratorical rituals of the colonial college coexisted with new vernacular literary and intellectual trends. This was a trend that had its origins in the second half of the seventeenth century, but came into full bloom in the middle decades of the eighteenth century in the post-humanist oratory of the Hispanic Economic Societies, before merging into the neoclassical form that would continue through much of the nineteenth century. The chapter will then turn to the early national oratory of Mexico. Although the ideas espoused by these enlightened reformers and founding fathers may have been radical, their rhetorical education and oratorical practice were continuations of the larger classical rhetorical tradition transmitted through the colonial colleges in both the Atlantic and the Pacific, much in the same way as the political thought of the Age of Revolutions represented to a large extent a repurposing of existing ideas, rather than the creation ex nihilo of a new political ideology.[4] At the same time, some elements of this long-standing tradition were, in fact, also strengthened by this rekindled republicanism, as classicizing public speaking was the archetypal civic practice of the archetypal republic, Rome. This created a synergistic relationship that would continue for much of the nineteenth century.

---

[4] Jaime E. Rodríguez, "*We Are Now the True Spaniards*": *Sovereignty, Revolution, Independence, and the Emergence of the Federal Republic of Mexico, 1808–1824* (Stanford, CA: Stanford University Press, 2012); James E. Sanders, *The Vanguard of the Atlantic World: Creating Modernity, Nation, and Democracy in Nineteenth-Century Latin America* (Durham, NC: Duke University Press, 2014).

Defining "Post-Humanism"

Before going any further, it is worth taking a closer look at "post-human-ism," which is a coinage of this book. Whereas most cultural and intellec-tual histories of the Atlantic and Pacific worlds emphasize the changes that took place between 1650 and 1800, post-humanism points to the fre-quently overlooked continuities. Reflecting neither the humanist world of the early seventeenth century nor the neoclassical rhetorical culture of the early nineteenth, post-humanism combines elements of two apparently different epochs, one colonial or early modern, the other national or modern. It is thus an attempt to do justice to the cultural practices of the early to mid-eighteenth century, which are normally wrenched apart by the gravitational forces of periodization. In other words, it is a way to underline that while the culture of late humanism did indeed come to an end, it did so in a gradual fashion merging almost unperceptively with new trends rather than suddenly disappearing.[5]

Between 1650 and 1800 profound and lasting changes did, of course, take place in the ways orators in the Iberian World were trained and how they practiced the scholarly, literary and oratorical skills they had learned in neo-European educational institutions in the Americas, Europe and Asia. Perhaps the most obvious change was that Latin was largely replaced by Castilian and other prestige local vernaculars. The growth in vernacular literacy, the creation of "national" language academies, the meteoric rise of vernacular print culture and the development of vibrant public spheres in Castilian and French all contributed to a loosening of Latin's stranglehold, although this was in some respects just the final stage in a process that had roots in the "vernacular humanisms" of earlier centuries. Alongside this linguistic shift came a changing of the guard in the texts read and cited. Whereas the authors of pagan and Christian antiquity studied by aspiring orators remained fairly stable, the humanist authors of the sixteenth and early seventeenth centuries fell away precipitously, becoming subjects of

---

[5] The most concise summaries of the decline of late humanism is to be found in April G. Shelford, *Transforming the Republic of Letters: Pierre-Daniel Huet and European Intellectual Life, 1650–1720* (Rochester, NY: University of Rochester Press, 2007), 2–3 and Sietske Fransen, "Latin in a Time of Change: The Choice of Language As Signifier of a New Science?" *Isis*, 108 (2017), 629–635. The existing literature that stresses continuity in the classical tradition tends to skirt around the issue of what did in fact change, for example, Bas van Bommel, *Classical Humanism and the Challenge of Modernity: Debates on Classical Education in 19th-Century Germany* (Berlin: de Gruyter, 2015). Conversely, the literature focused on change tends to ignore all continuities, for example, William James Bouwsma, *The Waning of the Renaissance, 1550–1640* (New Haven, CT: Yale University Press, 2000).

historical rather than practical interest. This all combined with a growing distaste for the erudite world of the late humanists whose methods and writings ceased to be mainstream.[6]

All this is well known. However, there were also important continuities in both education and practice. By the mid-eighteenth century, these had produced a culture of classicizing public speaking that was heir to the humanist tradition, but had not inherited all of its features. Whereas the classicizing form and content of "vernacular humanism" in the fifteenth to seventeenth centuries had been constantly nourished by a rich culture of humanist Latin eloquence and erudition, post-humanism was the result of the continuities in humanist education models that outlived the Latinate world of the late-humanists by at least a generation in most cases.[7] In the territories of the Hispanic Monarchy and other Catholic regions of the Republic of Letters, it was only the suppression of the Jesuits in 1767 that definitively cut oratorical culture adrift from late humanism. As a result, a plausible periodization of post-humanism might span much of the late seventeenth and all of the eighteenth centuries depending on local conditions and personal inclinations. As we shall see, the most important factor determining where an orator stood on the sliding scale from late humanism to neoclassicism occupied by post-humanism was not the date when the oration was delivered, but the culture that had predominated during the orator's formative years, although old dogs did occasionally learn new tricks. Given the overlaps in lifespans, this resulted in barely perceptible generational shifts that in the end amounted to considerable cultural change, as new species of orators began to inhabit the same ecosystem as preexisting ones whom they replaced over time.

It was the conservative nature of education (then as now) that stood at the heart of post-humanism. For much of the "Enlightenment," Latin declamation and late humanist handbooks or their translations remained the gymnasium in which speakers were trained for this new, largely vernacular context.[8] Right up until their expulsion from the territories of the crowns of Castile (1767) and Portugal (1759), Jesuit colleges

---

[6] Françoise Waquet came to similar conclusions in her examination of Protestant and to a lesser extent Catholic academies in France in the same period: *Latin or, the Empire of the Sign: From The Sixteenth to The Twentieth Century*, John Howe (trans.) (London: Verso, 2001), 10–11.

[7] Andrew Galloway, "John Lydgate and the Origins of Vernacular Humanism," *The Journal of English and Germanic Philology*, 107 (2008), 445–471 (445–50).

[8] This stress on continuity owes much to the insights of Anthony Grafton, "The Republic of Letters in the American Colonies: Francis Daniel Pastorius Makes a Notebook," *American Historical Review*, 117 (2012), 1–39.

continued to adhere to the letter, if not always the spirit of the *Ratio studiorum*, which was adapted only somewhat to the new vernacular and enlightened context.[9] This curricular continuity was reinforced by the stability of academic and ecclesiastical rituals in the Iberian World. These required that late humanist Latin orations be performed in colleges and cathedrals, and in turn cast a long shadow over the new ritual occasions that emerged in this period. Even in the third quarter of the eighteenth century, late humanist funeral oratory continued to be delivered by orators educated in the first half of the century. For instance, José Manuel Peramás (1732–1793), the author of an influential tract on the similarities between the Jesuit *reducciones* in Paraguay and Plato's ideal republic, delivered a series of five late humanist Latin orations in his capacity as professor of rhetoric at the Jesuit College of Monserrat in Córdova (modern Argentina) in the 1760s.[10] Similarly, following the Seven Years' War in 1764, the secretary of the cathedral chapter of Manila, Ignacio de Salamanca (1737–1802), delivered a Latin funeral oration for the Mexican-born archbishop, Manuel Antonio Rojo del Rio (1708–1764), who had died during the British occupation of the city.[11] This tradition, of course, was withering and would be wholly replaced in time by a vernacular neoclassical culture of rhetoric and oratory following the rise of *belles lettres* out of the ashes of late Renaissance literary culture. After this point, any public speaking in Latin that continued represented little more than a ritualized fossil that was wholly divorced from the world of the humanist orators.[12] However, even this did not stop the ossified remains of the Renaissance touching the lives of important figures in the modern Iberian World, such as the Christian Brahmin José Custodio de Faria (1756–1819), better known today as one of the pioneers of modern hypnotism, who delivered a Latin oration for Pope Clement XIV on Pentecost of 1775 while studying in Rome.[13]

---

[9] Jesuit education in eighteenth-century New Spain is discussed in detail in Chapter 5.

[10] In the printed edition, these were attributed to Bernabé Echenique, but are generally agreed to be the work of José Manuel Peramás: *Cinco Oraciones Laudatorias en Honor del Doctor don Ignacio Duarte y Quiros* (Córdoba, Argentina: Universidad Nacional, [1765] 1937).

[11] Manuel Antonio Rojo del Rio, *Heros Ecclesiasticus, Oratio Funebris in Exequiis Manilae Celebratis* (Mexico City, 1765).

[12] Latin funeral oratory continued in Mexico well into the nineteenth century, although in a much reduced state: Osorio Romero, *Tópicos sobre Cicerón en México*, 212–216.

[13] José Custodio de Faria, *De Adventu Spiritus Sancti Oratio*. Latin and classical rhetorical education continued in Goa after the expulsion of the Jesuits: "THESES de rhetorica defendidas em Goa," Biblioteca Publica, Evora, cod. CX/2–20 n. 14.

At the same time, the neoclassicism that succeeded the Janus-faced world of post-humanism as the dominant rhetorical culture was itself not a complete departure from earlier norms. Public speaking continued to be imagined in explicitly classicizing terms. Indeed, in some respects rhetorical theory and the models put forward for imitation began to rely more heavily on ancient precedents, as the mediating role of Renaissance humanism declined. In this context, Quintilian or collections of precepts taken directly from republican and early imperial Roman rhetoricians, albeit in translation, took on a renewed significance. This renewed classicism was, however, channeled almost exclusively through vernacular oratory, as the learned languages had declined in significance to such a degree that, apart from in a few niche scholarly fields like botany and classical philology, speaking and writing Latin became little more than a party trick. This was all accompanied by a "litterification" of rhetoric and oratory, as public speaking itself began to take a back seat to written eloquence and literary criticism within the larger context of rhetorical education and practice. From the turn of the nineteenth century, the Iberian World's neoclassical rhetorical culture thus increasingly began to reflect the priorities of the "New Rhetoric" of the Scottish Enlightenment, in which literary criticism, philosophical speculation and a system of aesthetics based on ideas of "good taste" became increasingly important tasks of rhetoric within the division of studies. In this way, models of public speaking as such, both ancient and modern, faded in importance in the education of orators and the production of orations, if not in the imagination of speakers. This neoclassical rhetorical culture was an identifiable part of the larger classical rhetorical tradition, but it also marked a distinct departure from the norms that had dominated in the Iberian World for several centuries.

"Post-Humanist" Eloquence in the Hispanic Economic Societies

Writing in the first years of the nineteenth century, Alexander von Humboldt observed that urbanites in the Indies were *aficionados* of the Enlightenment:

> [The inhabitants of the countryside are] better acquainted with the history of the sixteenth century than with that of our own times, [and] imagine that Spain continues to possess a decided preponderance over the rest of Europe. To them the peninsula appears the very center of European civilization. It is otherwise with the Americans of the capital. Those of them who are acquainted with French or English literature fall easily into a contrary

extreme; and have still a more unfavorable opinion of the mother country than the French had at a time when communication was less frequent between Spain and the rest of Europe. They prefer strangers from other countries to the Spaniards; and they flatter themselves with the idea that intellectual cultivation has made more rapid progress in the colonies than in the peninsula.[14]

The view that Spain was untouched by the Enlightenment was, of course an exaggeration. The truth was that there were champions of new ideas, many of which did indeed originate in France, Britain and elsewhere, throughout the Iberian world. Unbeknownst to Humboldt, however, these defenders of the Enlightenment across the Iberian World also had something else in common: They were the heirs to the humanist tradition who advocated revolutionary ideas using the classicizing post-humanist rhetorical tools they had learned in colleges in the Americas, Europe and elsewhere. Although not on Humboldt's itinerary, New Spain's Pacific frontier in the Philippines was not immune from the trend whereby enlightened theories found expression within the context of long-standing classicizing norms.

On May 6, 1781 the Governor of the Philippines, José Basco y Vargas (1733–1805), inaugurated the Royal Patriotic Society of Manila (*Real sociedad patriótica de Manila*) with a short speech in which he lamented the economic decline of the Philippines and heralded the foundation of a learned society that would encourage the arts, sciences and industry. This was one of the *sociedades* that appeared in the Hispanic Monarchy in the second half of the eighteenth century as part of a wider movement in the Republic of Letters to create institutions to support local economic, scientific and cultural development in an enlightened mode. Following the founding of the first economic societies in Zurich (1747), Paris (1761) and the Basque Country (1763), by 1790 there were seventy such organizations across Spanish America, Iberian Asia and the European territories of the Bourbons.[15] Although Basco, famed more for his anti-Jesuit

---

[14] Alexander von Humboldt, *Ensayo Político sobre el Reino de la Nueva España Estudio Preliminar*, Juan A. Ortega y Medina (ed.), 4th ed. (Mexico City: Porrúa, 1984), 78–79.
[15] Robert Jones Shafer, *Economic Societies in the Spanish World (1763–1821)* (Syracuse, NY: Syracuse University Press, 1958) is the authoritative history of the economic societies of the Hispanic World. On the Manila Society, see *ibid.*, 145–151. Miguel Luque Talaván, "Descubriendo las Luces de un Rico Diamante. El Progreso de las Filipinas en el Pensamiento Económico del Siglo Ilustrado," in Martínez Lopez-Cano, María del Pilar; Leonor Ludlow (eds.), *Historia del Pensamiento Económico: del Mercantilismo al Liberalismo* (Mexico City: Universidad Nacional Autónoma de México, 2007), 169–209.

sentiments and dedication to the royalist cause than his learning, did not rely heavily on classical precepts when composing his oration, he began a tradition of enlightened public speaking in Manila that would draw heavily on the post-humanist tradition, combining established patterns of argumentation and thought with the reforming agenda of the Hispanic Enlightenment.

As the governor reminded his audience in this inaugural oration, in the wake of the Seven Years' War and the British Occupation of Manila (1762–1764), the Philippines was not faring particularly well. This was despite its abundant resources, excellent geographical position and population of over two million.[16] In particular, the reliance on the Manila Galleon Trade had created a huge deficit, which meant that the Philippines was a constant drain on royal coffers. In the newly founded society particular attention was therefore to be paid to the possibility of producing silk for export to the Americas, which would then favor the development of other local textile and dye industries. This, Basco suggested, could be facilitated by encouraging literacy among Spanish and indigenous inhabitants of the Philippines through Spanish grammar competitions and the founding of schools beyond the central *Intramuros* area of the city.[17]

Despite all these efforts, there was considerable resistance from local elites who were unwilling to give up their interests in the Manila Galleon Trade. This hostility was perhaps best expressed by Manuel Zumalde (*c.* 1745–1782), a Philippine-born Spanish soldier and man of letters whose widely circulated manuscript satire, the *Bascoana*, lampooned the governor for his ignorance and attacks on the "liberty" of local merchants.[18] In the face of this recalcitrance, the governor set out to convince the local elite of the need for reform, setting out his ideas in a number of printed letters and tracts, which, despite his best efforts, had limited effect.[19] Given the urgent need for economic reform and the degree of resistance to it, the annual

---

[16] Eduardo Malo de Luque, *Historia Política de los Establecimientos Ultramarinos de las Naciones Europeas*, 5 vols. (Madrid, 1784–1790), V, Appendix 1, 4–7.

[17] The details of the proposed economic reforms are outlined in: José Basco y Vargas, *Plan General Económico* (Manila, 1779).

[18] Manuel Zumalde, "La Bascoana: Dichos y hechos de Don Joseph Dasco Governador de Philipinas," in Worcester Philippines Collection, University of Michigan Library, ms. M19. There is another manuscript preserved in Biblioteca del Colegio de Padres Agustinos de Valladolid, Valladolid, 177.

[19] Regalado Trota José, *Impreso: Philippine Imprints, 1593–1811* (Makati: Fundación Santiago, 1993), 227–235.

orations delivered at the meeting of the Royal Patriotic Society of Manila on the King's birthday took on renewed significance.

The Society's second annual oration delivered by Archbishop of Manila, Basilio Sancho de Santa Justa y Rufina (1728–1787), offers the most striking example of how training in post-humanist rhetoric could be used to espouse enlightened economic ideas in this hostile political climate. Born in Villanueva del Rebollar de la Sierra in Aragon, the future archbishop received his early education in the local Jesuit college, before moving to an *escuela pía*, part of a network of religious schools founded by the Order of Piarists to teach poor children. There, he followed the familiar curriculum of grammar, Latin authors and two years of rhetoric, much like his contemporaries in Jesuit colleges. Piarist schools in this period were, however, particularly well known for their enthusiasm for studying classical authors in the vernacular, and so the curriculum he followed can probably be characterized as post-humanist, in that classical literary works, such as the orations of Cicero, were the object of intense study in both Latin and vernacular editions, alongside late humanist handbooks, such as Augustín de Juan Bautista's *Artificiosae orationis sive rhetoricarum institutionum epitome* (Zaragoza, 1730). At the same time, the applications for this still heavily humanist training were almost wholly vernacular, both inside the classroom and out. This then was a Janus-faced education, structured according to the humanist models of previous centuries, but qualitatively different in terms of its stress on translating the traditional humanist skills of Latin eloquence into vernacular contexts.

Having shown particular promise in the Piarists' twin tenets of *pietas et litterae*, Don Basilio was sent to study philosophy and theology in nearby Daroca and then in Zaragoza. He subsequently returned to Daroca to teach rhetoric and philosophy before being summoned to teach theology at Valencia, from where his meteoric rise in the church and at court began.[20] As a rhetoric teacher in an *escuela pía*, Don Basilio was required both to

---

[20] Don Basilio's career culminated with his nomination by Clement XIII as Archbishop of Manila in 1756 and after some dragging of his feet, perhaps due to his popularity at court, he made his way to Manila via Canton in 1767 on a boat belonging to the Swedish East India Company. For an overview of his career, see Marta M. Manchado López, *Conflictos Iglesia-Estado en el Extremo Oriente Ibérico Filipinas (1767–1787)* (Murcia: Universidad de Murcia, 1994), 29–52. For the education in the *escuela pía*, see Joaquín Lecea, *Las Escuelas Pías de Aragón en el Siglo XVIII* (Madrid: Publicaciones ICCE, 1972), 238–241 278, 380–385, 508. On contemporary rhetorical handbooks, see Rosa María Aradra Sánchez, *De la Retórica a la Teoría de la Literatura: Siglos XVIII y XIX* (Murcia: Universidad de Murcia, 1997), 55–75.

teach the precepts of classical rhetoric from late humanist Latin handbooks and to deliver Latin orations for the inauguration of the academic year.[21] In this way, he became intimately familiar with both the theory and practice of the institutionalized form of late humanist oratory, which he then applied in Castilian sacred panegyrics delivered in his capacity as court preacher to Charles III. Such was Don Basilio's devotion to classicizing eloquence that we find it expressed in the most unexpected places. For example, in 1768, he wrote a Latin letter to Clement XIII praising the beatification of Juan de Palafox y Mendoza (1600–1659) and criticizing the regular clergy who were resisting episcopal authority, in which he could not hold himself back from rhetorical flourishes, including an allusion to Cicero's *First Catilinarian Oration*, replacing the murderous Roman traitor with the unruly Filipino regular clergy: "lo, Holy Father, when will there be an end to the unbridled audacity of the regular clergy?"[22]

The Archbishop of Manila was therefore the perfect choice to deliver the annual oration at the Royal Patriotic Society of Manila, as he possessed the right combination of high office and reforming zeal, alongside profound erudition and an excellent knowledge of classical rhetoric. Thus, on January 20, 1783, following a mass in the Cathedral to celebrate the King's birthday, the governor and the members of the Economic Society crossed Manila's *plaza de armas* and entered the governor's palace to hear Don Basilio speak (Figure 6.1). The archbishop did not disappoint. Having studied and taught from late humanist handbooks, he carefully constructed an *exordium*, which justified the ritual circumstances of the oration, namely the annual celebrations of the Economic Society and the tradition of celebrating the King's birthday in an effort to make the audience "benevolent, attentive and docile" (*benevolum, attentum et docilem*):

> We have gathered here this evening, not to undertake a mere ceremony, but rather to fulfill the requirements of the statutes of our Society, which, motivated of course by love for our monarch, instruct us to observe his birthday with a public celebration of his successes. It is an admirable statute, which, while it requires us to bring to the assembled company something that is both new and of use to the fatherland, encourages us to do so

[21] Joaquín Lecea, *Las Escuelas Pías de Aragón en el Siglo XVIII*, 289.
[22] Basilio Sancho de Santa Justa y Rufina, *Sanctissimo Domino Nostro Clementi XIII* (Manila, 1768), fol. 5r: "En, Beatissime Pater, quem ad finem sese effrenata iactet Regularium audacia!" Cf. Cicero, *In Cat.* 1.

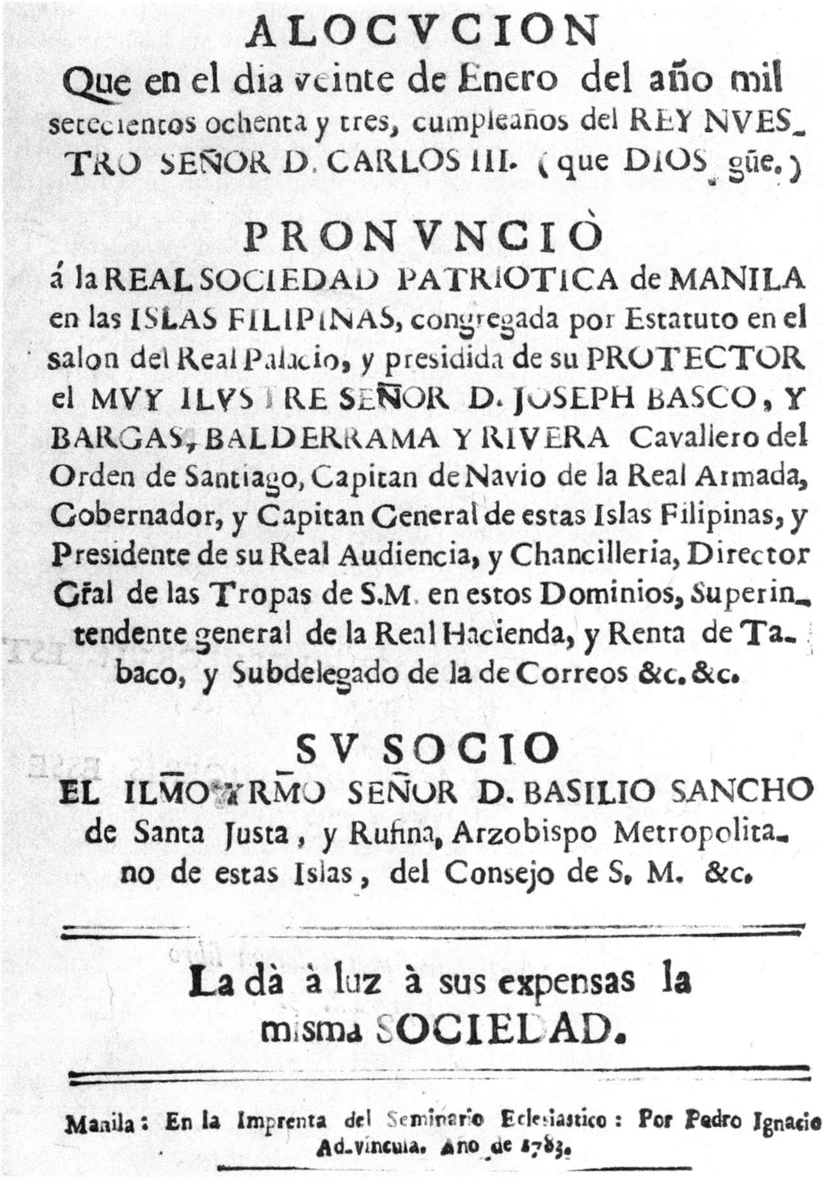

ALOCVCION

Que en el dia veinte de Enero del año mil setecientos ochenta y tres, cumpleaños del REY NVES_ TRO SEÑOR D. CARLOS III. (que DIOS gṹe.)

PRONVNCIÒ

á la REAL SOCIEDAD PATRIOTICA de MANILA en las ISLAS FILIPINAS, congregada por Estatuto en el salon del Real Palacio, y presidida de su PROTECTOR el MVY ILVSTRE SEÑOR D. JOSEPH BASCO, Y BARGAS, BALDERRAMA Y RIVERA Cavallero del Orden de Santiago, Capitan de Navio de la Real Armada, Gobernador, y Capitan General de estas Islas Filipinas, y Presidente de su Real Audiencia, y Chancilleria, Director Gral de las Tropas de S.M. en estos Dominios, Superin_ tendente general de la Real Hacienda, y Renta de Ta_ baco, y Subdelegado de la de Correos &c. &c.

SV SOCIO

EL ILMō Y RMō SEÑOR D. BASILIO SANCHO de Santa Justa, y Rufina, Arzobispo Metropolita_ no de estas Islas, del Consejo de S. M. &c.

La dà à luz à sus expensas la misma SOCIEDAD.

Manila: En la Imprenta del Seminario Eclesiastico: Por Pedro Ignacio Ad_vincula. Año de 1783.

Figure 6.1 Title page of Basilio Sancho de Santa Justa y Rufina, *Alocución que en el día veinte de enero del año mil setecientos ochenta y tres, cumpleaños del nuestro Señor D. Carlos III* (Manila, 1783).
Image courtesy of the John Carter Brown Library

alongside a tribute to our beneficent king who, like a vigilant father, spends his every waking moment in preserving his domains and looking to their advancement.[23]

Throughout his discussion of the ceremonial occasion, which seamlessly blended enlightened sociability, absolutism and reformist zeal, the archbishop constantly referred to classical examples in his praise of Charles III and his policies. For example, he compared the Bourbon monarch to Augustus and the early emperors of Rome whose title of *pater patriae* he deserved equally, if not more than his ancient predecessors. Hard on the heels of this first "comparison of lesser things" (*comparatio minorum*), a common trope in the humanist tradition, the archbishop then added another. Augustus, as Roman historians like Suetonius and Tacitus had recounted, had made a poor choice of heir, which contributed directly to the decadence of Rome, whereas Charles III had produced a fine prince who would continue his father's good work. Although Don Basilio did not structure his praise according to the heads of classical epideictic, he did see himself in that tradition, describing Charles III and his "living image" (i.e. his son) in terms taken directly from Pliny the Younger's panegyric of Trajan:

> I mean that he will have left us a king – to give the subject most rightly to the *Panegyricus* of Pliny – who is chaste in his habits, pious in his deeds, and very similar to God in his kingly virtues.

Here, he was self-consciously echoing Pliny's words: "For what is a more excellent or noble gift from the gods than a chaste and pious prince who is very similar to the gods?"[24] The orator's tone then quickly shifted from classical antecedents and praises of Charles III to the matter in hand:

---

[23] Basilio Sancho de Santa Justa y Rufina, *Alocución que en el Día Veinte de Enero del Año Mil Setecientos Ochenta y Tres, Cumpleaños del Nuestro Señor D. Carlos III* ... (Manila, 1783), 1: "venimos a unirnos aquí esta tarde, no para la práctica de una mera ceremonia, sino para dar cumplimiento a un Estatuto de nuestra Sociedad, la qual por cierto motivo de amor acia el Monarca, quiso celebrásemos anualmente su Cumpleaños con pública manifestación de sus progresos. Admirable Estatuto, que al paso que nos pone en la precisión de traer todos los años algo de nuevo a esta numerosa Asamblea en utilidad de la Patria, nos alienta a esto mismo con la memoria de un Rey beneficio, que como Padre vigilante no cesa de consumir sus años en la conservación de sus dominios, y en mirar en sus aumentos. Con esto nos servirá también de renovar en nuestros pechos aquel natural amor, que tenemos a Carlos III."

[24] *Ibid.*, 6: "Quiero decir (dando sujeto más proprio al panegírico de Plinio) que nos habrá dexado un REY CASTO en sus costumbres, SANTO en sus obras, Y MUY SEMEJANTE a DIOS en sus virtudes reales." Cf. Pliny, *Panegy.*, 1: "Quod enim praestabilius est aut pulchrius munus deorum, quam castus et sanctus et diis simillimus princeps?"

In the past, even during the celebrated reigns of Charles V and Philip II, although there were efforts to introduce manufacturing to many cities in Spain, for some reason or other more attention was paid to political legislation than economic. Nowadays without omitting the former, we pay attention to the latter. A civilized kingdom put in good order need only instruct itself in economics and direct its attention to that. This is the field we should cultivate in the pursuit of consolidation and expansion.[25]

Thanks to royal foresight, the archbishop maintained, industry and popular education were both flourishing. Just like the sun, the king warmed the earth with his benevolence and brought fertility and wealth to all his kingdoms. The late antique poet Claudian who frequently drew on the Virgilian motif of a returning Golden Age could have been talking of the age of Charles III, the archbishop argued, when he described the triumph of the arts and sciences over poverty and the foundation of the Royal Patriotic Society.[26] At this point, some late humanist poetry even made its way into the oration, as Don Basilio cited a couplet from Jacques Vanière (1664–1739), a Jesuit poet, whose praises of Louis XIV were equally applicable to Charles III, the Sun King's great-great-grandson.[27]

If we peruse the footnotes to the edition of the oration printed in Manila the same year, we also find that the orator's intellectual points of reference were decidedly classicizing and to some degree post-humanist. Indeed, the archbishop did not just quote classical authorities, but also played erudite games with them. Praising Charles III's virtues in peace and war, he made him think of the following lines:

> *You, O great king, who holds sway over multitudes, remember this!*
> *Afterwards mete out justice to the English and impose the ways of peace,*
> *Spare the conquered and vanquish the proud.*

---

[25] Basilio Sancho de Santa Justa y Rufina, *Alocución que en el Día Veinte de Enero del Año Mil Setecientos Ochenta y Tres, Cumpleaños del Nuestro Señor D. Carlos III . . .*, 9: "En otros tiempos, aun en los más celebrados de Carlos V y Phelipe II, aunque en orden a fabricas se introduxo mucha aplicación en diversas ciudades de España, pero sea la que fuere la causa, se puso más atención a la legislación política, que a la económica. Oy día, sin omitir aquella, se atiende especialmente a esta. Un reyno civilizado, y puesto en el orden conveniente, no necesita más que de instruirse en la económica, y de entregarse a ella. Este es el fondo de donde ha de sacar con que mantenerse, y adquirir fuerzas."

[26] *Ibid.*, 13–14.

[27] On Vanière, see Yasmin Haskell, *Loyola's Bees: Ideology and Industry in Jesuit Latin Didactic Poetry* (Oxford: British Academy, 2003), 38–60.

This represented a reworking of Anchises' words to Aeneas in the under-world from Virgil's *Aeneid*:

> *You, O Roman, who holds sway over multitudes, remember this!*
> *These will be your arts: to impose the ways of peace,*
> *To spare the conquered and to vanquish the proud.*[28]

If we return to the words of the oration itself, we see that this combination of post-humanist learning and reformist ideas continued apace, as Charles III's decree allowing free trade between the ports of Spain and the Americas also came in for praise.[29] Persisting with his classical citations in the original Latin, but now in the service of praising the Bourbons' economic reforms, the archbishop then used examples from Cicero and St. Augustine to argue that the population of Manila should labor for the common good, especially considering they were idle for such a large part of the year while they awaited the arrival of the Acapulco Galleon. The archbishop then combined classical examples of civic responsibility with further exhortations clothed in the familiar garb of a humanist *comparatio minorum* with the ancients. In this case, he availed himself of Charles Rollin's (1661–1741) judgment of Pliny the Elder who donated his large library to the Roman people and endowed professorships and schools for orphans and the poor, all of which he afforded by living a frugal life. The Christians of Manila should be ashamed that they have been outdone in Christian virtue by a pagan like Pliny. This was a direct attack on the merchants involved in the Manila galleon trade who preferred, in the words of the Roman historian Valerius Maximus, "to be rich in a poor republic, than to be poor in a rich one."[30]

The product of post-humanist conditioning in Jesuit and Piarist colleges, Basilio Sancho de Santa Justa y Rufina exemplifies the ease with

---

[28] Basilio Sancho de Santa Justa y Rufina, *Alocución que en el Día Veinte de Enero del Año Mil Setecientos Ochenta y Tres, Cumpleaños del Nuestro Señor D. Carlos III . . .*, 20 n. 0:

> *Tu regere imperio populos, rex magne, memento,*
> *iuraque post Anglis, pacisque imponere morem,*
> *parcere subiectis et debellare superbos.*

Cf. Virgil, *Aen.* VI.851–3:

> *Tu regere imperio populos, Romane, memento*
> *Hae tibi erunt artes pacisque imponere morem,*
> *parcere subjectis et debellare superbos.*

[29] On the free trade, see: Gabriel B. Paquette, *Enlightenment, Governance, and Reform in Spain and Its Empire, 1759–1808* (Basingstoke: Palgrave Macmillan, 2008), 99–106.

[30] *Ibid.*, 17. Cf. Valerius Maximus, *Dicta et Facta Memorabilia*, VI.4.

which new ideas could find expression within the context of long-standing traditions of eloquence and erudition. The Latin-speaking world of late humanism may have ceased to be in any way mainstream sometime around the midpoint of the eighteenth century, but the practices and educational standards pioneered in Renaissance Italy continued to influence the training and performances of orators who stood on the shoulders of their humanist forebears even when championing new economic theories. This post-humanist movement would itself soon merge into the neoclassical form typical of the nineteenth century, albeit at different paces in different local contexts.

Neoclassicism and Republican Nationalism in the September Orations

Mexico's September Orations are emblematic of the next stage in the development of the classical rhetorical tradition in the Iberian World: neoclassical oratory. These speeches delivered annually in Mexico City on September 16 between 1825 and 1871 commemorated an important moment in the birth of the Mexican nation: the "call to arms" (*pronunciamento*) of a heretical and revolutionary priest, Miguel Hidalgo y Costilla (1753–1811), in his parish of Dolores near Guanajuato, an event that is still celebrated today as Mexican Independence Day.[31] The precise events surrounding Hidalgo's actions and their repercussions are still the subject of debate. However, the general outline can be traced. In the wake of the Napoleonic invasion of Spain, Hidalgo is said to have exhorted the people to resist the "bad government" (*mal gobierno*) of the viceroy in Mexico City whose authority had been severely compromised after Napoleon had forced Charles IV and his son Ferdinand to abdicate in favor of his own brother, Joseph Bonaparte. Hidalgo then led an ill-fated revolt that ended at the Battle of Calderón Bridge in January 1811 where his ramshackle army, marching under the banner of the Virgin of Guadalupe, was routed and Hidalgo captured and executed along with other prominent leaders of the revolt.[32] Revolutionary sentiments would bubble under the surface for

---

[31] The bibliography on Hidalgo is vast. The basic biographical details of his life are treated in: Bernice Scott, *The Grito of September Sixteenth: Biography of Padre Miguel Hidalgo, Father of Mexican Independence* (Ingleside: Hemisphere House Books, 1981). For a survey of recent historiography on Hidalgo, see Marta Terán y Norma Páez, "Introdución a la Historiografía Hidalguista Entre 1953 y 2003," in Marta Terán y Norma Páez (eds.), *Miguel Hidalgo: Ensayos sobre el Mito y el Hombre (1953–2003)* (Mexico City: Instituto Nacional de Antropología e Historia, 2004), 15–36.

[32] The classic study of the revolt is: Hugh M. Hamill, Jr., *The Hidalgo Revolt: Prelude to Mexican Independence* (Gainesville, FL: Praeger, 1966). On the *grito de Dolores*, see *ibid.*, 118–123.

some time, before the reinstatement of the liberal constitution of Cádiz of 1820 ignited the cause of the insurgents. After a brief period of imperial monarchy under Agustín de Iturbide, the *Estados Unidos Mexicanos* came into being as a republic in 1824. As a result of his early opposition to the government of peninsular Spaniards, Hidalgo became a martyr, albeit a controversial one, for the cause of resistance to "Spanish" rule in New Spain. A cult would quickly develop around the renegade priest that would only gain strength in the course of the nineteenth and twentieth centuries. Celebrations of the *grito de Dolores* and the associated practice of delivering orations on September 16 soon became common in Mexico City and spread to other cities in the new republic as part of an explosion in patriotic civic rituals that commemorated significant events in the Wars of Independence, as we saw in the case of Manuel Micheltorena in Monterey, California.

Despite fears that commemorating an armed peasant uprising might encourage violent Hispanophobia, the Mexican Congress chose the anniversary of Hidalgo's call to arms as a day of national celebration in 1825. For this important task, they selected Juan Wenceslao Sánchez de la Barquera y Morales (1779–1840) who they believed possessed both the requisite patriotic zeal and necessary powers of classicizing eloquence. In terms of the former, Barquera's credentials were indeed impeccable. During the tumultuous years following Napoleon's invasion of the Iberian Peninsula, he had been a member of the revolutionary junta (*junta secreta de los Guadalupes*), while during the brief First Mexican Empire (1821–1823) he had served as secretary of the Patriotic Economic Society (*sociedad económica de amigos del país*). Now under the Republic he was a member of Congress, president of the municipal council of Mexico City and the editor of the official newspaper.[33] His qualifications as a man of letters were equally impressive. He had received his basic education in Latin under the noted educationalist José María Alcántara in the colegio de San Javier, studied humanities and philosophy at colegio de San Buenaventura de Tlatelolco and received a degree *de utroque iure* in 1807 from the former Jesuit stronghold, the colegio de San Ildefonso. His eloquence was also not in doubt, although the standards by which this was measured were predominately literary rather than oratorical, reflecting

---

[33] For biographical details on Barquera see: Emilio del Castillo Negrete, *Galería de Oradores de México en el Siglo XIX*, 3 vols. (Mexico City: Tip. de S. Sierra, 1877–80), I, 242–253; Ernesto de la Torre Villar, "Las Sociedades de Amigos del país y Juan Wenceslao Barquera," *Estudios de Historia Moderna y Contemporánea de México*, 14 (1991), 11–51.

the changed scholarly climate of the early nineteenth century. He had contributed to a number of notable periodicals, edited Spanish legal texts, composed various well-received poetic odes for the coronation of Ferdinand VII (who he had initially hoped would resist Napoleon) and written treatises on such diverse subjects as politics and agriculture.[34] Indeed, his 1825 oration was not even the only piece of patriotic public speaking he performed that year, as in January he had recited a poetic ode, entitled "An Invocation and Dedication to Liberty," at an academic pageant performed for the president of the Republic at their shared alma mater the colegio de San Ildefonso.[35]

In this sense, the type of eloquence possessed by Barquera differed markedly from that of his predecessors in New Spain, such as Juan Gregorio de Campos y Martínez with whom he overlapped in his early years. Despite the continuities in educational models and continuing prominence of classical culture more broadly, post-humanist rhetorical culture had by 1800 fully and universally morphed into the neoclassical form that we associate with the *belles lettres* tradition. It was in this new rhetorical context, classicizing but no longer directly influenced by the humanist tradition, that Barquera was educated. By the time he began attending the colegio de San Javier in the 1790s, Charles III's 1768 decree that grammar, humanities and rhetoric were to be taught in the vernacular had been in force for some time. Notwithstanding this important change and the general rupture in institutional life caused by the suppression of the Jesuits, Barquera's education was not entirely unrecognizable in the light of the earlier Jesuit *Ratio studiorum*, with successive classes focused on grammar, rhetoric and philosophy serving as the basic introduction to higher studies like medicine, law and theology. The texts read in each class were also not so far removed from those formerly used in Jesuit classrooms. For example, in the grammar class, he studied Latin and Castilian grammar, read Cicero and other classical orators in the original, and was exposed to some classical rhetorical theory. However, the production of orations and the practice of declamation was probably marginal to his

---

[34] His literary production is summarized in: Justo Sierra, Luis G. Urbina, Pedro Henríquez Ureña and Nicolás Rangel, *Antología del Centenario, Estudio Documentado de la Literatura Mexicana Durante el Primer Siglo de Independencia*, 2 vols. (Mexico City: Universidad Nacional Autónoma de México, 1910), I, 229–231.

[35] *Certamen Científico que el Nacional y más Antiguo Colegio de S. Ildefonso de México Dedica a su Antiguo Alumno el Ciudadano Guadalupe Victoria: Primer Presidente de los Estados Unidos Mexicanos* (Mexico City, 1825), 1–3.

education, while the works of late humanist authors were nowhere to be seen.

His *vademecum* in the rhetoric class during the 1790s and early 1800s was probably Gregorio de Mayans y Siscar's *Rhetórica* (Valencia, 1757), the most common rhetorical textbook in the late eighteenth-century Hispanic Monarchy. Unlike the authors of the late humanist handbooks that were typical of the earlier period, Mayans eschewed regurgitations of humanist rhetorical principles and detailed discussions of now defunct late humanist genres, and composed a rhetoric that prepared students for speaking and writing in his own day. Earlier in his long life, Mayans may have cultivated the skills of a late humanist, writing Ciceronian Latin epistles and editing the Latin biography of his mentor, the last great Spanish humanist in the Renaissance mold, Manuel Martí, whom we met in the last chapter. However, like many of his contemporaries in Spain and elsewhere he soon abandoned the older tradition and sought to promote new ideas from home and abroad with the aim of reviving Castilian as a literary language.

Leafing through Mayans' handbook, as Barquera or his teachers must have done, the features of neoclassical rhetoric become clear. The art of speaking was, of course, imagined in classicizing terms with a strong reliance on precepts taken directly from well-known classical texts. For example, in his prefatory letter to Cardinal Juan Tomás de Boxadors, he recounted the history of rhetoric beginning with Corax and Tisias in ancient Sicily, passing through Plato, Aristotle, Cicero and Quintilian, before turning to the moderns who received decidedly less attention. Rhetoric and oratory were still very much in the shadow of the ancients.[36] However, Mayans went beyond this tradition in a number of ways. For example, in Book V, he offered specific instructions for non-oratorical genres (questions, answers, conversations, letters, dialogues, inscriptions and histories), which make up a much larger proportion of the work than the brief discussion of the different genres of orations (nuptial, genethliac, thanksgivings, consolation, reprehension, etc.), which had dominated late humanist handbooks.[37] Furthermore, the belletristic focus of the handbook on developing style for the production of literature was front and

---

[36] Gregorio de Mayans y Siscar, *Obras Completas*, 5 vols. (Valencia: Diputación de Valencia, 1983–1986), III (*Rhetórica*), 9–14, 56–73.

[37] On the genres of oration, see *ibid.*, III, 180–215. On contemporary rhetorics, see Don Paul Abbott, "Mayans' *Rhetórica* and the Search for a Spanish Rhetoric," *Rhetorica: A Journal of the History of Rhetoric*, 11 (1993), 157–179; *ibid.*, "The Influence of Blair's *Lectures* in Spain," *Rhetorica: A Journal of the History of Rhetoric*, 7 (1989), 275–289.

center. Throughout the work, Mayans takes his examples of usage almost exclusively from modern vernacular poetry with the occasional vernacular sermon and very few works by classical writers, and then generally historians rather than orators. In Barquera's education, this literary focus may have also been reinforced through his reading of Hugh Blair's *Lectures on Rhetoric and Belles Lettres* (1783), which circulated widely in Mexico in this period, and a copy of which is known to have been held later at the colegio de San Ildefonso.[38]

While neoclassical public speaking may have found a particularly fertile outlet with the rise of new nations in the Americas, it also existed independently of it in the academic oratory of the late colonial and early republican colleges, which also provides important context for understanding the September Orations. For instance, the 1816 oration "On the Necessity of Knowing the Nation's Laws" delivered by a young José Basilio Guerra (1790–1871) in the Royal Academy of Theoretic-Practical Jurisprudence in Mexico City exemplifies the polite style of neoclassical oratory that would soon be put to nation-building ends. In his oration, the future member of the Supreme Court and Mexican ambassador to Prussia who would marry a Belgian noblewoman and eventually die in Rome mixed discussions of ancient lawgivers such as Solon and Lycurgus with references to an idealized Enlightenment vision of imperial China in an opening that consisted of an overt *comparatio* between New Spain and these ancient and modern polities that put laws above arms. All this he did in a self-consciously classicizing style that inspired him to construct a *captatio benevolentiae* that highlighted his "rational modesty that must cover me when speaking in front of an audience of such learned orators."[39] It was law that linked all citizens together and held the king in a state of "liberty," while its absence distinguished "despotic" governments from "monarchical" and "republican" forms.[40] This style of neoclassical academic oratory also continued following the Wars of Independence in Mexico and elsewhere. For instance, the future Chilean orator, diplomat and statesman, Antonio García Reyes (1817–1855) impressed his fellow

---

[38] Archivo Histórico de la Universidad Nacional Autónoma de México, Mexico City, caja 54, exp. 34, doc. 108.

[39] José Basilio Guerra, *Oración Inaugural sobre la Necesidad de Saber las Leyes Patrias* (Mexico City, 1816), 2: "del pudor racional que me debe cubrir al perorar ante oradores tan peritos." On Guerra, see: María Teresa Guerra Medici, "En los Parlamentos del Viejo y Nuevo Mundo. José Basilio Guerra (Campeche, Yucatán, 1790/ Roma 1872)," *Diritto@Storia: Revista Internazionale di Scienze Giuridiche e Tradizione Romana*, 12 (2013): www.dirittoestoria.it/11/note&rassegne/Guerra-Medici-Parlamentos-Jose-Basilio-Guerra.htm.

[40] José Basilio Guerra, *Oración Inaugural sobre la Necesidad de Saber las Leyes Patrias*, 6.

graduating students at the Instituto Nacional in Santiago de Chile in 1834 with a classicizing Castilian oration that attacked Junius Brutus for executing his two sons following a conspiracy to reinstate monarchy in Rome.[41]

If there was considerable common ground between the intellectual preparation of Barquera and previous generations, there were also striking continuities in the ritual contexts in which he delivered his 1825 September Oration. Like the baroque *exequias* for the deaths of Kings of Spain with their classicizing funeral orations and virtue-driven iconography, the first September 16 celebration of the Mexican Republic took place mainly within the main square (*plaza de armas*) of Mexico City and the imposing edifices that surrounded it, such as the former viceregal palace and cathedral. Like the funeral commemorations for Habsburg and Bourbon monarchs during the colonial period, the September 16 celebrations in 1825 began with a mass, thus solidifying the connection between the new republic and the Catholic Church. This was followed by a reception in the presidential palace (*palacio nacional*) hosted by the president himself, Guadalupe Victoria (1786–1843), who received the good wishes of diplomats and officials. The organizing junta then joined the president and the assembled dignitaries who proceeded along a prearranged route decorated with flags and banners, before returning to the main square where a speaker's platform had been erected. There, the central element of the ritual was performed, which again mirrored earlier colonial ritual: a classicizing ceremonial oration delivered by an erudite authority figure, a task that in 1825 fell to Barquera, the learned lawyer and man of letters who stood in place of the educated cathedral canon or professor of rhetoric of the previous age. Drawing on his training in formerly Jesuit colleges, the orator was to "remind the Mexicans of the glorious era of their emancipation and exhort them to defend and preserve their liberty, which had been acquired by great sacrifice."[42] After the oration was delivered, the afternoon's festivities concluded with a short speech by the president in which he drew the attention of the large crowd

---

[41] Antonio García Reyes, "Acusación a Junio Bruto por Haber Hecho Ejecutar a sus dos Hijos y Demás Cómplices en la Conspiración contra la Republica. Discurso como Alumnos de la Clase de Literatura, 1834," Fondo Antiguo, Santiago de Chile, vol. 94 pieza 6ª, fols. 259r–264r. García also wrote an addition to Blair's famous Enlightenment treatise on rhetoric and *belles lettres*: Archivo Nacional de Chile, Fondo Antiguo, Santiago de Chile, vol. 94 pieza 5, fols. 243r–258v.

[42] Jorge Denegre Vaught Peña (ed.), *Dos Siglos de Discursos Patrióticos* (Mexico City: Universidad Nacional Autónoma de México, 2011), 14: "que se recuerde a los mexicanos la época gloriosa de su emancipación y los disponga a que defienden y conserven sus libertades adquiridas con inmensos sacrificios."

to the orphans of fallen patriots who had been brought in for the occasion. Mexico's first citizen also ceremonially freed a number of slaves in honor of the freedom of the *patria*, an act that reflected Mexico's particular support for abolitionism. The celebrations then concluded in the evening with musical entertainment and allegorical representations.

When Barquera mounted the rostrum, he imagined the task before him in classical terms that were a product of his conditioning in a late eighteenth-century colonial college:

> If in an earlier age, the Roman people met in the forum to pronounce their laws with the glory and majesty of a sovereign people, today you who enjoy the same rights, have assembled to celebrate with a victory hymn the propitious birth of your independence and liberty.[43]

There was no more suitable way for a "sovereign people" to celebrate their republican liberty than through the archetypal civic practice of the ancient republic that ultimately supplied many of the institutional and intellectual models for their new polity.

As there were fine examples of eloquent public speaking from both the republic and the principate, Roman educational and oratorical models could remain relevant across the colonial-republican divide, in each case providing a treasure trove of models for imitation and creating a symbiotic relationship between political thought and urban ritual. This neoclassical understanding of oratory was not limited to this occasion. In his "patriotic discourse" delivered in 1830 in Toluca to the west of Mexico City, Barquera would again stress the classical antecedents of the new republic's civic oratory:

> The ancient Greek and Roman peoples carried on this custom in their civic festivals. Fathers taught their sons to imitate the great deeds of their ancestors. The priests in the temple reinforced the sublime idea of the divinity and of the gods' favor in order to maintain the happiness of the people, while public orators presented stories of the most memorable successes in political life.[44]

---

[43] *Ibid.*, 16: "Si en otro tiempo el pueblo romano se convocaba para dictar sus leyes en la plaza pública con la Gloria y la majestad de un pueblo rey, hoy vosotros con la misma investidura os habéis reunido para celebrar con el himno del triunfo el fausto nacimiento de vuestra independencia y libertad."

[44] Juan Wenceslao Barquera, *Discurso Patriótico que en el Aniversario de nuestra Independencia Solemnizado en la Ciudad de Toluca Residencia Provisional de los Supremos Poderes del Estado Soberano de México* (Toluca, 1830), 4: "Los antiguos pueblos de Grecia y Roma, llevaban siempre esta costumbre en sus fiestas cívicas. Los padres enseñaban a sus hijos a imitar las grandes acciones de sus antepasados. Los sacerdotes en el templo, fijaban la idea sublime de la divinidad, en la consignación de sus escogidos para conservar la felicidad de los pueblos, y los oradores públicos

The neoclassical trend in the classical rhetorical tradition also influenced Barquera's oratory in other subtle ways. For example, in the opening line of his 1825 September Oration, he borrowed directly from the structural conventions of classicizing oratory, opening with an *exordium de circumstantiis*:

> What a noble end, Mexicans, has brought you here today, filled with that patriotic fervor, which can inspire in righteous hearts the holy fire of liberty![45]

Imagining himself as a Roman patrician orator, Barquera replaced the "Romans" (*quirites*), "judges" (*iudices*) or "senators" (*patres conscripti*) of the orations of Cicero that he had read as part of his early education with "Mexicans" (*mexicanos*). Barquera then proceeded to justify the occasion for his speech with a *captatio benevolentiae*, arguing that future generations, when listening to orators in his position on September 16, would stand in silent admiration upon hearing the deeds of the "liberators" (*libertadores*), which he was about to recount. As classical rhetorical theory in general and Mayans's treatise in particular dictated, in "honorable cases" where the orator was supporting a just cause, the *captatio benevolentiae* should stress the honor of the occasion (*cosa*), and seek to render the audience "attentive" (*dócil*) to the orator's words. As the events of September 16 became more conventional and familiar, this technique also gained prominence as orators sought to gain the goodwill of their listeners by means of self-deprecating statements. For example, in the 1828 September Oration the orator apologized for the unoriginality of the subject matter: "this sort of thing contains nothing new or exceptional, but is very suitable to these circumstances."[46]

For the elites of the early Mexican Republic whose rhetorical training and republican traditions owed much to Greek and Roman models, channeling the classical rhetorical tradition chimed perfectly with their ambitions of reviving an ancient political form and its attendant values and

---

presentaban la historia de los sucesos más memorables de su carrera política." Barquera's 1830 oration makes greater reference to biblical examples than his 1825 speech, as well as having a more nuanced account of the events surrounding the Mexican Revolution.

[45] Jorge Denegre Vaught Peña (ed.), *Dos Siglos de Discursos Patrióticos*, 21: "¡Qué objeto tan sublime, mexicanos, os ha reunido hoy en este lugar, llenos de júbilo patriótico, que sabe inspirar en los pechos generosos el sacrosancto fuego de la libertad!" To take two examples from popular school texts: Cicero, *In Catilinam*, 1: "Tandem aliquando, Quirites, L. Catilinam furentem audacia"; Cicero, *Pro Milone*, 1: "Etsi vereor, iudices, ne turpe sit."

[46] *Ibid.*, 54: "nada tiene de nuevo o singular; pero es muy propia de las circunstancias."

civic practices.[47] For instance, both Rome and Mexico shared a reverence for the spirits (*manes*) of the glorious dead:

> It was not long ago, citizens, that our love and gratitude placed their venerable remains in this august temple of eternal sanctity in order to immortalize the memory of their virtues, and today their holy spirits (*manes*) arise from the underworld of their tombs to celebrate with us the abundant fruit of their heroic sacrifices and to mix the jubilation of the immortals with the joyful song of the free Mexican citizen.[48]

Recently liberated Mexico was, as Barquera put it, seeking to "bring back the days of Athens and Rome," in two related senses.[49] However, to what extent it was a revival is, of course, a matter of perspective. In the colonial colleges and the mouths of eighteenth-century orators, the ancients had never left.

Later orators who delivered the annual oration in the main square in Mexico City would to a greater or lesser extent follow the neoclassical precedent set by Barquera. Even those who espoused an indigenizing political ideology that sought to deny the role of any tradition with origins, however distant, in Europe, could not do without a classical frame of reference in their role as civic orators. For example, José María Tornel y Mendívil (1795–1853) who delivered the September Oration in 1827, challenged the primacy of Mediterranean antiquity, claiming that the Romans were criminals whose modern reputation was the product of the propaganda of their own historians. The true virtuous ancients were the Aztecs who were, he argued, far more peaceful than the ancient civilizations of Europe and Asia:

> Numa, Seleucus, Solon, Lycurgus, the pontiffs and the wise men of the Old World did not do a better job of correcting dissension and civic discords than the legislators of the Aztecs, the Zipas and the Incas ... However, even in the sullied variegations in which the pristine purity fell in later times, you will not

---

[47] In 1823 a panegyric of Washington was published in Mexico City, which may have reinforced the long-standing tradition of classicizing public speaking in New Spain and its association with republicanism: John Simon Chaudron, *Oración Funebre al Ciudadano Jorge Washington: Pronunciada el 1. de Enero de 1800, en una Sociedad Francesa en Filadelfia* (Mexico City, 1823).

[48] Jorge Denegre Vaught Peña (ed.), *Dos Siglos de Discursos Patrióticos*, 16: "No ha mucho tiempo, ciudadanos, que nuestro amor y gratitud depositaron sus restos venerables en ese templo augusto de la santidad increada, para eternizar la memoria de sus virtudes, y hoy sus manes sacrosantos se levantan del abismo de los sepulcros para congratularse con nosotros en el fruto opimo de sus heroicos sacrificios, y para mezclar los júbilos de los inmortales, con el alegre cantico del mexicano libre."

[49] *Ibid.*, 20: "renovar los días de Atenas y de Roma."

find the debasement, the extravagance or the violence of Rome; you will not find the frenzied ambition of the Syrians and the other peoples of Asia.[50]

According to Tornel, when Hidalgo called on the Mexican people to revolt, the Roman Emperors Tiberius and Caligula appeared in spirit as the representatives of tyranny to resist him, another sign of the perfidiousness of the Greeks and Romans. However, ancient Mediterranean history and culture, although ostensibly rejected, remained an important point of reference for Tornel who imagined his role as an orator in decidedly classicizing terms. For instance, when calling on Congress to uphold the Enlightenment ideas of Montesquieu and the Abbé Raynal, he exhorted them to do so with the "dignity of the Athenian orator against Philip and the Roman orator against Catiline."[51] Although eager to distance themselves from Greece and Rome, when it came to defending truth with eloquence and exhorting their fellow citizens to love virtue and defend the *patria*, even the most indigenizing among the Mexican orators could not do without the classical rhetorical tradition, and above all its patron saint, Cicero.

Conclusion

Mirroring other social, cultural and intellectual continuities that existed across the colonial-national divide in the Iberian World, Mexico's revolutionary neoclassical civic oratory was not a rejection of the sermon culture of the earlier epoch, but a subtle reworking of long-standing traditions of classicizing public speaking, both secular and sacred.[52] Public oratory may have been the archetypal civic practice of Mexico's republican government. However, it did not have to be revived for the new national states, since it had never fallen into disuse. As the classicizing oratory of Mexico City's

---

[50] Ernesto de la Torre Villar and Ramiro Navarro (eds.), *La Conciencia Nacional y su Formación: Discursos Cívicos Septembrinos (1825–1871)* (Mexico City: Universidad Nacional Autónoma de México, 1988), 43: "Numa, Zeleuco, Solón, Licurgo, los pontífices y los sabios del Viejo Mundo no corrigieron mejor las disenciones y discordias civiles, que los legisladores de los aztecas, de los zipas y los incas ... Pero aun en las variaciones en que sucesivamente degeneraba el candor primitivo, no se encontrarán el envilecimiento, la extravagancia y los atentados de Roma; no hallaremos el furor de la ambición de los sirios y de otros pueblos de Asia." On Tornel's education and his other classizing orations, see María del Carmen Vázquez Mantecón, *La Palabra del Poder: Vida Pública de José María Tornel, 1795–1853* (Mexico City: Universidad Nacional Autónoma de México, 2008), 34–35, 46–47, 53–55.

[51] Jorge Denegre Vaught Peña (ed.), *Dos siglos Siglos de Discursos Patrióticos*, 49: "no tardó en conocerse que la fuerza de la verdad y de nuestra justicia se sostendría en las juntas populares con el vigor y dignidad del orador de Atenas contra Filipo, y del orador de Roma contra Catilina."

[52] Jeremy Adelman, "The Problem of Persistence in Latin American History."

Royal Academy of Theoretic-Practical Jurisprudence and Manila's Economic Society shows, classicizing public speaking was a vibrant and versatile tradition long before Hidalgo's *grito de Independencia*. A new race of Ciceros did not spontaneously appear. Instead, the Iberian world already possessed a veritable phalanx of educated individuals whose training in colonial institutions like the colegio de San Ildefonso could easily be repurposed for new ritual occasions.

This said, there were of course deep and lasting changes that took place between 1700 and 1825, and the classical rhetorical tradition was not immune from these. For the first fifty years or so, late humanist practices such as Latin declamation, the use of late humanist rhetorical handbooks and the oratorical rituals of the colonial colleges coexisted with new literary and intellectual trends. As a result, we see many of the features of humanist oratory directly reflected in the identifiably post-humanist oratory of Santa Justa y Rufina and others. However, this was not to last. By the time of Barquera and his contemporaries, humanist handbooks played little role in rhetorical education, Latin declamation was now rare and rhetoric was firmly under the sway of *belles lettres*. Yet, the classical rhetorical tradition itself had not vanished. Far from it. Barquera and others relied heavily on classical rhetorical theory, often taken directly from ancient handbooks and oratory, with influence also coming from the not entirely un-classicizing New Rhetoric of the Scottish Enlightenment. More importantly, they continued to imagine their role as civic orators in neoclassical terms donning figurative togas to harangue their fellow citizens in the *plaza mayor*, the modern equivalent of the Roman forum. As deliberative oratory became more common in the republics that dotted the Atlantic world, leading figures, like Simón Bolívar (1783–1830) who delivered a famous address at the Congress of Angostura (1819–1821), similarly drew on the classical rhetorical tradition as they argued for new constitutional arrangements, discussing the models provided by the Roman republic, Britain's unwritten constitution and the works of Montesquieu and Volney in speeches that also often included a *captatio benevolentiae* and other recognizable features.[53]

---

[53] Simón Bolivar, *Discurso del general Bolívar al Congreso de Angostura* (1819), Archivo del Libertador, retrieved from: www.archivodellibertador.gob.ve/escritos/buscador/spip.php?article9987. On Bolívar's oratory in its Atlantic context, see Sandra M. Gustafson, *Imagining Deliberative Democracy in the Early American Republic* (Chicago: University of Chicago Press, 2011), 71–96. In general, the ceremonial oratory discussed in this chapter does not refer with any regularity to canonical thinkers in the history of political thought (e.g. Montesquieu, Rousseau, etc.), as their aim was not to create republics but to celebrate them. This is not to say that these ideas do not underpin their arguments. Rather, in order not to overburden their audiences with unnecessary philosophical claims, they chose not to cite and discuss them at length.

As the "modern" period dawned in the Americas and elsewhere, the shadow of Mediterranean antiquity's archetypal urban practice in some ways grew even more pronounced, as knowledge of it became a prerequisite for positions of authority in the new republics of the Americas and elsewhere. As the journalist and poet José Joaquín de Mora (1783–1864) put it in his inaugural lecture for a course on oratory at the short-lived liceo de Chile in Santiago, classicizing oratory was the archetypal republican practice, and it was in ancient Greece and Rome that it had enjoyed its Golden Age:

> Will I remind you of the splendor of the ancient republics, the first ornament and germ of whose growth and splendor was none other than the irresistible voice of their orators? If perhaps I wanted to continue in this vein, it would be enough to cite Cicero who personifies the highest achievements of the art of speech; I would make you see in the conqueror of Catiline in the author of *On Duties*, in the defender of Archias and Murena the most noble triumphs that the human mind has ever achieved in the most noble of pursuits.[54]

This was a classicizing conception of public speaking that would only fade away entirely in the twentieth century.

---

[54] José Joaquín de Mora, *Oración inaugural del curso de oratoria del Liceo de Chile, pronunciada el día 20 de abril de 1830* (Santiago de Chile, 1830), 2: "¿Traeré a vuestra memoria el lustre de las repúblicas antiguas, cuyo primer ornamento, cuyo primer jermen de engrandecimiento y esplendor no era otro que la voz imperiosa de sus oradores? Si quisiera valerme de este jenero de razones, me bastaría nombrar a Cicerón, para simbolizar en este augusto personaje el más alto encomio del arte de la palabra; os haría ver en el vencedor de Catalina, en el autor de los Oficios, en el defensor de Arquias y de Murena los triunfos más nobles que ha obtenido jamás el jenio del hombre en la más noble de las carreras."

Bibliography

ARCHIVAL SOURCES

Mexico

Archivo General de la Nación, Mexico City
Archivo Histórico de la Provincia de los Carmelitas Descalzos en México, Mexico City
Archivo Histórico de la Universidad Nacional Autónoma de México, Mexico City
Biblioteca Lafragua, Puebla
Biblioteca Nacional de México, Mexico City
Biblioteca Palafoxiana, Puebla

Peru

Archivo General de la Nación, Lima
Biblioteca Nacional del Perú, Lima

Chile

Archivo Nacional de Chile, Santiago

United States of America

Hispanic Society of America, New York, NY
University of Michigan Library, Ann Arbor, MI

Spain

Archivo General de Indias, Seville
Archivo General de Simancas, Valladolid
Biblioteca del Colegio de Padres Agustinos de Valladolid, Valladolid
Real Academia de Historia, Madrid

Portugal

Biblioteca da Ajuda, Lisbon
Biblioteca Nacional de Portugal, Lisbon
Biblioteca Publica, Braga
Biblioteca Publica, Évora

Italy

Archivum Romanum Societatis Iesu, Rome
Biblioteca Nazionale, Naples
Biblioteca Riccardiana, Florence

India

Directorate of Archives and Archaeology, Panjim, Goa

Philippines

National Archive of the Philippines, Manila

Japan

Kirishitan Bunko, Sophia University, Tokyo
Tōyō Bunko, Tokyo

PRIMARY SOURCES

Acquaviva D'Aragona, Tomaso. *L'Aquila Grande: Orazione per la Morte di Filippo Quarto il Grande Monarca delle Spagne*. Naples, 1666.
Acta Consistorii Publice Exhibiti a S. D. N. Gregorio Papa XIII Regum Iaponiorum Legatis Romae, Die XIII Martii MDLXXXV. Rome, 1585.
de Almeida, Miguel. *Jardim dos Pastores*, 5 vols. Goa, 1658–1659.
de Almoguera, Juan. *Oración Panegyrica Funebre en las Exequias del Rey n. Senor d. Felipe Quarto el Grande, que Dios aya. Celebrolas la Ciudad de Arequipa en la Santa Iglesia Catedral della el Año de 1666*. Lima, 1667.
Álvares, Manuel. *De Institutione Grammatica Libri Tres. Coniugationibus Accessit Interpretatio Iapponica*, Carlos Assunção and Masayuki Toyoshima eds. Tokyo: Yagi Bookstore, 2012.
Antonio, Nicholás. *Bibliotheca Hispana Nova*, 2 vols. Rome, 1672.
de la Anunciación, Juan. *Sermonario en Lengua Mexicana*. Mexico City, 1577.
Arcamone, Ignazio. *Purgatorii Commentarium Concannice Compositum Mortuorum Christi Fidelium Immortalibus Animabus Purgatorii Poenas Patientibus*. Rachol, 1663.
Conciones per Annum Concannice Compositae. Rachol, 1668.

Argelati, Filippo. *Bibliotheca Scriptorum Mediolanensium, seu Acta, et Elogia Virorum Omnigena Eruditione Illustrium, qui in Metropoli Insubriae, Oppidisque Circumiactibus Orti sunt.* Milan, 1745.

de Arrate y Acosta, José Martín Félix. *Llave del Nuevo Mundo, Antemural de las Indias Occidentales. La Habana Descripta: Noticias de su Fundación, Aumentos y Estados,* 4th ed. Havana: Comision Nacional Cubana de la UNESCO, 1964.

de Avendaño, Fernando. *Sermones de los Misterios de Nuestra Santa Fe Catolica, en Lengua Castellana, y La General del Inca: Impugnanse los Errores Particulares que los Indios Han Tenido.* Lima, 1648.

de Azevedo, Alfonso. *Commentarii Juris Civilis in Hispaniae Regias Constitutiones,* 6 vols. Lyon, 1737.

de Balbuena, Bernardo. *Grandeza Mexicana,* 2 vols. Mexico City, 1604.

Balli, Juan Bautista. *Oración en Elogio de la Jurisprudencia,* Daniel Kuri Breña and Salvador Ugarte eds. Mexico City: Editorial Jus, 1950.

Barquera, Juan Wenceslao. *Discurso Patriótico que en el Aniversario de nuestra Independencia Solemnizado en la Ciudad de Toluca Residencia Provisional de los Supremos Poderes del Estado Soberano de México.* Toluca, 1830.

Basco y Vargas, José. *Plan General Económico.* Manila, 1779.

Bautista, Juan. *A Iesu Christo S.N. Ofrece Este Sermonario en Lengua Mexicana.* Mexico City, 1606.

Benci de Arimino, Jorge. *Economia Christãa dos Senhores no Governo dos Escravos.* Rome, 1705.

Bompiani, Ignazio. *Philippus Quartus Catholicus Hispaniarum Rex Magnanimus, laudatus inter Solemnes eius Exequias in Basilica S. Mariae Maioris.* Rome, 1666.

de Bonifacio, Juan. *Christiani Pueri Institutio (1588).* Salamanca, 1575.

  Christiani Pueri Institutio (1588): Fac-simile da Edição (Existente na Biblioteca da Ajuda) do Mais Antigo Livro Impresso Pelos Missionários Europeus na China. Lisboa: Centro de Estudos do Livro e da Edição, 1988.

Brucker, Johann Jacob. *Pinacotheca Scriptorum Nostra Aetate Literis Illustrium, Exhibens Auctorum Eruditionis Laude Scriptisque Celeberrimorum, qui Hodie Vivunt, Imagines et Elogia.* Augsburg, 1741.

Campos y Martínez, Juan Gregorio. *Oratio Apologética.* Mexico City, 1746.

Cartas Ânuas do Colégio de Macau: (1594–1627), João Paulo Oliveira e Costa and Ana Fernandes Pinto eds. Macau, 1999.

Cartas que los Padres y Hermanos de la Compañía de Jesús, que Andan en los Reynos de Japón. Alcalá, 1575.

Caussin, Nicolas. *Eloquentiae Sacrae et Humanae Parallela Libri XVI.* Cologne, 1634.

de Chasseneuz, Barthélemy. *Catalogus Gloriae Mundi.* Cologne 1692.

Chaudron, John Simon. *Oración Funebre al Ciudadano Jorge Washington: Pronunciada el 1. de Enero de 1800, en una Sociedad Francesa en Filadelfia.* Mexico City, 1823.

Cicero, Marcus Tullius. *M. Tullii Ciceronis Orationes Duodecim Selectae... quibus Accesserunt Compendium Rhetoricae R.P. Cypriani Soarii S. J. et Lachrymae Sancti Petri R. P. Sidonii Hoschii.* Mexico City, 1756.

Clavigero, Francisco Javier. *Historia antigua de México*, Mariano Cuevas ed. Mexico City: Editorial Porrua, 1964.

de Cobarrubias Orozco, Sebastián. *Tesoro de la Lengua Castellana o Española.* Madrid, 1611.

Compendium Catholicae Veritatis, 3 vols. Tokyo: Sophia University, 1997.

Conciones, sive, Orationes ex Graecis Latinisque. Paris, 1570.

do Couto, Diogo. *Diogo do Couto Orador: Discursos Oficiais Proferidos na Câmara de Goa*, Maria Augusta Lima Cruz, Rui Manuel Loureiro and Nuno Vila-Santa eds. Lisbon: Arandis, 2016.

de la Cruz, Sor Juana Inés. *Obras Completas*, Alfonso Méndez Plancarte and Alberto G. Salceda eds., 4 vols. Mexico City: Fondo de Cultura Económica, 1951–1957.

Deza, Francisco. *Cenotaphio Real de la Catholica Magestad de Philippo Quarto el Grande Rey de las Españas, y Emperador de las Indias.* Manila, 1668.

Días, Pedro. *Arte da Lingua de Angola.* Lisbon, 1697.

Dictionarium Latino-Lusitanicum ac Japonicum ex Ambrosii Calepini Volumine Depromptum. Amakusa, 1595.

Doctrina Christiana en Legua Española y Mexicana. Mexico City, 1550.

Drexel, Jeremias. *Aurifodina Artium et Scientiarum Omnium: Excerpendi Solertia, Omnibus Litterarum Amantibus Monstrata.* Antwerp, 1641.

de Echevarria, Juan. *Fúnebre Memoria de la Muerte del Rey N Señor D. Felipe Quarto el Grande. Piadosa Seña de la Gloria en que Descansa su Magestad Cesárea. Panegírico Cenotaphio en las Exequias, que la S. Iglesia Cathedral de Durango, y Reyno de la Nueva Vizcaya le Consagraron a sus Cenizas Reales.* Mexico 1667.

Eguiara y Eguren, Juan José de. *Biblioteca Mexicana*, Ernesto de la Torre Villar ed., 5 vols. Mexico City: Universitdad Nacional Autónoma de México, 1986–1989.

Eguiara y Eguren, Juan José. *Bibliotheca Mexicana, sive Eruditorum Historia Virorum, qui in America Boreali Nati, vel Alibi Geniti, in Ipsam Domicilio aut Studiis Asciti quavis Lingua Scripto aliquid Tradiderunt. Eorum Praesertim qui pro Fide Catholica et Pietate Amplianda Fovendaque Egregie Factis et quibusvis Scriptis Floruere Editis aut Ineditis Ferdinando VI Hispaniarum Regi Catholico Nuncupata.* Mexico City, 1755.

Epigrammata Aliqua ad Faciliorem Epigrammatis Componendi. Mexico City, 1641.

Esequie di Filippo IV. Cattolico Re di Spagna: Celebrate in Firenze dal Serenissimo Ferdinando II. Gran Duca di Toscana Descritte da Giovanni Batista Borgherini Canonico Fiorentino. Florence, 1665.

Eseqvie Reali alla Catt. Maestà del Rè D. Filippo IV. Celebrate in Milano alli 17. Decembre 1665. Milan, 1665.

*Faguo Guojia Tushuguan Ming-Qing Tianzhujiao Wenxian*法國國家圖書館明清天主教文獻, 26 vols., Adrianus Dudink, Nathalie Monnet and Nicolas Standaert eds. Taipei: Taipei Ricci Institute, 2009.

Filipp, Alegambe. *Bibliotheca Scriptorum Societatis Iesu.* Antwerp, 1676.

Flosculi ex Veteris ac Novi Testamenti, S. Doctorum et Insignium Philosophorum Floribus Selecti per Emanuelem Barretum Lusitanum Presbyterum Societatis IESV (Nagasaki, 1610). Tokyo, 1978.

de Frias, António João. *Aureola dos Indios & Nobiliarchia Bracmana, Tratado Historico, Genealogico, Panegyrico, Politico, & Moral.* Lisbon, 1702.

Frois, Pedro. *La Première Ambassade du Japon en Europe,* eds. J. A. Abranches Pinto, Yoshitomo Okamoto and Henri Bernard. Tokyo: Sophia University, 1942.

Gaubil, Antoine. *Correspondance De Pékin: 1722–1759,* Simon Renée ed. Geneva: Librairie Droz, 1970.

Giovanni Calenzani, Pietro. *Descrizione del Funerale Fatto dalla Serenissima Republica di Genova al Catolico Filippo Quarto.* Genoa, 1666.

Guerra, José Basilio. *Oración Inaugural sobre la Necesidad de Saber las Leyes Patrias.* Mexico City, 1816.

de Hailly, Charle-François Amounet. *Harangue Funebre Prononcée aux Exeques de Philippe le Grand Roy Catholique des Espagnes et des Indes.* Brussels, 1665.

Hara, Martinho. *Oratio Habita a Fara D. Martino Iaponio, suo et Sociorum Nomine, cum ab Europa Redirent ad Patrem Alexandrum Valignanum Visitatorem Societatis IESU, Goae in D. Pauli Collegio Pridie Non. Iunii Anno Domini 1587.* Tokyo: Yushodo Booksellers, 1978.

Honorario Túmulo Pompa Exequial y Imperial Mausoleo que más Fina Artemisa la Fe Romana por su Sacrosanto Tribunal de Nueva España Erigió y Celebró llorosa Egeria a su Catholico Numa y Amante Rey Philippo Quarto. Mexico City, 1666.

Houbraken, Iudocus. *Oratio Funebris in Exequiis Philippi IV., Hispaniarum ac Indiarum Regis Catholici.* Antwerp, 1666.

von Humboldt, Alexander. *Ensayo Político sobre el Reino de la Nueva España Estudio Preliminar,* Juan A. Ortega y Medina ed., 4th ed. Mexico City: Porrúa, 1984.

St Ignatius Loyola. *Exercitia Spiritualia.* Amakusa, 1596.

de Iturriaga, Jose Mariano. *La Californiada,* Alfonso Castro Pallares ed. Mexico City, 1979.

Jnāneshvari (Bhāvārthadipikā), Vitthal Ganesh Pradhan and Hester Marjorie Lambert eds. and trans., 2 vols. London: Allen & Unwin, 1967.

Kouduo Richao: Li Jiubiao's Diary of Oral Admonitions. A Late Ming Christian Journal, Erik Zürcher ed., 2 vols. Oxford: Routledge, 2007.

Labbé, Philippe. *Bibliothecae Bibliothecarum.* Rouen, 1672.

Lascari, Antonio. *Real Panteón, Oratorio Fúnebre: Sermón que el Sr. Antonio Lascari Beneficiado del Partido de Tututepec, en el Obispado de Oaxaca.* Mexico City, 1667.

Lazaro de Velasco, Antonio. *Funesto Geroglífico, Enigma del Mayor Dolor, que en Representaciones Mudas Manifestó la muy Noble, Antigua, Leal, Insigne, y Coronada Ciudad de Valencia, en las Honras de su Rey Felipe el Grande IV en Castilla y III en Aragon.* Valencia, 1666.

de León Pinelo, Diego. *Hypomnema Apologeticum pro Regali Academia Limensi in Lipsianam Periodum.* Lima, 1648.

de Linares Urdanivia, Francisco. *Oración Fúnebre . . . en las Exequias que Celebró a la Sacra y Real Magestad de Nuestro Catholico Rey y Señor D. Felipe IV. El Grande.* Mexico City, 1667.

Lipsius, Justus. *De Constantia Libri Duo, qui Alloquium Praecipue Continent in Publicis Malis.* Antwerp, 1584.

Llanto del Occidente en El ocaso del más Claro Sol de las Españas: Fúnebres Demonstraciones que Hizo Pyra Real, que Erigió en las Exequias del Rey N. Señor D. Felipe IIII el Grande. Mexico City, 1666.

López, Baltasar. *Oratio pro Instauratione Studiorum Habita in Collegio Mexicano Societatis Iesu.* Mexico City, 1644.

López, Vicente. *Diálogo de Abril: Acerca de la Bibliotheca del Señor Doctor Juan José de Eguiara y del Ingenio de los Mexicanos,* Silvia Vargas Alquicira ed. Mexico City: Universidad Nacional Autónoma de México, 1987.

López de Mendizábal, Gregorio. *Oratoria Parentatio, qua Caesareae Angelorum Urbis Americanae Magnum, Meritumque Dolorem Testatus est in Acerbo Philippi IV Magni Hispaniarum & Indiarum Regis Funere.* Mexico City, 1666.

Loyens, Henricus. *Oratio Fvnebris, in Exequijs Serenissimi ac Catholici Hispaniarum ac Jndiarum Regis Philippi Qvarti dum illi Academia Lovaniensis in Æde Divo Petro Sacra Lugibri & Solemni Pompa Parentaret . . .* Louvain, 1665.

Lubrani, Giacomo. *L'Anfiteatro della Constanza Vittoriosa Oratione Funerale del P. Giacomo Lubrani della Compagnia di Giesù. Detta nel Duomo di Palermo per le Solenni Essequie Celebrate alla Cattolica Maestà di Filippo IV il Grande re delle Spagne e di Sicilia.* Palermo, 1666.

de Luque, Eduardo Malo. *Historia Política de los Establecimientos Ultramarinos de las Naciones Europeas,* 5 vols. Madrid, 1784–1790.

Machiavelli, Niccolò. *Opere Politiche,* 2 vols. Rome: Salerno Editrice, 2006.

Mahābhārata. Book Six. Bhīṣma, Alex Cherniak trans. New York: New York University Press, 2008.

Martí, Manuel. *Epistularum Libri Duodecim,* 2 vols. Madrid, 1735.

Matranga, Girolamo. *Le Solennità Lugubri e Liete in Nome della Fedelissima Sicilia nella Felice e Primaia Città di Palermo Capo del Regno Celebrate in Due Tempi,* 3 vols. Palermo, 1666.

de Mayans y Siscar, Gregorio. *Emmanuelis Martini, Ecclesiae Alonensis Decani, Vita,* Luis Gil ed. Valencia: Ayuntamiento de Oliva, 1977.

Obras Completas, 5 vols. Valencia: Diputación de Valencia, 1983–1986.

de Meneses, Garcia. *Garsias Menesius Eborensis Praesul quum Lusitaniae Regis Inclyti Legatus & Regiae Classis Aduersus Turcas Hydruntem in Apulia Praeesidio Tenentes Praefectus ad Vrbem Accederet, in Templo diui Pauli Publice Exceptus apud Xistum iiii Pontificem Maximum & apud Sacrum Cardinalium Senatum, Huiuscemodi Orationem Habuit.* Coimbra, 1561.

Micheltorena, Manuel. *Discurso Pronunciado en México el Día 27 de Septiembre de 1840*. Mexico City: A. Diaz, 1840.

Oración Cívica que Elegido por la junta Patriótica de la Capital del Departamento de Californias Pronunció en Solemnidad del 27 de Septiembre, el exmo Sor. D. Manuel Micheltorena Actual Gobernador Comandante General e Inspector Ayudante General de la Plana Mayor del Ejército. Monterey, CA, 1844.

Nova Acta Eruditorum. Leipzig, 1738.

Osio, Antonio María. *The History of Alta California: A Memoir of Mexican California*, Rose Marie Beebe and Robert M. Senkewicz eds. Madison: University of Wisconsin Press, 1996.

Páez, Baltezar. *Sermão que Fez o Doutor Fr. Baltezar Páez Provincial da Orden da Santissima Trinidade no Convento da Mesma Orden Desta Cidade de Lisboa. Em hum Officio, que os Irmãos da Irmandade de Todos os Sanctos dos Officiaes e Criados de sua Magestade Fizerão, Conforme ao su Compromisso. Pela Magestade Catholica del Rey Dom Philippe II de Portugal*. Lisbon, 1621.

de Palafox y Mendoza, Juan. *Estatutos y Constituciones Hechas con Comisión Particular de su Magestad*. Mexico City, 1688.

de Palma, Juan Antonio. *Lágrimas en las Honras que a la Magestad Real de N Rey y Señor Filipo IV el Grande Celebró el Real Acuerdo de Lima, Gobernando en Vacante, en su Santa Iglesia Metropolitana en 17. Días del Mes de Septiembre de 1666*. Lima, 1666.

Peramás, José Manuel. *Cinco Oraciones Laudatorias en Honor del Doctor don Ignacio Duarte y Quiros*. Córdoba: Universidad Nacional, [1765] 1937.

Pérez de Rúa, Antonio. *Funeral Hecho en Roma en la Yglesia de Santiago de los Españoles à 18 de Diciembre de 1665: a la Gloriosa Memoria del Rei Catolico de las Españas Nuestro Señor D. Felipe Quarto el Grande en Nombre de la Nación Española*. Rome, 1666.

Peter Martyr of Angleria, *Opera*, Erich Woldan ed. Graz: Akademische Druck und Verlagsanstalt, 1966.

Pichardus, Atonius. *Commentariorum in Quatuor Institutionum Iustinianearum Libri*, 2 vols. Salamanca, 1620.

de Poblete, Juan. *Oración Fúnebre Panegyrica a las Honras del Rey Nuestro Señor don Felipe Qvarto el Grande*. Mexico City, 1666.

Pomey, François. *Novus Candidatus Rhetoricae Praecepta*. Mexico City, 1726.

Pompe Funebri Celebrate all'Augusto Monarca Filippo Quarto il Grande. Lecce, 1666.

Ribeiro, Diogo. *Vocabulario da Lingoa Canarim*, Tōru Maruyama ed. Nagoya: Nanzan University, 2005.

Ricci, Matteo. *De Christiana Expeditione apud Sinas*, Nicolas Trigault ed. Cologne, 1617.

Rodrigues, João. *João Rodrigues's Account of Sixteenth-Century Japan*, Michael Cooper ed. And trans. London: Routledge, 2001.

Rojo del Rio, Manuel Antonio. *Heros Ecclesiasticus, Oratio Funebris in Exequiis Manilae Celebratis*. Mexico City, 1765.

de Salazar, Francisco Cervantes. *Túmulo Imperial de la Gran Ciudad de México.* Mexico City, 1560.

de Salazar, Francisco Cervantes. *México en 1554*, Joaquín García Icazbalceta ed. Mexico City: Universidad Nacional Autónoma de México, 2001.

de Salinas y Córdova, Buenaventura. *Memorial, Informe, y Manifiesto.* Madrid, 1646.

de San Antón Muñón Chimalpahin Cuauhtlehuanitzin, Domingo Francisco. *Annals of His Time: Don Domingo De San Antón Muñón Chimalpahin Quauhtlehuanitzin*, James Lockhart, Susan Schroeder and Doris Namala eds. Stanford, CA: Stanford University Press, 2006.

de Sande, Duarte. *De Missione Legatorum Iaponensium ad Romanam Curiam.* 1590

Diálogo Sobre a Missão dos Embaixadores Japoneses à Cúria Romana, Sebastião Tavares Pinho and Américo da Costa Ramalho eds., 2 vols. Coimbra: Imprensa da Universidade de Coimbra, 2009.

Japanese Travellers in Sixteenth-Century Europe: A Dialogue concerning the Mission of the Japanese Ambassadors to the Roman Curia (1590), J. F. Moran trans., Derek Massarella ed. London: Routledge, 2012.

de Santa Justa y Rufina, Basilio Sancho. *Sanctissimo Domino Nostro Clementi XIII.* Manila, 1768.

Alocución que en el Día Veinte de Enero del Año Mil Setecientos Ochenta y Tres, Cumpleaños del Nuestro Señor D. Carlos III . . . Manila, 1783.

Schulz, Johann Henry. *Commentarius de Vita Friderici Hoffmanni*, in Friederick Hoffmann, *Opera Omnia Physico-Medica*, 6 vols. Geneva, 1761.

Soáres, Cipriano. *De Arte Rhetorica Libri Tres.* Madrid, 1597.

Solemníssimas Exequias, que la S. Iglesia Cathedral de Valladolid, Provincia de Mechoacan, Celebró a la Inclita y Grata Memoria del Catholicíssimo y Magnánimo Monarcha D. Felipe Quarto El Grande N. Rey, y Señor. Mexico City, 1666.

de Solórzano Pereira, Juan. *Politica Indiana.* Madrid, 1648.

Solutae Orationis Fragmenta. Mexico City, 1641.

Stephens, Thomas. *Father Thomas Stephens' Kristapurāṇa: Purāṇa I & II*, Nelson M. Falcao ed. and trans. Bengaluru: Kristu Jyoti Publications, 2012.

Tianxuechuhan 天學初函, 6 vols. Taipei: Student Book, 1965.

de Toledo, Pero Díaz. *Libro Llamado Fedrón: Plato's Phaedo*, Nicholas Grenville Round ed. Rochester, NY: Tamesis Books, 1993.

Toppi, Nicoló. *Biblioteca Napoletana et Apparato a Gli Huomini Illustri di Napoli e Del Regno, delle Famiglie, Terre, Città, e Religioni, che Sono nello Stesso Regno, dale Loro Origini per Tutto l'Anno 1678.* Naples, 1678.

de Totanés, Sebastián. *Arte de la Lengua Tagala, y Manual Tagalog, para la Administración de los Santos Sacramentos.* Sampaloc, 1745.

Urna Sacra y Fúnebre Pompa con que los Señores President y Oidores de la Real Audiencia Desta Ciudad de Guatemala Celebraron las Reales Exequias, a las Augustas Memoriales de la Catholica Magestad de D. Felipe Quarto el Grande Rey de las Españas y de las Indias que esté en el Cielo. Guatemala, 1666.

Valadés, Diego. *Retórica Cristiana*, Tarsicio Herrera Zapién ed. Mexico City, 1989.

Valignano, Alessandro. *Sumario de las Cosas de Japón (1583); Adiciones del Sumario de Japón (1592)*, José Luis Álvarez-Taladriz ed. Tokyo: Sophia University, 1954.

van den Venne, Franciscus. *Oratio Fvnebris, in Exequiis Magni & Catholici Hispaniarum Indiarumque Regis, Belgarum Principis Philippi IV*. Brussels, 1665.

Vieira, António. *Obra Completa*, João Francisco Marques ed., 30 vols. Lisbon: Círculo de Leitores, 2014.

Wicki, Josef ed. *Documenta Indica*, 18 vols. Rome, 1948–1988.

Yapuguay, Nicolás. *Sermones y Exemplos en Lengua Guarani*, Guillermo Furlong ed. Buenos Aires: Editorial Guarania, 1953.

Zapata y Mendoza, Juan Buenaventura. *Historia Cronológica de la Noble Ciudad de Tlaxcala*, Luis Reyes García and Andrea Martínez Baracs eds. Tlaxcala: Centro de Investigaciones y Estudios Superiores en Antropología Social, 1995.

SECONDARY SOURCES

Abbot, Don Paul. "*La Retórica y el Renacimiento*: An Overview of Spanish Theory," in James Jerome Murphy ed. *Renaissance Eloquence: Studies in the Theory and Practice of Renaissance Rhetoric*. Berkeley: University of California Press, 1983: 95–104.

"The Influence of Blair's *Lectures* in Spain," *Rhetorica: A Journal of the History of Rhetoric*, 7 (1989): 275–289.

"Mayans' *Rhetórica* and the Search for a Spanish Rhetoric," *Rhetorica: A Journal of the History of Rhetoric*, 11 (1993): 157–179.

Abbott, Don Paul. *Rhetoric in the New World: Rhetorical Theory and Practice in Colonial Spanish America*. Columbia: University of South Carolina Press, 1996.

Adelman, Jeremy. "The Problem of Persistence in Latin American History," in Jeremy Adelman ed. *Colonial Legacies: The Problem of Persistence in Latin American History*. New York: Routledge, 1999: 1–13.

"Latin American and World Histories: Old and New Approaches to the Pluribus and the Unum," *Hispanic American Historical Review*, 83 (2004): 399–409.

Aili, Hans. *The Prose Rhythm of Sallust and Livy*. Stockholm: Almqvist & Wiksell International, 1979.

Alden, Dauril. *The Making of an Enterprise: The Society of Jesus in Portugal, Its Empire, and Beyond: 1540–1750*. Stanford, CA: Stanford University Press, 1996.

Alden, Dauril, James S. Cummins and Michael Cooper. *Charles R. Boxer: An Uncommon Life: Soldier, Historian, Teacher, Collector, Traveller*. Lisbon: Fundacao Oriente, 2001.

Allen, W. Sidney. *Accent and Rhythm: Prosodic Features of Latin and Greek.* Cambridge: Cambridge University Press, 1973.

Alonso Acero, Beatriz. *Orán-Mazalquivir, 1589–1639: Una Sociedad Española en la Frontera de Berbería.* Madrid: Consejo Superior de Investigaciones Científicas, 2000.

Anderson, Benedict. *Imagined Communities: Reflections on the Origin and Spread of Nationalism,* rev. ed. New York: Verso, 2006.

Ando, Clifford. *Imperial Ideology and Provincial Loyalty in the Roman Empire.* Berkeley: University of California Press, 2000.

Aradra Sánchez, Rosa María. *De la Retórica a la Teoría de la Literatura: Siglos XVIII y XIX.* Murcia: Universidad de Murcia, 1997.

Armitage, David. "What's the Big Idea? Intellectual History and the *Longue Durée," History of European Ideas,* 38 (2012): 493–507.

von Arnim, Hans. *Leben und Werke des Dio von Prusa: mit einer Einleitung, Sophistik, Rhetorik, Philosophie in ihrem Kampf um die Jugendbildung.* Berlin: Wentworth Press, 1898.

Arrom, Silvia Marina. "New Directions in Mexican Legal History," *The Americas,* 50 (1994): 461–465.

de Ataíde, Mousinho. *Rachol: Jesuit College, 1610–1759.* Goa: Rachol Jesuit Seminary, 2012.

Axelrod, Paul and Michelle Fuerch, "Flight of the Deities: Hindu Resistance in Portuguese Goa," *Modern Asian Studies,* 30 (1996): 387–421.

Baber, R. Jovita. "The Construction of Empire: Politics, Law and Community in Tlaxcala, New Spain, 1521–1640." Ph.D. Dissertation, University of Chicago, 2005.

Báez Rubí, Linda. *Mnemosine Novohispánica: Retórica e Imágenes en el Siglo XVI.* Mexico City: Universidad Nacional Autónoma de México, 2005.

Bailey, Gauvin A. *Art on the Jesuit Missions in Asia and Latin America, 1542–1773.* Toronto: University of Toronto Press, 1999.

Baker, Patrick. *Italian Renaissance Humanism in the Mirror.* Cambridge: Cambridge University Press, 2015.

Barreto Xavier, Ângela. *A Invenção de Goa: Poder Imperial e Conversões Culturais nos Séculos XVI e XVII.* Lisbon: Imprensa de Ciências Sociais, 2015.

Barreto Xavier, Ângela and Ines G. Županov, *Catholic Orientalism: Portuguese Empire, Indian Knowledge (16th–18th Centuries).* Oxford: Oxford University Press, 2015.

"Ser Brâmane na Goa da Época Moderna," *Revista de História,* no. 172 (2015): 15–41.

Bartsch, Shadi. *Actors in the Audience.* Cambridge, MA: Harvard University Press, 1994.

Bayley, Peter. *French Pulpit Oratory, 1598–1650: A Study in Themes and Styles, with a Catalogue of Printed French Pulpit Oratory.* New York: Cambridge University Press, 1980.

Bayly, Christopher A. *Birth of the Modern World, 1780–1914.* Malden, MA: Wiley-Blackwell, 2004.

Behringer, Wolfgang. "Communications Revolutions: A Historiographical Concept," *German History*, 24 (2006): 333–374.

Beltrán, Joaquín Rodríguez. "La Agudeza del Ingenio Vista por un Humanista Novohispano: Estudio, Edición y Traducción de la *Oratio pro Instauratione Studiorum* de Baltasar López." Master's Thesis, Universidad Nacional Autónoma de México, 2012.

Bennett, Herman L. *Colonial Blackness: A History of Afro-Mexico*. Bloomington: Indiana University Press, 2009.

Benton, Lauren and Adam Clulow, "Empires and Protection: Making Interpolity Law in the Early Modern World," *Journal of Global History*, 12 (2017): 74–92.

Berbara. Maria Louro and K. A. E. Enenkel eds. *Portuguese Humanism and the Republic of Letters*. Leiden: Brill, 2012.

Berchet, Guglielmo. *Le Antiche Ambasciate Giapponesi in Italia*. Venice: Visentini, 1877.

Bergmann, Emilie L. "Language and 'Mothers' Milk': Material Roles and the Nurturing Body in Early Modern Spanish Texts," in Naomi J. Miller and Naomi Yavneh, *Maternal Measures: Figuring Caregiving in the Early Modern Period*. Aldershot: Routledge, 2000: 105–120.

Bermejo Vega, Virgilio. "Acerca de los Recursos de la Iconografía Regia; Felipe IV, de Rey Sol a Nuevo Salomón," *NORBA-ARTE*, 12 (1992): 163–186.

Beuchot, Mauricio. "Algunos Opositores de Maquiavelo en España y la Nueva España," *Signos Filosóficos*, 6 (2004). www.redalyc.org/articulo.oa?id=34301103.

"Perfil del Pensamiento Filosófico de Fray Alonso de la Vera Cruz," *Nova Tellus*, 29 (2011): 201–214.

Bireley, Robert. *The Counter-Reformation Prince: Anti-Machiavellianism or Catholic Statecraft in Early Modern Europe*. Chapel Hill: University of North Carolina Press, 1990.

Black, Robert. *Humanism and Education in Medieval and Renaissance Italy: Tradition and Innovation in Latin Schools from the Twelfth to the Fifteenth Century*. Cambridge: Cambridge University Press, 2001.

Education and Society in Florentine Tuscany. Boston: Brill, 2007.

Blair, Ann. *Too Much to Know: Managing Scholarly Information before the Modern Age*. New Haven, CT: Yale University Press, 2010.

Bleichmar, Daniela. *Visible Empire: Botanical Expeditions and Visual Culture in the Hispanic Enlightenment*. Chicago: University of Chicago Press, 2012.

Bohman, George V. "Rhetorical Practice in Colonial America," in Karl R. Wallace ed. *History of Speech Education in America; Background Studies*. New York: Forgotten Books, 1959: 60–79.

van Bommel, Bas. *Classical Humanism and the Challenge of Modernity: Debates on Classical Education in 19th-century Germany*. Berlin: de Gruyter, 2015.

Boncompagni-Ludovisi, Francesco. *Le Prime Due Ambasciate Dei Giapponesi a Roma (1585–1615)*. Rome: Forzani & Company, 1904.

Bono, Diane M. *Cultural Diffusion of Spanish Humanism in New Spain: Francisco Cervantes de Salazar's Diálogo De La Dignidad Del Hombre.* New York: Peter Lang, 1991.

Borah, Woodrow Wilson. *Justice by Insurance: The General Indian Court of Colonial Mexico and the Legal Aides of the Half-Real.* Berkeley: University of California Press, 1983.

Borges, Charles J. "The College of St. Paul's and Jesuit Education in Goa," in *Jesuits and Education in India*, Herman Castellino ed. Anand: Gujarat Sahitya Prakash, 2005: 1–14.

Bouwsma, William James. *The Waning of the Renaissance, 1550–1640.* New Haven, CT: Yale University Press, 2000.

Boxer, Charles Ralph. *The Christian Century in Japan: 1549–1650.* Berkeley: University of California Press, 1951.

The Portuguese Seaborne Empire, 1415–1825. London: Hutchinson, 1969.

"Portuguese and Spanish Projects for the Conquest of Southeast East, 1580–1600," *Journal of Asian History*, 3.2 (1969): 118–136.

Boyajian, James C. *Portuguese Trade in Asia under the Habsburgs, 1580–1640.* Baltimore: The Johns Hopkins University Pres, 1993.

Brading, David A. *The Origins of Mexican Nationalism.* Cambridge: Centre of Latin American Studies, University of Cambridge, 1985.

The First America: The Spanish Monarchy, Creole Patriots, and the Liberal State, 1492–1867. Cambridge: Cambridge University Press, 1991.

Bristol, Joan Cameron. *Christians, Blasphemers, and Witches: Afro-Mexican Ritual Practice in the Seventeenth Century.* Albuquerque: University of New Mexico Press, 2007.

Bronner, Fred. "Urban Society in Colonial Spanish America: Research Trends," *Latin American Research Review*, 21, (1986): 7–72.

Buescu, Ana Isabel. *Imagens do Príncipe: Discurso Normativo e Representação (1525–1549).* Lisbon: Edições Cosmos, 1996.

Burke, Peter, Luke Clossey and Felipe Fernández-Armesto. "The Global Renaissance," *Journal of World History* 28 (2017): 1–30.

Burkhart, Louise M. "2014 Presidential Address: Christian Salvation As Ethno-Ethnohistory: Two Views from 1714," *Ethnohistory*, 63 (2016): 215–235.

Burnett, Charles. "Humanism and the Jesuit Mission to China: The Case of Duarte de Sande (1547–1599)," *Euphrosyne*, 24 (1996): 425–471.

Caciagli, Giuseppe. *Lo Stato dei Presidi*, 2nd ed., Pisa: Arnera, 1992.

di Camillo, Ottavio. "Humanism in Spain," in A. Rabil, Jr. ed. *Renaissance Humanism: Foundations, Forms, and Legacy*, 3 vols. Philadelphia: University of Pennsylvania Press, 1988.

"Interpretations of Humanism in Recent Spanish Renaissance Studies," *Renaissance Quarterly*, 50 (1997): 1190–1201.

Campanelli, Maurizio. "L'Oratio e il 'Genere' delle Orazioni Inaugurali dell'Anno Accademico," in Silvia Rizzo ed. *Lorenzo Valla, Orazione per l'Inaugurazione dell'Anno Accademico 1455–1456. Atti di un Seminario di Filologia Umanistica*, Rome: Roma nel Rinascimento, 1994: 25–61.

Campos, Francisco Javier and Fernández de Sevilla, *Fiestas Barrocas en el Mundo Hispánico: Toledo y Lima*. Madrid: Ediciones Escurialenses, 2012.

Cañeque, Alejandro. *The King's Living Image: The Culture and Politics of Viceregal Power in Colonial Mexico*. New York: Routledge, 2004.

"El Arco Triunfal en el México del Siglo XVII como Manual Efímero del Buen Gobernante," in José Pascual Buxó ed. *Reflexión y Espectáculo en la América Virreinal*. Mexico City: Universidad Nacional Autónoma de México, 2007: 199–218.

"Imaging the Spanish Empire: The Visual Construction of Imperial Authority in Habsburg New Spain," *Colonial Latin American Review*, 19 (2010): 29–68

Cañizares-Esguerra, Jorge. *How to Write the History of the New World: Histories, Epistemologies, and Identities in the Eighteenth-Century Atlantic World*. Stanford, CA: Stanford University Press, 2001.

Cañizares-Esguerra, Jorge and Benjamin Breen. "Hybrid Atlantics: Future Directions for the History of the Atlantic World," *History Compass*, 11 (2013): 597–609.

Calneck, Edward. "The Calmecac and Telpochcalli in Pre-Conquest Tenochtitlan," in J. Jorge Klor de Alva et al. eds. *The Work of Bernardino de Sahagún: Pioneer Ethnographer of Sixteenth-Century Aztec Mexico*. Albany, NY: Institute for Mesoamerican Studies at SUNY-Albany, 1988: 169–178.

Cardim, Pedro. *Portugal Unido y Separado: Felipe II, la Unión de Territorios y el Debate Sobre la Condición Política del Reino de Portugal*. Valladolid: Ediciones Universidad de Valladolid, 2014.

Cardim, Pedro, Tamar Herzog, José Javier Ruiz Ibáñez and Gaetano Sabatini eds. *Polycentric Monarchies. How Did Early Modern Spain and Portugal Achieve and Maintain a Global Hegemony?* Brighton: Sussex Academic Press, 2012.

del Carmen Vaquero Serrano, María. "Hacia una Reconstrucción de la Librería del Colegio del Espíritu Santo de Puebla: Inventario de sus Libros, Siglos XVI–XVIII." Thesis for the *Licenciada en Historia*: Benemérita Universidad Autónoma de Puebla, 2006.

"El Maestro Alonso Cedillo (1484–1565): Escritos, Testamento e Inventario: Su Biblioteca," *Lemir: Revista de Literatura Española Medieval y del Renacimiento*, 21 (2017): 33–106.

del Carmen Vázquez Mantecón, María. *La Palabra del Poder: Vida Pública de José María Tornel, 1795–1853*. Mexico City: Universidad Nacional Autónoma de México, 2008.

Carlo, Agustín Millares. *Apuntes para un Estudio Bibliográfico del Humanista Francisco Cervantes de Salazar*. Mexico City: Universidad Nacional Autónoma de México, 1958.

del Castillo Negrete, Emilio. *Galería de Oradores de México en el Siglo XIX*, 3 vols. Mexico City: Tip. de S. Sierra, 1877–1880.

Castillo Ramírez, Elena. *Tusculum I: Humanistas, Anticuarios y Arqueólogos tras los Pasos de Cicerón: Historiografía de Tusculum (Siglos XIV–XIX)*. Rome: L'Erma di Bretschneider, 2005.

Castro Morales, Efraín. *Las Primeras Bibliografías Regionales Hispanoamericanas: Eguiara y sus Corresponsales*. Puebla: Ediciones Altiplano, 1961.

"Los cuadros de castas de la Nueva España," *Jahrbuch für Geschichte von Staat, Wirtschaft, und Gesellschaft Lateinamerikas*, 20 (1983): 671–690.

Cerdan, Francis. "La *Oración Fúnebre* del *Siglo* de *Oro*, entre *Sermón Evangélico y Panegírico Poético Sobre Fondo* de *Teatro*," *Criticón*, *30* (1985): 79–102.

Chakravarti, Ananya. *The Empire of Apostles: Religion, Accommodation, and the Imagination of Empire in Early Modern Brazil and India*. New Delhi: Oxford University Press, 2018.

Chocano Mena, Magdalena. "Colonial Printing and Metropolitan Books: Printed Texts and the Shaping of Scholarly Culture in New Spain, 1539–1700," *Colonial Latin American Historical Review*, 6 (1997): 69–90.

Cieslik, Hubert. "The Training of a Japanese Clergy in the Seventeenth Century," *Studies in Japanese Culture* (1965): 41–78.

Clossey, Luke. *Salvation and Globalization in the Early Jesuit Missions*. New York: Cambridge University Press, 2008.

de los Cobos, Andrés Úbeda. *El Palacio del Rey Planeta. Felipe IV y el Buen Retiro*. Madrid: Museo Nacional del Prado, 2005.

Cohen, Leonardo. *The Missionary Strategies of the Jesuits in Ethiopia (1555–1632)*. Wiesbaden: Harrassowitz, 2009.

Conrad, Sebastian. *What Is Global History?* Princeton, NJ: Princeton University Press, 2016.

Cooper, Michael. *The Japanese Mission to Europe 1582–1590: The Journey of Four Samurai Boys through Portugal, Spain and Italy*. Folkestone: Global Oriental, 2005.

Conover, Cornelius. "Reassessing the Rise of Mexico's Virgin of Guadalupe, 1650s–1780s," *Estudios Mexicanos*, 27 (2011): 251–279.

Coronati, Lia. *Obras Poéticas Latinas de Cayetano de Cabrera y Quintero: Catálogo*. Mexico City: Universidad Nacional Autónoma de México, 1988.

da Costa Nunes, M. *Documentação para a História da Congregação do Oratório de Santa Cruz dos Milagres do Clero Natural de Goa*. Lisbon: Centro de Estudos Históricos Ultramarinos, 1966.

da Costa Ramalho, Américo. *Para a História do Humanismo em Portugal* Coimbra: Imprensa da Universidade de Coimbra, 1988.

de la Costa, Horacio. *The Jesuits in the Philippines, 1581–1768*. Cambridge, MA: Harvard University Press, 1961.

Crewe, Ryan Dominic. "Brave New Spain: An Irishman's Independence Plot in Seventeenth-Century Mexico," *Past and Present*, 207 (2010): 53–87.

Christensen, Mark Z. *Nahua and Maya Catholicisms: Texts and Religion in Colonial Central Mexico and Yucatan*. Stanford, CA: Stanford University Press, 2013.

Cummins, James S. and Nicholas P. Cushner, "Labor in the Colonial Philippines: 'The 'Discurso Parenetico' of Gomez de Espinosa," *Philippine Studies*, 22 (1974): 117–203.

Cutter, Charles. "The Legal System As a Touchstone of Identity in Colonial New Mexico," in Luis Roniger and Tamar Herzog eds. *The Collective and the*

Public in Latin America: Cultural Identities and Political Order. Portland, OR: Sussex Academic Press, 2000: 57–70.

Dandelet, Thomas James. *Spanish Rome, 1500–1700.* New Haven, CT: Yale University Press, 2001.

The Renaissance of Empire in Early Modern Europe. Cambridge: Cambridge University Press, 2014.

D'Elia, Anthony F. *The Renaissance of Marriage in Fifteenth-Century Italy.* Cambridge, MA: Harvard University Press, 2004.

Dean, Carolyn. *Inka Bodies and the Body of Christ: Corpus Christi in Colonial Cuzco, Peru.* Durham, NC: Duke University Press, 1999.

Dench, Emma. *Empire and Political Cultures in the Roman World.* Cambridge: Cambridge University Press, 2018.

Denegre Vaught Peña, Jorge ed. *Dos Siglos de Discursos Patrióticos.* Mexico City: Universidad Nacional Autónoma de México, 2011.

van Deusen, Nancy E. *Global Indios: The Indigenous Struggle for Justice in Sixteenth-Century Spain.* Durham, NC: Duke University Press, 2015.

Doi, Tadao. "Das Sprachstudium der Gesellschaft Jesu in Japan im 16. und 17. Jahrhundert," *Monumenta Nipponica,* 2 (1939): 437–465.

Doyle, John Patrick. "Hispanic Scholastic Philosophy," in James Hankins ed. *The Cambridge Companion to Renaissance Philosophy.* Cambridge: Cambridge University Press, 2007: 250–269.

Durston, Alan. *Pastoral Quechua: The History of Christian Translation in Colonial Peru, 1550–1650.* Notre Dame, IN: University of Notre Dame Press, 2007.

Earle, Rebecca. "If You Eat Their Food …": Diets and Bodies in Early Colonial Spanish America," *The American Historical Review,* 115 (2010): 688–713.

Elliot, J. H. "A Europe of Composite Monarchies," *Past and Present,* 137 (1992): 48–71.

Elison, George. *Deus Destroyed: The Image of Christianity in Early Modern Japan.* Cambridge, MA: Harvard University Press, 1988.

Elisonas, J. S. A. "Journey to the West," *Japanese Journal of Religious Studies,* 34 (2007): 27–66.

Evans, Susan Toby. *"Aztec Palaces and Other Elite Residential Architecture,"* in Susan Toby Evans and Joanne Pillsbury eds. *Palaces of the Ancient New World.* Washington, DC: Dumbarton Oaks Research Library and Collection, 2004: 7–58.

Fabrício, Arnaldo, Sebastião de Pinho and Maria José Pacheco eds., *Orações de Sapiência, 1548–1555.* Coimbra: Imprensa da Universidade de Coimbra, 2011.

Fanego Pérez, Tomás. "'Ad Illustrissimos Fernandum et Helisabeth Hispaniarum Regem et Reginam Potentissimos Alfonsi Ortiz Doctoris Oratio' de Alfonso Ortiz: Edición Crítica de las Versiones Latina y Castellana," *Humanistica Lovaniensia,* 50 (2001): 91–117.

Fantham, Elaine. *The Roman World of Cicero's De Oratore.* New York: Oxford University Press, 2004.

Farge, William J. *The Japanese Translations of the Jesuit Mission Press, 1590–1614: De Imitatione Christi and Guía de Pecadores*. New York: Edwin Mellen Press, 2002.

de Faria, José Custódio. *De Adventu Sancti Spiritus Oratio*. Rome, 1775.

Faulhaber, Charles B. *Latin Rhetorical Theory in Thirteenth and Fourteenth Century Castile* Berkeley: University of California Press, 1972.

Fernandes, Lagrange. "Uma Descrição e Relação 'de Sasatana Peninsula' (1664) do Padre Inácio Arcamone," *AHSI*, 50 (1981): 76–120.

Fernandes Pereira, Belmiro. *Retórica e Eloquência em Portugal na Época do Renascimento*. Lisbon: Imprensa Nacional-Casa da Moeda, 2012.

Fernández-Armesto, Felipe. "The Stranger-Effect in Early Modern Asia," *Itinerario*, 24 (2000): 80–103.

Fernández López, Jorge. "Rhetorical Theory in Sixteenth-Century Spain: A Critical Survey," *Rhetorica: A Journal of the History of Rhetoric*, 20 (2002): 133–148.

Findlen, Paula, Suzanne Sutherland Duchacek, Iva Lelková, "A Jesuit's Letters: Athanasius Kircher at the Edges of his World," forthcoming *American Historical Review*.

Foucault, Michel. *Surveiller et Punir*. Paris: Gallimard, 1975.

Fransen, Sietske. "Latin in a Time of Change: The Choice of Language As Signifier of a New Science?" *Isis*, 108 (2017): 629–635.

Fumaroli, Marc. *L'Age de l'Eloquence: Rhétorique et "Res Literaria," de la Renaissance au Seuil de l'Époque Classique*. Geneva: Librairie Droz, 1980.

Gallagher, John and Ronald Robinson, "The Imperialism of Free Trade," *The Economic History Review*, second series, 6 (1953): 1–15.

Galloway, Andrew. "John Lydgate and the Origins of Vernacular Humanism," *The Journal of English and Germanic Philology*, 107 (2008): 445–471.

García-Abásolo, Antonio. "Mestizos de un país Sin Mestizaje. Mestizos Españoles en Filipinas en la Época Colonial," in Marta Maria Manchado López y Miguel Luque Talaván eds. *Un Mar de Islas, un Mar de Gentes. Población y Diversidad en las Islas Filipinas*. Córdoba: Editorial Universidad de Córdoba, 2014: 223–246.

García Hernán, David. *La Nobleza en la España Moderna*. Madrid: Marcial Pons Historia, 1992.

van Gelderen, Martin. "So Meerly Humane: Theories of Resistance in Early Modern Europe," in Annabel Brett and James Tully eds. *Rethinking the Foundations of Modern Political Thought*. Cambridge: Cambridge University Press, 2006): 149–170.

George, Edward V. "Humanist Traces in Early Colonial Mexico: Texts from the Colegio de Santa Cruz de Tlatelolco," in Ferran Grau Codina, José María Maestre Maestre and Jordi Pérez Durà eds. *Litterae Humaniores: Del Renacimiento a la Ilustración*. Valencia: Universidad de València, 2009: 279–291.

Gerbi, Antonello. *Diego de Leon Pinelo contra Justo Lipsio; una de las Primeras Polémicas sobre el Nuevo Mundo*, 2 vols. Lima: Editorial Lumen, 1945–1946.

von Germeten, Nicole. *Black Blood Brothers: Confraternities and Social Mobility for Afro-Mexicans*. Gainesville: University Press of Florida, 2006.

Gibson, Charles. *Tlaxcala in the Sixteenth Century*. Stanford, CA: Stanford University Press, 1967.

Gil Fernández, Luis. *Panorama Social del Humanismo Español (1500–1800)*, 2nd ed. Madrid: Tecnos, 1997.

Golvers, Noël. *Libraries of Western Learning for China: Circulation of Western Books between Europe and China in the Jesuit Mission (ca. 1650–ca. 1750)*. Leuven: Leuven University Press, 2012.

Gomes, Olivinho J. F. *Konkani Manasagangotri: An Anthology of Early Konkani Literature*. Chandor: Konkani Sorospot Prakashan, 2000.

Gómez Moreno, Ángel. *España y la Italia de los Humanistas*. Madrid: Gredos, 1994.

González Rul, Francisco. *Urbanismo y Arquitectura en Tlatelolco*. Mexico City: Instituto Nacional de Antropología e Historia, 1998.

Grafton, Anthony. *Worlds Made by Words: Scholarship and Community in the Modern West*. Cambridge, MA: Harvard University Press, 2009.

"The Republic of Letters in the American Colonies: Francis Daniel Pastorius Makes a Notebook," *American Historical Review*, 117 (2012): 1–39.

Grafton, Anthony and Lisa Jardine, *From Humanism to the Humanities: Education and the Liberal Arts in Fifteenth- and Sixteenth-Century Europe*. Cambridge, MA: Harvard University Press, 1986.

"Studied for Action: How Gabriel Harvey Read His Livy," *Past and Present*, 129 (1990): 30–78.

Gray, Hanna H. "Renaissance Humanism: The Pursuit of Eloquence," *Journal of the History of Ideas*, 24 (1963): 497–514.

Grendler, Paul F. *Schooling in Renaissance Italy: Literacy and Learning, 1300–1600*. Baltimore: The Johns Hopkins University Press, 1989.

Gruzinski, Serge. *Les Quatre Parties Du Monde: Histoire D'une Mondialisation*. Paris: Points, 2004.

Guerra Medici, María Teresa. "En los Parlamentos del Viejo y Nuevo Mundo. José Basilio Guerra (Campeche, Yucatán, 1790/Roma 1872)," *Diritto@Storia: Revista Internazionale di Scienze Giuridiche e Tradizione Romana*, 12 (2013). www.dirittoestoria.it/11/note&rassegne/Guerra-Medici-Parlamentos-Jose-Basilio-Guerra.htm.

Guillen-Nuñez, Cesar. *Macao's Church of Saint Paul: A Glimmer of the Baroque in China*. Hong Kong: Hong Kong University Press, 2009.

Gustafson, Sandra M. *Imagining Deliberative Democracy in the Early American Republic*. Chicago: University of Chicago Press, 2011.

Habinek, Thomas. *Ancient Rhetoric and Oratory*. Hoboken, NJ: Wiley-Blackwell, 2008.

Hagemann, Matthias. *Iniuria: von den XII-Tafeln bis zur Justinianischen Kodifikation*. Cologne: Böhlau, 1998.

Hamann, Byron Ellsworth. *The Translations of Nebrija: Language, Culture, and Circulation in the Early Modern World*. Amherst: University of Massachusetts Press, 2015.

Hamill, Hugh M. Jr. *The Hidalgo Revolt: Prelude to Mexican Independence.* Gainesville, FL: Praeger, 1966.

Hankins, James. "Renaissance Crusaders: Humanist Crusade Literature in the Age of Mehmed II," *Dumbarton Oaks Papers* 49 (1995): 111–207.

"Exclusivist Republicanism and the Non-Monarchical Republic," *Political Theory*, 38 (2010): 452–482.

"Machiavelli, Civic Humanism, and the Humanist Politics of Virtue," *Italian Culture*, 32 (2014): 98–109.

Virtue Politics: Soulcraft and Statecraft in Renaissance Italy. Cambridge, MA: Harvard University Press, 2019.

Harada, Hiroshi. *Kirishitan Shisai Goto Migeru no Latengo no Shi to Sono Insatsusha Saisho Migeru wo Megutte* キリシタン司祭後藤ミゲルのラテン語の詩とその印刷者税所ミゲルをめぐって. Tokyo: Kindaibungeisha, 1998.

Haskell, Yasmin. *Loyola's Bees: Ideology and Industry in Jesuit Latin Didactic Poetry.* Oxford: British Academy, 2003.

Helmrath, Johannes. "Diffusion des Humanismus. Zur Einführung," in Johannes Helmrath, Ulrich Muhlack and Gerrit Walther eds. *Diffusion des Humanismus: Studien zur Nationalen Geschichtsschreibung Europäischer Humanisten.* Göttingen: Wallstein Verlag, 2002: 9–29.

"Der Europäische Humanismus und die Funktionen der Rhetorik," in Thomas Maissen und Gerrit Walther eds. *Funktionen des Humanismus. Studien zum Nutzen des Neuen in der Humanistischen Kultur.* Göttingen: Wallstein Verlag, 2006: 18–48.

Henn, Alexander. *Hindu-Catholic Encounters in Goa: Religion, Colonialism, and Modernity.* Bloomington: Indiana University Press, 2014.

Heredia, Roberto. "Eguiara y Eguren, las Voces Concordes," *Literatura Mexicana*, 8 (1997): 511–549.

Herrejón Peredo, Carlos. *Del Sermón al Discurso Cívico: México, 1760–1834.* Zamora: El Colegio de Michoacán A.C., 2003.

Herrera, Arnulfo. "Los traspiés de un sermón famoso: 'Fe de erratas al licenciado Suazo de Coscojales,' de Pedro de Avendaño," in Ignacio Arellano Ayuso, Antonio Lorente Medina eds. *Poesía Satírica y Burlesca en la Hispanoamérica Colonial.* Madrid: Iberoamericana Editorial, 2009: 191–206.

Herzog, Tamar. "¿Letrado o Teólogo? Sobre el Oficio de la Justicia a Principios del Siglo XVIII," in Johannes Michael Scholz ed. *Fallstudien zur Spanischen und Portugiesischen Justiz (16.–20. Jahrhundert).* Frankfurt: Rechtsprechung, 1994: 697–714.

Defining Nations: Immigrants and Citizens in Early Modern Spain and Spanish America. New Haven, CT: Yale University Press, 2003.

Upholding Justice: Society, State, and the Penal System in Quito (1650–1750). Ann Arbor: University of Michigan Press, 2004.

"Los Americanos Frente a la Monarquía: el Criollismo y la Naturaleza Española," in Antonio Álvarez-Ossorio Alvariño and Bernardo J. García García eds. *La Monarquía de las Naciones. Patria, Nación y Naturaleza en la Monarquía de España*. Madrid: Fundación Carlos de Amberes, 2004: 77–92.

Frontiers of Possession: Spain and Portugal in Europe and the Americas. Cambridge, MA: Harvard University Press, 2015.

Hesselink, Reiner H. "The *Capitães Mores* of the Japan Voyage: A Group Portrait," *International Journal of Asian Studies*, 9 (2012), 1–41.

"*I Go Shopping in Christian Nagasaki*: Entries from the Diary of a Mito Samurai, Ōwada Shigekiyo (1593)," *Bulletin of Portuguese/Japanese Studies*, ser. II, 1 (2015): 27–45.

The Dream of Christian Nagasaki: World Trade and the Clash of Cultures, 1560–1640. Jefferson, NC: McFarland, 2016.

Hoffman, Martha K. *Raised to Rule: Educating Royalty at the Court of the Spanish Habsburgs, 1601–1634*. Baton Rouge: Louisiana State University Press, 2011.

Hsia, Adrian and Ruprecht Wimmer, *Mission und Theater: Japan und China auf den Bühnen der Gesellschaft Jesu*. Regensburg: Schnell & Steiner, 2005.

Hsia Po-Hsia, Ronnie. *A Jesuit in the Forbidden City: Matteo Ricci 1552–1610*. New York: Oxford University Press, 2010.

Hugo-Brunt, Michael. "The Jesuit Seminary and Church of St. Joseph, Macao," *Journal of the Society of Architectural Historians*, 15 (1956): 24–30.

Ieong, Helen Hoi Keng, "An Exploration of Documents from Catholic and Buddhist Sources in Macao Libraries," *Revista de Cultura (Macau)*, 5 (2003): 6–25.

Irving, D. R. M. *Colonial Counterpoint. Music in Early Modern Manila*. New York: Oxford University Press, 2010.

Israel, Jonathan. "Mexico and the 'General Crisis' of the Seventeenth Century," *Past and Present*, 63 (1974): 33–57.

Jones, Jacqueline. "Performing the Sacred: Song, Genre, and Aesthetics in *Bhakti*." Ph.D. dissertation: University of Chicago, 2008.

José, Regalado Trota. *Impreso: Philippine Imprints, 1593–1811*. Makati: Fundación Santiago, 1993.

Kagan, Richard. *Students and Society in Early Modern Spain*. Baltimore: The Johns Hopkins University Press, 1974.

Kamen, Henry. *Empire: How Spain Became a World Power, 1492–1763*. New York: Harper Perennial, 2004.

Karttunen, Frances. "From Court Yard to the Seat of Government: The Career of Antonio Valeriano, Nahua Colleague of Bernardino De Sahagún," *Amérindia*, 19 (1995): 113–120.

Kawamura, Shinzo. "Humanism, Pedagogy, and Language: Alessandro Valignano and the Global Significance of Juan Bonifacio's Work Printed in Macao (1588)," in *O Humanismo Latino e as Culturas do Extremo Oriente*. Treviso: Fondazione Cassamarca, 2006: 143–155.

Keeline, Thomas J. *The Reception of Cicero in the Early Roman Empire: The Rhetorical Schoolroom and the Creation of a Cultural Legend*. Cambridge: Cambridge University Press, 2018.

Keeline, Thomas and Stuart M. McManus, "Benjamin Larnell, the Last Latin Poet at Harvard Indian College," *Harvard Studies in Classical Philology*, 108 (2015), 621–642.

Kellogg, Susan. *Law and the Transformation of Aztec Culture, 1500–1700*. Norman: University of Oklahoma Press, 1995.

Keṇī, Candrakānta and Murgaon Mutt Sankul Samiti. *Saraswats in Goa and Beyond*. Goa: Murgaon Mutt Sankul Samiti, 1998.

Kennedy, George A. *Comparative Rhetoric: An Historical and Cross-Cultural Introduction*. New York: Oxford University Press, 1998.

Classical Rhetoric and Its Christian and Secular Tradition from Ancient to Modern Times. Chapel Hill: University of North Carolina Press, 1999.

Kirk, Thomas Allison. *Genoa and the Sea: Policy and Power in an Early Modern Maritime Republic, 1559–1684*. Baltimore: The Johns Hopkins University Press, 2005.

Kishimoto, Emi. "The Adaptation of the European Polyglot Dictionary of Calepino in Japan: *Dictionarium Latino Lusitanicum, ac Iaponicum* (1595)," in Otto Zwartjes and Cristina Altman eds. *Missionary Linguistics II/Lingüística Misionera II: Orthography and Phonology*. Philadelphia: John Benjamins Publishing Company, 2005: 205–223.

Kittel, Ferdinand. *A Kannada-English Dictionary*. Mangalore: The Basel Mission Book & Tract Depository, 1894.

Klaus, Susanne. *Uprooted Christianity: The Preaching of the Christian Doctrine in Mexico Based on Franciscan Sermons of the 16th Century Written in Nahuatl*. Markt Schwaben: Saurwein, 1999.

Klor de Alva, Jorge. "Colonialism and Postcolonialism As (Latin) American Mirages," *Colonial Latin American Review*, 1 (1992): 3–23.

"The Postcolonialism of the (Latin) American Experience: A Reconsideration of 'Colonialism,' 'Postcolonialism,' and 'Mestizaje,'" in Gyan Prakash ed. *After Colonialism: Imperial Histories and Displacements*. Princeton, NJ: Princeton University Press, 1994: 241–275.

Konrad, Herman W. *A Jesuit Hacienda in Colonial Mexico: Santa Lucía, 1576–1767*. Stanford, CA: Stanford University Press, 1980.

Kostyanovsky, Lucy Wooding. "From Tudor Humanism to Reformation Preaching," in Peter McCullough, Hugh Adlington and Emma Rhatigan eds. *The Oxford Handbook to the Early Modern Sermon*. Oxford: Oxford University Press, 2011: 329–347.

Kraye, Jill. "Marcus Aurelius and Neostoicism in Early Modern Philosophy," in Marcel van Ackeren ed. *Blackwell Companion to Marcus Aurelius*. Oxford: Wiley-Blackwell, 2012: 515–531.

Kristeller, Paul Oskar. *The Classics and Renaissance Thought*. Cambridge, MA: Harvard University Press, 1955.

"The European Diffusion of Italian Humanism," *Italica*, 39 (1962): 1–20.

"An Unknown Humanist Sermon on St. Stephen by Guillaume Fichet," in *Mélanges Eugène Tisserant*, 7 vols. Vatican City: Biblioteca Apostolica Vaticana, 1964): VI, 459–497.

Studies in Renaissance Thought and Letter, 4 vols. Rome: Edizioni di storia e letteratura, 1996.

Krause, Miller Stanley. "Prose Rhythm in the Orations and Epistles of Marcus Antonius Muretus." Masters Thesis, University of Kentucky, 2009.

Kulkarni, A. "Marathi Records on Village Communities in Goa Archives," *The Indian Economic and Social History Review* 19, (1982): 377–385.

Lach, Donald Frederick. *Asia in the Making of Europe*, 2 vols. Chicago: University of Chicago Press, 1965.

Lafaye, Jacques. "Literature and Intellectual Life in Colonial Spanish America," in Leslie Bethell ed. *The Cambridge History of Latin America*, 11 vols. Cambridge: Cambridge University Press 1984.

Laird, Andrew. "Patriotism and the Rise of Latin in Eighteenth-Century New Spain: Disputes of the New World and the Jesuit Constructions of a Mexican Legacy," *Renaessanceforum*, 7 (2012): 163–193.

"Nahuas and Caesars: Classical Learning and Bilingualism in Post-Conquest Mexico; An Inventory of Latin Writings by Authors of the Native Nobility," *Classical Philology*, 109 (2014): 150–169.

Lane, Kris E. *The Colour of Paradise: Emeralds in the Age of the Gunpowder Empires*. New Haven, CT: Yale University Press, 2010.

Lawrance, Jeremy N. H. "Humanism in the Iberian Peninsula," in Anthony Goodman and Angus MacKay eds. *The Impact of Humanism on Western Europe*. London: Routledge, 1990: 220–258.

Lavallé, Bernard. *Las Promesas Ambiguas: Ensayos sobre el Criollismo Colonial en los Andes*. Lima: Pontificia Universidad Católica del Péru, 1993.

Lecea, Joaquín. *Las Escuelas Pías de Aragón en el Siglo XVIII*. Madrid: Publicaciones ICCE, 1972.

Leibsohn, Dana and Stuart M. McManus. "Eloquence and Ethnohistory: Indigenous Loyalty, Chinese Treachery and the Making of a Tagalog *Letrado*," *Colonial Latin American Review*, 27 (2018): 522–574.

León-Portilla, Miguel. "La Embajada De Los Japoneses En México, 1614. El Testimonio En Nahuatl Del Cronista Chimalpahin," *Estudios de Asia y Africa*, 16 (1981): 215–241.

Lewis, Martin W. and Kären Wigen, *The Myth of Continents: A Critique of Metageography* Berkeley: University of California Press, 1997.

Lewy, Guenter. *Constitutionalism and Statecraft during the Golden Age of Spain: A Study of the Political Philosophy of Juan de Mariana*, S. J. Geneva: Librairie E. Droz, 1960.

van Liere, Katherine Elliot. "Humanism and Scholasticism in Sixteenth-Century Academe: Five Student Orations from the University of Salamanca," *Renaissance Quarterly*, 53 (2000): 57–107.

Lletget, Alejandro Coroleu. "Angelo Poliziano in Print: Editions and Commentaries from a Pedagogical Perspective (1500–1560)," *Cahiers de l'Humanisme*, 2 (2001), 191–222.

Lockhart, James. *The Nahuas after the Conquest: A Social and Cultural History of the Indians of Central Mexico, Sixteenth through Eighteenth Centuries*. Stanford, CA: Stanford University Press, 1992.

Lockhart, James. *Of Things of the Indies: Essays Old and New in Early Latin American History*. Stanford, CA: Stanford University Press, 1999.

Lopez-Gay, Jesus. "La Primera Biblioteca de los Jesuitas en el Japón (1556). Su Contenido y su Influencia." *Monumenta Nipponica*, 15 (1959): 350–379.

Lopez-Portillo, Jose-Juan. *"Another Jerusalem" Political Legitimacy and Courtly Government in the Kingdom of New Spain (1535–1568)*. Leiden: Brill, 2017.

Lorca, Arnulf Becker. *Mestizo International Law: A Global Intellectual History 1842–1933*. Cambridge: Cambridge University Press, 2014.

Lourenço, José. *The Parish Churches of Goa: A Study of Façade Architecture*. Margao: Amazing Goa Publications, 2005.

Lowe, Kate. "'Representing' Africa: Ambassadors and Princes from Christian Africa to Renaissance Italy and Portugal, 1402–1608," *Transactions of the Royal Historical Society*, 17 (2007): 101–128.

Luk, Bernard Lung-Kay. "Aleni Introduces the Western Academic Tradition to Seventeenth-Century China: A Study of the *Xixue Fan*," in Tiziana Lippiello and Roman Malek eds. *"Scholar from the West." Giulio Aleni S. J. (1582–1649) and the Dialogue between Christianity and China*. Brescia: Fondazione Civiltà Bresciana, 1997: 479–518.

Luque Talaván, Miguel. "Descubriendo las Luces de un Rico Diamante. El Progreso de las Filipinas en el Pensamiento Económico del Siglo Ilustrado," in Martínez Lopez-Cano, María del Pilar and Leonor Ludlow eds. *Historia del Pensamiento Económico: del Mercantilismo al Liberalismo*. Mexico City: Universidad Nacional Autónoma de México, 2007: 169–209.

MacCormack, Sabine. "Latin Prose Panegyrics: Tradition and Discontinuity in the Later Roman Empire," *Revue d'Etudes Augustiniennes et Patristiques*, 22 (1976): 29–77.

On the Wings of Time: Rome, the Incas, Spain, and Peru. Princeton, NJ: Princeton University Press, 2007.

MacKay, Ruth. *The Limits of Royal Authority: Resistance and Obedience in Seventeenth-Century Castile*. New York: Cambridge University Press, 1999.

MacLachlan, Colin M. *Spain's Empire in the New World: The Role of Ideas in Institutional and Social Change*. Berkeley: University of California Press, 1988.

Mack, Peter. *A History of Renaissance Rhetoric (1380–1620)*. Oxford: Oxford University Press, 2011.

Madrigal, José Luis. "Cervantes de Salazar, Francisco," *Real Academia de la Historia*. http://dbe.rah.es/biografias/11971/francisco-cervantes-de-salazar.

Makdisi, George. *The Rise of Humanism in Classical Islam and the Christian West with Special Reference to Scholasticism*. Edinburgh: Edinburgh University Press, 1990.

Malpan, Varghese. *A Comparative Study of the Bhagavad-gītā and the Spiritual Exercises of Saint Ignatius of Loyola on the Process of Spiritual Liberation*. Rome: Gregorian & Biblical Press, 1992.

Manchado López, Marta M. *Conflictos Iglesia-Estado en el Extremo Oriente Ibérico Filipinas (1767–1787)*. Murcia: Universidad de Murcia, 1994.

Maravall, José Antonio. *Estado Moderno y Mentalidad Social (Siglos XV a XVII)*, 2 vols. Madrid: Revista de Occidente, 1972.

La Cultura del Barroco: Análisis de una Estructura Histórica. Barcelona: Esplugues de Llobregat, 1975.

Teoría del Estado en España en el Siglo XVII. Madrid: Centro de Estudios Constitucionales, 1997.

Marques, João Francisco. *A Parenética Portuguesa e a Dominação Filipina*. Porto: Imprensa Nacional Casa da Moeda, 1986.

Martín, Luís. *La Conquista Intelectual del Perú. El Colegio Jesuita de San Pablo 1568–1767*. Barcelona: Editorial Casiopea, 2001.

Martínez, María Elena. *Genealogical Fictions: Limpieza de Sangre, Religion, and Gender in Colonial Mexico*. Stanford, CA: Stanford University Press, 2008.

Martínez Peláez, Severo. *La Patria del Criollo: Ensayo de Interpretación de la Realidad Colonial Guatemalteca*, 4th ed. Guatemala City: Fondo de Cultura Económica, 1976.

Masferrer León, Cristina Verónica. "Por las Ánimas de Negros Bozales: Las Cofradías de Personas de Origen Africano en la Ciudad de México (Siglo XVII)," *Cuicuilco*, 18 (2011): 83–104.

Masters, Adrian. "A Thousand Invisible Architects: Vassals, the Petition and Response System, and the Creation of Spanish Imperial Caste Legislation," *Hispanic American Historical Review*, 98 (2018): 377–406.

Mattingly, Garrett. *Renaissance Diplomacy*. London: Jonathan Cape, 1955.

Mawson, Stephanie. "Philippine Indios in the Service of Empire: Indigenous Soldiers and Contingent Loyalty," *Ethnohistory*, 63 (2016): 381–413.

Maxson, Brian. *The Humanist World of Renaissance Florence*. Cambridge: Cambridge University Press, 2014.

Mazín, Óscar and José Javier Ruiz Ibáñez eds., *Las Indias Occidentales: Procesos de Incorporación Territorial a las Monarquías Ibéricas (siglos XVI a XVIII)*. Mexico City: El Colegio de México, 2012.

Menegus Bornemann, Margarita. "El Cacicazgo en Nueva España," in Margarita Menegus Bornemann and Rodolfo Aguirre Salvador eds. *El Cacicazgo en Nueva España y Filipinas*. Mexico City: Plaza y Valdes, 2005: 13–70.

Menegus Bornemann, Margarita and Rodolfo Aguirre Salvador, *Los Indios, el Sacerdocio y la Universidad en Nueva España, Siglos XVI–XVIII*. Mexico City: Plaza y Valdes, 2006.

Mestre Sanchis, Antonio. *Manuel Martí, el Deán de Alicante*. Alicante: Gil-Albert, 2003.

McCrea, Lawrence. "Standards and Practices: Following, Making, and Breaking the Rules of Śāstra," in Yigal Bronner, Whitney Cox and Lawrence McCrea eds. *New Directions in South Asian Studies: Critical Engagements with Sheldon Pollock*. Ann Arbor MI: Association for Asian Studies, 2011: 229–244.

McDonogh, Gary W. *Iberian Worlds*. New York: Routledge, 2009.

McDonough, Kelly S. *The Learned Ones: Nahua Intellectuals in Postconquest Mexico*. Tucson: University of Arizona Press, 2014.

McGuinnes, Frederick J. *Right Thinking and Sacred Oratory in Counter-Reformation Rome.* Princeton. NJ: Princeton University Press, 1997.

McManamon, John M. *Funeral Oratory and the Cultural Ideals of Italian Humanism.* Chapel Hill: The University of North Carolina Press, 1989.

McManus, Stuart M. "The Art of Being a Colonial *Letrado*: Learned Sociability and Urban Life in Eighteenth-Century Mexico City," *Estudios de Historia Novohispana,* 56 (2017): 40–64.

"*Classica Americana*: An Addendum to the Censuses of Pre-1800 Latin Texts from British North America," *Humanistica Lovaniensia: Journal of Neo-Latin Studies,* 67.2 (2018): 421–461.

"The *Bibliotheca Mexicana* Controversy and Creole Patriotism in Early Modern Mexico," *Hispanic American Historical Review,* 98.1 (2018): 1–41.

"Imperial History without Provincial Loyalty? Reading Roman History in Renaissance Japan," *KNOW: A Journal on the Formation of Knowledge,* 3.1 (2019): 123–157.

"World Philology: Indo-Humanism and Jesuit Indigenous-Language Scholarship in the Americas and Asia," in Ines G. Županov ed. *Oxford Handbook of Jesuit History.* New York: Oxford University Press, 2019: 737–758.

Meliá, Bartomeu. *La Lengua Guaraní Del Paraguay: Historia, Sociedad y Literatura.* Madrid: Editorial MAPFRE, 1992.

de Melo, Carlos Mercês. *The Recruitment and Formation of the Native Clergy in India (16th–19th Century): An Historico-Canonical Study.* Lisbon: Agência Geral do Ultramar, 1955.

"El cacicazgo en Nueva España," in Margarita Menegus Bornemann and Rodolfo Aguirre Salvador eds. *El Cacicazgo en Nueva España y Filipinas.* Mexico City: Plaza y Valdes, 2005: 13–70.

Merola, Alberto. *Dizionario Biografico Degli Italiani,* 81 vols. Rome: Istituto della Enciclopedia Italiana, 1960–2014.

Meznar, Joan. "Our Lady of the Rosary, African Slaves, and the Struggle against Heretics in Brazil, 1550–1660," *Journal of Early Modern History,* 9 (2005): 371–397.

Mignolo, Walter D. *The Darker Side of the Renaissance: Literacy, Territoriality, and Colonization.* Ann Arbor: University of Michigan Press, 1995.

Milner, Stephen J. "'Le Sottili Cose non si Possono Bene Aprire in Volgare': Vernacular Oratory and the Transmission of Classical Rhetorical Theory in the Late Medieval Italian Communes," *Italian Studies* 64 (2009): 221–244.

Miranda, Rocky. *The Old Konkani Bhārata.* Mysore: Central Institute of Indian Languages, 2011.

Moran, Joseph. *The Japanese and the Jesuits: Alessandro Valignano in Sixteenth Century Japan.* New York: Routledge, 1993.

Morstein-Marx, Robert. *Mass Oratory and Political Power in the Late Roman Republic.* New York: Cambridge University Press, 2004.

Moss, Ann. *Printed Commonplace Books and the Structuring of Renaissance Thought*. Oxford: Clarendon Press, 1996.

Mouren, Raphaële. "La Rhétorique Antique au Service de la Diplomatie Moderne: Piero Vettori et l'Ambassade Florentine au Pape Jules III," *Journal de la Renaissance*, 1 (2000): 121–154.

Mundy, Barbara E. *The Death of Aztec Tenochtitlan, the Life of Mexico City*. Austin: University of Texas Press, 2015.

Murphy, James J. and Michael Winterbottom, "Raffaele Regio's 1492 Quaestio Doubting Cicero's Authorship of the Rhetorica Ad Herennium: Introduction and Text." *Rhetorica: A Journal of the History of Rhetoric*, 17 (1999): 77–87.

Nauwelaerts, Marcel A. "Humanisme en Onderwijs," in *Antwerpen in de XVIde eeuw*. Antwerp: Mercurius, 1975: 257–300.

Nemser, Daniel. "Archaeology in the Lettered City," *Colonial Latin American Review*, 23 (2014): 197–223.

Norden, Eduard. *Die Antike Kunstprosa: vom VI. Jahrhundert v. Chr. bis in die Zeit der Renaissance*, 2 vols. Berlin: Nabu Press, 1915.

Nunes Pereira, António. *A Arquiectura Religiosa Cristã de Velha Goa: Segunda Metade do Século XVI – Primeiras Décadas do Século XVIII*. Lisbon: Fundação Oriente, 2005.

Núñez González, Juan María. "Las cláusulas métricas Latinas en el Renacimiento," *Latomus*, 53 (1994): 80–94.

Oestreich, Gerhard. *Neostoicism and the Early Modern State*. Cambridge: Cambridge University Press, 1982.

O'Hanlon, Rosalind and Christopher Minkowski. "What Makes People Who They Are? Pandit Networks and the Problem of Livelihoods in Early Modern Western India," *The Indian Economic & Social History Review*, 45 (2008): 381–416.

Okenfuss, Max J. *The Rise and Fall of Latin Humanism in Early-Modern Russia: Pagan Authors, Ukrainians, and the Resiliency of Muscovy*. New York: Brill, 1995.

Oliveira Costa, João Paulo and Vítor Luís Gaspar Rodrigues, *Conquista de Goa, 1510–1512: Campanhas de Alfonso de Albuquerque*. Lisbon: Tribuna da História, 2008.

O'Malley, John W. *Praise and Blame in Renaissance Rome: Rhetoric, Doctrine, and Reform in the Sacred Orators of the Papal Court, c. 1450–1521*. Durham, NC: Duke University Press, 1979.

  The First Jesuits. Cambridge, MA: Harvard University Press, 1993.

Orso, Steven N. *Art and Death at the Spanish Habsburg Court: The Royal Exequies for Philip IV*. Columbia: University of Missouri Press, 1989.

Osgood, Josiah. *Rome and the Making of a World State, 150 BCE–20 CE*. Cambridge: Cambridge University Press, 2018.

Osorio, Alejandra B. *Inventing Lima: Baroque Modernity in Peru's South Sea Metropolis*. Basingstoke: Palgrave Macmillan, 2008.

Osorio Romero, Ignacio. *Tópicos sobre Cicerón en México*. Mexico City: Universidad Nacional Autónoma de México, 1976.

Colegios y Profesores Jesuitas que Enseñaron Latín en Nueva España (1572–1767). Mexico City: Universidad Nacional Autónoma de México, 1979.

Floresta de Gramática, Poética y Retórica en Nueva España (1521–1767). Mexico City: Universidad Nacional Autónoma de México, 1980.

La Enseñanza del Latín a los Indios. Mexico City: Universidad Nacional Autónoma de México, 1990.

El Sueño Criollo: José Antonio de Villerías y Roelas (1695–1728). Mexico City: Universidad Nacional Autónoma de México, 1991.

Owensby, Brian Philip. *Empire of Law and Indian Justice in Colonial Mexico*. Stanford, CA: Stanford University Press, 2008.

Pacheco, Diego. "Diogo de Mesquita, S. J. and the Jesuit Mission Press," *Monumenta Nipponica*, 26 (1971): 431–443.

"Los Cuatro Legados Japoneses de los Daimyos de Kyushu Después de Regresar a Japón," *Boletín de la Asociación Española de Orientalistas*, 10 (1973): 19–58.

Padron, Ricardo. "A Sea of Denial: The Early Modern Spanish Invention of the Pacific Rim," *Hispanic Review*, 77 (2009): 1–28.

Pagden, Anthony. "Identity Formation in Spanish America," in Nicholas Canny and Anthony Pagden eds. *Colonial Identity in the Atlantic World, 1500–1800*. Princeton, NJ: Princeton University Press, 1987: 51–93.

Lords of All the World: Ideologies of Empire in Spain, Britain and France c. 1500–c. 1800. New Haven, CT: Yale University Press, 1995.

Paquette, Gabriel B. *Enlightenment, Governance, and Reform in Spain and Its Empire, 1759–1808*. Basingstoke: Palgrave Macmillan, 2008.

Parker, Geoffrey. *The Army of Flanders and the Spanish Road 1567–1659: The Logistics of Spanish Victory and Defeat in Low Countries' Wars*. Cambridge: Cambridge University Press, 1972.

The Dutch Revolt. Ithaca, NY: Cornell University Press, 1977.

"Crisis and Catastrophe: The Global Crisis of the Seventeenth Century Reconsidered," *The American Historical Review* 113 (2008): 1053–1079.

Patil, Urmila Rajshekhar. "Conflict, Identity and Narratives: The Brahman Communities of Western India from the Seventeenth through the Nineteenth Centuries." Ph.D. Dissertation, University of Texas at Austin, 2010.

Pawling, Perla Chinchilla. *De la Compositio Loci a La República de las Letras: Predicación Jesuita en el Siglo XVII Novohispano*. Mexico City: UIA, 2004.

Pereira, Antonio. *The Makers of Konkani Literature*. Goa: Pilar, 1982.

Pereira, José. "Gaspar de S. Miguel's *Arte da Lingoa Canarim, Parte 2a, Sintaxis Copiossisima na Lingoa Bramana e Pollida*," *Journal of the University of Bombay*, 36 (1967): 1–155.

Konkani: A Language; A History of the Konkani Marathi Controversy. Dharward: Karnatak University, 1971.

Phillips, Carla Rahn. *Six Galleons for the King of Spain: Imperial Defense in the Early Seventeenth Century*. Baltimore: The Johns Hopkins University Press, 1986.

Pinto, J. A. Abranches and Henri Bernard, "Les Instructions du Père Valignano pour l'Ambassade Japonaise en Europe. (Goa, 12 Décembre 1583)," *Monumenta Nipponica*, 6 (1943): 391–403.

Pinto, Jeanette. *Slavery in Portuguese India, 1510–1842*. Bombay, NY: South Asia Books, 1992.

Pissurlencar, Panduronga. "A Propósito dos Primeiros Livros Maratas Impressos em Goa," *Boletim do Instituto Vasco da Gama*, 73 (1956): 55–79.

Pollmann, Judith. *Catholic Identity and the Revolt of the Netherlands, 1520–1635*. Oxford: Oxford University Press, 2011.

Pollnitz, Aysha. "Old Words and the New World: Liberal Education and the Franciscans in New Spain, 1536–1601," *Transactions of the Royal Historical Society*, 27 (2017): 123–152.

Pollock, Sheldon. *The Language of the Gods in the World of Men: Sanskrit, Culture, and Power in Premodern India*. Berkeley: University of California Press, 2006.

"Literary Culture and Manuscript Culture in Precolonial India," in Simon Eliot, Andrew Nash and Ian Willison eds. *History of the Book and Literary Cultures*. London: British Library, 2006: 77–94.

Pomplun, Trent. *Jesuit on the Roof of the World: Ippolito Desideri's Mission to Eighteenth-century Tibet*. New York: Oxford University Press, 2010.

Ponce Cárdenas, Jesús. "El *Panegírico al Duque de Lerma*. Trascendencia de un Modelo Gongorino (1617–1705)," *Mélanges de la Casa de Velázquez*, 42.1 (2012): 71–93.

Ponce Leiva, Pilar. "Séneca en los Andes. Neoestoicismo y Crítica Social en Quito a Fines del Siglo XVII," *Histórica (Lima)*, 31 (2007): 43–68.

Portilla, Miguel León. *Aztec Thought and Culture: A Study of the Ancient Nahuatl Mind*. Norman: University of Oklahoma Press, 1963: 137–143.

Prabhudesai, V. B. "Vanavályãñcô Maḷô by Father Miguel de Almeida", *Nagpur University Journal (Humanities)*, 21 (1970–1): 1–110.

Premo, Bianca. *The Enlightenment on Trial: Ordinary Litigants and Colonialism in the Spanish Empire*. New York: Oxford University Press, 2017.

Primmer, Adolf. *Cicero Numerosus. Studien zum Antiken Prosarhythmus*. Vienna: Bohlau, 1968.

Priolkar, Anant Kakba. *The Goa Inquisition: Being a Quatercentenary Commemoration Study of the Inquisition in India*. Bombay: Bombay University Press, 1961.

Priyadarshini, Meha. *Chinese Porcelain in Colonial Mexico: The Material Worlds of an Early Modern Trade*. Cham: Springer International Publishing, 2018.

de la Puente Luna, José Carlos. *Andean Cosmopolitans: Seeking Justice and Reward at the Spanish Royal Court*. Austin: University of Texas Press, 2018.

Rabil, Albert Jr. *Knowledge, Goodness and Power: The Debate over Nobility among Quattrocento Italian Humanists.* Binghamton, NY: Medieval & Renaissance Texts & Studies, 1991.

Rafael, Vicente L. *Contracting Colonialism: Translation and Christian Conversion in Tagalog Society under Early Spanish Rule.* Ithaca, NY: Duke University Press, 1988.

Rama, Ángel. *La Ciudad Letrada.* Hanover, MD: Ediciones del Norte, 1984.

Ramírez, Rueda. "Libreros y Librerías: la Ofera Eultural en el Mundo Moderno," in Marina Garone Gravier ed. *Miradas a la Cultura del Libro en Puebla: Bibliotecas, Tipógrafos, Grabadores, Libreros y Ediciones en la Época Colonial.* Mexico City: Gobierno de Puebla, 2012: 377–400.

Rappaport, Joanne. *The Disappearing Mestizo: Configuring Difference in the Colonial New Kingdom of Granada.* Durham, NC: Duke University Press, 2014.

"Ratio atque Institutio Studiorum Societatis Iesu [1599]," in *Monumenta Paedagogica Societatis Iesu*, Ladislaus Lukács ed., 5 vols. Rome, 1965–86: V, 355–454.

Relationi della Venvta Degli Ambasciatori Giaponesi a Roma Fino alla Partita di Lisbona: con le Accoglienze Fatte Loro da Tutti i Principi Christiani per Doue Sono Passati. Rome, 1586.

Relatione delle Sontuose Esequie Fatte dall'Illustriss. e Reuerendiss. Capitolo, e Canonici della Sacrosanta Basilica di S. Maria Maggiore in Roma, alla Gloriosa Memoria di Filippo Quarto, Re delle Spagne: con Alcune Osseruationi sopra i Particolari del Funerale. Rome, 1666.

Rerum Aethiopicarum Scriptores Occidentales Inediti a Saeculo XVI ad XIX, Camillo Beccari ed., 15 vols. Rome, 1903–1917.

Restall, Matthew. *Seven Myths of the Spanish Conquest.* New York: Oxford University Press, 2003.

del Rey Fajardo, José. *La República de las Letras en la Venezuela Colonial.* Caracas: Fuentes para la Historia Colonial de Venezuela, 2007.

Ricard, Robert. *La "Conquète Spirituelle" Du Mexique.* Paris: Institut d'Ethnologie, 1933.

Rico, Francisco. *El Sueño de Humanismo.* Madrid: Editorial Crítica, 1993.

Rivas Sacconi, José Manuel. *El Latín en Colombia: Bosquejo Histórico del Humanismo Colombiano*, 3rd ed. Bogota: Instituto Caro y Cuervo, 1993.

Rodríguez, Jaime E. *"We Are Now the True Spaniards": Sovereignty, Revolution, Independence, and the Emergence of the Federal Republic of Mexico, 1808–1824.* Stanford, CA: Stanford University Press, 2012.

Rovira, José Carlos. *Entre dos Culturas. Voces de Identidad Hispanoamericana.* Alicante: Universidad de Alicante, 1995.

Ruderman, David B. ed. *Preachers of the Italian Ghetto.* Berkeley: University of California Press, 1992.

Ruiz Bañuls, Mónica. *El Huehuetlatolli: Como Discurso Sincrético En El Proceso Evangelizador Novohispano El Siglo XVI.* Rome: Bulzoni, 2009.

Ruiz Ibáñez, José Javier. "Les Acteurs de l'Hégémonie Hispanique, du Monde à la Péninsule Ibérique," *Annales. Histoire, Sciences Sociales*, 69 (2014): 927–954.

Rummel, Erika. "Marineo Sículo: A Protagonist of Humanism in Spain," *Renaissance Quarterly*, 50 (1997): 701–722.

Saarinen, Risto. "Virtus Heroica. 'Held' und 'Genie' als Begriffe des Christlichen Aristotelismus," *Archiv für Begriffsgeschichte*, 33 (1990): 96–114.

Salgado, Félix Herrero. *La Oratoria Sagrada Española de los Siglos XVI y XVII*, 2 vols. Madrid: Fundación Universitaria Española, 1996–1998.

de Santa María, Carmelo Sáenz. *Historia de la Educación Jesuítica en Guatemala*. Madrid: Instituto Gonzalo Fernández de Oviedo, 1978.

Sarreal, Julia J. S. *The Guaraní and Their Missions: A Socioeconomic History*. Stanford, CA: Stanford University Press, 2014.

Sato, Masaki. "Revisando a Criollos y al Criollismo en el Virreinato Peruano del Siglo XVII: el Caso de Fray Buenaventura de Salinas y Córdova," *Historia y Cultura* (Lima), 27 (2015): 83–114.

Sánchez Aguilera, María. "Jesucristo, Pontífice de los Bienes Futuros: Un Sermón en Náhuatl de Fray Bernardino de Sahagún," *Estudios de Cultura Náhuatl*, 48 (2014): 265–299.

Saulini, Mirella. "Tra Erasmo e Cicerone: l'Eclettismo Oratorio di Stefano Tuccio, S.J. (1540–1597)," *AHSI*, 78. 15 (2009): 141–221.

Sanders, James E. *The Vanguard of the Atlantic World: Creating Modernity, Nation, and Democracy in Nineteenth-Century Latin America*. Durham, NC: Duke University Press Books, 2014.

Schaub, Jean-Frédéric. *Portugal na Monarquia Hispânica*. Lisbon: Livros Horizonte, 2001.

Schäfer-Sevilla, Ernst. "Der Verkehr Spaniens mit und in seinen amerikanischen Kolonien," *Ibero-amerikanisches Archiv*, 11 (1937/38): 435–455.

Scheidel, Walter ed., *Rome and China: Comparative Perspectives on Ancient World Empires*. Oxford: Oxford University Press, 2009.

Schloesser, Stephen. "Accommodation As a Rhetorical Principle: Twenty Years after John O'Malley's *The First Jesuits* (1993)," *Journal of Jesuit Studies*, 1 (2014): 347–372.

Schmidt, Peer. "Neoestoicismo y Disciplinamiento Social en Iberoamérica Colonial" in K. Kohut and S.V. Rose eds. *Pensamiento Europeo y Cultura Colonial* (Madrid: Vervuert-Iberoamerica, 1997): 181–204.

Schütte, Josef Franz. "Christliche Japanische Literatur, Bilder und Druckblätter in einem Unbekannten Vatikanischen Codex aus dem Jahre 1591," *AHSI*, 9 (1940): 226–280.

Valignanos Missionsgrundsätze für Japan, 2 vols. Rome: Edizioni di storia e letteratura, 1951–1958.

Monumenta Historica Japoniae. Rome: Monumenta Historica Soc. Iesu, 1975.

Scott, Bernice. *The Grito of September Sixteenth: Biography of Padre Miguel Hidalgo, Father of Mexican Independence*. Ingleside: Hemisphere House Books, 1981.

Scott, William Henry. *Barangay: Sixteenth-Century Philippine Culture and Society.* Quezon City: Ateneo de Manila University Press, 1994.

Seijas, Tatiana. *Asian Slaves in Colonial Mexico: From Chinos to Indians.* New York: Cambridge University Press, 2014.

Sellers-García, Sylvia. *Distance and Documents at the Spanish Empire's Periphery.* Stanford, CA: Stanford University Press, 2014.

Shafer, Robert Jones. *Economic Societies in the Spanish World (1763–1821).* Syracuse, NY: Syracuse University Press, 1958.

Shelford, April G. *Transforming the Republic of Letters: Pierre-Daniel Huet and European Intellectual Life, 1650–1720.* Rochester, NY: University of Rochester Press, 2007.

Sierra, Justo, Luis G. Urbina, Pedro Henríquez Ureña and Nicolás Rangel, *Antología del Centenario, Estudio Documentado de la Literatura Mexicana Durante el Primer Siglo de Independencia,* 2 vols. Mexico City: Universidad Nacional Autónoma de México.

Skinner, Quentin. *The Foundations of Modern Political Thought, 2 vols.* New York: Cambridge University Press, 1978.

Liberty Before Liberalism. Cambridge: Cambridge University Press, 1998.

van Skyhawk, Hugh. "'. . . In this bushy land of Salsette. . .': Father Thomas Stephens and the *Kristapurāṇa*," in A. Entwistle, C. Salomon, H. Pauweis and M. Shapiro eds. *Studies in Early Modern Indo-Aryan Languages, Literature and Culture.* Delhi: Manohar Publishers & Distributors, 1999: 363–378.

Smith, Hilary Dansey. *Preaching in the Spanish Golden Age: A Study of Some Preachers of the Reign of Philip III.* New York: Oxford University Press, 1978.

Snowden, Frank M. *Before Color Prejudice: The Ancient View of Blacks.* Cambridge, MA: Harvard University Press, 1983.

Song, Gang. *Giulio Aleni, Kouduo Richao, and Christian-Confucian Dialogism in Late Ming Fujian.* Oxford: Routledge, 2018.

Sorge, Giuseppe. *Matteo de Castro (1594–1677): Profilo di una Figura Emblematica del Conflitto Giurisdizionale tra Goa e Roma nel Secolo XVII.* Bologna: Clueb, 1986.

de Sousa, Lúcio. *The Portuguese Slave Trade in Early Modern Japan: Merchants, Jesuits and Japanese, Chinese, and Korean Slaves.* Boston: Brill, 2019.

Spence, Jonathan D. *The Memory Palace of Matteo Ricci.* New York: Penguin Books, 1984.

Stacey, Peter. *Roman Monarchy and the Renaissance Prince.* Cambridge: Cambridge University Press, 2007.

Stegmüller, Friedrich. *Filosofia e Teologia nas Universidades de Coimbra e Évora no Sécula XVI.* Coimbra: Universidade de Coimbra, 1959.

Steiger, Johan Anselm. "*Oratio Panegyrica versus Homilia Consolatoria.* Ein Exemplarischer Vergleich Zwischen einer Römisch-katholischen Trauerrede (Wolfgang Fuchs) und einer Lutherischen Leichenpredigt (Johann Gerhard)," in Birgit Boge and Ralf Georg Bogner eds. *Oratio Funebris. Die katholische Leichenpredigt der frühen Neuzeit. Zwölf Studien.*

Mit einem Katalog Deutschsprachiger Katholischer Leichenpredigten in Einzeldrucken 1576–1799 aus den Beständen der Stiftsbibliothek Klosterneuburg und der Universitätsbibliothek Eichstätt. Amsterdam: Rodopi, 1999: 103–130.

Stelzer, Winfried. "Zum Scholarenprivileg Friedrich Barbarossas (Authentica 'Habita')," *Deutsches Archiv für Erforschung des Mittelalters,* 34 (1978): 123–165.

Stoneman, Richard, Kyle Erickson and Ian Richard Netton eds. *The Alexander Romance in Persia and the East.* Groningen: Barkhuis, 2012.

Strand, David. "Citizens in the Audience and at the Podium," in Merle Goldman and Elizabeth J. Perry eds. *Changing Meanings of Citizenship in Modern China.* Cambridge, MA: Harvard University Press, 2002.

Subrahmanyam, Sanjay. *The Portuguese Empire in Asia, 1500–1700: A Political and Economic History.* London: John Wiley & Sons, 1993.

Three Ways to Be Alien: Travails and Encounters in the Early Modern World. Waltham, MA: Brandeis University Press, 2011.

"Global Intellectual History Beyond Hegel and Marx," *History and Theory,* 54 (2015): 126–137.

Sullivan, Thelma D. "*The Rhetorical Orations, Or Huehuetlatolli,* Collected by Sahagun," in Munro S. Edmundson ed. *Sixteenth-Century Mexico: The Work of Sahagún.* Albuquerque: University of New Mexico Press 1974: 83–89.

Tanner, Marie. *The Last Descendant of Aeneas: The Hapsburgs and the Mythic Image of the Emperor.* New Haven, CT: Yale University Press, 1993.

Tau Anzoátegui, Víctor. *Casuismo y Sistema: Indagación Histórica Sobre el Espíritu del Derecho Indiano.* Buenos Aires: Instituto de investigaciones de historia del derecho, 1992.

Tavárez, David Eduardo. *The Invisible War: Indigenous Devotions, Discipline, and Dissent in Colonial Mexico.* Stanford, CA: Stanford University Press, 2011.

Taylor, Gérald. *Sermones y Ejemplos: Antología Bilingüe Castellano-quechua, Siglo XVII.* Lima: Instituto Francés de Estudios Andinos, 2002.

Tenorio-Trillo, Mauricio. *Latin America: The Allure and Power of an Idea.* Chicago: University of Chicago Press, 2017.

Terán y Norma Páez, Marta. "Introdución a la Historiografía Hidalguista Entre 1953 y 2003," in Marta Terán y Norma Páez eds. *Miguel Hidalgo: Ensayos sobre el Mito y el Hombre (1953–2003).* Mexico City: Instituto Nacional de Antropología e Historia, 2004: 15–36.

Thauren, Johannes. *Die Akkommodation Im Katholischen Heidenapostolat; Eine Missionstheorethische Studie. Teil I. Inaug.-diss.* Münster: Aschendorff, 1926.

Thesaurus Linguae Latinae, 11 vols. Leipzig: Teubner, 1900–2012.

Thompson, I. A. A. "Spain, Castile and the Monarchy: The Political Community from *Patria Natural* to *Patria Nacional,*" in Richard L. Kagan and Geoffrey Parker eds. *Spain, Europe and the Atlantic World: Essays in Honour of John H. Elliot.* Cambridge: Cambridge University Press, 1995: 125–159.

Thornton, John. "The Development of an African Catholic Church in the Kingdom of Kongo, 1491–1750," *Journal of African History,* 25 (1984): 147–167.

Africa and Africans in the Making of the Atlantic World, 1400–1800. New York: Cambridge University Press, 1998.

"Conquest and Theology: The Jesuits in Angola, 1548–1650," *Journal of Jesuit Studies*, 1 (2014): 245–259.

Tiliander, Bror. *Christian and Hindu Terminology: A Study in Their Mutual Relations with Special Reference to the Tamil Area*. Uppsala: Religionshistoriska institutionen i Uppsala, 1974.

Tomasi, Massimiliano. *Rhetoric in Modern Japan: Western Influences on the Development of Narrative and Oratorical Style*. Honolulu: University of Hawaii Press, 2004.

de la Torre Villar, Ernesto. *Historia de la Educación en Puebla (Época Colonial)*. Puebla: Universidad Autónoma de Puebla, 1988.

"Las Sociedades de Amigos del país y Juan Wenceslao Barquera," *Estudios de Historia Moderna y Contemporánea de México*, 14 (1991): 11–51.

de la Torre Villar, Ernesto and Ramiro Navarro de Anda eds., *Testimonios Históricos Guadalupanos*. Mexico City: Fondo de Cultura Económica, 1982.

de la Torre Villar, Ernesto and Ramiro Navarro eds., *La Conciencia Nacional y su Formación: Discursos Cívicos Septembrinos (1825–1871)*. Mexico City: Universidad Nacional Autónoma de México, 1988.

Truman, Ronald W. *Spanish Treatises on Government, Society and Religion in the Time of Philip II: The "De Regimine Principum" and Associated Traditions*. Boston: Brill, 1999.

Tulpule, Shankar Gopal and Anne Feldhaus, *A Dictionary of Old Marathi*. Mumbai: Popular Prakashan, 1999.

Tuori, Kaius. *The Emperor of Law: The Emergence of Roman Imperial Adjudication*. Oxford: Oxford University Press, 2016.

Turnbull, Stephen R. *The Samurai: A Military History*. New York: Routledge, 1977.

Urrejola, Bernarda. "El Panegírico y el Problema de los Géneros en la Retórica Sacra del Mundo Hispánico. Acercamiento Metodólogico," *Revista Chilena de Literatura*, 82 (2012): 220–247.

Villarroel, Fidel. *A History of the University of Santo Tomas: Four Centuries of Higher Education in the Philippines (1611–2011)*, 2 vols. Manila: University of Santo Tomas Publishing House, 2012.

Villella, Peter B. *Indigenous Elites and Creole Identity in Colonial Mexico, 1500–1800*. New York: Cambridge University Press, 2016.

Waquet, Françoise. *Latin or, the Empire of the Sign: From the Sixteenth to the Twentieth Century*, John Howe trans. London: Verso, 2001.

Watanabe, Akihiko. "Hara Maruchino no Varinyāno Raisan Enzetsu: Koten Juyō no Ichirei toshite" (原マルチノのヴァリニャーノ礼讃演説 －古典受容の一例として－), *Otsuma Journal of Comparative Culture* 大妻比較文化：大妻女子大学比較文化学部紀要, 13 (2012): 3–19.

"Diego Yūki no 1615-nen 8 tsuki 2 hidzuke Kuraudio akuavu-īvu-a ate shokan (ARSI Jap. Sin. 36. 245 R. - 246 V.): Ratengo genbun to chūkai" (ディエゴ結城の1615年8月2日付クラウディオ・アクアヴィー

ヴァ宛書簡(ARSI Jap.Sin. 36.245r.-246v.): ラテン語原文と注解),
Otsuma Journal of Comparative Culture 大妻比較文化 : 大妻女子大学
比較文化学部紀要, 14 (2013): 94–112.

"Neo-Latin in 17th Century Japan: Two Epistles from Japanese Seminarians to
the Jesuit Superior General (ARSI Jap.Sin.33.75, 78)," *Japan Studies in
Classical Antiquity*, 2 (2014): 137–154.

Wendt, Reinhardt. "Philippine Fiesta and Colonial Culture," *Philippine Studies*,
46 (1996): 3–23.

Wicki, Josef. "Zum Humanismus in Portugiesisch-Indien des 16. Jahrhunderts,"
in *Studi sulla Chiesa Antica e sull'Umanesimo: Studi Presentati nella Sezione di
Storia Ecclesiastica del Congresso Internazionale per il IV Centenario della
Pontificia Università Gregoriana, 13–17 Ottobre, 1953*. Rome: Universitatis
Gregorianae, 1954: 193–246.

Windmuller-Luna, Kristen. "Guerra Com a Lingoa: Book Culture and
Biblioclasm in the Ethiopian Jesuit Mission," *Journal of Jesuit Studies*, 2
(2015): 223–247.

Witt, Ronald G. *In the Footsteps of the Ancients: The Origins of Humanism from
Lovato to Bruni*. Leiden: Brill, 2000.

Wolfe, Cary. *What Is Posthumanism?* Minneapolis: University of Minnesota Press,
2010.

Worcester, Thomas. "The Catholic Sermon," in Larissa Taylor ed. *Preachers and
People in the Reformations and Early Modern Period*. Boston: Brill, 2001:
3–33.

Yates, Frances A. *Astraea: The Imperial Theme in the Sixteenth Century*. London:
Pimlico, 1975.

Yhmoff Cabrera, Jesús. *Una Muestra de los Actos Académicos en el Virreinato de la
Nueva España*. Mexico City: Universidad Nacional Autónoma de México,
1979.

van Young, Eric. "Brading's Century: Some Reflections on David A. Brading's
Work and the Historiography of Mexico, 1750–1850," in Susan Deans-
Smith and Eric Van Young eds. *Mexican Soundings: Essays in Honour of
David A. Brading*. London: Institute of Latin American Studies, 2007:
42–64.

Yun Casalilla, Bartolomé. *Iberian World Empires and the Globalization of Europe,
1415–1668*. Singapore: Palgrave Macmillan, 2019.

Yuuki, Diego. *Os Quatro Legados dos Dáimios de Quiuxu após Regressarem ao
Japão*. Macau: Instituto Cultural de Macau, 1990.

Index